STRATEGIES *for* MANAGERIAL WRITING

STEVEN H. GALE
Kentucky State University

MARK GARRISON
Kentucky State University

THOMSON
™
SOUTH-WESTERN

Australia · Canada · Mexico · Singapore · Spain · United Kingdom · United States

THOMSON

SOUTH-WESTERN

Strategies for Managerial Writing
Steven Gale, Mark Garrison

VP/Editorial Director:
Jack W. Calhoun

Acquisitions Editor:
Keith Paul Chassé

Developmental Editor:
Taney H. Wilkins

Marketing Manager:
Larry Qualls

Production Editor:
Heather Mann

Manufacturing Coordinator:
Diane Lohman

Technology Project Editor:
Amy Wilson

Web Coordinator:
Kelly Reid

Design Project Manager:
Michael H. Stratton

Production House:
Rebecca Gray Design

Internal Designer:
Creatives On Call/Barb Northcott

Printer:
Edwards Brothers
Ann Arbor, MI

FOREWORD

...

In my almost forty years of management—from first-line supervisor, through second-, third-, and fourth-level positions to chief operating officer and member of the board of directors of AT&T Alascom—I have seen only one successful manager who did not have good control of his or her written communications. Although this particular VP's personal brilliance and enormous drive led others to tolerate his lack of skill in writing, his failure to use writing as a tool certainly prevented even him from achieving all that was possible. During the same time, I have seen a great many otherwise talented managers flounder because they did not give sufficient time and attention to learning to communicate well in writing.

Many managers prefer to have an opportunity to present their ideas in person. Oral presentations allow for greater flexibility or mid-course corrections based on audience reaction. However, even when oral presentations are made, it is almost universally true that follow-through requires writing. I recall one third-level manager who addressed a meeting of engineering and operations vice presidents at AT&T. He was very good verbally with high personal impact. His ideas were sound. His proposal received nods of encouragement. However, at the end of his presentation, he was told to summarize his proposal and circulate it for formal approval. He never did. He avoided at all costs exposing his lack of skill in writing. The result was that a good idea, which might have brought the company benefits and the creator rewards, died at the point writing was required to bring it to life.

I have seen many good ideas poorly presented in writing and many written communications thrown in the trash or deleted from the screen without having been read because too many errors convinced the recipient that the content could not be worth the effort to decipher what was intended from what was sent. Frankly, the level of tolerance for poor writing is low. People are too busy to take the time to try to solve puzzles. Good writing communicates efficiently as well as effectively.

I have also seen good writing save the day. One second-level manager who confided in me was clearly in trouble. Metrics and feedback from both internal sources and customers indicated that this manager was not doing his job. His boss confronted him with the expectation that he would resign. He did not. What he did was write a very well-thought-out and executed defense of his poor performance. Failures were explained as less than what others would have experienced or as unavoidable under the circumstances. His poor performance numbers were discussed in a larger context of market and competitive issues that made his results seem actually good in the proper context. The manager prevailed. His performance that had been viewed as unacceptable was now seen as almost heroic. The facts had not changed. The difference was in the manager's writing skill.

I have seen relatively obscure managers (that is, at lower levels in the organization and either geographically or politically not close to the power brokers) catapult themselves to the attention of senior leadership by presenting a well-written argument for pursuing a particular course of action. I have done it more than once myself. Good writing is not sufficient for success in these endeavors, but it is essential.

It is a common and serious error to think that written communications are subjected to less critical appraisal than oral. It surprises me how many managers will prepare extensively for an oral presentation, often practicing repeatedly and sometimes hiring a professional coach, but will then dash off an ill-conceived and poorly written report without pause. Electronic messaging seems to exacerbate this tendency. Serious managers should take care to avoid this mistake.

Clearly, the academic community recognizes the importance of managerial writing. For instance, for the two accelerated five-week courses that I teach at the University of Phoenix, the standard syllabus for the first course requires nine written papers and seven are required for the second course.

There are many reasons why *Strategies for Managerial Writing* is important. Managerial writing is unique. It is different from business, academic, or general writing. Although managerial writing conforms to basic composition, grammar, and spelling conventions, there are critical subtleties that distinguish it as an area worthy of special study and continual practice. Those subtleties are the focus of this text.

Managerial writing, like all aspects of management, changes over time. What is expected and what is excellent today is different from what was expected and excellent not long ago. The impact of increased electronic communications, a far greater number of communications between individuals in different locations who may never have actually met one another in person, and the ever-increasing velocity of doing business, all have contributed to a focused need for clear and concise writing structured for maximum impact. Excellent managerial writing is now the equivalent of a television sound bite. Like a television sound bite, far more effort is required than most imagine. So, while many core themes with respect to good writing have not changed, there are new ways of executing written communications that are critical to managerial success.

Serious professional managers will study and train themselves in the practices described in this text. Managerial writing is a distinct discipline that is an inseparable part of management. A manager's writing ability is a significant factor in determining his or her and the organization's level of success.

I am aware of no other text like this one. Here those who intend to be professional managers will find this book clear and well-written; easy to follow; full of good advice; based on relevant, real-world examples, and full of valuable information and applicable lessons. Much of the information presented was previously only available through mentoring. Mentoring by senior managers and grooming of junior managers is actually less common than not too many years ago. Lawsuits have cooled the mentoring practice. A manager who mentors may be guilty of misleading the mentored and of discriminating against those not mentored. One result of this litigation is less information shared personally, making the information in this text even more valuable.

Major themes in this text include strategies for managerial writing, techniques for being an effective communicator in writing, and illustrations of the logic that supports good writing. "Fuzzy-headed" thinking will be reflected as poor writing. A manager who is "wooden-headed," as Barbara Tuchman uses in her *The March of Folly: From Troy to Vietnam* (1984), may attempt to overrun facts with words. I have seen many examples of well-presented data pointing to one conclusion only to find that the managers have ignored what they have written (or perhaps has been provided by a staff member) and that they have presented contrary conclusions in the same communication. It is almost as if the authors did not read their own arguments. Clarity and consistency are hallmarks of good managerial writing.

Managerial writing is a tool, and like most tools, it may also be used as a weapon. Managers will make such ethical choices for themselves. However, only managers skilled in writing will be able to choose to use writing as an effective tool. Good writing can obfuscate poor management. It can buy the manager time to recover his or her performance.

Managerial writing is not an arcane discipline appropriate to only a handful of practitioners who specialize in writing for managers. Managers cannot hire a writer as they do an accountant. Good managerial writing is far too intimate and is used far too often to entrust to just anyone. Therefore, the intended audiences for this text are those who manage, from the new supervisor to the chairperson of the board.

Terry Elfers
Director of Quality, Corvis Corporation
Practitioner Faculty, University of Phoenix

BRIEF CONTENTS

...

CONTENTS
...

The Next Step

PREFACE

...

Managerial professionals—and those who aspire to successful careers as managers—must be able to communicate effectively. We have written *Strategies for Managerial Writing* in response to this critical need. In this text, the reader will explore the strategies and processes necessary to write successful managerial communications. The approaches are grounded in strategy, process, and product rather than on the more common, formulaic approaches of typical business communication texts. We do not focus on the basics of written and oral communication; instead, we have kept the text brief and compact, and we have organized the text according to the products of managerial writing. These products include memoranda, e-mail, press releases, a wide variety of reports, letters of evaluation, and so forth.

As students, you must master the many forms of workplace and interpersonal communications, their particular structures and formats, and the styles appropriate to them—yet the formulae for types of communication will be useless to managerial students without careful instruction concerning the strategies that guide effective managerial writing. To the discussion of careful pre-writing and writing processes, we have added a detailed discussion of reasoning, including a review of the major logical fallacies that often undermine one's best arguments. To focus learning experience on both strategy and process, the writing exercises in the workbook sections at the end of each chapter are designed as "inbox" exercises. These exercises provide an opportunity to put into practice the concepts introduced and developed in the chapter. To enhance the learning experience, we employ real-world examples of corporate and organizational communication, scenarios requiring students to adopt a point of view, and opportunities to develop written communications from that specific point of view. The text and its accompanying exercises focus on teaching you how to communicate to produce positive outcomes.

The initiating concept behind *Strategies for Managerial Writing* was two-fold. First, we felt that there were few choices in the textbook market for someone who wanted to learn about how to write as a manager. Managers grow out of the world of business, but there are differences between business writing and managerial writing. We address those differences in this text. Second, we envisioned a book that is unique in content and format, fitting the needs of a specific group of students.

The primary difference between business writing and managerial writing is subtle but telling; it has to do with how one approaches a writing task. Thus, we stress the strategies that guide managerial writing. For instance, we explain the *rationale* for utilizing the individual common elements of writing from pre-writing to the finished product—determining the objective of the writing, identifying the nature of the target audience, and choosing the proper and most effective format to achieve a goal. We explain the characteristics of various kinds of writing so that you, the student, understand why a particular format is appropriate for a given assignment.

All businesses rely on internal and external communication. Much of this communication is managerial in nature and, as a manager, your writing ability can be a significant factor in determining your company's success and your personal success. Because this text is designed for students who are at an advanced level, we include real-world elements that go beyond business alone because recognizing and using these elements are integral to success. Twenty-first-century business is dramatically different from the business of the era it follows. In larger numbers than ever before, people who are trained in business schools, many of whom hold MBAs, now work in the public and not-for-profit sectors.

This includes jobs at all levels of government, working in the arts, and a plethora of other nontraditional areas. Accordingly, while we draw upon illustrations that are taken purely from business experiences, we also acknowledge that material from nonbusiness fields may provide useful insights as well.

Furthermore, the globalization that began in the late twentieth century increasingly demands a larger worldview for a business to succeed than has been necessary to date. Taking this worldview into account, we stress that part of knowing one's audience is being aware of history and of national and cultural differences.

Finally, in a time of corporate and personal fallibility—including Enron, Martha Stewart, Merrill-Lynch, and countless other financial disasters brought about by ethical failures—we have included discussions of these ethical matters where appropriate.

These and many other topics are discussed and explained in this text. The more tools you as a manager have at your command, the better your writing will be and the greater the success you will enjoy.

The text is divided into four sections. The first section, the Introduction, includes two chapters: Chapter 1 addresses the concept of strategy and how it applies to managerial writing and Chapter 2 addresses the key aspects of the organization of writing, beginning with the pre-writing activity of outlining but also examining the use of logic and reasoning in managerial writing. Part 1: Classic and Contemporary Forms includes five chapters devoted to the importance of writing memos and letters (Chapter 3), analytic reports (Chapter 4), assessment and recommendation reports (Chapter 5), developing proposals (Chapter 6), and using writing as a means of managing people (Chapter 7). In the discussions throughout Part 1, topics touched upon include various types of analysis, persuasive writing, letters, coaching and mentoring through writing, and other managerial tasks that demand effective writing. Part 2: Essential Tools for Managerial Writing includes three chapters. In them, we will explore ways to master the managerial tasks associated with the electronic tools found in the office (Chapter 8), important corporate communications such as press releases and professional presentations (Chapter 9), and basics related to using graphics in a document (Chapter 10). Finally, in the concluding section, "The Next Step," we discuss the role of writing in job searches and career advancement (Chapter 11).

Throughout the text, we have employed several types of examples. Many examples are drawn from real life, while many are modeled on actual experiences but fictionalized to protect the original case. The fictional company, SHG General, provides a context for some of the discussions. Insight Boxes have been included in each chapter to address important tangential concerns. The pedagogy of each chapter includes division of the chapters into Key Concept sections that have an introductory key concept statement, a section summary, and a challenge problem for review. A glossary of important terms also has been included for reference. Each chapter has three or four pre-writing exercises and four or five writing exercises. The concluding activity is the In-Box activity that is based on various divisions of SHG General.

Overall, we have sought to provide a text balanced with examples, exercises, discussion, and learning opportunities appropriate to managerial writing. We hope that *Strategies for Managerial Writing* becomes a foundation for your future success in management and a resource to which you can return for information and advice throughout your business career.

Steven H. Gale

Mark Garrison

DEDICATION

...

To Kathy, Shannon, Ashley, and Heather; Diane, Erik, Astrid, and Nels; and to all the Gales, Garrisons, Wetzels, Goodwins, Johnsons, and Gavendas, and in memory of Norman A. Gale, Mary Wilder Hasse, and William Franklin Gale—as always, with all our love and thanks.

ACKNOWLEDGMENTS

...

A great many people and organizations contributed to *Strategies for Managerial Writing* in numerous ways. Our thanks go to Jeffrey Gale, Segway, The Vermont Teddy Bear Company, British Airways, and Neuberger Berman for providing us with real-world examples. Bill Coffey and the Paul Sawyier Gallery deserve special thanks for an extended example. Terry Elfers' perspective on business communications was wide-ranging, accurate, and invaluable, as was Stanley Schatt's input. Uncle Bernard was a source of inspiration and encouragement.

Kim Bickers and Diane Garrison helped in the manuscript preparation, and Kathy Gale proofread the manuscript and offered constructive and insightful suggestions. The editorial staff at South-Western/Thomson recognized our vision and helped make it concrete and viable.

Finally and most importantly, we would like to thank our families, Kathy, Shannon, Ashley, and Heather and Diane, Erik, Astrid, and Nels, for their support and patience.

ABOUT *the* AUTHORS

...

STEVEN H. GALE is the University Endowed Chair in the Humanities in the Whitney Young, Jr., College of Leadership Studies at Kentucky State University. He has taught at the University of Southern California, the University of California at Los Angeles, the University of Puerto Rico, the University of Liberia (as a Fulbright Professor), the University of Florida, and Missouri Southern State. He was head of the Department of English and Director of the University Honors Program at Missouri Southern.

Gale earned his bachelors degree at Duke University, his masters at UCLA, and his doctorate at the University of Southern California. He has also studied at San Diego City College, San Diego State College, Massachusetts Institute of Technology, and Christ Church College at Oxford University.

He is the author of twenty-three scholarly books (including several award winners), 160 articles and essay-reviews on a wide variety of subjects, and a textbook on writing. He is a past president of the Frankfort Arts Foundation, the founding president of the Harold Pinter Society, founding co-editor of a scholarly journal, and the general editor of two book series. He has also served as a consultant to Pacific Bell Telephone and local companies.

MARK GARRISON currently serves as the Interim Director of Graduate Studies at Kentucky State University in Frankfort, Kentucky, where, as professor of psychology, he has taught for twenty years. He earned his doctorate from Emory University, a masters degree from the University of Dallas, and a bachelors degree from Shimer College in Illinois. His more that seventy-five publications include *Human Relations: Productive Approaches for the Workplace*, with Margaret Bly, and *Introduction to Psychology*, which was translated into Spanish. Instructional areas include courses in social psychology and industrial/organizational behavior. In the pubic and private sector, he has worked as a consultant for Toyota Motor Manufacturing Company and many state and federal government agencies. Through successful grant writing, he has helped bring more than a million dollars to Kentucky State University.

Garrison's awards include being named the Kentucky State University Distinguished Professor for 2004 and 2005, an honor conferred on one professor each year at the university. Other recent recognitions include an award in 2002 for "Excellence in Online Teaching" given statewide by the Kentucky Council on Postsecondary Education. He was named 2001–2002 Faculty Fellow in the Center for Innovation in Teaching, Learning, and Assessment.

...

INTRODUCTION

CHAPTER 1
...
STRATEGIES *for* EFFECTIVE MANAGERIAL WRITING

LEARNING OUTCOMES
...

Upon completion of this chapter, you will be able to accomplish the following tasks:

1. Define strategy in managerial writing.

2. Describe how communication and management processes constitute managerial writing.

3. Distinguish reasoning and argument from assertion.

4. Describe how aspects of the communicator, the audience, and the message become strategic issues.

5. Define culture and distinguish the concept of organizational culture.

6. Describe the role of a corporate mission statement in guiding corporate actions.

7. Describe the many types of formal and informal communication processes in the workplace.

8. Identify the types of personal goals and values necessary for success as a manager.

9. Discuss the relationship between self-image and corporate image.

10. Outline the basic ethical guidelines for communication that control professional conduct for a manager.

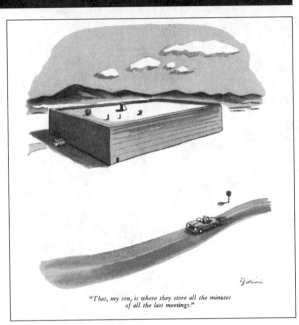

"That, my son, is where they store all the minutes
of all the last meetings."

Writing is a process. Successful managerial writers follow specific procedures and strategies. Before the process begins, decide where you are going and how you want to get there. You must know the message that you want to send and the way the message should be sent. In fact, you should begin with the knowledge of the impact you want the message to have on your audience and how the message will influence that audience to act. You must be aware of the procedures that will lead you to your goal. In this book, you will learn what strategies and procedures work best in the variety of tasks that you will encounter as a manager in the contemporary workplace.

To begin, you must be aware that words are the basic building blocks of writing. As writers, managers must be especially sensitive to the impact that words can have. When speaking of those who plan acts of terrorism, do not call them "masterminds." This word gives credibility in the minds of followers and victims alike by making it sound as though the terrorists are bright and reasonable people. It would be more accurate and rhetorically effective to call them "plotters." This word diminishes their stature and places the emphasis on their innocent victims.

The effect of words is seen in many personal experiences. Some years ago, the Pacific Bell Telephone Company in Southern California contracted Professor Gale to serve as a consultant. Its marketing department serviced military communications from just north of San Bernardino (including a NORAD command installation) to the Mexican border. Two managers were in charge of that department.

Upper management began receiving nonspecific complaints about the department. After some preliminary internal inquires, a decision was made to hire an outside consultant to write an analytic report (see Chapter Four). Through a series of individual interviews with department members and their military clients, Professor Gale realized that one word in the department's mission statement was subject to two contradictory interpretations. Unfortunately, no one recognized that both managers were instructing the sales force to do the opposite of what the other was directing them to do. The reason for the confusion was that the two managers thought that they were instructing the sales team in the same way because they were using the same word. Once the problem was diagnosed, the solution was simple. The two managers agreed on a single definition of the word and then made sure that everyone in the sales force operated within that definition. The irony is that the word itself has been long-forgotten, while the turmoil it caused continues to be remembered.

When you understand the importance of individual words, you have begun the writing process. Your next step on this journey is to understand the role of strategy in successful managerial writing. Learn to identify the context in which you write. Both the communications context and the management context are critical; neither can be ignored. Strategic issues help you focus on the nature of your role as a communicator, on the audience that you are addressing, and on the message that you are trying to transmit.

Throughout the writing process, concentrate on the character of your workplace. What cultures are involved—**microculture**, **organizational culture**, or **macroculture**? How do these relate in the mix of corporate goals and leadership style? Determining these factors helps you make crucial choices, such as selecting a formal or informal style or a positive or negative tone. These choices shape how your audience receives your message. For instance, writing a congratulatory note to be read to the company's sales team at an internal conference requires a different style (informal) and tone (positive) than writing a response to proposed legislation prejudicial to your organization (formal and negative).

Once critical contextual elements are identified, you can organize the procedural elements of your writing strategy. Begin with a **controlling idea**, the main purpose of the piece. Next, determine the depth of analysis needed to support your message. Analysis leads to the selection of supporting evidence and the formation of a logical argument. For example, responding to an RFP (request for proposal) for equipment will require more technical data than writing to invite a customer to attend a golf outing.

After acquiring and practicing these skills in the context of managerial writing, you will be prepared to apply your knowledge to appropriate tasks. For instance, when composing memoranda and letters, you will find that selecting an effective tone, identifying your purpose and audience, characterizing your message, and specifying your results are no longer difficult or challenging elements. Formatting a memo according to its function will be a simple matter. These skills required for determining and using the context become tools for success. The same set of equations will operate when you write a business letter, prepare a report, or summarize an evaluation.

Other kinds of writing might involve navigating corporate communications—that is, writing a press release, a product announcement, or a corporate profile. You are likely to write analytic reports and incorporate graphic illustrations. Through time, mastery of the managerial writing processes will become a central fixture of your managerial style. This will make you highly marketable. Your familiarity with essential procedures and strategies will give you an advantage as you move toward the next level of professional success.

The Role of Strategy in Successful Managerial Writing

Successful writing of any kind follows a carefully conceived strategy. Writers of all types, from novelists to speechwriters, plan their work.

Few successful activities in life begin without a plan; even fewer begin without a purpose. However, some people sit down to write a report or compose a memo and have *no idea of what they are going to write.* Professional writers never engage the writing process in this manner; in a sense, managers are professional writers. In fact, becoming an excellent managerial writer is vital to becoming a successful manager. Like professional writers, managerial writers do not begin with a blank page. Instead, they start by employing a technique called prewriting. **Prewriting** is the process involved in preparing to write. Developing a writing strategy is part of prewriting.

What is meant by a writing strategy? In a formal sense, a **strategy** is the means of thinking about, and organizing, a project that is guided toward a specific goal. A scientist must design an experiment before starting it. The hypothesis, the variables, the means of collecting the data, and the tools for analysis that will support the hypothesis, all must be planned before the experiment can be conducted. Imagine starting an experiment and deciding what the variables will be after it is already underway! Writers use strategy to organize resources, information, analysis, and delivery in a manner that forms the message to fit the audience. The strategy guides writing toward the optimum effect.

Strategies employed in managerial communication are always part of a larger managerial strategy. Management has a general purpose that generates specific goals. These goals lead to actions, and these actions lead to additional goals. That is why writing strategies flow from these larger strategies that serve the corporate mission. In the most general sense, the guiding purpose of any manager is to influence people. Managers may employ a variety of actions to exert this influence. Each of these managerial acts requires some form of communication, and much of that communication is written.

What options other than strategic approaches are there? The **blank page approach** provides one class of approach. Although few people begin a writing project completely "blank," many begin without any formal planning or prewriting. They have an idea of what they want to say, but they have only a faint idea of what they expect to happen when someone reads their message. Only the most gifted natural writer can be successful with such an approach over an extended period. While a few "stream-of-consciousness" writers have won Nobel Prizes in literature, this approach is not recommended for managers.

Another approach is the **formula approach**. There are well-established formulas for each major form of communication. These even include formulas for developing the tone and content of message types. However, rote application of a formula may lead to overlooking context and long-term plans. Happily, formulas can be flexible, and a good strategist has many at hand to use when appropriate. The formula approach offers efficient, practical solutions. An experienced manager who uses them frequently can be quite successful and can employ them within the context of a strategy, though perhaps intuitively and unconsciously.

The **behavioral approach** is another popular method. This approach follows the psychological theory called "observational learning" in which we learn by observing others. The writer simply imitates a successful model. Indeed, the behavioral model can be employed without the writer actually knowing why particular techniques are used. Unfortunately, the scripted imitation of structure, tone, or phrasing may make the writing awkward and unnatural. Success with this approach takes time, because it requires a feedback loop that may be missing when the message is unsuccessful. It is unlikely that you will become skillful merely through imitation. Remember, a good strategy integrates resources, information, analysis, and delivery.

So, what is the role of strategy in managerial writing? Strategies provide plans of action from a project's conception to its completion. Strategy is the tool for organizing the elements of a project. With this tool, the writer matches context, audience, and message in pursuit of a clearly articulated goal. The writer must focus the message within the parameters of the managerial strategy, the corporate mission, and the organizational culture.

Writing in Context

Managerial writing always involves a context. For our purpose, there are two intersecting processes that define the context of managerial writing: the *communication process* and the *managerial process*. Both of these processes may be considered part of a larger context of information management, but a discussion of this distinction belongs in a management theory class.

We have already noted that at least one key purpose of management is to exercise influence. Let us examine the role of two processes, communication and management, in influencing others.

Communication Process

In traditional descriptions, the **communication process** involves three elements: the *sender* of the message, the *message*, and the *receiver* of the message. A fourth element, *feedback* from the receiver to the sender, should be included because it is an integral element in the process (although technically, feedback is another communication cycle with the receiver becoming a new sender). The communication channel (described later) refers to the manner in which a message is sent, such as by e-mail or on corporate letterhead, and may be considered a fifth element in communication. Typically, the message grabs the focus of attention. The message helps identify other components of communication, such as the source (the sender) and the target (the receiver). The suggestion that the message can reveal aspects of the source and the intended target implies that the message encapsulates more information than the words and their immediate meanings.

The sender has a specific role in communication and must follow a few basic rules. The sender's main role is to encode a message in such a way that the receiver will be able to understand it as the sender intends. You might think this is not a difficult task. Misunderstood messages are probably the most prominent force in the breakdown of human interaction. In the book *A Civil Action*, the main character has gone to New York to meet with an attorney representing one of the defendants in the court case. He meets the attorney at the Harvard Club, one of the most prestigious clubs in America, and is asked, "What do you want?" He begins to list the settlement demands of his clients, when his host stops him. He is forgiven, because this is his first visit to the Harvard Club, but business is never discussed at the club. What the host meant was, "What do you want *to drink*?" (Harr, 1996).

The sender of a message must follow what is called the "cooperative principle." The **cooperative principle** is the idea that communication is a process of sharing information, that the creator of the message is making an honest attempt to be understood. Managers might subvert this principle by knowingly manipulating a message in such a way as to ensure misunderstanding. In rare instances, such as protecting a subordinate from disciplinary action or unfair scapegoating, the manager's lack of cooperation in communication serves an important purpose. On the other hand, this subversion may be unethical or inappropriately used, but it is common enough to warrant attention. A suspicious view of uncooperative communication may reflect a Westernized, overly pragmatic view of communication. Some cultures employ metaphor and innuendo regularly. Nevertheless, the typical receiver assumes that a message was designed to follow the principle of cooperation. When we talk with someone, we may be surprised when the discussion includes cryptic or veiled references that we cannot understand. Understanding is such a basic part of communication that cooperation is a tacit, shared assumption. Even if we cannot understand a single word of a visitor's language, we understand that when a foreigner speaks, something meaningful is being said and that he or she wants to be understood.

A message can take many forms and serve many purposes. The form a message takes is considered a **communication channel**. The three basic channels are written, oral, and nonverbal. A message may be communicated through several channels. In fact, every message, even one that is written, is thought to have a nonverbal component. The format of a letter and the mode of delivery of the letter are parts of the message, and they convey their own message elements. A letter brought by a courier can have a significant impact on the receiver. A hand-delivered letter conveys a sense of urgency and importance. We might be confused if a hand-delivered letter was an invitation to lunch from a coworker, yet an invitation to lunch with the company president might be hand delivered. In that case, the message and the manner of its delivery would be consistent. The manner of delivery, the formality of an internal address, the use of special stationary, and many other physical cues are part of the nonverbal channel. They are part of the **encoding process** undertaken by the sender and interpreted by the receiver. If a manager hands a memorandum to an employee concerning a specific behavior, such as informing the employee of a particular workplace rule, then the manager is sending a different message than what would be conveyed with a verbal reminder of the rule. If the manager greets an employee on Monday with "Casual dress day is Friday" rather than "I disapprove of what you are wearing," the core message may be the same, but the nonverbal elements are much different.

Which message has a stronger impact on the employee—the indirect reference to the rule or the direct comment of disapproval? The answer: it depends on the relationship between the manager and the employee. This relationship involves what is called common ground. **Common ground** comprises the shared and mutually understood aspects of a communication. These aspects include a common language, shared goals, a common cultural background, and shared experiences. The company's rulebook represents shared information that constitutes part of the common ground between the manager and the employee. If the employee has been trying to convince the manager that a casual dress day should be implemented, then the greeting "Casual dress day is Friday" has a different meaning because of the common ground of an ongoing conversation. Workplace diversity has narrowed common ground; nuance and inflection carry different meanings among people of different backgrounds. Diversity requires increasingly comprehensive, clear, and concise writing. Using cryptic statements that rely on common culture can easily fail in a diverse workplace. Writing the equivalent of a verbal "you know" may fail to communicate with those who, in fact, do not know. Finally, the more words and sentences it takes to say something, the greater the opportunity for cultural miscommunication.

In Western cultures, the role of the receiver is primarily straightforward. Unfortunately, people can easily garble a perfectly clear message. The responsibility of the receiver is twofold: first, to decode the message; second, to acknowledge the message. If the sender exercises skill when encoding the message, the receiver's attempt to decode it should be effortless. The receiver is responsible for establishing some form of feedback. People often send an acknowledgment of having received a message even if they have not had time to formulate an adequate response. A "thank you for submitting the report" tells the author of the report that it has been received and that the recipient knows that it has arrived. Managers often "read between the lines" in an attempt to determine what is really being said. For example, one manager noticed that unless the names were in alphabetical order, the order in which names were listed on a memo reflected the order in which the president of the company thought of each individual when writing the memo. If the memo was complimentary or critical, the recipients knew who was being praised or blamed, in order. Knowing that the recipients of his memos understood his practice, the president could choose to list the recipients in order of importance or mask that information by using alphabetical order. Subtle emphasis like this usually comes only from experience and alert attention to detail.

Management Process

The second process that greatly influences the context of managerial writing is the management process itself. Managers serve many roles in an organization. These roles shift according to the level of the manager within the organization and according to whether the organization is a corporate, profit-oriented organization, a nonprofit entity, or a government bureaucracy. The emphasis on profit in business organizations differs from the emphasis on service in public and nonprofit organizations. The manager is expected to implement the corporate mission, to specify the company goals and objectives, and to guide subordinates as they contribute to the success of the company. Managers thus must understand and convey rules for the completion of work, regulations imposed by internal and external entities, and other appropriate directives. They are also responsible for the members of a work group whom they oversee.

Organizational structures define specific management processes that move all types of information up and down the organizational structure. These processes provide the mechanisms for individuals to control the work activity within their respective domains of the organizational structure. The particulars of how information flows and how work is controlled depend greatly on the type of organizational structure, the mission of the organization, the size and geographic diversity of the organization, and the values that guide it. As a context for managerial writing, the relevant components of the management process are information flow and the control of work (see Table 1.1). Communication allows the manager to exercise influence over others and a substantial part of this communication will be in a written form. Effective managerial writing requires that the writer be familiar with the specifics of the management process that establish the context of the writing.

Context is critical for strategy. It shapes the sender, the message, the channel, and the receiver. The resources, information, analysis, and delivery elements all occur within specific communication and management contexts. These include the concepts of common ground and the cooperative principle. Effective strategy cannot be formulated without certain and confident knowledge of these contexts.

Reasoning and Argument

Analysis is a component of communication that is often overlooked in approaches that focus on established routines of communication. The formula approach to managerial writing provides the writer with many tools for preparing a message. However, the necessary

TABLE 1.1
...

Summary Table: Communication and Managerial Processes

	Communication Processes
Sender	The individual or group that constructs a message and conveys it to recipients. The sender places the message in a specific form or code.
Message	The encoded information constructed and sent to the receiver. The coding may include the words, inflection, and format of the message.
Receiver	The intended and unintended individual or group that gets and then interprets the message sent by the sender.
Feedback	A return message from a receiver that indicates that the message was received. Also may include a response to the message itself.
Channel	The method by which the message was sent, including verbal, oral, written, imagistic, nonverbal gestures and inflections, or some combination of these modalities of expression.
Common Ground	The culture, experience, and knowledge shared by two or more people.
Cooperative Principle	The fundamental assumption that when one speaks, one is intending to communicate.
	Managerial Processes
Information Flow	A critical management role involves transmitting information to individuals, units, teams, or groups that need the information in order to achieve common corporate goals.
Control of Work	A critical management role that involves scheduling, guiding, organizing, and controlling others in order to achieve the common goal of work.

analyses of information and opportunities that form a foundation of the strategic approach cannot necessarily be conveyed in a formula because analysis requires reasoning and argument. Although these two concepts are often used interchangeably, they have different definitions for writers. **Reasoning** refers to the formal process of logical analysis that provides the means of using evidence to reach a conclusion. Logicians typically distinguish two classes of reasoning: deductive reasoning and inductive reasoning (reasoning processes are examined in detail in Chapter 2). Reasoning can be used to analyze a set of possible alternatives without offering a decision about which is correct or offers the best opportunity.

In common usage, an argument occurs in the context of a disagreement and is better known as argumentativeness. For formal writing and reasoning purposes, an **argument** combines specific reasoning methods with documented evidence. When a writer makes a choice and then justifies that choice, the justification would be called the argument. The argument should stand on its own without anyone expressing agreement or disagreement.

One of the most pervasive errors in writing is the confusion of assertion with argument. Arguments can be strong or weak, correct or incorrect. They may be presented as potentially fallible with the intention of initiating healthy and productive debate. People freely employ assertion as if stating a claim about something makes the claim valid. **Assertions** are empty claims without supporting evidence, reasoning, or logic. Assertions offer little to the receiver of the message that can be used to analyze the soundness of the claim. They are vague prescriptions for conduct like "the customer is always right." To this comment, a disgruntled customer service representative, might—with fallacious logic—answer: "That means, because you are wrong, you must not be a customer." These difficulties can prove minor in contrast to costly decisions made on the basis of unsubstantiated assertions. Nevertheless, managers frequently rely on assertion when their positional authority entitles them to impose their will without convincing others of the merits of a case. While this autocratic style of management has been maligned for years, it is still common, especially in dispatching minor issues. For example, the ranking manager in a group may simply tell the others what the agenda will be, what the dress code is, how their vouchers will be processed, and so forth, with no attempt whatsoever to justify these decisions.

When an entire state government (and the federal government as well) decides to use a particular software package because "that's what everyone else uses," then a major purchasing decision has been based on a faulty assertion. Because others use it does not make it good or appropriate for a particular company or use. For instance, one might hear that a certain incompatible desktop computer executes superb graphics. Yet, current models of the compatible leading desktop platform can perform all of the same graphic manipulation tasks and have a greater number of software packets available. What is heard then, rather than well-reasoned arguments, are the assertions that people make supporting their views. In fact, the claim "I prefer Macintosh computers" is itself an argument with evidence. However, the evidence is personal, and personal preferences do not carry as much weight as other types of evidence. If you are expected to use a computer and you prefer a specific model, if it is just as functional as the options, then preference is a good argument. Making an assertion without revealing a preference, though, is not a good argument. As is noted in the next chapter, reasoning and argument are the key aspects of analysis—an essential component of a writing strategy.

Managers are extremely jealous about time. There are always more demands on their time than can be met reasonably. Therefore, managers often favor methods that shortcut thorough analyses. To extend the previous software example, it may be argued that using a popular software is enough evidence to make the choice rather than squandering corporate resources on a more exhaustive study that will almost certainly lead to the same conclusion. It is common to hear that reports must be no more than one or two pages, because busy managers will not read more. Trying to achieve balance between communicating information important enough that it should be considered and staying within guidelines for length is why a great deal of managerial writing includes charts, tables, and graphs.

Strategic Issues

Which aspects of communication are most critical for understanding the role of strategy in managerial writing? Certainly, the more comprehensive your knowledge of any given writing context, the more successful your strategy will be. A good strategy guides us so that we can identify elements of a situation that require special attention and focus on those details. The following are specific aspects of the communicator, the audience, and the message that should always be kept in mind.

1. *Communicator*. You may have an accurate self-appraisal of your skills and limitations as a writer, manager, and team member. Your audience may not share that knowledge. Your position and reputation will always be major points of consideration for anyone reading a message that you send. You must be aware of the impression that the audience has of you, not just as a writer, but in all

aspects of your relationship with the audience. Do you have recognized authority, a reputation for hard work, a track record of successful recommendations, or a specialized expertise? Does the audience know these details? If they do not, is there a reason why they should believe you? Reputation must be established or proven, not merely asserted. You must learn to read your writing as if you are a member of your audience.

2. *Audience.* Audiences can be hard to judge. However, the skill of assessing the readiness of an audience to receive your message is crucial. The readiness of the audience must always enter into the strategy developed for a particular communication. Just as you must know yourself, you must know your audience. In later chapters of this book, we will see that managers concerned with making proposals and evaluations must take special effort to ascertain the readiness of their audience. Will the audience understand your context or will they interpret your analysis within their own context and point of view? Do they share your goals? Do you have any sense of their goals, expectations, and values?

   Another related concern that shapes a writing project is how much effort the audience is likely to put into reading the message. A busy audience expects you to appreciate their time constraints and to make the message succinct and clear. Another audience may anticipate a thorough, detailed, and in-depth analysis that requires a longer narrative with greater detail and precise explanations.

3. *Message.* Many misunderstandings can arise in the interpreting of a message. These misunderstandings may occur not only because the words are unclear or confusing, but because the context is misread, the nonverbal cues are overinterpreted, or unintended implications are present. The message itself should be composed late in the process of implementing a writing strategy. A sales presentation should follow a careful assessment of the customer's needs, resources, plans, and personnel. The proposal is written only when all of this information has been gathered. The writing process is an extension of a careful and systematic research process, of collecting as much information as can be reasonably gathered; a successful and effective managerial writer balances time, resources, the importance of the message, and the readiness of the audience. Strategy guides the balancing act.

SECTION SUMMARY

A strategy-based approach to managerial writing contrasts with approaches that draw upon formulas, imitate models, or simply count on personal skill. The strategy approach provides a guiding plan that coordinates resource, information, analysis, and delivery in pursuit of a specific communication goal. Managerial writing occurs at the intersection of the communication process and the management process. Both of these processes are more effective in influencing people to behave in a desired way, because they are focused on justification for action rather than assertions. Reasoning and arguments are hallmarks of good writing. Finally, special characteristics of the communicator, the audience, and the message are the foundation for many elements in the development of a writing strategy.

CHALLENGE PROBLEM FOR REVIEW

When was the last time someone told you that you had to do something a certain way because "that is how it is always done"? What was your response to this assertion? A rationale, even some evidence, should be available for your response. What would be a better supporting answer than "that is how it is always done"?

Understanding the Workplace

Managerial writing occurs in the broader context of the workplace. Contemporary concerns about the workplace influence the nature of this managerial task.

The workplace has been the flashpoint of global transformation and progress, although many management approaches remain slow to change and conservative. The marketplace puts endless pressure on companies to make adjustments to extend profitability and competitiveness. Today's business world is experiencing an ongoing, increasing globalization of the marketplace in which an information-based economy makes global issues into local ones. Governmental agencies, educational institutions, and nonprofit organizations must respond to these global pressures just as intensely as the corporate sector does. Government must become more efficient and responsive, educational systems must prepare a globalized workforce, and nonprofit organizations must serve increasingly diverse populations and worldwide missions.

These broad influences on work have consequences on management style and the very way that work itself is organized. More than ever, government and other service organizations have turned to workplace models to reinvent the way their "not-for-profit" work is done; soon after work teams appeared in the business world, they appeared in government. Self-managed teams became popular in business, and work teams became self-managed in government as well. The movement toward quality management approaches began in business, moved on to government, and then to the management of educational institutions.

Microculture, Organizational Culture, and Macroculture

The term **culture** once applied only to a collection of people who shared a common ethnic background, common methods of artistic expression, a common language, and a common geographic origin. Members of a culture share a sense of membership or identity with others in that culture. Today, the term culture refers to any group of people who share common goals, physical spaces, and shared experiences.

Just as the definition of culture is changing at the broadest levels, we now find reference to organizational and corporate cultures. Recognizing that each group evolves its own style, we can improve our personal fit within the group's culture as we also find ways to express our personal style. As with the older concept of culture, for those newly defined groups to have a "culture," there must be an expectation of common membership or shared identity. For instance, the authors of this book share an identification with their university in the same way you identify with your institution, and recognize that their university has an organizational culture of its own, as does yours.

Broadly defined, culture has at least three distinct levels: (1) the immediate *micro*culture level of a work group or other cohesive entity, (2) the broader *organizational* culture level in which work groups collaborate and strive toward a common goal, and (3) the larger *macro*culture level. Macroculture usually refers to the cultures of the society or at least to a large segment of a society, such as East Coast or the Southwest. Corporate culture can range from a small business to an international business. There is no limitation on size or geographic location on these terms; they are used primarily for convenience in making distinctions among different types of cultural identity.

Workers who share a common identity with a large corporation may recognize the existence of a corporate culture that is geographically dispersed. For example, Home Depot is a nationwide organization. It has a distinctive corporate culture that it encourages with closed circuit television broadcasts made on a regular basis by the company founders, Bernie Marcus and Arthur Blank (Soslow, 1992). They convey their sense of humor and commitment to the employees in these television communiqués and to customers in commercials. At the same time, Lowe's Home Improvement management has chosen to support American Olympians as a part of emphasizing its group-oriented culture. Wal-Mart stresses the friendliness of Wal-Mart employees and the low prices of merchandise, encapsulated in the yellow smiley-face symbol. People like to work at Home Depot, Lowe's, and Wal-Mart and identify with the respective corporate values.

At the other end of the spectrum, a company with only one plant and few outlets has its own distinctive style. Employees have a sense of "the way we do business" that affects every activity from production to sales and service. This style evolved over time and requires employee commitment and "buy in" to be successful. Although this type of corporate culture easily develops in a small business, large corporations have seen the value in these approaches and have tried to re-create the small business feel. Even the giant Wal-Mart strives to make employees and customers feel like they belong to a common culture.

Other considerations include the mix of ethnic cultures and the actual geographic location of a company. The division of an American business in India will have different work and dress habits than will a division of the company located in France. Whether these local differences affect the corporate culture depends on the characteristics of each company.

The local culture influences how a company conducts business in a locality. To succeed, an American business in Mexico follows Mexican business protocol in dealing with Mexican suppliers, corporate partners, and employees. The same business in Japan must adjust its interactions with Japanese businesses to fit that culture. For example, an evening visit to a karaoke bar in Tokyo is considered a standard business practice, whereas in the United States, it is seen as frivolous entertainment. In either case, the company's organizational culture dictates the norm; the person or business that holds the greatest power determines the style. If a company is seeking to become a supplier of parts to a Korean automobile company, then the negotiations will probably follow Korean protocols. If the Korean company is seeking to sell parts to an American manufacturer, then American protocols will be followed. The person or entity that holds the bargaining power controls the interaction. This can occur without anyone articulating the rules or consciously attempting to assert control.

An effective writing strategy that spans two macrocultures requires research into the protocols of both cultures. An experienced manager should be familiar with those cultural differences and know how to navigate the potential barriers both in writing and in face-to-face contact. Likewise, the more unusual a factor arising from organizational culture, the more cautious one must be when approaching someone outside the organization. The writer must be aware of organizational idiosyncrasies and remove them from communications with someone who may not understand them. Failure to do so can result in alienation of the audience, if even for minor reasons. Consider the sales representative who visits a toy manufacturer to promote the top-of-the-line, most modern, high-tech sewing system for stuffed toys. The system produces stuffed animals

© VERMONT TEDDY BEAR. USED WITH PERMISSION.

without any human intervention and can save (once it is paid for) thousands of employee hours annually. Imagine this salesperson trying to sell this machine to the makers of teddy bears at the Vermont Teddy Bear Company. Vermont Teddy Bear is the largest maker of hand-crafted teddy bears in American ("Not Your Average Bear," February 2002). The teddy bears are cut, sewn, and stuffed by hand. To make them individualized and special, they are also dressed by hand with names embroidered on their clothing and then placed in special shipping boxes that include an air hole. What would the world think if they were machine made? In reality, cuts are made by machines (hand guided) and stitching is done on a sewing machine (though some is literally done by hand). Computers help, but the factory is not noticeably high tech. In fact, the factory has become a popular tourist attraction. This sewing system salesperson would need a convincing strategy to become a provider of any of the machines used in the hand-made processes. Perhaps the sales representative could suggest that the blower that helps stuff the bears produces less dust than the older models, or the cutting edges stay sharp longer on the high-tech machine. In the end, though, the culture of the hand-made teddy bears provides the final point for a decision. Will the new machines undermine the core mission of this charming and successful manufacturer?

Culture contributes to the personal and organizational style of an organization. Successful managerial writing follows a strategy that consciously incorporates significant elements of the microcultural, organizational, and macrocultural. For example, in one organization, "as soon as possible" means "immediately" whereas in another it means "whenever you get around to it." Obviously, if a manager wants to drive the correct behavior with a memo to his or her staff, using the phrase "as soon as possible" appropriately for the organizational context is important.

Corporate Goals

Companies publish their mission and goal statements in documents for public consumption. For example, annual reports sent to stockholders and potential investors articulate missions and goals. More than ever, corporate mission statements have become a force in the development of the strategic plan of the company. Strategic plans often contain three to five long-range goals and a number of specific objectives derived from a mission statement. A clothing company's executives may promote a mission to become the top provider of outdoor clothing. A specific goal might be to develop and launch an interactive Web site for customers to order online and to learn about each season's new fashions. The planning executive would develop a project flow chart with specific time frames for each stage of the development.

For the most part, managers have a responsibility to specific parts of an overall action plan and particular goals. Some aspects of the mission may address a value system from which goals are derived. The company may place high value on serving customers in a friendly and prompt manner. Sometimes, a value-based mission statement empowers

INSIGHT BOX 1.1
...

That "Quality" Word

Words such as total quality management (TQM), quality management, and Ford's motto, "Quality is Job 1," have developed lives of their own. The quality movement, as it is sometimes called, has very specific guidelines that dictate implementation of such concepts as TQM. Quality may be considered an absolute, but it is usually measured in relative terms and can be measured in many ways.

The corporate approach always begins with the identification of quality in the context of the organization's product or service. In products, quality may be measured in terms of zero defects. Quality service may be measured in zero customer complaints, on-time service calls, replacements within a specified time period, and so on. Merely announcing or proclaiming quality to be a goal does not ensure that the company's mission will be met.

lower-level employees to take independent action in order to satisfy customers. The values may be articulated in writing and shared with employees and customers or they may be part of the image that employees and customers have come to know without it being written and publicized. All of the manager's activities, including writing and other forms of communication, must reflect the corporate mission.

Many of America's top companies have embraced new management styles that have altered the traditional role of the manager. Included in these new styles are flattened corporate structures with fewer steps between the lowest level employees and the senior management. Two consequences of the flattened structure model are a wider span of control for individual managers and the delegation of more authority to employees down the management chain. A prevalent concept in today's workplace is that of **empowerment**, the extension of responsibility and authority to workers at all levels of the corporate hierarchy. The delegation of authority to employees at the line and staff levels is a form of empowerment. Making people responsible for their own quality control is another. The introduction of the quality circle in manufacturing and assembly plants has further empowered workers. In most cases, worker empowerment is limited to the scope of work. The Harley-Davidson Motor Company, for instance, empowered its workers to select the milling machines used to bore the engine blocks for their motorcycles. This meant that skilled machinists were responsible for selecting and purchasing the quarter-million dollar machines they would be using in their own work. As you can imagine, this was a significant step for Harley-Davidson and for its employees. (Boyett and Conn, 1991, and Garrison and Bly, 1997).

Another major shift in the contemporary workplace includes a range of phenomena that on one hand adds to the empowerment of the employee and on the other hand intensifies the employee-work relationship. Just-in-time delivery of materials, excessive reliance on contract workers, telecommuting, and **internal entrepreneurship** are representative of shifts in the workplace. Add to these trends the dramatic increase in electronic communication. Information technology expanded the power of a single person to communicate and accomplish work. At the same time, technology has magnified the stress of work because work is increasingly time sensitive.

Managers must learn to survive in the corporate culture just described, which makes effective communication is a must. Challenges for managers will not diminish, and the need to polish and exercise writing skills continues to gain in importance. More of the modern manager's job requires managing information, thus placing additional emphasis on writing skills. Moreover, these skills serve both the corporate mission and the manager's personal goals. The better you are at managing information, the more valuable you become in a world of work dominated by the flow of information.

Formal and Informal Processes

All environments where groups develop—work, play, school, place of worship, and so on—have many modes of communication. Most groups develop some type of formal communication and organizational structures, several informal communication systems, and informal relationships among components beyond the formal structures. These formal and informal structures invoke their own rules and routines. A successful manager needs to be highly knowledgeable about all of the structures operating within the group. He or she must be able to negotiate these structures and use them to personal and corporate advantage.

In this book, we examine many of the formal writing processes and products. The writing products include the letter and memorandum, e-mail, reports, news releases, and, to a lesser extent, special items such as the resume and procedural instructions. With rare exception, the sequence of planning, prewriting, draft, review, and final draft applies to all written products. Each product of managerial writing requires special processes, like that of collecting information or developing a graphic illustration program for a major proposal. These processes, and the products created using them, are part of the formal activity of management. They have specialized protocols for delivery and dissemination that are critical paths to follow as they make their way up through the chain of command. New management styles and structures are causing chains of command to flex, and in some cases, strain. However, flexibility can lead to improved efficiency, innovation, and responsiveness to the changing business environment.

Each writing project has its own context, rules for sharing, and methods of response or feedback. These factors constitute the formal code of conduct for the writing process that must be followed. Most of these rules arise in the informal process of communication and are never articulated. This applies even to casual communications such as e-mails, which should not be read by a third party without the recipient's or the sender's permission. It is common practice to forward e-mails, usually with the recipient's comments added. It is also common practice at many companies to use commercial software to monitor all e-mails for improprieties. Considering these issues, in some organizations, the cultural expectation is that an e-mail that the sender does not want forwarded is clearly marked "DO NOT FORWARD" or "PRIVATE." The recipient should not have to guess whether the sender is willing to share the information.

The workplace environment encompasses both formal and informal procedures, relationships, and communications. Any effective strategy for writing must recognize and incorporate these aspects. This does not mean that at every moment you must employ a strategy that contains data about who is friends with whom or which department is working with what other department on a special project. Nonetheless, awareness of existing tensions and affinities, conflicts and coalitions, or who is "in" and who is "out" will help you gauge how the audience will receive a message. These subtleties can provide powerful tools for influencing others. Merely following the rules as formally specified is like following the rule of driving. Sure, the other driver should have seen your vehicle, and sure, you had the right of way. The car went through the stop sign and hit your car anyway. Could some defensive driving on your part—even though you were in the "right"—have helped avoid the accident? Attending to the informal relationships and interactions while preparing even the most innocuous communication will be beneficial in the long run. Remember, not only must you know yourself, but you must know other people as well; a realistic dose of awareness and sensitivity is always a prudent component of any strategy for communicating in any context.

SECTION SUMMARY

Effective managerial writing occurs in the context of the workplace and reflects the critical features of the successful workplace. Strategies for managerial writing must be attuned to organizational structures, current trends in the ever-changing business environment, and special aspects of the contemporary corporation. The goals and mission of a company are primary ingredients in the setting of corporate long-range plans. Mission statements are taken seriously as guides to almost every action, official and unofficial, in the conduct of business. Writing is part of the complete picture of the workplace, and it occurs in the context of formal and informal relations throughout that environment. Successful managerial writing depends on an informed perspective.

CHALLENGE PROBLEM FOR REVIEW

Locate a corporate mission statement, a nonprofit organization's mission statement, and a government agency's mission statement (they are easily found on the Web). Your university has a mission statement; include it as well. Do the mission statements seem reasonable, even laudable? Now determine which is most believable, which most accurately reflects the daily practices of the organization, and which is least believable. What is the responsibility of middle managers to follow these mission statements?

Professional Conduct and Personal Success

Strategies for managerial writing evolve from the writer's personal goals and ambitions. To be effective as a writer, you must have a good grasp of your goals, the corporate image, and the professional rules of conduct.

The final element introduced concerning a strategy for managerial writing underlies all others: Each writer is an individual with personal goals and ambitions. You have a self-image, and to some extent, you have become immersed in the corporate image. The confidence with which self-image directs actions and influences decisions should be reflected in the confident writing style that you use in every communication. This final piece of the puzzle is the all-important aspect of ethical behavior. Writing is a part of your professional conduct, and awareness of the professional ethical concerns must be included in the writing process.

Personal Goals

We all have dreams, aspirations, and hopes for the future. In terms of our careers, these take the form of personal goals. Unfortunately, most of us do not all put much effort into clarifying these goals and the steps needed to achieve them. Just as efforts to improve the quality of our writing, we should take steps to improve the effectiveness of our goal attainment. Consider how few people you know who undertake an effort to clarify goals on a regular basis. How can we assess our progress toward our goals without clearly stating the goals in the first place? What measure would we use to mark each step of the achievement?

Personal and professional goals are closely related, and personal values influence the selection of goals. Consider the personal conflict that would arise in this case: A devoted environmental activist who works for a small alternative energy company discovers that Exxon has bought the company. Can someone committed to saving the environment work for a company that has been vilified for environmental disasters such as the *Exxon Valdez* oil spill? Will the goal of developing new energy resources override the value of environmental protection? Will the conflict between personal values and employer perceptions cause problems as the employee tries to do his or her job? The best way to be prepared for these kinds of potential conflicts is to engage in some form of **values clarification** and goal-setting exercises in a regular manner.

Simple Goal Setting

Goals must be realistic and attainable. A goal of becoming a millionaire by the age of twenty-five is realistic because some have accomplished it. However, it is not easily attainable because, of the many who want to become millionaires at an early age, very few do so. The goal of beginning a career by the age of twenty-five with a company in the telecommunications sector is both realistic and attainable. Many jobs are available in this sector, even with the unsettling swings in the telecommunications market. In addition, this goal defines special skills that must be acquired. These include several types of technical skills. Managerial skills will also be helpful. Skills in sales and human relations may be another avenue of opportunity.

The concept of developing concrete goals means that there are specific steps which can be identified and taken. If you want to become a city planner or a civil engineer, you must take courses in municipal governance to understand how government regulation will affect your work. These courses are steps along the way, although they do not in themselves make you a city planner.

A simple first step is to make a list of reasonable goals that you expect to attain by the end of this week, by the end of the term, and by the end of a year. Add to this list where you would like to be in your career in five and/or ten years. Do you expect to have a family along the way? Are you willing to relocate? Have you been doing things recently that move you forward toward your goals? Conversely, have you been doing things that distract you from your goals?

Now, with this list in hand, identify things that you must do to reach these goals. What skills do you need to acquire? Will there be any certifications that you must obtain? How will you know that you have achieved one of your goals? Will there be concrete evidence? How will you know that you have reached the goal satisfactorily: Is there something still missing or are you happy with what you have achieved? After answering these questions, compare your answers to the goal statements. Table 1.2 provides a sample of how this listing might look.

After you complete this exercise, you might be pleased that you have made good progress. On the other hand, you should pay close attention to the "distracters" that you have encountered. What do the distracting events say about your commitment to your primary goals? Can you devise a plan to correct the distraction? Does the distraction hint at alternatives that you have failed to consider?

Values Clarification

Many strategies can be followed to help you clarify your goals. If you enjoy watching the news, your reactions to daily events are part of an ongoing values-clarification process. Sometimes, such startling things happen that this process may be labeled "value realization." We often are unaware of specific attitudes and values that we have until they are brought to our consciousness by the shock of a current event. People who opposed the death penalty may have been so overwhelmed by the events of September 11, 2001, that their opinions about the death penalty were shaken and their values undergone clarification and change. School shootings that occur with alarming frequency across the country may lead us to question the safety of our children and, in turn, to value them more in face of the realization that life is fleeting.

Several good books have been written to help clarify values. Perhaps the most popular is the best seller, *Values Clarification: A Practical, Action-Directed Workbook*, by Simon, Howe, and Kirschenbaum (1995). These colleagues provide a detailed and organized approach to personal values clarification and include steps and activities to guide the reader through the process. Another "guru" of self-improvement who stresses values and integrity is Stephen Covey. Covey is a popular writer who simplifies the complex issues of values, conduct, and ethics in his various *Seven Habits of . . .* books, tapes, and guided programs. His first book on the topic, *Seven Habits of Highly Effective People* (1989), continues to be a popular, best-selling book. A book is only a helpful starting point, however. A simple list of issues and some type of rating can be extremely effective. List the top ten events of the week as they appear in news headlines (from the newspaper or the broadcast news) and rate these items on a scale of one to five, or mark them as "important," "not important," or "not given much thought." These ratings will provide a beginning for making sense of what you believe and why. If family stories rate high, then what does that mean for you? If the stock market has you concerned, what does that mean? Use Table 1.3 on page 20 to rate these stories. By the way, you may also want to note what you can do about each of the stories. Some are beyond your individual control and influence; how do you handle such a situation?

Why are these clarification and value realization activities so important? A truly good writer and manager always works from a foundation of self-knowledge. You must be aware of your interests and ambitions if you expect to be successful at supporting the work and ambition of those you supervise. The act of clarifying these values is but one of many ways to learn your own focus. Another critical benefit is that self-aware people are also confident people—and successful managers must be confident. One of the first places that a lack of confidence will appear is in communicating with others.

TABLE 1.2
...

Simple Goal-Setting Task

Setting Goals

Today and this week

1. What will I achieve this week?

2. What will distract me from my plans this week?

This term

1. What will I achieve this term?

2. What skill or knowledge do I need to achieve this term?

3. What will distract me from this plan?

This year

1. What will I achieve this year?

2. What skill or knowledge do I need to achieve this year?

3. What will distract me from this plan?

In ten years

1. What will I achieve in ten years?

2. What skill or knowledge do I need to achieve in ten years?

3. What will distract me from this plan?

Self-Image and Corporate Image

Progress toward a meaningful set of life goals and a well-articulated set of personal values is important as you acquire and practice communication skills in general and writing skills in particular. These skills require sensitivity to others, to your own self-image, and to the impression that you make on others. The question you need to ask yourself is, are you willing to accept the kind of image that you project in comparison to the goals and values that you have identified?

Self-image is important for the manager who is expected to adopt the corporate image as if it were an extension of his or her own self. Managers consciously become corporate citizens and take on the mannerisms and identity of the company. Even though sacrifice of individuality seems odd in a culture defined by rugged individualism, this emulation of the corporate ideal is almost universal.

There are several reasons for this. First, the manager represents someone who must influence others to act in a way consistent with corporate goals. Projecting an identity fused with the corporate image, a manager may have a strengthened sense of confidence. Moreover,

TABLE 1.3
...

Rating News Events

News Event	Rating: 1 = high interest; 5= low interest				
	1	2	3	4	5
	1	2	3	4	5
	1	2	3	4	5
	1	2	3	4	5
	1	2	3	4	5
	1	2	3	4	5
	1	2	3	4	5
	1	2	3	4	5
	1	2	3	4	5
	1	2	3	4	5

image is certainly a means of establishing authority. Second is a concern for mobility. Most managers expect to have upward mobility through the corporate hierarchy. The projected image is another means of fitting into the expected role of a good corporate citizen.

Does producing high-quality managerial writing require you to embrace this corporate image and fuse it with your own? Probably not. Still, written communication from an officer or staff member of a company is usually perceived as a message from the company, not necessarily from the individual author. The corporate logo on a company letterhead ensures that the receiver understands that the message is an official communication from the company. Care must be taken to recognize this effect on the reader. Writers who include personal opinions in a letter or memorandum are cautioned to make it clear that the opinion is that of the writer and not the official stance of the company.

At the same time, the audience may impose the corporate image on the writer. Not in itself a bad thing, this image can be a useful component of the communication. The corporate image may convey to the reader a certain amount of authority and identify the nature of the company. It may remind the reader of the power of the corporate interests and concerns or it may strengthen the intentions expressed in the communication. These impressions are not difficult to manage. They can be used to your advantage to focus the reader's attention on the high quality of your product or service by stressing the connection between the product or service and the organizational image.

Communication Ethics

Ethical guidelines governing managerial communications are not articulated in any standard booklet or publication; there is no published code of **ethics** for writers. Common sense should be enough, but news of individual wrongdoings constantly amazes. Because written communications create a record that has legal weight, care to be truthful and honest should be considered the first ethical rule. The second rule would be to recognize the written work of others as their property. Plagiarism is wrong no matter where it takes place, and copyright violations can lead to serious legal difficulties. These two rules engender the respect of others and establish the integrity of your own work. Professional standards of behavior for your specialty or discipline are as important in written communications as they are in the course of professional activities. Aside from the requirement that you must be sure that what you say or write is truthful, all other recommendations regarding the conduct of writing are a matter of etiquette. The habit of practicing appropriate etiquette—using proper titles, showing respect, and saying thank you—enhances your self-image, makes you an appreciated colleague, and gives you a step up on the ladder to corporate success.

Each type of writing has its own protocol. This protocol may shift from time to time, but it will prescribe specific formats to be used, to whom a message is delivered, and to whom copies should be sent. Different types of communication carry expectations of confidentiality, but the extent to which confidentiality can be honored changes as laws (such as open-record laws) change and become more broadly applied. Many companies now maintain required as well as suggested rules for all communications (both verbal and written forms). These specify, often for legal reasons, how each type can be utilized, what kinds of uses the company sanctions, and what kinds of uses the company disallows.

In addition to the sets of rules now existing on the corporate scene, professional conduct should be a guide. If you are unsure of the protocol, find an experienced colleague to ask for guidance. An employee evaluation, as discussed in a later chapter, must follow certain guidelines yet must be respectful even if brutally honest. In any case, truth should not be compromised. Hints and innuendos can be more dangerous than silence—especially if the reader is left to speculate and read between the lines. Furthermore, there are some issues about how managers do this in actuality. There are a number of *shoulds* that are correct from an ethical perspective, yet many managers know better than to follow this advice, based on their experience.

As in all other aspects of management activity, writing must follow the expectations of professional conduct. Knowledge of these expectations is required as one prepares a strategy for writing. Although direct ethical influences may have only minor effects on the finished product, authority and reputation are part of the tone of every form of communication. The reputation of being a professional is the best reputation to have and is achieved by the consistent application of these principles to your writing.

Culture and Ethics

Over the last couple decades, vast changes have taken place in the world of business. With the end of the Cold War, political relationships shifted, and the status and power

Why the Emphasis on Other Cultures?

Textbooks in every field seem to raise the issue of globalization, sensitivity to other cultures, tolerance for differences between groups, and acceptance of people of differing ethnic backgrounds. Why is this so important? First, many people find the differences between themselves and others to be quite fascinating and informative. Even more critical, knowing how others respond to situations helps us be more responsive to them. Such sensitivity makes us more likely to be accepted and thus more likely to be successful in business situation with them. It just makes sense that we all need to understand our clients' needs in the fullest possible way.

of many nations changed dramatically. New—and different—markets emerged. To a large extent, advances in technologies enhanced the speed and the range of political changes. As the impact of the Pacific Rim has waxed, that of Western Europe waned. The influence of France and Russia has been diminished by the increasing importance of China's economy. Those companies that do not recognize shifts in focus and make corresponding adjustments in how they conduct business will suffer in an increasingly competitive world marketplace.

Among the changes that need to be made is the recognition of cultural differences. When everything was modeled after an American-European template, it was easy for businesspeople to fit into a single pattern, whatever their native culture was. That has changed. Travel to and interaction between cultures is so rapid and so ubiquitous that the American-European model often is outdated and occasionally inoperative. As attention to a particular section of the world increases, the overall picture becomes ever more complicated and multifaceted. Traditional activities and approaches that are acceptable now may well be ineffective or discarded in a few years.

The first step to learning how to be acclimated in the contemporary world of business is to be aware of ongoing changes. The second step is to be ready to incorporate new realities into business operations. The third step is to learn what those realities are, and the fourth step is to practice them in your business transactions.

This means that you must be sensitive to your host culture. For example, you probably know that Jews and Muslims do not eat pork. Did you know that in many countries eating with your left hand is considered inappropriate? In many countries, you should not cross your legs in public. The Japanese consider exposure of the sole of one's shoe to be quite rude; in that same country, you must remove your shoes before entering a house.

The color white, not black, signifies death in a number of cultures. The Japanese word for six and the word for death are the same; the number is avoided whenever possible. Inhabitants of Islamic countries try to avoid numbers with four in them. A large, modern hotel might not have any rooms numbered four, so room 420 would be numbered 520.

If these practices seem impractical or even silly to an American, think about actions that you take which might seem unreasonable to a foreigner. Do you knock on wood or throw salt over your shoulder? Do you walk around ladders instead of under them, and do you keep away from broken mirrors? Do you fear the number 666? Have you been in a hotel that has floors numbered twelve and fourteen but not thirteen? The point is, all cultures contain rituals that may seem illogical to people of other cultures; you need to know the standards of the society with which you are interacting and to adopt them when appropriate.

Interestingly, this may require your company to create a standard of ethics, too. In the United States, bribery is not only morally and ethically wrong, it is also illegal. What do you do in countries where bribery is an accepted way of life? In West Africa, "dashing" is a common practice. To dash someone who is in power is to give them a gift. In a sense, this is a method of showing respect; at the same time, dash is also a gift given in advance of a favor. How is that different from a bribe, especially in a culture in which people are expected to supplement their meager incomes with such favors? How does this differ from the tips taxi drivers and restaurant servers receive in our own country. In some cultures, taxi drivers and restaurant servers are not allowed to accept tips. Not many years ago, the only nations that had lotteries were in the third world, and the only legal casino gambling in the United States was in Nevada. Will the same pattern be followed with bribery?

SECTION SUMMARY

Subtle influences of personal ambition, values, and goals condition the writing process by giving the writer a clear sense of direction. Writing managerial communications also invokes identification with the corporate image, and you must be aware of this throughout the process. Finally, writing must follow a simple ethical code and work within the appropriate protocol. By their very nature, managerial communications evoke elements of authority and reputation purely by originating from a managerial position with a corporate organization.

CHALLENGE PROBLEM FOR REVIEW

Image is an extraordinarily powerful aspect of the corporate world, government, and nonprofit organizations. Reflect on recent crises in the business world: improprieties in the stock market, corporate scandals, or government programs in which the projected and public image contradicted what was occurring behind the scenes. How damaging is this? What is the role of the manager in helping to prevent or rectify this kind of image problem? How does managerial writing support this? Finally, what might be the ethical concerns raised for the manager who faithfully pursues organizational goals even when serious issues are brewing?

CHAPTER SUMMARY
...

In this chapter, you have introduced to the importance of strategy in managerial writing. Effective managerial writing requires that you recognize the context of your writing, the audience for whom it is intended, and the importance of offering a reasonable argument for your requested actions. Complexities of the workplace make managerial writing easier to accomplish but more difficult to be effective. You must at all times be alert to corporate and organizational nuances, ranging from the mission statement to specific objectives. Your personal goals must also match in some way the corporate goals that you have accepted.

EXERCISES
...

1. Locate and review speeches given by two politicians, one liberal and one conservative, on a subject such as tax cuts (These are usually on the Web at a politician's Web site). Summarize their logical arrangements and then analyze the language that they use to express those arguments. Do their words reflect their ideas logically? Given their choice of words, do you believe and/or trust their motives? Which words led you to your conclusions? Why?
2. Use Table 1.2: Simple Goal-Setting Task, to complete a goal-setting exercise and value-clarification exercise. Your goals reflect your values, even if you have never articulated the value. For instance, if you expect to achieve corporate success, one of your values would be financial success as well. If you hope to achieve a leadership position in local, state, or federal government, you probably do not feel a need to achieve great wealth. Use your goals to find hidden or unspoken values.

WRITING EXERCISES
...

1. Write a letter from yourself in the future to yourself in the present. Explain why writing has been an important part of your successful career.
2. Begin a collection of samples of writing (memoranda, e-mail, business letter, proposals from another class). Look for examples of writing: good and bad, clear and unclear, well-reasoned and poorly reasoned, and so on.
3. Choose the Web site of a national or international corporation with a strong and well-received corporate image. Analyze how the image is conveyed and what makes it effective. For instance, in addition to written mission and values statements, what other channels of

communication are used to strengthen the image? How is the image transmitted to the general public?

4. Review the definitions for types of cultures given in the glossary at the end of the book. In 100 words, describe the microcultures, organizational cultures, and macrocultures in which you are involved. Include your school, work, and family life. You might compare and contrast the school, work, and family cultures.

_____

_____

_____

_____

_____

_____

_____

_____

_____

_____

_____

_____

_____

_____

_____

_____

_____

_____

_____

_____

_____

_____

_____

_____

_____

_____

_____

_____

_____

_____

_____

_____

_____

_____

IN-BOX EXERCISE
...

Welcome to the first In-Box Exercise. This assessment activity has been designed to provide you with a real-world application of your writing skills. The concept of an in box is simple and quite comparable to types of activity that managers in all fields and all types of organizations face every day.

Typically, you will find in your in box a set of memos, e-mails, notes regarding phone messages, and other forms of written communication. You then evaluate and prepare responses to the items and direct others to take specific actions needed to resolve the problem. Usually, the items focus on one or two core problems, but sometimes there are items that are not relevant and are meant to distract you—as will be the case in an actual business environment.

In these In-Box Exercises, you play the role of a newly appointed manager required by your supervisor to respond to these items in writing. The idea of the exercises is to test your skill at using written communications to direct others and to do so in a manner that anticipates events.

You have an administrative assistant, Kim, and the main office has assigned a secretary, Pat, to your unit. For each chapter, this scenario will be the same, but the nature of the messages will be different in order to reflect the chapter contents.

For your convenience, the items are numbered as they appear in your in box and identify the form of the communication: memo, e-mail, handwritten note, and so forth. Item 1 would be the top item in the stack. Remember, some of the items may be distractors; you must organize your responses. You can use the space provided or add your own paper. You will need to indicate whether your responding communication is an e-mail, letter, or memo, or some other kind of note. A blank page titled "Notes" has been included on which you can give Kim directions or keep a list of actions for yourself.

Important points about this activity:

1. You are newly appointed to a management position and must respond to these items in writing.

2. You have an administrative assistant, Kim, and a secretary, Pat.

3. Upon "arrival," you find several items in your in box. The items are numbered according to when they arrived in your in box. (1 being the most recent.)

4. You must organize your responses. You will need to indicate whether your instructions and messages are to be sent as an e-mail, letter, memo, or some other kind of message. Be sure to identify the persons to whom you are sending them.

5. Your task is to solve problems and take action using written instructions and communications.

6. You may be asked by your instructor to justify and/or explain your responses.

IN-BOX

You have been employed by SHG General, an international conglomerate. Your first assignment is as a new unit manager for Widgets International, Inc., a company that makes a variety of items used in interior construction. One division makes electrical fixtures, another makes specialty moldings, and another makes flooring products. Your division makes and assembles door hardware that includes locksets, hinges, drawer pulls, and other upscale accessories.

ITEM 1: TYPED NOTE FROM JERRY We only have about one day's worth of raw brass stock for the Victorian fixtures. I checked with our brass plate supplier, and they can't get us the extra thick plate we use on the Victorian stuff anytime soon without a special order. Should I place a rush order?

Your Response

Check one: ☐ Memorandum   ☐ E-mail   ☐ Letter   ☐ Note   ☐ Other

To: _____

_____

_____

_____

_____

_____

_____

_____

_____

_____

_____

_____

_____

_____

_____

_____

_____

_____

_____

_____

_____

_____

_____

_____

_____

_____

_____

ITEM 2: E-MAIL FROM JAN, INVENTORY CLERK The computer shows about 500 Vintage Victorian interior door sets and 100 entry door sets. The hinges seem to be completely out of stock. Jim told me that we would be making more soon. There is no standing order for these, and the ones we have been around for a while.

Your Response

Check one: ☐ Memorandum   ☐ E-mail   ☐ Letter   ☐ Note   ☐ Other

To: _____

_____

_____

_____

_____

_____

_____

_____

_____

_____

_____

_____

_____

_____

_____

_____

_____

_____

_____

_____

_____

_____

_____

_____

_____

ITEM 3: NOTE FROM LYNN, LINE SUPERVISOR Welcome to the unit! I was watching one of those home improvement shows Saturday when I noticed they were using our "Vintage Victorian" line for the door hardware and other trim. Last time the show used one of our products, I think it was a crown molding, all the major home improvement stores sold out and we didn't have enough stock to fill all the orders. I think the molding division had to work a lot of overtime just to fill orders. We don't keep much of the Vintage Victorian in the warehouse, and you may not know this, but we have to do extra maintenance when we make the stuff. It uses our thickest brass plating, and that wears the stamps and cutters down really fast. Those solid brass doorknobs are forged, and have to be ordered from another division. So, I think we probably need to get some of the lines running the hardware. We might need to plan for overtime too.

Your Response

Check one: ☐ Memorandum ☐ E-mail ☐ Letter ☐ Note ☐ Other

To:

KEY TERMS
...

Argument (p. 9)

Assertions (p. 10)

Behavioral approach (p. 6)

Blank page approach (p. 5)

Common ground (p. 7)

Communication channel (p. 7)

Communication process (p. 6)

Controlling idea (p. 5)

Cooperative principle (p. 7)

Culture (p. 12)

Empowerment (p. 15)

Encoding process (p. 7)

Ethics (p. 20)

Formula approach (p. 6)

Internal entrepreneurship (p. 15)

Macroculture (p. 4)

Microculture (p. 4)

Organizational culture (p. 4)

Prewriting (p. 5)

Reasoning (p. 9)

Strategy (p. 5)

Values clarification (p. 17)

REFERENCES
...

Boyett, Joseph, and Henry Conn (1991). *Workplace 2000*. New York: Penguin Books.

Covey, Stephen (1989). *The Seven Habits of Highly Effective People*. New York: Simon and Schuster.

Garrison, Mark, and Margaret Bly (1997). *Human Relations: Productive Approaches for the Workplace*. Boston: Allyn and Bacon.

Harr, Jonathan (1996). *A Civil Action*. New York: Random House.

"Not Your Average Bear," *Business People*, February 2002, at the Vermont Teddy Bear Company, http://ir.vtbearcompany.com/index.php?id=139 (accessed June 15, 2004).

Simon, Sidney, Leland Howe, and Howard Kirschenbaum (1995). *Values Clarification: A Practical, Action-Directed Workbook*. New York: Warner Books.

Soslow, Robin (1992). "Master of Motivation," *Business Atlanta* 21, no. 4 S1, p. 24.

CHAPTER 2

...

ORGANIZING YOUR WRITING STRATEGY

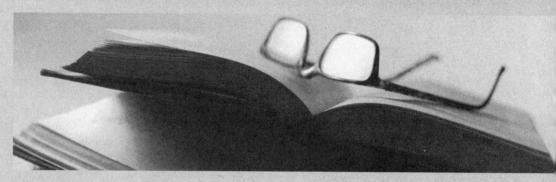

LEARNING OUTCOMES

...

Upon completion of this chapter, you will be able to accomplish the following tasks:

1. Identify the controlling idea of the writing project.

2. Select an appropriate organizing principle for the writing project.

3. Apply the appropriate organizational structure to create an effective outline.

4. Develop the writing project using comparison-and-contrast or cause-and-effect analysis.

5. Identify the four guiding procedures for effective business writing.

6. Demonstrate an understanding of the role of logic and reasoning in supporting and utilizing evidence.

7. Recognize and avoid logical and reasoning fallacies.

8. Create logical arguments.

9. Employ critical and lateral thinking in the process of organizing writing projects.

"And now at this point in the meeting I'd like to shift
the blame away from me and onto someone else."

You might wonder why we focus on organizing written communication when there are so many tools to help us organize all aspects of life and communication. Ironically, the more organizing tools we have, the more it appears that we have become disorganized. We face many pressures: diversity in the workplace, corporate restructuring, and a frenzy of news and information, just to name a few. The area that has the greatest impact on our writing is electronic communication, especially e-mail and the Web. Reflection on the communication environment will reveal this influence and the potential dangers that accompany it.

Electronic media dominates the communication environment. The impact of information technology on writing is so significant that it threatens the quality of written communication. Core aspects of communication must be considered. Whatever your writing task, it must be guided by clear, unambiguous logic. Numerous strategies are available to establish, reinforce, or complement the logic in your writing. The speed of the Internet and e-mail, combined with their ease of use, outpaces the mental tasks of thoughtfully constructing our messages. This rapid cycle from thought to sent message will get shorter and faster as we move to more speech-based messages and bypass the mechanics of word processing. Effective communication depends on tools of planning and reasoning no matter what the medium. Many managers have regretted sending a message too quickly, failing to give it the careful consideration appropriate to a professional communication.

The Internet is a virtually endless medium for communication. As a means of conveying electronic mail, it has revolutionized corporate and institutional communication. One of the most exciting aspects of the Internet lies in the individual's ability to place information in a single location that can be viewed by many. However, there are side effects to this overly exposed information that are not widely recognized. The very speed of Internet information is a major concern. Although sites on the Internet tend to offer details in an abbreviated, to-the-point fashion, the desire to get the point across quickly encourages the sender to present the results and little else. The consequence is a writing style that depends upon what we called assertion in Chapter 1. The reader is expected to trust that the author has the necessary evidence and reasoning to support the conclusions presented. Visitors to a Web site typically have little patience for long downloads of details and supporting argument. Many professionals rely on the reputation of the site or the author or both to evaluate the validity of the assertions made.

Professional graphics, user interactions, and bulleted lists are fine for the purposes of the World Wide Web. When our other writing imitates that of the Internet, though, we chance the loss of the distinction between assertion and argument. When managerial communications are not justified based on assertion supported by sufficient personal, positional, or organizational authority, then the communication must include appropriate justification with the context of the message itself. This fact is too often lost on inexperienced managers who believe they always have the authority to rely on assertion alone. This justification distinguishes messages that merely contain claims (assertions) from those that convince their audience through reasoned arguments. Deciding which messages require internal justification and which do not is an important consideration for a manager during the strategy phase of writing. Including justification where assertion only is appropriate will communicate a lack of confidence or understanding of one's authority. Failing to include justification where it is required will communicate arrogance and a lack of understanding of one's relative position with respect to power and authority in the organization. Erring in either direction is a serious mistake for a manager to make.

In this chapter, we examine the important strategies of a controlling idea, the value of using a prescribed method for organizing ideas into messages, and the role of evidence and reasoning in developing a justification. *These elements represent the key components of your writing process strategy.* In addition, other strategic elements play crucial roles. These factors include the character of the message (positive, negative, request for action, etc.), the cultural contexts of the audience, and the authority and credibility of the writer.

Defining the Controlling Idea

A controlling idea provides the strategic guidance necessary to lead the writer from prewriting to completion of the work.

Janet Clark, an organic chemist, manages professionals and support staff for Certified Containment, Inc., a small corporation that provides consulting services to companies involved in large-scale government contracting. She was asked to supply a memorandum of support for a company that is trying to secure a contract from the U.S. Department of Agriculture. The project manager requested that she send the memorandum to him and address several points (see his letter in Figure 2.1).

How should Dr. Clark proceed? Before she composes the memorandum, she must develop a clear idea of what she wants to accomplish. This is the controlling idea, the

KEY CONCEPT 2.1
...

FIGURE 2.1
...

Project Director Marshall Edwards' Letter

CERTIFIED CONTAINMENT, INCORPORATED

A Division of *SHG General*   800.555.4321
Suite 1000, One SHG Boulevard
Dayton, Ohio 45439

Springfield,MN

Dr. Janet Clark
Director
Clark Chemical Consulting Services

February 27, 2005

Dear Dr. Clark:

Please submit to me a memorandum of support regarding the controlled packaging project for which we have asked you to serve as consultant. This memorandum is critical to the success of our proposal to the USDA. The contracting division needs evidence of your ability, experience, and track record on similar projects. I think that they are also a bit uncertain about the resources necessary for you to analyze and provide necessary control assessment in a timely fashion.

Please return the memorandum by Tuesday, March 5.

Thank you,

Marshall Edwards
Project Director
Project Number 18803

conceptualization of a writing task that incorporates the purpose of the task and the strategy required to achieve it. Dr. Clark realizes that the memorandum is actually not just for the project manager. She must convince the contract-granting agency that her company has the expertise, staff, and available time to provide the critical external guidance required by the contract. She begins by outlining her thoughts.

Outlining: Giving Your Ideas Order

In this case, successful business writing requires organized, logical reasoning. A logical structure provides the foundation for an effective argument. As the overall organizing device for a piece of writing, the **outline** establishes the order in which points are made and serves as the major unifying element of the writing. Typically, writers use an outline to define the structure of the planned writing. However, not all outlines look alike. Some writers prepare a list of three or four key points, associate evidence and analysis with these points, and then proceed to the writing stage. For more formal writing projects or difficult tasks, a more detailed outline may be used to establish the structure. In either case, the outline reflects the tactical plan for implementing the writing strategy.

While we will avoid writing that appears to be cut from template formulas, the common forms of outlines are routine and predictable. Outlines should be, and this suggests that formulas are not in themselves bad or sub-par. As the controlling idea unfolds, the reasoning and justifications offered to build the argument begin to shape the specific structure of the outline and ultimately determine the finished product. The preparation of an outline is the first step in implementing a writing strategy.

Organizing Principles

Dr. Clark identified four key phrases in the project manager's e-mail request and arranged them in a sensible order (see Figure 2.2). This list was the core of her outline, to which she added details. The list reflects her awareness of what the writing must convey; that her team can do the proposed work and that Certified Containment, Inc., should be selected for the contract.

When you begin preparing material for a writing project, you should list only the basic ideas that you want to discuss, information that you want to convey, evidence that you want to present, and the conclusions to which your analysis leads. How much outline do you need? The outline is for the writer's benefit and is the writer's guide to orderly

FIGURE 2.2
...

Dr. Clark's Rudimentary Outline with Notes

Notes for Memo to Marshall:

Expertise: Mine and staffs'

Experience: Last three similar projects

Available staff support:
   Each staff member has required time available, can add additional staff as needed

Material and physical resources:
   Have equipment required for this type of testing and chemical assessments
   Lab space can be controlled and secured

Order?
   Need by next Tuesday

Can I fax it to him?

---

expression. Even writing a routine e-mail can benefit from a short list of paragraph topics, and more formal letters and memos benefit from a carefully made list. Your list need not resemble a traditional outline, but rather it provides a **mnemonic** (memory) **device** in the form of a concrete record of selected ideas. Often one term at the head of an outline section reminds the writer of an entire set of ideas and data.

Of course, organizing one's ideas, data, and other supporting evidence into a meaningful whole is best accomplished through a formal outline: Arrange ideas and illustrations into an order that stipulates specific relationships among ideas, supporting evidence, and conclusions. Some points obviously fit into groups; others may be inappropriate for discussion and should be discarded. Many writers have difficulty deleting material that required effort to collect or write. An outline helps judge the usefulness of material. If the material does not contribute to the objective or the strategy, it probably distracts from the objective.

Some writers think through their subjects so thoroughly that they feel there is no need to create an outline. This approach requires skill and practice; few people can write proficiently without an outline guide. The highest praise that seventeenth-century dramatist Ben Jonson offered about his contemporary William Shakespeare was that he wrote with hardly a "blot" (he made no corrections). Even for experts and experienced managers, a formal outline is a useful tool. The act of creating an outline improves understanding of the material, strengthens the relationships between thoughts, and helps identify logical gaps. Sometimes unseen relationships between thoughts emerge, and clues to a more convincing order may become apparent. Finally, an outline works like a to-do list; all of the ideas and points are covered, assuring that everything is included. When preparing a major report of any length, an outline can become the table of contents and provide the organizational headings of the report.

The first step in creating an outline is to determine your controlling idea. Some of the aspects of the controlling idea will be implicit, such as whether your audience includes fellow professionals or is the general public. This form of categorizing represents a line of questioning to refine a controlling idea. For example, beginning a report on sales approaches, the first major division is clearly implied: Your topic concerns salespeople as opposed to technicians. Next, categorize sales representatives as either company employees or independent vendors. If you are interested in examining marketing techniques, a further distinction might be made between national and local sales. Your examination of marketing techniques indicates that there are two types of salespeople: those who handle inside sales and those who deal with outside sales. If you want to focus on outside sales, a further categorization might include those who are responsible for individual accounts and those who work with corporate accounts. *Remember, any reference to an excluded category will be a distraction to the reader!* Figure 2.3 on page 36 illustrates an outline of these divisions. Parenthetically, much of the time, a manager's topic is assigned rather than chosen, in which case the purpose of outlining is to develop the controlling idea, rather than to select it.

Another approach for focusing your controlling idea is to use a matrix. For instance, the decision regarding the most appropriate form of written communication can be placed on a matrix. Table 2.1 on page 36 is an illustration of the matrix of possibilities of written communication organized according to the purpose of the message and the nature of the audience.

Keep in mind the following points when creating an outline matrix. First, divide the subject according to a single, appropriate principle. In examining a series of topics, divide them into groups based on common characteristics. For example, the book market is divided into hardcover and paperback. Second, be sure that the categories are mutually exclusive (everything should fit into one category only). Hardcover books may be mysteries, science fiction, children's books, or romance or historical novels, but so also may paperbacks. Similarly, mysteries may be either hardcover or paperback. However, Sherlock Holmes stories are always mysteries, whether hardcover or paperback. Remember: Consistency is vital in the effort to focus the impact of your analysis.

FIGURE 2.3
...

Categories and Contents

Categories for Task Clarification

Nonhumans—Humans

Nonbusiness People—Business People

Manufacturing—Marketing

National—Local

Inside Sales—Outside Sales

Individual Accounts—Corporate Accounts

TABLE 2.1
...

Simple Decision Matrix of Purpose and Audience

The contents of these cells will be filled in throughout the course of the text. Where does Dr. Clark's memorandum fit? Where does Mr. Edwards' memo to her fit?

	Audience:						
Purpose:	Worker	Team	Group	Corporation	Vendors	Customers	Public
To Inform							
To Request Action							
To Persuade							
To Affirm or Confirm							

Layout: Mechanics of the Outline

The formal outline consists of three main divisions: the introduction, the body, and the conclusion. Twenty-five hundred years ago, the philosopher Aristotle suggested that in the introduction to a speech you tell your audience what you are going to tell them, in the body you tell them, and in the conclusion you tell them what you told them (Barnes, 1984). An outline of written documents must do this, too. Later, when you develop details, the outline governs the progression. That progression develops from logical relationships. These relationships provide increasingly more and more detailed definitions, exemplifications, and modifications.

The traditional approach for identifying outline components designates major units with capital Roman numerals (I, II, III, . . .). Major subheads are indicated by capital letters (A, B, . . .). Arabic numerals indicate subdivisions of the subheads (1, 2, . . .), and further subordinations are designated by lowercase letters (a, b, . . .), then numerals in parentheses [(1), (2), . . .]. These are followed by lowercase letters in parentheses [(a), (b), . . .], numbers set off with closing parentheses and punctuation marks [1.), 2.), . . .], and then lowercase letters set off with closing parentheses and punctuation marks [a.), b.), . . .]. However, only in extremely rare instances would you need to develop this level of detail. Indentation should reflect the degree of subordination. Major headings are aligned; subheadings of the first degree are indented equally; subsequent subheadings should be indented further, according to the degree of subordination. Figure 2.4 demonstrates how this system should appear.

Choices about the details of an outline enumeration vary only a little bit, yet publishers refer to headings as A level, B level, C level, and so on. Keep this in mind if you are writing a report or proposal that will be professionally printed for wider circulation or for submission to an outside group or agency. Even your in-house printing and publications staff will use this terminology, especially if they have professional experience in the publishing industry.

The parts of the outline should be arranged so that each major division contains a group of related ideas. The parts are arranged in a natural, parallel, and logical order throughout—both on the level of the overall outline and on the level within the individual segments. Headings should not overlap or be coordinated with unequal headings. Since headings indicate divisions between two or more parts, avoid using single headings or subheadings.

When you have completed your writing task, compare it with your original outline to make sure that you have included all pertinent data and followed the order that you intended. When writing a long or complex piece, some writers prepare an outline from their finished work and then compare this outline with the original one they had planned to follow. Not only can you determine whether you actually followed your plan and overlooked nothing, but you may discover new relationships or weaknesses. You can easily determine which outline is actually the most effective and logical. Discrepancies between the original outline and the final outline might indicate weaknesses, errors, or even opportunities for enhancement. Perhaps your material forced you to stray from your original plan. You may find that you need to go back and rearrange your material to fit your initial outline. Or, during the writing process, you might have developed a more effective structure that grew organically from your material as you committed it to paper.

Structural or Ordering Strategies

As your overall writing strategy is based on your goals, so the strategy for developing a structure for a writing task depends on what the outline is intended to accomplish. An

FIGURE 2.4
...

Parts of a Formal Outline

```
 I.  Introduction
II.  Body
     A. (Subhead of the first degree)
        1. (Subhead of the second degree)
           a. (Subhead of the third degree)
              (1) (Subhead of the fourth degree)
                  (a) (Fifth degree)
                      1.) (Sixth degree)
                          a.) (Seventh degree)
        2. (Repeat pattern)
     B.
III. Conclusion
```

outline guides the writer through one of three basic organizational tasks: (1) arrangement; (2) inducing structure; and (3) transformation (Greeno, 1978). The **arrangement task** involves taking existing elements and placing them in a meaningful pattern, much as one would complete a jigsaw puzzle. In the puzzle, there are elements of order and structure, such as corner pieces, edges, color groups, and so on. An organizational restructuring would be an example of this kind of problem solving. The **inducing-structure task** involves the creation of a structure or organization where none exists. The identification of causal relationships is a means of inducing structure in an argument. The creation of a new organizational unit, a new position, even a new process or procedure is an example of this task. A **transformation task** takes an existing order and requires that you analyze it. A series of questions that need answering should be answered in the form in which they are given; the questions imply a structure, and the writer merely needs to convert or *transform* the questions into responses (as well as add evidence and reasoning). In report writing, taking data and transforming it into a PowerPoint presentation exemplifies this task. See Table 2.2 for clarification of these tasks.

A half dozen common approaches for structuring material are available for creating a business report. Most of these can be used for any basic organization task. Using one of these common approaches ensures that readers can follow your ideas easily.

1. *Sequential Order.* **Sequential** or **chronological order** involves the presentation of a series of events in a particular order that may be time-ordered (moving from first to last in order of time, as in a narrative description of your daily routine), alphanumeric (abacus, barometer, computer; 1, 2, 3), or by rank (lieutenant, captain, major, or queen, king, ace). For example, the sequential order would be appropriate for a work instruction that specifies the activities that must be done, in order, to achieve some end, such as entering a sales order into the company's order control system.

2. *Spatial Order.* **Spatial order** places items according to their relationships with other items. This order consists of the movement from one object or physical location to another in a reasonable manner that may include a description of the physical relationship of the items being described, such as in a description of your position in a room. Another example is writing about corporate regions, organized by geographic territories. A variation of sequential order is *figurative spatial order*. Imagine describing the new organization chart for a recently merged company. Spatial terminology may help define roles, new

TABLE 2.2

Organizational Task Summary Chart

Concept	Definition	Example
Arrangement Task	This task involves taking existing elements and placing them in a meaningful pattern.	Jigsaw puzzle Organizational restructuring
Inducing-Structure Task	This task involves the creation of a structure or organization where none exists.	Number sequence Creation of new unit Creation of new position
Transformation Task	This task takes an existing order and requires that you analyze it in order to convert it into another order.	Rubic's cube puzzle Tower of Hanoi problem Formulation of new procedures

entities, and the relationships between units and corporate officers (Jeff is over John's group; John and Jack are now peers, and so forth). However, this order does not refer to actual space. Instead it is "figurative," and it refers to a relationship of power or authority.

3. *Simple-to-Complex Order.* In the **simple-to-complex order**, basic concepts are presented first, possibly in the form of an overview. These points are followed by a more detailed, in-depth discussion of the points. In this form, a general, briefly summarized claim would be followed by a detailed discussion of the reasoning and evidence. For example, a manager might assert that three lessons are to be learned from the recently completed audit, list them, and then proceed to describe each in order, with supporting evidence from the audit report.

4. *General-to-Specific Order.* Several patterns are utilized for this structure: **basic**, in which a general topic is introduced and then specific evidence or aspects of the issue are considered; **whole-to-part**, in which an overview is provided with subsequent attention being paid to the components; **major-to-subclass**, in which something is divided into units that are examined separately, though usually in relationship to each other and to the whole. For example, a manager might describe the entire process for realizing a new product, from initial design considerations through development, prototyping, and finally manufacturing, before addressing specific issues of concern with respect to current prototyping methodologies. This approach places the topic of interest into its larger organizational context, helping to identify its relative importance and its boundary conditions.

5. *Most-to-Least-Important Order.* Often the most direct approach and the best course of action is to present the strongest part of your argument at the very beginning. The **most-to-least important order** places the most critical or most convincing element of your argument at the beginning and points of decreasing importance follow. The focus of your justification will be on the most critical point. The less important components become supporting elements. This ordering method should be used to keep your audience's attention on your central argument or reasoning. A manager who has developed six reasons why she should be given the budget to hire another employee will usually list the strongest reason first, recognizing that it is unlikely anyone reading her message will actually take the time to get through the sixth reason.

6. *Least-to-Most-Important Order.* This approach mimics the inductive reasoning approach discussed later. The **least-to-most important order** creates a sequence that moves from subordinate and less critical points, issues, or reasons to the most critical points. The effect of this order is to create a dramatic "revelation" or conclusion. By encouraging the reader to agree with the less important reasons— sometimes these arguments are the easiest to accept or understand, the reader is already on your side by the time you reach the critical or most powerful parts of the rationale. This approach can be useful in outdoing others, for example. A manager might list the reasons for making a particular decision already given by others in reverse order of their merit, ending with his own, most important, reason. This positioning can leave the impression that the manager had the final say in the matter, thus enhancing the manager's perceived status.

These last two ordering principles draw upon two important psychological concepts called the *primacy effect* and *recency effect*. These two effects combine in memory to cause us to remember the first and the last items in a list more easily than the middle items (Glanzer and Cunitz, 1966). Depending upon how you emphasize your chosen order, and to some extent on the readiness of your audience, you can use these two effects to your advantage. For instance, you can place the most important data in your first item and the most important reasoning in your last. Your audience will have a greater chance of remembering these two critical points. See Table 2.3 for a chart that summarizes these organizational techniques.

Practical Style in Outlining

Does an outline need to follow formal organizing principles for headings and utilize one of these common ordering methods? These mechanical issues are of concern if you are working on a proposal or other large writing project with a team or over an extended period of time. If you leave your writing and return to it days later, a clear outline will make it easier to restart. You probably have returned to something that you worked on some time ago and found yourself needing to reconstruct your plan. Formal outlines help avoid the need to repeat work.

Some writers have their own individual, informal, yet systematic style of preparing an outline. The *systematic* quality of their approaches provides the key to success. One person may list brief topics, another may state the basic relationships and explanations

TABLE 2.3
...

Organizing Techniques Summary Chart

	Definition
Sequential Order	The presentation of a series of events in a chronological order.
Spatial Order	Consists of the movement from one object or physical location to another in a reasonable manner that may include a description of the physical relationship of the items being described.
Simple-to-Complex Order	Structure basic concepts are presented first, probably in the form of an overview.
General-to-Specific Order	1. Basic, in which a general topic is introduced and then specific evidence or aspects of the issue are considered. 2. Whole-to-part, in which an overview is provided, with subsequent attention being paid to the components. 3. Major-to-subclass, in which something is divided into units that are examined separately, though usually in relationship to each other and to the whole.
Most-to-Least-Important Order	Places the most critical or most convincing element of your argument at the beginning and points of decreasing importance follow.
Least-to-Most-Important Order	Creates a sequence that moves from subordinate and less critical points, issues, or reasons to the most critical points.

being used, a third may list each piece of evidence and data that will be incorporated. Yet another may write a series of topic sentences. These other elements include actual evidence and data, specific justifications, and especially the specific formulation of the goal that will be included in the writing (such as the request being made or the information being conveyed).

Mind-mapping is also commonly used to develop and display relationships more flexibly than in a traditional outline. This free-flowing **mind-map** approach allows for creativity and can be used to break artificial barriers and other blocks to problems solving. The technique is excellent for brainstorming. In its simplest form, you place your main thoughts on a page and then draw lines to show the connections between and among the ideas. This method helps you and other members of your team visualize a problem or challenge and all the relationships that may exist between the problem and its possible solutions. The technique can be used individually or in a group. Figure 2.5 illustrates mind mapping.

Remember, as you prepare your outline, keep in mind what you are trying to accomplish. Your objectives guide you as you select the order of points to be made and the method of analysis to be offered. Only when you have organized the analysis and the evidence into a meaningful structure should you begin writing. The following section looks at the methods of using evidence and analysis to build an idea into a successful message.

SECTION SUMMARY

Once you establish your controlling idea and determine your audience, outlining provides a logical structure for your writing. Outlines may be developed according to six patterns: sequential order, spatial order, simple-to-complex order, general-to-specific order, most-to-least-important order, and least-to-most-important order.

FIGURE 2.5
...

Mind Mapping

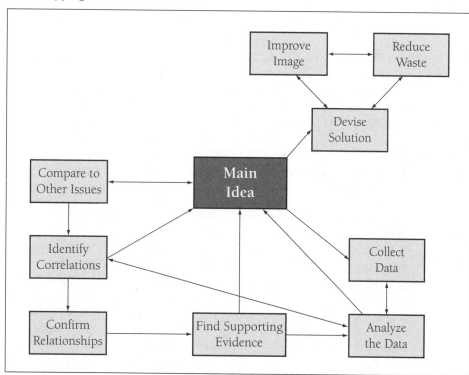

CHALLENGE PROBLEM FOR REVIEW

Reflect on the problem of profitability and its relationship to outsourcing. Construct a matrix and a mind-map of the issues involved. Now, once you visualize all the concerns, rationales, and management issues, consider which outline pattern would most elegantly present the aspects of the situation while offering a balanced place for each issue.

Analytic Tools and Basic Writing Guidelines

KEY CONCEPT 2.2
...

Successful execution of the controlling idea requires organizing the idea around the right analytic process and following a simple set of writing guidelines.

Will Dr. Clark's memorandum need to convince the reader that she and her team are the *best* candidates for the duties required in the contract or should she make the case that the team has all the necessary skills and experience to complete the job as required? (Basically, others can do the job, but her team is the best choice.) The first claim requires that her analysis lead to a specific cause and effect: If her team is not chosen, then the project will fail (cause and effect: if . . ., then). The second claim requires a comparative analysis of the other options. She could claim that she has done this kind of work before and has been successful, efficient, timely, and cost effective. Dr. Clark might offer these analyses directly or she might lead her reader to make the analysis and come to the same conclusion. In either case, she must address her audience in such a way that the analysis is made for it—contracting agencies have little time for lengthy and exhaustive reviews. Whether a contracting agency makes time for a lengthy and exhaustive review depends on the size and value of the project. For example, when evaluating potential suppliers who responded to an RFP (the RFP, or request for proposal, is discussed in detail in Chapter 6) for an $800 million dollar contract for telecommunications equipment, a company might structure the evaluation in three steps, spread out over six months: an evaluation of the written response; an evaluation team at the supplier's facilities; and, finally, cooperative testing at the buyer's test facilities.

Analysis: Tools for Building Ideas

Analysis refers to the means of identifying relationships between and among different components of an argument or a process of reasoning. An analysis may take a number of forms. Two of the simplest and most frequently used approaches are (1) comparison and contrast and (2) cause and effect.

Comparison and Contrast: Strategic Roles

Making a comparison and identifying a contrast comprise the simplest means of analyzing relationships. **Comparison and contrast** allow the illustration of differences between things normally considered similar and of similarities between things normally considered different. To paraphrase poet Alexander Pope, this pattern is useful for making unfamiliar things seem familiar. In fact, comparison is an essential tool of poets. However, managerial writing is not poetry, and extended metaphors belong in advertising or public speaking. Nevertheless, *appropriate* comparisons and contrasts make for convincing writing.

Comparison and contrast are two distinct techniques and the difference between them is simple. Using **comparison**, the emphasis is on points of similarity; with **contrast**, the emphasis is on points of dissimilarity (sometimes the term *comparison* is used—incorrectly —to designate a combination of both patterns). Writers apply the comparison-and-contrast technique for analyzing two or more options, choices, procedures, and so forth. Comparison primarily addresses similarities between things that are in the same class. However, one common type of comparison, **analogy**, examines likenesses between members of different categories and is useful in clarifying and explaining difficult or abstract concepts. Analogies are so popular, that some consider analogy a separate class of analytic tool. In an analogy, the writer expresses the focal concepts in terms of paralleling something simple or concrete with which the audience is already familiar. This pattern is seen when suggesting that there is a "ripple effect" in the economy when interest rates are raised or lowered. By analogy, the economy is like a pond. The actions of the Federal Reserve—sometimes just the ruminations of the Federal Reserve chairman—affect other entities, most notably the bond and stock markets. In turn, these entities affect other sectors of the economy. This process continues much as ripples spread over the surface of a pond when a stone is tossed into it. We are all familiar with what a rippling pond surface looks like, so we easily imagine a parallel in the effects of one person's actions spreading out to have an impact on a great many people.

Comparison-and-contrast processes may serve several purposes. They can function to provide an objective, informational comparison, merely listing qualities or characteristics and drawing distinctions between two or more things. A demonstration of the differences between two or more things allows readers to make choices based on which of the things examined best suits their needs. Comparison and contrast can be used to clarify complicated, unfamiliar issues by identifying similarities between the unfamiliar and the familiar. Explaining an expert system for assessing credit worthiness of applicants can be compared to the choice sets of operatorless telephone answering services. "If you wish to speak to the service department, press 2" kinds of choices are familiar. An automated expert-decision system works much the same way; that is, each automatic choice follows a specific rule (though no human has to make any active choice), and the comparison can make the explanation clear.

Comparison-and-Contrast Patterns The two most common patterns used in comparison and contrast are subject-by-subject and point-by-point. Both patterns follow a division by subject or by points; the difference appears in the organization of the presentation. In the subject-by-subject process, also known as whole-by-whole, information for one subject is given in full, followed by information for subsequent subjects. Figure 2.6a is an illustration of this pattern.

If you were in charge of purchasing and you were directed to obtain a new vehicle for your firm, your comparison might look like that in Figure 2.6b on page 44.

The advantages of the subject-by-subject format include providing for a full, unified discussion of each subject. Normally used for simple comparisons (the fewer the points being compared the better), it allows for discussion of one item at a time. Among the disadvantages are delays in reaching the conclusion and some difficulty in following the

FIGURE 2.6a
...

Subject-by-Subject Comparison Format

I.   Introduction
II. Body
    A. First Subject
        1. First Detail
        2. Second Detail
    B. Second Subject
        1. First Detail (parallel to above)
        2. Second Detail (parallel to above)
III. Conclusion

FIGURE 2.6b
...

Subject-by-Subject Comparison

Vehicle Comparison

I. Introduction
   Discussion of need, funds available, possible vendors, models available
II. Body (Comparison)
   A. Pickup truck
      1. Functionality
      2. Original cost
      3. Maintenance
      4. Gas mileage
      5. Safety features
      6. Resale value
   B. Van
      1. Functionality
      2. Original cost
      3. Maintenance
      4. Gas mileage
      5. Safety features
      6. Resale value
III. Conclusion

argument. If your audience is familiar with one of your subjects, then focus on presenting the unfamiliar subject in detail. Other disadvantages arise in the tendency to dispute comparisons and encourage readers to recall their own biases.

The point-by-point pattern, sometimes called part-by-part, alternates information about the subjects being compared. An outline of this pattern would appear much the same as in the subject-by-subject format, as illustrated in Figure 2.7a.

While the outline looks the same, it operates quite differently, as is seen in the presentation of the vehicle choice example in Figure 2.7b.

The advantages of the point-by-point format include a presentation of similarities or differences in items. It is the best approach for comparing complex subjects. It also lends itself to making lists of pluses and minuses for a side-by-side comparison. A disadvantage is that the reader must juggle bits of information about each item. The reader must then try to bring them all together at the conclusion instead of having the complete presentation of each item's characteristics made in one block.

Comparison/Contrast Applications Whether you choose the subject-by-subject or the point-by-point pattern (and it certainly would be conceivable that you might want to employ both patterns in the same report), there are five factors that apply in either case.

1. *Consistency.* Your discussion must cover the same features for each subject and in the same order. Editors often refer to this consistency of order as the **principle of parallelism**. It would not be appropriate to talk about gas mileage in one case and gas tank size in another without making some sort of connection between the two. Another simple comparison would be the use of miles per gallon (mpg) in American cars and liters per 100 kilometers (L/100k) in Canadian cars. This

Point-by-Point Comparison Format

FIGURE 2.7a
...

```
I.   Introduction
II.  Body
     A.  First Point of Comparison
         1.  Subject 1
         2.  Subject 2
     B.  Second Point of Comparison
         1.  Subject 1
         2.  Subject 2
III. Conclusion
```

Point-by-Point Comparison

FIGURE 2.7b
...

```
I.   Introduction
     Could be the same as in the previous example
II.  Body (Comparison)
     A.  Functionality
         1.  Pickup Truck
         2.  Van
     B.  Original Cost
         1.  Pickup Truck
         2.  Van
     C.  Maintenance
         1.  Pickup Truck
         2.  Van
     D.  Gas Mileage
         1.  Pickup Truck
         2.  Van
     E.  Safety Features
         1.  Pickup Truck
         2.  Van
     F.  Resale Value
         1.  Pickup Truck
         2.  Van
III. Conclusion
```

comparison requires the reader to invert one or the other ratio and then convert between metric and English measurement so a comparison can be made. Initially, the two ratios are not parallel.

2. *Significant points.* If you are trying to communicate something, you generally want to be as effective and efficient as possible. Include pertinent points, but *never* introduce a point that has no bearing on your argument, no matter how

interesting. Irrelevant points confuse the reader and undermine the coherence if not the logic of your presentation. Gas tank size, for instance, is not likely to have anything to do with maintenance costs.

3. *Completeness*. In order for your reader to make the best, most informed decision possible, you must supply all pertinent information. Among other things, this requires that you recognize the scope and limitation of your assignment. Thus, you may need to consider load capacity in the pickup truck–van example shown in Figure 2.6 and 2.7, but a discussion of the history of the Japanese-German competition for a segment of the American motor vehicle market would probably require justification.

4. *Clarity*. Your reader must know what to look for and how to deal with the information presented. Not only should readers be provided with a definition of your charge (that is, what you have been instructed to do), and your analytical approach, but they must be able to follow your thoughts and analytical process step by step as well. If not overused, transition words or phrases such as "but," "on the other hand," "likewise," "next," "similarly," and "finally" provide clues that help lead your reader in the direction that you want to go.

5. *Audience awareness*. As with any writing assignment you undertake, the effectiveness of your comparison or contrast depends on the appropriateness of the elements involved and your audience's readiness to understand them. Innovative technical details in an engine's construction would probably be of little interest to someone whose primary duty lies in moving supplies from one job site to another. It is commonly understood that engineers and managers with an engineering background expect to see tables of numbers and charts showing data over time, whereas managers with a marketing or less technical background favor bullet points and illustrations. If you show bullet points and illustrations to engineers, they will ask to see the data. If you show tables and charts of data to non-technical people, they will ask you for your conclusions based on the data.

See Table 2.4 for a summary of the strategic roles of comparison and contrast.

Cause and Effect

There are different types of causes, and the inherent complexity of some problems may require a logical presentation of what may be a series of causes and effects. The two primary categories of causes are immediate and underlying causes (sometimes called ultimate or root causes).

Immediate causes are those that have clearly accepted connections to their effects, usually because they are close to the effect. Lighter weight cars and more efficient engines are the immediate causes of increased fuel economy in autos.

The **underlying** (or **ultimate** or **root**) **cause** is normally more complex and at first glance may not seem related to the effect being examined. The underlying causes of improved fuel economy include inflationary costs of gasoline, concern in the buying public for more "green" automobiles, engineering improvements, and the dependency on a foreign oil supply that may be disrupted. A **causal chain** occurs when one cause leads to an effect that, in turn, leads to a new cause and again to a new effect. Furthermore, one cause may lead to several effects and an effect might derive from any number of causes. For instance, two underlying causes for thousands of technological innovations are the space program and the invention of lasers. These have led to unanticipated applications. They include communications, weather forecasting, surgical techniques, food processing, miniaturization, ceramics, metal working (alloys), plastics, aeronautical design, cryogenics, semiconductors, photography, and many more.

TABLE 2.4

Comparison-and-Contrast Summary Chart

Pattern	Description
Subject-by-subject process	Also known as *whole-by-whole*, information for one subject is given in full, followed by information for subsequent subjects.
Point-by-point pattern	Sometimes called part-by-part, alternates information about the subjects being compared.

Critical Factors	
Consistency	The comparison must cover the same features for each subject, and in the same order. This is also called **principle of parallelism**
Significant points	To be as effective and efficient as possible, focus on the main points.
Completeness	For the reader to make the best, most informed decision possible, one must supply all pertinent information.
Clarity	The reader must know what to look for and how to deal with the information.
Audience awareness	The effectiveness of a comparison or contrast depends on the appropriateness of the elements involved and the audience's readiness to understand them.

Causes may also be classified by subdividing them according to their importance in producing an effect:

- *Contributory causes* may be a factor in the creation of an effect, but they must be present in combination with other factors since they are not sufficient to create the effect by themselves. In the mid-1960s, a new social freedom allowed the Beatles to be accepted. Because of their popularity, their hair styles, clothing fashions, social attitudes, and so on, influenced hair styles, clothing fashions, and social attitudes of millions of their fans, an influence that crossed over into the general public. As a result, the Beatles may have been an ultimate (obscure) or contributory cause that led to an effect that no one could have foreseen: the invention of seamless pantyhose. Pantyhose came about of necessity with the introduction of miniskirts and evolved into a billion-dollar business that has no apparent connection with the Beatles. Imagine trying to convince upper management that the Beatles are going to cause women to need pantyhose! Today, it is recognized that many trend-setting musical groups influence all manner of preferences. Artistic success may not be too far from business and marketing success as well.
- *Necessary causes* are needed for an effect to take place, but like contributory causes they are not sufficient in themselves to create an effect. Chemistry students are well acquainted with catalysts. Catalysts are necessary for some chemical reactions to take place, but the catalysts are not changed by the reaction and

can typically be reused. Also, catalysts are not sufficient causes because something more is required. Will a total quality management (TQM) program result in improved productivity? Can such a program work like a chemical catalyst? A catalyst like TQM may be necessary for change, but will not in itself cause the change; other ingredients must be present.

- *Sufficient causes* are in themselves adequate to create an effect. In some cases, only sufficient causes should be addressed. When recommending that someone be terminated from a position, a single, sufficient cause is all that should be offered. Adding other contributory causes can confuse the rationale for the termination. Often, these other causes open the door for the affected employee to claim that he or she was singled out or was never properly warned. Multiple causes occur over time, and co-workers may have committed the same violation yet not have been fired. In some circumstances, though, the entire sequence of causes can help support the analysis and your interpretation of events.

Cause-and-Effect Patterns To some extent, the principle of cause and effect guides every analysis. Having a purpose (effect) in mind, you must decide how best to bring it about (cause). The two common cause-and-effect structures are the progression from cause to effect and the progression from effect to cause. In organizing your writing, you need to determine which of these approaches is most effective for your purpose. Do you want to explain how one thing led to another, or do you want to start with the consequences and then explain why they came about?

The effect-to-cause pattern is often best for complicated issues because it is the easiest to follow. Although there may be some loss of dramatic suspense, the chronological nature of this pattern allows the reader to understand how each step is related to the next step and to trace how each step grows out of those that precede it. The reversed cause-to-effect progression is useful when you want your audience to be aware of what happened from the beginning of the presentation. When you explain how each step happened, the reader will be cognizant of the ultimate consequences of each step. The structure of the communication may be arranged so that your points are made in a climactic order: the most important or convincing point is the last one presented. There can also be a listing of causes and effects, a tracing of a series of events (the causal chain), or a discussion of the relationships between causes and effects. Normally, a natural order is derived from the material itself.

So, which is more important: the cause or the effect? A dramatic, convincing analysis can begin with either. Furthermore, you can make your writing more effective if you employ suspense or understatement with an awareness of how the audience will respond to your analysis.

Procedures for Organizing Analysis

During the preparation and execution of the managerial writing process, your analysis should be guided by five rules:

1. Strive for objectivity.
2. Keep the presentation simple.
3. Use sufficient evidence and present it logically.
4. Let the evidence speak for itself.
5. Avoid guilt by association.

Be Objective

Consider all possible causes and effects. We opened this chapter noting that electronic communications have encouraged writing by assertion rather than by argument. Unless assertion is sufficiently supported by personal, organizational, or referent power, it must be supported by argument. Assertions are blanket claims that often hide biases, disguise a lack of evidence, or cover a weak reasoning process. Be certain that you relate your examples to your points; you cannot give an example and expect your audience to understand exactly how it relates to your point unless you provide some guidance. Remember, your primary purpose in writing is normally to communicate, so you want to make your argument as easy to follow as possible. If your true purpose is to obfuscate, then these principles can be subverted to that purpose. Also, do not assume that you know the cause before you have studied your problem in detail; this assumption often leads only to evidence that supports your point of view. However, you must know where you are going before you begin the writing. If you do not, you may change your mind part way through, creating what is called a *broken back report*. Broken back reports have no credibility. This reinforces why having a good outline or mind map as a guide prior to beginning to write avoids this unfortunate possibility.

We suggest a simple rule that no matter how valid your argument may be, or how much the reader may want to agree with the premise, if you cannot prove it by identifying supportive details (e.g., A + B = C), your argument is not acceptable. Similarly, even if the reader disagrees with the argument, if the evidence supplied supports the argument, that argument must be considered valid. This rule can be applied to any form of analysis. If you cannot demonstrate a direct cause-and-effect relationship, there probably is none. Worse yet, a weak relationship can lead you to become embroiled in making claims rather than in conveying your message. Finally, present the evidence without distortion. Be aware, however, that not all writers are conscientious or capable of doing this, so assess other people's writing carefully. In the real world of managers, power alliances and conflicting agendas can easily overcome truth and reason. Be aware of and allow for political aspects in the writing of others.

Strive for Simplicity

To avoid complicating and obscuring your argument, concentrate solely on those causes that are pertinent to your argument. This rule is often called the law of parsimony (also known as Ockam's Razor). The **law of parsimony** states that when faced with two equally valid and acceptable answers to a given problem, use the simpler one. Simplicity decreases the chance of error and has more impact on the reader; it is also easier to manage. Other causes may be legitimate but of little importance to the immediate purpose of your message. If you are late to a meeting, the proximate cause may be that you ran out of gasoline. The fact that congressional actions in the late 1980s shifted much of the burden of road repair from the national level to the state level, which caused states to raise the tax on gasoline, thus making it too expensive for you to keep your gas tank filled, is a remote cause and not relevant when you are trying to explain your tardiness to your supervisor. While both explanations may be correct, the second one sounds like an effort to ask for a raise (which could be considered inappropriate if you just arrived late for an important meeting!).

Use Sufficient Evidence and Present It Logically

In an analysis of President Harry Truman's decision in 1945 to drop atomic bombs on Hiroshima and Nagasaki, the argument that he did it to stop the war is compelling, perhaps, but still insufficient (Gale, 1971). A number of issues were present: Human suffering, ethical considerations, the destructive nature of the new weapon, a lack of full comprehension of its force, and the ramifications of its very existence; the number of lives lost due to the bombing versus the number of lives that may have been saved by shortening the war; the Japanese high command's attitude against surrender; the probability that an extended land invasion supplied over vast distances of water would be necessary; and myriad additional factors would all have to be examined too. Some might still disagree with the decision, but they would understand why it was made. One almost never has all the evidence needed to make an irrefutable decision. Gathering evidence takes time and is expensive. At some point, the decision process stops because action must be taken and sufficient evidence has been accumulated. Furthermore, Truman's motto was, "The buck stops here."

Let the Evidence Speak for Itself

Your reader is not likely to be convinced if you either over- or understate your case. In the first instance, the reader wonders whether the argument is too weak to stand by itself if you have to push the topic so hard (much political rhetoric falls into this area). In the second instance, words such as "perhaps," "generally," and "probably," suggest that you are not sure of your argument. Seek an appropriate balance determined by the nature of your topic, your knowledge of it, and your audience.

Avoid Guilt by Association

The Post Hoc, Ergo Propter Hoc Logical Fallacy   The post hoc, ergo propter hoc fallacy occurs when two things appear in sequence thereby encouraging the assumption that the first was the cause of the second. Consider the extreme example, that "All managers drank milk when they were babies. Therefore, drinking milk leads to managerial positions." Technically, the association here is a weak correlation. A correlation does not demonstrate causality. Causality has three criteria:

1. time order (one *always* follows the other)
2. covariation (if one changes, the other changes)
3. eliminate confounding variables (that is, demonstrate that something else was not the cause)

The milk-drinker-to-managerial-success fallacy depends upon the first two criteria but ignores the third and most critical one. While it confuses causal and associational (i.e., correlational) elements, it is also an example of the consequences of an undistributed middle in constructing a syllogism (a discussion of syllogisms follows). Sometimes both things may be symptoms of something else (the real cause); sometimes there may be no connection whatsoever.

A common application of guilt by association in management is to attribute to the individual the stereotype characteristics of his or her professional training, experience, or position. For example, someone is disparaged as being a salesperson; that is, he or she is too optimistic and dismissive of the shortcomings of the company's product or service. Similarly, categorizing someone as an engineer implies someone lost in technical detail with no strategic vision for the company; an MBA is someone with too many useless theories interfering with his or her ability to think. Using these categories may be appropriate or not, depending on the writer's purpose.

SECTION SUMMARY

Choosing the most effective analytical process is vital. The two most common forms of analysis are: (1) comparison and contrast and (2) cause and effect. Comparison and contrast patterns are subject-by-subject and point-by-point. In both cases, the elements of the analysis must be consistent, significant, complete, clear, and tailored to your audience. Causes are either underlying or immediate, and they may be contributory, necessary, or sufficient in nature. The cause-and-effect structure can be either from cause to effect or from effect to cause. In an analysis, strive for objectivity and simplicity, use sufficient evidence, let the evidence speak for itself, and avoid guilt by association.

CHALLENGE PROBLEM FOR REVIEW

When was the last time you tried to win a point simply making an assertion (such as, "well, that is the way it is done," or "I just know that I am right")? Record this assertion and develop a reasoned argument in favor of it and one against it. Use either cause and effect or comparison and contrast. The core of the challenge is constructing the argument against your own assertion—this will help you understand how others heard your claim.

Evidence, Logic, and Reason

Confident mastery of evidence, judicious use of logic, and well-argued and reasoned appeals for audience agreement enhance well-organized writing.

The final component of a well-organized writing plan rests on the development of evidence to support your logic and reasoning. Offering accurate interpretations of events and data develops evidence. Numerous logic pitfalls can be avoided if you are aware of them. The most common of these, as well as several techniques for developing evidence, are described in this section. Merely proclaiming that a truck's gas mileage is ten miles per gallon proves little about the efficiency of the truck compared to other vehicles. Comparing the gas mileage of one truck to another demonstrates some of the advantage, but comparing it to an average of all similar trucks develops the data fully as supportive evidence.

Using Evidence to Support Logic and Reasoning

One thing that is constant in all analyses is the *interpretation of evidence*. Evidence can be presented in the form of quotations, summaries, paraphrasing, tables, or charts. Proper attribution must always be included. Like many writers, managers are notoriously poor at remembering to provide attribution. The most compelling reason for providing attribution is the ability to produce a valid source for the data, if challenged. For example, if a writer enumerates the benefits of attaining CMM level 2, the weight of the argument is only as strong as the writer's reputation within the software community. However, if the writer cites the benefits from Carnegie Mellon's Software Engineering Institute Web site, and then enumerates the benefits of CMM level 2, the weight of the argument is increased to reflect that of this prestigious organization. Attribution validates claims.

The interpretation of evidence may involve either deductive or inductive reasoning. Normally, *your analysis will be stronger if you use deductive reasoning*, since this kind of reasoning depends upon logical connection of your points, evidence, and conclusions. The nature of your evidence may determine which kind of reasoning you can utilize, though, sometimes it is impossible to gather evidence that can be used deductively. When this happens, you need to acknowledge that you are working with inferences rather than directly connected evidence and logical conclusions.

Deductive reasoning is a process in which the conclusion necessarily follows from stated premises (the prefix "de" means "from," so you are reasoning from a starting assumption). If you know that all bananas are yellow, you know that any individual banana is going to be yellow. In the following syllogism, an inference is reached by reasoning from the general to the specific.

Here are several syllogisms:

> All managers have subordinates.
> Julie is a manager.
> Therefore, Julie has subordinates.

All managers were born.
Ashley is a manager.
Therefore, Ashley was born.

Inductive reasoning is the opposite of deductive reasoning. In inductive reasoning, a conclusion is reached about all members of a category from studying a sample of members of that category. Inductive reasoning proceeds from the particular to the general. If you taste three hard, green apples and they are all sour, then you inductively presume that all hard, green apples are sour. Since the prefix "in" denotes "not," you can remember that the reasoning involved is not inherent in your evidence. Thus, an example of inductive reasoning:

Toyota uses the team approach.
Honda uses the team approach.
Mitsubishi uses the team approach.
Therefore, all Asian automobile companies use the team approach.

Although the conclusion *may* be correct, the process cannot produce the conclusive, logical proof that is demonstrated in deductive reasoning. All Asian automobile manufacturers have not been shown to use the team approach, only these three have. Inductive reasoning is an attempt to establish reasonable probability, and the larger the sample observed, the more likely it is that the findings will be accurate.

Analysis and Logic

Many writers find it useful to distinguish between argumentative and persuasive modes. If you want to convince someone to use your product or service, the most effective way to do so is to demonstrate logically how your product or service is superior to your competitor's. It would be nice to create an emotional bond as well, but ultimately the consumer is going to choose what works best. When you decided to major in an area of business, your choice should have been made based on an analysis of your own goals in life, your personal abilities and talents, opportunities to match your goals and abilities in various fields, and other such information. Persuasion, on the other hand, can be emotionally or motivationally based and is the technique employed when trying to move someone to a decision. Logic is often a secondary concern for persuasive techniques.

Word choice and writing tone are important in helping you convince your audience that the writer's logic is valid. The care required to avoid or knowingly use fallacies in logic cannot be overstated. For one thing, the presence of fallacies in logic could undermine your analysis under the reader's close scrutiny. Further, if your reader recognizes that you are using fallacies in logic, your credibility will be damaged. Nevertheless, at times for certain purposes with certain audiences, the proper use of fallacies in logic might be the most effective writing technique. The fallacy may help emphasize a point or may draw on the expectations people have. To avoid or use fallacies in logic, you must be able to recognize them. The most common fallacies in logic include the following.

Ignoring the Burden of Proof

Simply asserting that something is so does not prove that it is. You must demonstrate the validity of your statement by offering sufficient evidence that confirms your statement. For example, the assertion that, "Science majors have no understanding of or liking for subjects in business," is a generalization for which no evidence is offered as proof. Of course, if the manager has sufficient authority to enforce the truth of the statement, then there is no burden to prove it. For example, if the general manager of a factory declares that work hours are 8:00 A.M. to 5:00 P.M., with an hour break for lunch, then that's the end of the matter, unless someone challenges the legality of those hours.

Circular Reasoning or Begging the Question

You cannot assume that something is true and then "prove" it merely by restating your original assumption in different words. Consider this example: "Of course he's guilty; why else would he have been arrested?" In begging the question, the premises include the assumption that the conclusion is true. Another, specialized form of this fallacy is called the **complex question fallacy**. Here is our variation on this fallacy: "What year did you stop cheating on your taxes?" The question implies that you are a taxpayer and a cheater in the first place!

Evading the Issue

This fallacy is common in advertising and politics. It appears in numerous forms.

Name Calling   Name calling involves belittling an opposing view by applying labels rather than addressing the issues. Consider this example: "Corporations motivated only by corporate greed are moving their headquarters offshore to avoid paying taxes and to escape government regulation." This emotionally charged declaration of greed and selfishness avoids discussing the merits or drawbacks of the practice in question. Legitimate reasons for relocating one's headquarters do exist.

Ad Hominem   *Ad hominem* means, literally, "argument against the man." In this case, the person is attacked rather than the argument. For example: "We can't accept the president's foreign policy. As you know, he had never left the country before he became president." There is, of course, no relationship between touring foreign countries and possessing foreign policy acumen.

Ad Populum   *Ad populum* fallacy appeals to popular prejudices, patriotic feelings, and so forth, in an attempt to cloud the issue with emotionalism. The current tendency in the United States to fear or suspect people who look like they may be of Middle Eastern descent is only the latest anxiety to grip Americans. Perhaps one of the most extreme cases of ad populem is the Sacco-Vanzetti Case in the 1920s. It has become a classic example of how potent this fallacy can be. Nicola Sacco and Bartolomeo Vanzetti were admitted anarchists who were convicted of murder and subsequently executed on the basis of their political beliefs rather than as a result of the presentation of hard evidence to link them to a fatal bombing incident. Then, of course, there was the internment of Japanese-Americans during World War II and the "Red Scare" search for communists during the 1950s. A current anxiety is also developing with immigrants, primarily from Latin America, but also from other foreign lands, where cheap immigrant (documented and undocumented) labor has become suspect for the appearance of stealing jobs from American citizens (who, ironically, are almost entirely descendents of immigrants).

Bandwagon   The basis for this fallacy is the suggestion that you should do something because everyone else does it. Some fashion designers and salespeople make a living because of the power of this fallacy, and politicians rely on it. For example: A famous song in the 1920s insisted, "Fifty million Frenchmen can't be wrong!" Why can't they? In fact, when it was written, there were not fifty million French people.

Appeal to Authority   This approach implies that someone who is an authority or well-known figure in one field is equally an authority in an unrelated field. For example: The use of movie stars and athletes in advertising is one of the most obvious exploitations of this fallacy. In an amusingly invalid television commercial in the late 1980s, for instance, an actor dressed in a white lab coat was seen sitting behind a desk in a posh professional's office. Admitting that he was not a doctor, even though he portrayed one on a popular television soap opera, the actor went on to advocate the use of a medicinal product as though he were a doctor. By drawing attention to the medical profession in his disclaimer, the actor managed to establish his appeal to authority. Presumably, the fact that he was actually a recognized actor, a double twisting of the appeal fallacy reinforced his claims.

Appeal to Pity The appeal to pity relies on an emotional appeal for support. For example: "My family has suffered great misfortune over the years, so you should be especially good to me to make up for this." What others have done or experienced has no bearing on the logic of an argument.

Distraction: The Red Herring Fallacy In an old tale, a character dragged a fish across his trail in order to throw a pack of pursuing hound dogs off the scent. Thus, this fallacy refers to any attempt to confuse the audience or to make it forget the real issue by raising irrelevant points. Consider this contemporary example: In an effort to minimize the impact of a small salary increase for line workers, a CEO suggests that the current contribution level to the pension plan may be in jeopardy. Anxiety over the pension distracts the workers from paying attention to how small their raises are.

Extension: The Straw Man Fallacy This fallacy involves distorting an opposing argument by exaggerating it to such an extent that it is no longer valid. The distorted opposing claim is easier to attack than the actual issue. "Straw man" refers to a non-existent target. The straw target not only has all of the unfavorable characteristics, it is easy to tear down. Consider this example: The federal government presents an easy target for ridicule as a source of endless *unnecessary* regulation and *excessive* taxation. However, many of those regulations keep us safe, support economic development, and encourage business. For someone, the regulations are considered *necessary* and certainly taxation that pays for the programs that benefit society might be considered excessive if we took in more than we spent. Roads, education, defense, and other critical services have been funded by our taxes. When presented in an abstract, oversimplified depiction, the federal government is a monster of unnecessary regulation, bureaucracy, and seeming waste. As an abstract target, the regulation and taxation represent extensions of fact and are thus "straw man" targets.

Hasty Generalization

This fallacy derives from making a general statement that is based on a sample too small to be accurate or representative. For example: "Because several CEOs have been caught 'cooking' the books, all CEOs have been cooking the books." A generalization based on a few notable instances out of thousands is no more valid than the conclusion that the fact that former professional quarterback Frank Ryan earned a doctorate in mathematics demonstrates that all professional quarterbacks are brilliant scholars.

Equivocation

In a sense, equivocation is a fallacy based on improper or changing definitions. **Equivocation** takes place when a meaning is applied to a word that is either different from the meaning of the word when it is used elsewhere in the message or when the word is used in an ambiguous manner. The following statement is an example of equivocation:

> *Today's unethical CEOs subvert the ideals upon which our society was founded and upon which the welfare of our country rests: justice, freedom, and liberty. They have no regard for these ideals when they exploit the environment, workers, and standard accounting practices. This isn't a dictatorship of the powerful who are free to act as they please because they can. Maybe if they had to work unpaid overtime and have no health insurance they would understand these ideals. That would be an example of justice in action.*

Clearly, this passage contains a shift in the definition of the words and concepts of justice, freedom, and liberty. The concept of liberty propounded in the Declaration of Independence and the Constitution, for instance, does not amount to individual license to do whatever one wants regardless of how the desired action impinges on the rights of another.

Oversimplification

This occurs when the complexities of a problem are either ignored or downplayed so that it may be "solved" easily. Typically, this is accomplished through one of two methods:

Either/or Hypothesis Only two contradictory solutions are suggested for a problem. For example: "America, love it or leave it!" A popular reactionary battle cry in the mid-1960s, this exhortation ignored the many alternatives to these mutually exclusive options. Why do so many people fear criticism? We discipline our children and still love them. Is it possible to love a country and still feel that it can be even better?

Post Hoc, Ergo Propter Hoc *Post hoc, ergo propter hoc* means "After this, therefore because of this" and is a common fallacy based on the mistaken correlation of two or more unrelated events. Most superstitions are examples of this fallacy, from those concerning black cats to those about spilled salt or broken mirrors. Just because one thing precedes another does not make it a cause. If individual worker productivity increases when a team member is out sick, the productivity may be a result of others compensating for the missing team member. It does not mean that absenteeism causes an increase in productivity (and the extra effort on the part of others may not be a sustainable change).

Personifying Abstractions

The treatment of an abstract subject, such as history, as though it has human attributes or as though it represents a single voice is called *personification*. For example: "History has shown that we are doomed to repeat our mistakes." Not being human, or even alive, history cannot show anything. (Common patterns can be traced through history, though there will be historians who interpret incidents differently, so the comment quoted is applicable because it does not recognize this fact.)

False Analogy

That there are similarities between things in some respects does not necessarily mean that they are alike in all respects. Consider the errors in this example: "The state of Kansas does not have a death penalty, and the murder rate there is lower than that in Florida, a state with capital punishment. Florida could lower its murder rate by revoking its death penalty." The differences between Kansas and Florida (geography, size and composition of the population, and other factors) preclude drawing such a conclusion from this comparison.

INSIGHT BOX 2.1
...

Superstitious Behavior Fallacy

This fallacy in which a person believes that a given repeated behavior can affect the outcome of an event appears commonly in sports. For example, in 1978 when Cincinnati's Pete Rose hit safely in forty-four consecutive baseball games to tie Wee Willie Keeler's mark, his manager, Sparky Anderson, walked along the dugout wall each time that Rose came to bat because he had done this prior to Rose's tying Tommy Holmes's National League mark of thirty-seven consecutive games. Anderson felt that his outfielder would continue to hit as long as he followed this practice. No matter how praiseworthy Rose's feat was, Joe DiMaggio's record of hitting in fifty-six consecutive games still stands—despite Anderson's pacing, Rose did not get a hit in his forty-fifth game.

Fallacy of the Undistributed Middle

This is a problem in deductive reasoning that occurs when a syllogism has been incorrectly devised on the assumption that things that belong to the same class are shared (called distributed). For example: "Not all students will graduate. Maria is a student. Therefore, Maria will not graduate." The middle (shared) term, student, does not have the same role in each premise, so the syllogism is invalid. Maria, being a student, belongs to the class of "all students" while the nongraduating portion of the class of "all students" may or may not include Maria. The quality of Maria being a student is not shared with the quality of "not all students will graduate." Logicians thus declare the term "undistributed." Another way to visualize this is to consider the variation: "Some students do not graduate; Maria is some student; therefore, Maria will not graduate." The middle term "students" is qualified in both premises, and nothing guarantees that being a student in one premise puts everyone in the restricted class of the other premise. Another label for this fallacy is the *shared characteristic*.

Non Sequitur

Non sequitur means, literally, "it doesn't follow" and refers to one line of reasoning that follows another as though the two were related, but where there is actually no connection or the conclusion is not related to the premise. A common observation from the teaching field serves as an excellent example: "Since Professor G publishes so much, Professor G cannot be a good teacher." This argument does not take into account the possibility that some people can operate successfully in more than one area.

Critical Thinking, Lateral Thinking

In analyzing your material, you need to employ critical thinking. Essentially, **critical thinking** is the formal application of logic in the problem-solving process. Common patterns can be learned; many of them are based on mathematical models, though a facility for mathematics is not vital to utilizing the approaches. For the most part, critical thinking refers to a process of evaluating ideas, arguments, and claims of others by first analyzing the material and assessing its validity. One may look for fallacies of logic and errors in reasoning, poorly documented evidence, and so on.

Related to critical thinking is the concept of **lateral thinking**. Sometimes the solution to a problem is best determined when the problem is looked at from a different or alternative perspective. Suppose, for example, that you have a flask with a dime in it. The neck of the flask is large enough for the dime to fit through, but it is stopped up with a cork. Your problem is to remove the dime from the flask without either pulling the cork, breaking the flask, or in any other way destroying the integrity of the flask (such as cutting a hole in it).

Solve This Challenge!

MARK GARRISON

By reversing your normal mode of thinking, you might arrive at the answer, which is given at the end of this chapter. See the Coin Challenge, page 59.

The reason that lateral thinking is important has to do with flexibility in approaching problems in managerial dealings. For example, consider the negotiation of the terms for a position. If the potential employer cannot give you what you think you should receive because this would put you out of line with those who are already working for the company, you might find the use of a company car or the payment of retirement or health insurance could make up the difference. You would both get what you need without causing undue discomfort. In real estate transactions, "creative financing," which is another example of lateral thinking, is sometimes used to effect a transaction that has otherwise come to an impasse—as in a Starker Exchange, when like real estate properties are exchanged. However, there is a caveat: Creative does not mean by any means; the application must be legal and should be ethical. Unfortunately, the term "creative financing" has recently been associated with unethical practices and even a few recent scandals. Real estate brokers no longer refer to creative financing, and instead speak of conventional, nonconventional, and even "nonconforming" loans.

SECTION SUMMARY

Evidence, logic, and reason are crucial in analysis. Evidence can be interpreted deductively or inductively. Logic can be either argumentative or persuasive. The most common logical fallacies are ignoring the burden of proof, circular reasoning, evading the issue, hasty generalization, equivocation, oversimplification, personifying abstractions, false analogy, fallacy of the undistributed middle, and non sequitur. Critical thinking and lateral thinking are useful extensions of everyday logic.

CHALLENGE PROBLEM FOR REVIEW

How does something like mind mapping help you overcome barriers to problem solving and thus become a lateral thinker?

CHAPTER SUMMARY
...

In this chapter, you learned about important strategies in the writing process. The first is establishing a controlling idea. Having done this, you can create an outline for your document. Based on your outline, you can approach your subject using either a comparison-and-contrast or cause-and-effect method or a combination of the two. You present evidence in a logical manner to convince your reader through argumentation or persuasion. Finally, you can identify and define many fallacies of logic, all of which must be avoided or used with care in your writing.

CHECKLIST: ORGANIZING YOUR WRITING
...

_____ 1. Be sure that you understand your purpose.
   a. What are you expected to find out, what resources are at your disposal (budget, personnel)?
   b. What are the timelines?
   c. What is the length requirements for the finished report?
   d. Who is your audience?
   e. Are you to provide recommendations as well as conclusions?
   f. How will the results be used?
   If you have any questions about any of these items, think through your purpose or check with your supervisor or the person who made the assignment. If there are still questions, write a memo so that you will have a record of the questions and the answers to them.
_____ 2. Have you designed an appropriate controlling question?
_____ 3. Is your data sufficient and accurate?
_____ 4. Are your analyses logical?
_____ 5. Does your evidence support your conclusions?
_____ 6. Do your recommendations logically follow from your conclusions?

EXERCISES

...

Prewriting Exercises

Assume that you are going to write an evaluative report on a chapter from one of your texts in another course for students who would probably not take a course of that nature. For example, if you chose an accounting text, the report would be for nonaccounting majors.

1. Create an outline or mind map for your report.
2. What is your controlling question or controlling idea?
3. What elements would you consider?
4. What organizational strategy would you employ?
5. Would you utilize any materials other than the text? If so, what would they be? Why would you use them? How could you use them?
6. Would you use graphics in your report?
7. What would your tentative conclusions be?

Writing Exercises

1. Choose an article in a business magazine such as *Business Week*, *Money*, *Forbes*, and so forth, and explain how the author used a prescribed method for converting ideas into messages and how evidence and reasoning were used to develop a justification.
2. For a writing assignment in another class, create an outline according to one of the organizing principles discussed in this chapter and explain why you chose that principle.
3. Using the Internet as your primary tool, research the concept of "lateral thinking" and summarize your findings. How might you apply the concept in your daily life? At work?
4. Would you buy a Buick because golfer Tiger Woods advertises for Buick?
   a. Explain why or why not in a one-paragraph deductive argument.
   b. Present an inductive argument for the opposite point of view for the Tiger Woods argument.
   c. Explain which answer to items 4a and 4b is best and why.
5. Examine several advertisements each for several different products (shoes, automobiles, dietary products, and so forth). Comment on the use of logic in these advertisements, both individually and by category of product.

COIN CHALLENGE

...

Answer to the dime-within-the-flask problem: The dime can be removed from the flask if you push the cork *into* the bottle.

MARK GARRISON

IN-BOX EXERCISE

...

In this assignment, SHG General has acquired a contract employee service. The new division has millions of dollars in federal contracts for cleaning and regular maintenance of military housing and some federal office buildings. You have been transferred to this division temporarily, and the unit you manage does the cleaning for military housing and base offices. For the housing, the unit provides basic repairs and maintenance and cleans apartments of military personnel who have moved. The company's name is Government Services International (GSI). It supplies services overseas as well.

IN-BOX

ITEM 1: FORMAL MEMO FROM BOBBIE, CONTRACTS COORDINATOR FOR SHG MILITARY DIVISION. Please be advised that a new set of reporting regulations have been issued by the DMA for reporting damage done to military-provided housing by military personnel and their dependents. The report forms are to be completed with copies kept in your office, copies to the housing department at your base, copies sent to our main office. We will handle forwarding to DMA. These forms are important for proper charges to be made. They affect our profit.

Your Response

Check one: ☐ Memorandum ☐ E-mail ☐ Letter ☐ Note ☐ Other

To: _____

_____

_____

_____

_____

_____

_____

_____

_____

_____

_____

_____

_____

_____

_____

_____

_____

_____

_____

ITEM 2: HANDWRITTEN NOTE FROM BILL, AN ELECTRICIAN. My request to be transferred to another crew has not been completed. I asked Mr. Benjamin, the guy you replaced, to move me from Thomas's crew. I think he is unsafe and he doesn't complete all the work records.

Your Response

Check one: ☐ Memorandum ☐ E-mail ☐ Letter ☐ Note ☐ Other

To: _____

_____

_____

_____

_____

_____

_____

_____

_____

_____

_____

_____

_____

_____

ITEM 3: E-MAIL FROM BRANDY, NONMILITARY QUALITY CONTROL INSPECTOR FOR THE BASE COMMANDER. You have not responded to the itemized list of non-compliant inspections I sent you last week. Since this is an extraordinary number of failed inspections, our contract allows us to delay payment until the problems are corrected. We have personnel who must be moving in this week.

Your Response

Check one: ☐ Memorandum ☐ E-mail ☐ Letter ☐ Note ☐ Other

To:

ITEM 4: E-MAIL FROM BARRY, CLEANING CREW CHIEF. Twice now I have seen the base QC person walk right into a freshly cleaned apartment while it was raining. Both of these apartments where in section 1—where the sidewalk is being redone and there is mud everywhere. Then she writes us up for not having the apartment clean. I think she is out to get us.

Your Response

Check one: ☐ Memorandum ☐ E-mail ☐ Letter ☐ Note ☐ Other

To: _____

_____

_____

_____

_____

_____

_____

_____

_____

_____

_____

_____

_____

_____

_____

_____

_____

_____

_____

_____

_____

_____

_____

ITEM 5: NOTE FROM BEN, PAINTING CREW. I don't know where you got this paint, but it takes three coats to cover some of the you-know-what I've been finding on the walls. We need better paint. I can't keep going back and forth to repaint apartments. Also, that nosy Brandy keeps checking on us. She comes in and won't say anything, then acts important and leaves.

Your Response

Check one: ☐ Memorandum ☐ E-mail ☐ Letter ☐ Note ☐ Other

To: _____

_____

_____

_____

_____

_____

_____

_____

_____

_____

_____

_____

_____

_____

_____

_____

_____

_____

_____

_____

_____

_____

_____

_____

_____

_____

_____

_____

ITEM 6: BRAD, A CARPENTER.   I told Mr. Benjamin that somebody broke three doors in Apartment 10-5. I had to replace all of them, and now the painters are mad because they have to paint the doors. We only had two doors in the warehouse, so I took one from the empty apartment that had the fire in it. I think it was 10-11. It didn't smell too bad.

Your Response

Check one: ☐ Memorandum   ☐ E-mail   ☐ Letter   ☐ Note   ☐ Other

To: _____

_____

_____

_____

_____

_____

_____

_____

_____

_____

_____

_____

_____

_____

_____

_____

_____

_____

_____

_____

_____

_____

_____

_____

_____

_____

_____

_____

_____

ITEM 7: HANDWRITTEN NOTE FROM BOB, ELECTRICAL MAINTENANCE
CREW CHIEF.   Now that SHG has finally replaced that so and so Benjamin, I do not plan to keep filling out all the forms he made for us. They were a pain, and I was in his office once and saw that he threw
most of them out. I think they just made him look good or busy or something. You better tell us which of
these forms we are supposed to use, because I plan to use only the original work order.

Your Response

Check one: ☐ Memorandum   ☐ E-mail   ☐ Letter   ☐ Note   ☐ Other

To: _____

_____

_____

_____

_____

_____

_____

_____

_____

_____

_____

_____

_____

_____

_____

_____

_____

_____

_____

_____

_____

_____

_____

_____

_____

_____

KEY TERMS
...

Analogy (p. 42)

Analysis (p. 42)

Arrangement task (p. 38)

Basic order (p. 39)

Causal chain (p. 47)

Comparison (p. 42)

Comparison and contrast (p. 42)

Complex question fallacy (p. 53)

Contrast (p. 42)

Critical thinking (p. 56)

Deductive reasoning (p. 51)

Equivocation (p. 54)

Immediate causes (p. 46)

Inducing-structure task (p. 38)

Inductive reasoning (p. 52)

Lateral thinking (p. 56)

Law of parsimony (p. 49)

Least-to-most-important order (p. 39)

Major-to-subclass order (p. 39)

Mind map (p. 41)

Mnemonic device (p. 35)

Most-to-least-important order (p. 39)

Outline (p. 34)

Principle of parallelism (p. 44)

Sequential (chronological) order (p. 38)

Simple-to-complex order (p. 39)

Spatial order (p. 38)

Transformation task (p. 38)

Underlying (or ultimate or root) cause (p. 46)

Whole-to-part order (p. 39)

REFERENCES
...

Aristotle, *Rhetoric*, Book III (1984). In Jonathan Barnes (ed.), *The Works of Aristotle*. Princeton: Princeton University Press. II 2152-2269.

Gale, Steven H. "What Hiroshima 1945 Means Today." *The San Juan* [Puerto Rico] *Star*, August 1, 1971, E-10.

Glanzer, M. and A.R. Cunitz (1966). "Two Storage Mechanisms in Free Recall." *Journal of Verbal Learning and Verbal Behavior* 5, 351–360.

Greeno, J. G. "A Study of Problem Solving." In R. Glaser (ed.), *Advances in Instructional Psychology* 1 (1978): pp. 13–75. Hillsdale, NJ: Lawrence Erlbaum Associates.

PART 1

...

CLASSIC *and* CONTEMPORARY FORMS

CHAPTER 3
...
COMPOSING MEMOS *and* LETTERS

LEARNING OUTCOMES
...

Upon completion of this chapter, you will be able to accomplish the following tasks:

1. Determine the tone of a memorandum by analyzing its purpose, audience, and the character of the message.

2. Determine what you want the message to accomplish from how the message needs to be worded.

3. Recognize the various formats for memoranda and employ them successfully.

4. Understand, distinguish, and prepare the types of memos that inform, create a record, transmit a report or proposal, request action, and review a previously agreed-upon relationship or arrangement.

5. Determine the tone appropriate for letters by identifying the purpose, the audience, and the character of the message.

6. Recognize when the motive for sending a letter may be different from the content of the letter.

7. Recognize when the desired results may differ from the requested action.

8. Create a formal business letter using the preferred styles of formatting.

9. Distinguish and use the key types of letters that request information and action.

10. Prepare letters that inform the reader of good or bad news, transmit a proposal, or confirm a previous action.

"Miss Caldwell, write twenty letters, make five Xerox copies of each, feed the whole lot into the shredder, and then, if it's five o'clock, you may go home."

In today's large companies, most communications are electronic. At Corvis Corporation, for instance, instead of using follow-up memoranda after meetings, employees post their notes in a meeting action item register on the firm's intranet. Other employees can read the postings and respond to them in the register. Many of these online documentation systems are formatted. That is, there are areas to complete for the subject, attendees, distribution beyond those who attended, actions assigned to individuals with due dates, and so forth. Small businesses that do not have this capability may use memos to communicate internally. Whether those small companies use the Internet for external messaging depends on the particulars of their business, the number of employees, and the nature of the owners. Significantly, both the companies that rely primarily on electronic communication and the companies that rely primarily on hard-copy, paper-based documents have something in common: The format is essentially the same. While methods of transmission differ, an e-mail memorandum is structured like a paper memo.

Memos and letters constitute a major portion of managerial communication. A full understanding of the range and impact of the message and its tone must guide the writing of this form of communication. Memos get leaked, misreported, misunderstood, and are sometimes even lost. However, the memo and letter writer must not be frightened by these possibilities. Composed with care, planning, and honesty, memos and letters serve as tools for successful interactive management.

Three standard formats for written communication exist in any organization: the memorandum, the letter, and the report. In this chapter, we examine the memo and the

INSIGHT BOX 3.1

Rejection Letters

Some people keep their favorite rejection letters as reminders of what it takes to get where they are or of where they could be. College admission applicants, authors, and job seekers all share the experience of rejection letters. One of our favorite rejection letters boasted of the large number of applications, the serious effort and time spent by the selection committee, and the well-worded praise for the applicant's credentials. The application was for a faculty appointment at one of the nation's most prestigious small liberal arts colleges. The letter-writer announced that an outstanding candidate had accepted the position. An obligatory wish for success closed the letter. In the body, the chair of the selection committee emphasized how the recipient's application had been carefully reviewed by the entire committee and that they were universally impressed with the applicant's background, training, references, and experience. What made the applicant suspicious of the letter, other than that it was addressed to "Dear Applicant," was that it came in return mail and had been photocopied crooked on the page. Worse yet, the application deadline was still weeks away. An applicant for another job received a 3″ × 5″ pink carbonless copy of a form that consisted of an address and several boxes on it. The box next to the word "Rejected" had been checked. There was nothing else in the envelope. Although these classic rejections were written in an era before computers were common secretarial tools, a bit more care should have been taken.

letter. E-mail, proposals, presentations, evaluations, and the other writing products that are examined in later chapters are all derivatives or variations of these formats.

No special skills are required for writing memos and letters, but there are many techniques that one can use to be successful. Each medium depends on a conventional format, has special and specific purposes, and allows a wide range of message content and impact. In fact, these forms of written communication are so fundamental that the memorandum should be considered the **paradigm** (the ultimate model) for internal communication and the letter should be considered the paradigm for external communication.

The Memorandum

KEY CONCEPT 3.1
...

A well-written memorandum contributes to the success of a manager as much as supervisory training or other special interpersonal skills.

The **memorandum** or **memo** is the most common form of business writing. Because it is so common, it may serve any of several purposes. All of these purposes have a common denominator: The memo is used for messages inside a company (as opposed to letters, which are sent outside the company). Memos normally concern a single topic. The only common exception to this rule is a routine report in the form of a memo. Even in this case, the memo covers only the material germane to the report.

Letters must be carefully prepared because they represent your business to the outside world. Similarly, memos must be carefully written because they represent you in your corporate environment, so it is imperative that you know your audience. Sometimes, like letters, memos go to people whom you do not know well, such as supervisors or personnel in other departments. In such cases, the memos represent you or your department in the same way that letters represent your company.

Memos are important even when they are addressed to people whom you see every day. These people are the ones with whom you must maintain harmonious relationships. Thoughtless or poorly worded memos can damage in seconds your reader's trust and confidence in you, trust and confidence that may have taken months or years to develop. So, though memos are often swiftly or hastily written, audience analysis and appropriate tone remain critical concerns. Too often, managers feel that because they are in positions of authority they can write memos any way they please. The resulting memo can be confusing, internally inconsistent, or incomplete.

Strategy: Finding the Appropriate Tone

Because of its brevity, a memorandum seems to distill the tone of the writer into a single expression. That tone is usually clearly pleasant, angry, upset, or neutral. Mixed emotional tone in a short written message presents a "red flag" and calls for quick action. The reader's expectation of brevity compounds the effect of a focused tone, and the reader often interprets the tone as an abbreviation of a larger feeling or attitude on the part of the sender. Consequently, great care must be taken in finding the appropriate way to express your message. The best approach requires a systematic analysis of your purpose, audience, and message itself.

Identify the Purpose

Memos can be utilized to provide information (inform or remind), establish a record, present a report, or direct action. The five general types of memos—informational, record, report, action, and memorandum of understanding—reflect these purposes. In conceiving the memo, the first step is to determine what you want to accomplish. In fact, you should focus on what the message is meant to do before you focus on how it is worded. To force other managers to comply with existing procedures for purchasing, the purchasing director should focus her analysis on the kinds of mistakes that need correction and the steps that should be taken to change the behavior of the managers. She might ask several questions: "Do they know what they are doing incorrectly?"; "Are they purposely ignoring the procedures because of an inefficiency in the procedures?", or/and "Does the mishandling of the orders occur somewhere else in the process?" These and other kinds of inquiries will clarify the purpose of the memo and set the required tone.

Simply dictating that procedures must be followed provides neither an adequate nor a helpful message. A friendly reminder of the specific errors being made should help those who are unaware that they are failing to follow procedures. For someone who is purposely subverting the order system, a request that the procedures be followed can be combined with a suggestion that complaints about the procedures be submitted for consideration. In this case, the purchasing director must state that following procedures until they are changed prevents auditing problems. She might also promise to examine procedures or at least explain the reasons why these procedures cannot be changed. In the latter circumstance, she should request the aid of other managers in locating where the problems occur. In a carefully written memo, she can use this approach to gain compliance with procedures without blaming anyone for the problems even while identifying the problem areas. In some circumstances, the director may simply want to enforce the current procedures. In this case, she may simply inform her audience that, in the future, bills or vouchers will not be paid until they are submitted correctly.

Identify the Audience

The purchasing director needs to know her fellow managers before she asks them to identify problem areas in the process. Some managers may be willing to blame others for causing the problems. If this potential exists, the director should avoid the tactic of asking her managers for a blanket response. She should ask them only to address problem areas in their own administrative domains. For procedural problems, errors may be occurring at subordinate levels that can be addressed through a broader approach—perhaps a memorandum to all staff in which she identifies the specific procedural problems and requests compliance. Internal audiences have strong and sometimes even willful personalities. Knowledge of these characteristics can be advantageous and disadvantageous. A memo written one way may please one reader and upset another.

Even the simplest memos require knowledge of their audience for the message to be successful. The memo will likely become part of a permanent record. Someone will see it long after it has met its original purpose—this reader is also part of the audience. Internal memoranda and letters sent among U.S. tobacco companies that were originally marked "Confidential" later surfaced to demonstrate that for years tobacco companies knew about the dangers of their products and additives. Memos and hand-written notes that emerge for national, public scrutiny regularly embarrass government officials. Our best advice: "Don't write it if you don't want your mother to read it." However, this rule is not meant to be an excuse for avoiding tough issues and responsibilities or for engaging in unethical practices. It is also wise to have an active records management system that regularly removes outdated documentation from the organization's files. This helps restrict the future audience. Sometimes a memo appropriate at the time it was written can be misconstrued later when circumstances and cultural contexts have changed. If electronic records are being deleted appropriately, it is prudent to engage the information technology department to ensure that these records are not recoverable from the software.

Characterize the Message

Memos have effects that go beyond the specific message that they are intended convey. An emphatic memo can impact on issues not covered in the memo. A friendly recommendation can suggest to the reader that the sender might be considered for help with other projects.

A few questions will help you analyze the character of the message:

- Is the message good news or bad news for the receiver?
- Is the news welcome or unwelcome?
- Is the message expected or unexpected?
- Have the recipients been waiting for this information or action? If so, for how long?
- Is this the kind of message that you feel you need to offer an apology for having sent?
- How would you feel if this message came to you?

During prewriting and writing, these questions should be constant referents as you select words and phrases, make requests, and offer criticism. You may wish to make your own list, but these are good starting points.

The last two questions are particularly important. Putting yourself in the position of the recipient requires that you understand the audience. To do so, you must know the reader and empathize with his or her needs, responsibilities, and anxieties. You do not need to be a psychologist or a psychic, though. You merely need to appreciate the point of view of the person or group who will receive your memo. If, from that perspective, you say, "The author of this should really be embarrassed," then you have answered the question about apologizing. If you need to apologize for the message, something is wrong and you must reconsider what you are writing or how you are expressing your message. If you have failed to complete a task on time or are admitting another shortcoming, then an apology is warranted. However, *you should never need to apologize for the message itself*. It may also be your purpose to upset, embarrass, or anger the reader. As long as you have thought through the likely impact of your memo, and you expect it to be what you want it to be, then you have done the writing job successfully.

Specify the Results

One of the most overlooked or neglected managerial skills is that of establishing appropriate control. **Administrative control** refers to giving clear directions to subordinates requesting feedback in a given form by a specified time. The three main components of establishing control are *delegation*, *feedback*, and *time frame*. While failure to delegate authority and responsibility is a failure to manage, failure to specify the form of feedback and a time frame results in inefficiency and completion problems. Most administrators learn to delegate actions, but many learn the hard way about the control measures of feedback and time frame. Sometimes, administrative control is the primary reason for creating a hard copy of a memorandum. These memos are placed in the file for the project or activity, thereby becoming reminders that aid in monitoring the progress of the activity. More recently, electronic messaging systems offer automatically generated follow-up messages to the person responsible for completing the task assigned. In many of these systems, after a specified number of reminders or the passing of a specified number of days, escalation notices are automatically issued up the chain of command. The process continues until the action item is formally closed in the system. Here is an example:

Corrective action implementation plan to Action Request #03030222 issued to Nick Newguy with a due date of 08-AUG-05 is now overdue. The delinquency is being automatically escalated to you to ensure that a corrective action plan is developed, documented, and implemented. The success of these improvement initiatives depends on everyone's involvement to ensure that actions are carried out and results are effective.

You are requested to contact the above Assignee/Owner of Action Request #03030222 to see that appropriate actions are being taken to meet assigned due dates and entered into the system. If a response is not received by [24 hours after this alert], an escalation alert will be sent to the next level of management.

Should you have any questions, please contact the Corrective Action Coordinator at x5555.

http://qa-apps/car/index.jsp?mode=edit&AR=03030222 (fictional address)

Process: Formatting the Memo

Memos can come in written or electronic form. Written memos were pervasive before the electronic era, but electronic memos have largely replaced them. It is important to understand the general formatting that applies for both forms of memos.

Memos are formatted for maximum convenience and clarity and are developed according to some variation of a standard format. In fact, the memo is designed to convey the key elements of the basic managerial writing task. Authority is expressed in the heading, the identification of the sender, and the corporate letterhead. Brevity, clarity, and directness are the hallmarks of excellent memo writing. Even the subject declaration (RE: or SUBJECT:) should be clear and direct, allowing the reader to determine why the memo needs to be read. This simple yet powerful format should be used to the writer's advantage. The format includes at least four headings, TO:, FROM:, DATE:, and SUBJECT:, as Figure 3.1 illustrates.

A glance at these headings orients the recipient of the memo. If the first thing you notice about a memo is that it comes from the company president or that it is marked "Critical Problems in Standard Procedures," you will give it high priority.

In a written memo, the four headings are often printed on company letterhead or a standardized memo form. Variations occur in the order of the headings, simply based on the preference of the company. TO: and FROM: come first. Sometimes they are printed one underneath the other, as in Figure 3.1; sometimes they are printed on the same line. Occasionally, the FROM: heading is omitted, and the sender signs at the bottom of the page. More commonly, though, the sender writes his or her initials after the typed name to indicate that the memo has been proofread and authorized.

DILBERT reprinted by permission of United Feature Syndicate, Inc.

INSIGHT BOX 3.2
...

Details of Spacing, Templates, and E-mail

The greatest efficiency provided by word processing programs is the instant availability of templates for all manner of communication. E-mail takes it a step further by standardizing virtually all communication, even making it impossible to send an e-mail without the proper recipients listed (no recipients, the e-mail goes nowhere). Appropriate and consistent use of spacing, tabs, centering, and fonts becomes more a matter for the operator.

Block formatting is nearly the standard pattern: Each paragraph ends with a line added, and the next paragraph starts without any indentation. E-mail programs do not have commonly used centering and tab functions, so this straightforward block technique is used. Anything that requires careful columns and other formatting issues is often placed in an attached word-processed file or in an attached spreadsheet file.

FIGURE 3.1

Typical Memo Format

SHG GENERAL   **Providing Quality Services Worldwide**

Suite 1000, One SHG Boulevard   800.555.4321
Dayton, Ohio 45439

MEMORANDUM

TO:
FROM:
DATE:
SUBJECT: (or RE:)

[The body is composed of paragraphs without indentation. Instead, an extra blank line separates each paragraph.]

The order of the date and the subject lines may be reversed. Our example with the subject line last demonstrates the most common version, since it clearly highlights the purpose of the memo. At the same time, some managers like the subject line above the date as a way of reflecting an order of importance. The abbreviation "RE:" for "REGARDING" is sometimes used in place of "SUBJECT." When writing a memo in response to one that you have received, use the same subject line that was used in the original memo. People other than the recipient often determine where to file a memo; repeating the wording indicates that both memos are to be filed together. After the subject line, some companies may add other items that pertain to their particular business, such as a file number or a pair of approve or disapprove check boxes.

Memos may be addressed to several people, so there are a number of different ways of addressing and circulating memos. The group simply may be named after the FROM: heading, or all members of the group may be listed. Sometimes a routing slip is attached to the memo, especially when it explains some item that needs to be circulated. A routing slip is a list of all of the intended recipients with a line after each name for initials. It may include a simple note asking each recipient to sign or initial and to pass on the memo to the person next on the list. It may also ask the last person on the list to return the memo to the sender to confirm that everyone has seen it. Figure 3.2 on page 76 is a typical routing slip.

The advantage of a routing slip is that the need to initial it encourages people to deal with the memo quickly and pass it on. A common variation is to list the names from the routing slip at the bottom of the memo and to write LIST after the TO: heading.

The body of the memo is single spaced, with double spacing between paragraphs. Each paragraph begins at the left margin without indentation. In memos longer than one page, pages after the first one are treated like the later pages of a letter and are headed by the recipient's name, the date, and the page number. After the body of the memo, include the additional information that typically appears in letters—perhaps the typist's initials and a list of people to whom copies have been sent. Other things that appear in a standard business letter do not appear in memos. For instance, normally a memo does not use a return address or an inside address. Some do not include a salutation, or a complimentary close, and your initials above replace the formal signature at the end. These last elements differ with individual style. Many people include a greeting-like salutation, a closing thank you, and a signature over the typed "FROM:" name.

The differences between an electronic memorandum and a paper one are important at this point in our exploration. The setup of an e-mail automatically generates the format

FIGURE 3.2

...

A Typical Routing Slip

INTEROFFICE ROUTING SLIP

For your: ☐ Approval; ☐ Review; ☐ Information

Subject: _____

(Check when reviewed, and send to the next person on the list.)

☐ Mr. Jones

☐ Ms. Smith

☐ Mr. Burns

☐ Ms. Sharma

☐ Ms. James

☐ Mr. Johnson

of a memorandum, even if one is e-mailing someone outside the company. Thus what were once informal letters to friends and associates now automatically take the form of a memorandum. The e-mail allows quick and easy addressing of both individuals and groups, and the requirements of requesting a reply, notification of receipt, and even controlling the time an e-mail is sent. These features make the electronic format extremely manager friendly. With a bit of advanced planning, you can automate the electronic filing of messages you send and receive.

Products: Types of Memos

Four main purposes exist for memos: They are used to inform or remind, provide a written record, present a report, or direct action. These functions are not mutually exclusive. A reminder or a report also serves as a record. Nevertheless, each of your memos will be more effective if during prewriting you decide the main purpose of the memo. Also, keep in mind that many forms of memoranda can be sent in electronic mail. However, if the message is important, consider that an e-mail can easily be lost in the hundreds of e-mails most managers receive each day. It is now common to require electronic receipt for a message, to ask that you be informed when the recipient has read (opened) your message, and to assign a priority to a message. Thus losing a business e-mail is not likely and is no longer accepted as an excuse for not knowing what the sender had to say. Before sending a memo, think through the choice of electronic format versus print format while considering the necessary impact of the message, the urgency it carries, and the mechanics of the format. Because e-mail or electronic messages are now the norm, receiving a hard-copy, written memo causes the recipient to pay attention. It is almost certainly something important.

Informational Memos

As a general rule, memos should be one page or less. Memos written to inform or remind are the shortest and most frequently used. Examples of this type are usually brief because each covers only one small topic. Notice the brevity of Figure 3.3, a reminder memo of only four sentences.

FIGURE 3.3
...

A Reminder Memo

SHG G**ENERAL**   **Providing Quality Services Worldwide**

Suite 1000, One SHG Boulevard   800.555.4321
Dayton, Ohio 45439

MEMORANDUM

TO: Purchasing Staff
FROM: Debbie Pallett *DP*
             Director of Purchasing
DATE: August 18, 2004
RE: Staff Meeting, August 24, 2004, Room 313

Please check your calendars and be sure that you keep 9:00 A.M. free for our full
staff meeting. The agenda is short but has three important items for discussion
and your information.

Note the room change to Rm 313 from 204.

Plan to be there!

Why would it be necessary to send a one- or two-line memo? Are not businesses trying to reduce paperwork? Yes, but sometimes short memos are the most efficient way
of getting things done. This memo is addressed to the purchasing staff. Its direct purpose is to remind them to attend the staff meeting; its indirect purpose is to remind
them to keep their calendars free and to inform them of the limited number of items on
the agenda. It took the writer less time to type this brief message, photocopy it (or print
multiple copies), and put it in several mailboxes in a central location than it would have
taken her to phone or locate all the purchasing staff in their offices. In addition to saving time, another advantage is that each recipient was given a written reminder of the
time and place, information to help assure that they will appear for the meeting.

An e-mail may work, but some people check their e-mail infrequently. However, no
longer can those in business afford to check their e-mail infrequently. Most are logged on
constantly throughout the day and hear an audible alert when a new message is received.
If a manager is in meetings or traveling, he or she will log on and check messages as soon
as possible. In fact, Microsoft Office and other electronic messaging systems now offer an
electronic calendar that allows the user to check everyone's schedule for availability for a
meeting, to schedule that meeting by sending an invitation to each participant, and to
include in the invitation the agenda, the minutes from the last meeting, or other documentation for consideration (such as the proposal to be discussed or the procedure to be modified). Another consideration is that a physical memo can have more dramatic impact on
some people than can forms such as voice mail or e-mail. The impact will be different, but
the difference will depend on organizational culture. In many organizations, e-mail and
voice mail have a greater sense of urgency than a physical memos, even though the physical memo may be more important.

When choosing between writing a memo or speaking to someone, decide whether
putting the information in writing is useful and whether writing a memo will save time.
If you write a long memo to one individual about a complicated situation instead of
talking about it face-to-face, you spend too much time and you run a great risk of not
being understood or possibly alienating the person. The phrase "managing by memo"

is used to describe administrators who substitute written for oral communication; it is not a complimentary description.

Control of tone is important in memos that inform and remind, though this point is often neglected. To avoid alienating your readers, remember that they may not welcome the information you bring or they may not want to be reminded about your subject. Of course, your intent may be to alienate, anger, or upset the recipient. If that is the purpose, then your contemptuous or aggressive tone may be just the thing. Review the sections on message in Chapter 1 (see page 11) and on argument in Chapter 2 (see page 32), and apply these principles whenever you write to inform or remind. Remember that reminding is actually persuasion. In general, try to be polite. However, you need to recognize that there are times when the reminder is directive in nature, not persuasive. Also, there comes a time in business when it is no longer appropriate to be polite. But, being direct and forceful does not mean rude and arrogant. If, for example, a subordinate has ignored your directive, it might be time to make it clear that you are angry with him or her, and that further inaction will lead to disciplinary action, perhaps even dismissal. It is possible to be angry and not rude. We know a corporate vice president who was clear that if you received an e-mail from him in all capital letters, he was "yelling" at you. He wanted it to be clearly understood.

Words like "please" and "appreciate" are not signs of weakness but convey courtesy and respect (and, in fact, require courteous and respectful responses). When writing to your peers or subordinates about routine matters, be informal; use first names and a relaxed style. When writing to supervisors, be courteous and clear. When writing to supervisors or people in another department in the company, avoid jargon and spell out acronyms, because those people may not share your specialized background.

Reminder memos may present a particularly touchy problem because the writer feels that they should not have to be written; that the recipients should not have to be reminded. Still, tone is important. Informality may characterize early reminders. Later reminders, while courteous, may be more forceful. Study Figure 3.4 and compare the tone of the original memo with the effect of the handwritten note added later.

The memo refers to an earlier meeting, held August 24, during which instructions about new procedures were introduced. Now in November, few people have implemented the procedures. The supervisor added a bold and italicized comment to the memo to let people know that the procedures were still required. An emphatic tone is established through the bold lettering, the italicizing, and the exclamation point. A follow-up memo should be sent only to those people who continue noncompliance with the instructions. Contrast this firmness with the straightforward tone in the reminder about the room change in Figure 3.3 where it is assumed that everyone will be at the meeting.

Record Memos

Serving as a record is a function of many memos. A copy of almost every memo ever written is filed away somewhere, at least for a time. Record keeping is the secondary purpose of memos written to inform, remind, or present a report, but it is the primary purpose of some memos. They serve as a written record of phone calls, discussions, or meetings. Such memos provide essential documentation of information that is important to a company. Later, if a disagreement arises about the issues, the memo can be used for clarification. Record-keeping memos, therefore, must be particularly clear and detailed, because the writer has no idea who will read them or how well the readers will understand the situation. With such a large secondary audience, being too detailed is better than being too brief.

In Figure 3.5, the purchasing director uses a memo to record a notification to an employee who has not implemented new procedures. Because the primary purpose of this memo is to provide a record, full names and titles are given, as well as details about the possible courses of action. This is no longer a reminder memo. This kind of memo should usually be a printed memorandum with a handwritten signature, although electronic memos have

FIGURE 3.4

Tone in a Reminder Memo

SHG GENERAL   **Providing Quality Services Worldwide**

Suite 1000, One SHG Boulevard   800.555.4321
Dayton, Ohio 45439

MEMORANDUM

TO: Purchasing Staff
FROM: Debbie Pallett *DP*
         Director of Purchasing
DATE: November 15, 2004
RE: Purchasing Procedures

In our staff meeting on August 24, 2004, I clarified two new procedures required by the accounting department for quick processing of purchase orders. Please review the procedures I handed out to everyone at that meeting. We are still not in conformance with these new procedures, and I am beginning to receive complaints from the accounting department. Although they may cause difficulties for you as you try to adjust your routine, please take the extra time to get familiar with them.

This is the third reminder to follow these procedures, so please try!

FIGURE 3.5

A Memo for the Record

SHG GENERAL   **Providing Quality Services Worldwide**

Suite 1000, One SHG Boulevard   800.555.4321
Dayton, Ohio 45439

MEMORANDUM

TO: Larry Frank
         Purchasing Support
CC: Director's File
         Personnel File
FROM: Debbie Pallett *DP*
         Director of Purchasing
DATE: December 7, 2004
RE: Failure to Follow Purchasing Procedures

You have been advised repeatedly to follow the new procedures for direct purchasing. Failure to comply with company policies and procedures are grounds for disciplinary action and possible termination. If you have any questions about this memorandum, the procedures, or the possible sanctions, please make an appointment to see me.

---

been held by various authorities (courts, labor boards, the Equal Employment Opportunity Commission, and so forth) to be fully satisfactory documentation if created in the normal course of business.

Sometimes memos of record are written about a conversation that is confidential but important enough that a record needs to be preserved. In such cases, the writer may address the memo to a file by putting the word "File" after the heading TO:, where the recipient's name usually goes. This type of memo is common in the work of people such as personnel directors; it is uncommon in most managerial jobs because supervisors should always receive copies of this kind of memo. Still, this type of memo is useful for two reasons. Instead of merely being filed, it can be addressed to and sent to the person with whom you had the conversation. It serves to express your understanding of what was said (and by whom) and to confirm your recollection. If there is a difference of opinion, the addressee has an opportunity to help set the record straight. Moreover, whether sent to the other party or merely filed, the memo establishes a record for reference as evidence in the case of a dispute.

Remember that memos must be substantive. Managers sometimes make the mistake of writing memos simply to impress the boss with their ideas for changes or to humble their subordinates with their knowledge. Unsolicited memos are often seen as pretentious or pompous. Review the material on audience analysis in Chapter 1 (see page 11) and the section on unsolicited proposals in Chapter 6 (see page 178) to avoid wasting your time writing unnecessary memos for the record.

Report Memos

When most of us think of memos, we envision very short pieces, but memos that serve as reports can be quite long. Report memos are similar to informational memos, but instead of dealing with only one small topic, they cover either a single topic in greater detail or a much broader range of topics. Indeed, the memo format is used for many of the types of reports, including recommendation reports, evaluations, feasibility studies, and progress reports. The memo format is used for these reports when they are addressed to people within the writer's company. When addressed to people outside the company, the formats used are those of formal reports, as discussed later.

Like most business letters, report memos typically have a large secondary audience that may be more important than the primary audience. This secondary audience determines the memo's content and tone. Report memos must be clear and detailed, for they serve to preserve information. Background details are given and explanations are developed because members of the secondary audience may not be familiar with the subject. The tone is semiformal. Unless the writer is certain that the potential readers share his or her level of technical expertise, jargon is minimized and explained, and highly technical supporting details are presented in appendices.

If the memo report is more than one page long, headings might be used to clarify the structure of the content. Each heading is a single word or a short phrase that identifies the content of the following section. The headings are boldfaced or underscored to make them stand out, and, if there is enough room on the page, each stands on a line by itself. If space is at a premium, the text of the paragraph can begin on the same line as the heading.

Notice that the short report memo in Figure 3.6 gives background about the sales trends in Regions I and III that the writer and the recipient already know. This information may not be known to secondary readers, such as members of an executive committee who will have to approve reassignment of duties. Specific names are not used because the subject is not the performance of personnel but the job descriptions for certain positions. The writer sets aside personal emotions even though the situation involves problems in her department, and she uses a straightforward, neutral tone. Her plan is not presented as the best or the only solution; such an approach would be presumptuous, because she has only been asked to make suggestions. She does, however, explain the feasibility of her proposals and stress their advantages.

FIGURE 3.6
...

A Short Memo Report

SHG GENERAL   **Providing Quality Services Worldwide**

Suite 1000, One SHG Boulevard   800.555.4321
Dayton, Ohio 45439

MEMORANDUM

TO: Rick Shannon, Vice President
FROM: Dorothy Kring DK *D.K.*
            National Sales Manager
DATE: April 12, 2004
RE: Problems in Regions I and III

The sales trends provided in the attached report reflect weaknesses in Regions I and III that are resulting in trends below projections. Each region has five sales representatives, and one of the representatives in each region acts as regional manager. While these are our two smallest regions, and they do not justify full-time managers on the basis of current sales productivity, the failure to have a full-time manager in each region may be preventing the regions from meeting sales goals, despite their large potential base. Some of the sales representatives have expressed concern that another sales representative is acting as manager while being responsible for sales as well. One suggestion has been that the part-time manager is taking the best accounts and then not able to service the accounts because of managerial duties.

The problem may be more one of perception than fact. The best answer would be to create a full-time sales manager in each of these two regions for an eighteen-month period and see if sales and morale improve. National sales are strong enough to compensate for this modest increase in costs (check the financial reports you received last week). If I am right, Regions I and III will increase their sales productivity. Alternately, absorbing the regions into neighboring regions is geographically difficult and might create one region too large to be managed effectively. I am open to this possibility, though I am concerned that it may disrupt two or three of our best-performing regions.

A meeting with other upper management team members might provide guidance. The problem must be solved, and I believe that input from all the affected units is necessary.

Action Memos

One of the four primary purposes of communication defined in Chapter 1 is to direct and control action. In written organizational communications, that is the primary purpose of a memo. Clear and direct instructions can be conveyed in a memo, and the record established by the very existence of the memo should leave duties and assignments stated in a clear and straightforward manner. It is common practice to incorporate these memos into a series of written procedures that are placed under document control and formally released (approved). As changes are made, a revision number or letter indicates an update. An online document control system may be used to create, route for approval, store, and retrieve such documentation. The critical advantage to the use of these systems is that it is always clear what instructions are in force and what revision is the current one. See Figure 3.7 for a memo requesting action.

Memos of Understanding

When two or more individuals, distinct groups within an organization, or separate organizations agree to share a responsibility, join together on a project, enter a contract for services, end a dispute, or other similar activity, a common means of detailing that understanding is called a **memorandum of understanding**. This special memo is a legal document. Monetary commitments and other legal issues need not be specified. Rather, the memo indicates that the parties have agreed to the terms of undertaking a specific venture or have agreed to develop an association or to end one. At times, this kind of memo is used as a predecessor to a formal contract. See Figure 3.8.

The typical memorandum of understanding includes signatures from authorized individuals representing each party involved. Normally, these parties are the executive officers of the organizations or, in the case of two different departments within the same organization, the chief administrators of each department. Frequently, these memos will be written, reviewed, and edited by legal counsel. Sometimes, a contract will specify that a mutually signed memorandum of understanding can nullify the contract.

Consider a final caveat about memos. If there is any chance that you may be misunderstood, you should pick up the phone or walk into the office of the person with whom you are trying to communicate. This has the advantage of immediate feedback so that you can explain or expand or otherwise modify your message based on the recipient's reactions. Ineffective managers avoid this straightforward approach because they are afraid that they will appear weak and that their authority will be called into question. They may be right. If they persist in taking an easy way out, this may lead to a worse situation—they confirm their own weakness in writing. Problems that could be solved eas-

FIGURE 3.7
...

Memo Requesting Action

SHG GENERAL   **Providing Quality Services Worldwide**

Suite 1000, One SHG Boulevard   800.555.4321
Dayton, Ohio 45439

MEMORANDUM

TO: Regional Managers
FROM: Dorothy Kring   D.K.
           National Sales Manager
DATE: April 13, 2005
RE: First Quarter Reports

Excellent news! I am pleased to find that a scan of each region's sales figures reveals that we are experiencing record growth! Production is concerned that without new figures, production may not be able to keep up with orders. I would like each of you to revise your sales expectations based on this new data. We need to adjust our production schedules based on projections from your expected sales activity. Please complete this analysis by April 22. I will convene a meeting of the managers at that time to discuss our projections.

Congratulations to everyone for such aggressive and successful work! Now we need to keep ahead of the game and make these very welcome adjustments.

FIGURE 3.8
...

Memorandum of Understanding

Memorandum of Agreement

Between Certified Containment, Inc. (CCI), and Clark Chemical Consulting Services

July 14, 2004

Agreement to Provide Consulting Services for Project 18803

Following our discussion, we understand that Clark Chemical Consulting Services has been asked to serve as a quality control consultant on project 18803. Clark Chemical will regularly inspect and certify each hazardous chemical container constructed by CCI and submit appropriate qualifying reports for federal government inspectors. We understand that the schedule for these reports is to be transmitted to CCI from the agency contact, and that CCI will provide regular updates regarding when these reports must be filed. In return, we also understand that CCI will pay Clark the standard federal rate for inspections of this type, and that these rates will be adjusted according to any changes made in the federal rate schedule.

Finally, we understand that an agreement specifying the terms of this arrangement will be prepared by CCI. If it is satisfactory, Clark Chemical will sign and return a copy of this agreement.

If these conditions are not in accord with your understanding, please let me know as soon as possible.

Signed:

_____

George Boxer
President and CEO
Certified Containment, Inc.

_____

Dr. Janet Clark, Principal Partner
Clark Chemical Consulting Services

ily can spin out of control because someone does not take the time to make sure that others understand the problem. This can create hard feelings and tension. Instead of harmonious cooperation, people may end up working against one another even when they share the same goals. If necessary, the "for-the-record" memo can be sent as a follow-up to make sure that everyone involved shares the same understanding of the discussion.

SECTION SUMMARY

The memorandum is a standard format for communication in business. It is the most common form and the paradigm for internal communication. Memos may be defined by their function: to inform or remind, to provide a record, to present a report, to direct action, or to provide a standardized way of responding to routine business situations. In composing a memo, find an appropriate tone. This involves identifying the problem, identifying the audience, characterizing the message, and specifying the results. This is essential in reminder or informational memos because their indirect purpose is to persuade. Record memos must be detailed and exact, as well as comprehensible to a secondary audience. In report memos, you must also present sufficient information for a secondary audience, clarify the structure with headings, and use a semiformal tone.

CHALLENGE PROBLEM FOR REVIEW

Collect samples of memos, memo-like notices, and e-mail messages you have recently received. Locate one of each type if possible. Compare the tone and format of each of those you have collected. What makes the tone appropriate to the message goal, physical format, and means of sending? Can you suggest better ways to make the points being made in the communications?

The Business Letter

KEY CONCEPT 3.2
...

The business letter is the formal means of communication between an organization and its clients, vendors, and partners.

The business letter is a crucial means of communicating. How well it is written tells the recipient a lot about you and your company. Suppose you received a poorly photocopied, mis-timed, and patronizing letter of rejection. What would you, as a potential client, customer, or employee, think about the rejecting organization? "Glad I won't be there!" might be the response. The official letter *represents* the organization. First impressions matter greatly, and sometimes they become the last impression—an impression that lingers for years. The letter should be written with the same care given to a memo to a close coworker or the company president.

Strategy: Finding the Appropriate Tone

With only a few exceptions, virtually everything about writing memos applies to letters. Unlike the memo, which we usually send to those in the same work environment, we often send letters to people unfamiliar with our work. This lack of familiarity limits the common ground that we can assume. Our interests may not be the same, and the recipient may even be from a different culture. Nevertheless, there are ways to bridge problems such as generational gaps and to get around the lack of common ground. Tone can be used to secure a willingness to share interests. Deciding on the degree of formality, the extent of friendliness, and even the kind of greeting are important elements in the strategy for writing successful business letters. Like memos, business letters today are frequently sent electronically. In many cases, contracts (or at least purchase orders) are executed electronically. In either case, the same writing principles apply.

Identify the Purpose

As with any writing project, you must decide what you want to accomplish with your letter before you begin writing. Are you sending good news or bad? Are you trying to persuade the reader or have you already established a commitment? You need to be careful, though: Over-selling yourself to the same person, especially after he or she has made a commitment, leaves the reader with a question about your confidence.

Often a letter writer has a number of motives for writing. However, all of these motives may not be made clear in the letter. For instance, a letter in which you offer an influential local businessperson your organization's support for a local fund-raiser may also be intended to gain a commitment of the other party to your organization's needs. Yet, you would never say, "We are helping with this and in exchange we expect you to help us by supporting our proposed zone change."

Good will can go a long way, and a letter sent with matter-of-fact kinds of information can also be an opportunity for building rapport. Sometimes, research into the hidden connections and networks—whether they are local, national, or international—can have larger, less obvious related pay-offs in the future.

First, decide what the "primary" purpose of the letter is, then identify the "secondary" purpose(s). Official letters require formal language. This can be achieved easily with the **bureaucratic style**. Phrases like "in regard to your request" or "pursuant to the contract stipulations in paragraph two" provide this formality. Formality does not always mean impersonal, though in the most official letters, the authority derives from the office, not the person. Do not stilt the language, however. Sometimes simply avoiding too familiar a tone is sufficient.

Look for opportunities to advance the secondary purposes, but avoid letting these subordinate motives interfere with your primary purpose. A formal, official letter is not the place to build rapport or develop networks. Nevertheless, if completion of a contract requires an official notice of completion in the form of a letter, an attached, less formal or even handwritten, note can be included to enhance your compatibility. The end of a project provides an appropriate time for expressing how pleased everyone was with the working relationship.

Identify the Audience

As always, knowledge of your audience, even if some research is required, helps you determine a suitable level of expression. Will you be communicating to people in your field? If so, the special **jargon** of your profession is acceptable; if not, your letter should be jargon free. Jargon refers to the special "shorthand" and abbreviations used by members of a profession for quick communication. The specialized terms are usually highly embedded in the professional work context. Many people will use jargon with what appears to be unlimited glee. Customers in computer hardware and software stores often get either jargon or patronizing treatment. Do not do this to your audience. If you are uncertain about your audience's level of expertise, err on the side of intelligent but not quite expert. In conveying messages about machinery or technical systems, details with full names of parts or even descriptions of a problem that both name the part and describe its function can be used to educate the recipient. Technical jargon, especially systems with alphabetical abbreviations (as in accounting or computing: FIFO, LIFO, I/O, SCSI, etc.) can be frustrating. Furthermore, the same acronym may have different meanings within specialized areas of expertise. For example, ATM is an automated teller machine to some and a telecommunications protocol to others. It may be necessary to explain which you mean to a particular audience.

There are other issues to consider in this area. Do you know the recipient well or is this a first contact? Will a letter with a jovial tone be shared with someone other than your intended recipients? Keep this in mind even when you know the recipient very well. Like other warm greetings, you may want to separate the critical information from the friendly communication when you are unsure of the distribution of the letter.

If the letter is meant to persuade and there are competitors for the business that you are trying to capture, direct comparison should avoid the logical fallacies discussed in Chapter 2 (see pages 51–56). Asserting that the competitor is inferior without careful reasoning or justification can actually alienate the audience and may be deemed to be illegal. Careless and unsubstantiated attacks, even if they are true, reveal the hidden motive: "Get the order at all costs." Consider how advice such as "I think our product is wrong for you at this time" builds your credibility. In your next attempt, the recipients will remember that you are honest.

Finally, to what extent does the audience know and trust you? The extent to which you develop credibility depends on how you stand with the audience already. If you are not a recognized expert, how do you establish credibility? This has to be done through the message itself.

Characterize the Message

The message can be characterized as formal or informal, direct or indirect, and good or bad news. Are you eager to write the letter? For instance, writing a positive letter of reference for a well-qualified coworker and friend is more enjoyable than writing a letter for an employee with minimal skills who is nevertheless seeking a promotion. In writing a supportive letter for a friend, be careful that you are not overly effusive. An overworked letter of support can read like a cautiously contrived exaggeration. In writing a letter for the under-prepared employee, only describe the specific contacts with the employee and examples of specific, work-related activity. In such a letter (which the employee should be able to read, by the way), what you do not say can serve your purpose. Those missing elements characterize the message. If you cannot see how to write a letter that meets your purpose, you can always decline to do it.

For instance, to what stage of your current project does this letter pertain? Letters written in the early stages may require greater detail and justification for steps being taken; in later stages you may depend on shared information. When the message is one in a sequence of letters, balance the shared understanding and the need for the letter to stand on its own. Care should be taken that the letter would not be misunderstood if it were to be read out of context.

Specify the Results

As in a memo, a letter must include specific and detailed instructions whenever you expect the recipient to respond. If information is requested, indicate the form in which the information should be sent and when that information is needed. If you are planning a sales proposal, indicate the level of business activity. Requests for sensitive information should be made with care. For example, in order to compete for a copier service contract, you might need figures on the volume of paper used in each regional office. This kind of data is unlikely to be considered sensitive. To supply raw material or compete for service to a sales operation, the sales figures that you need may be considered more sensitive. Information about profit margins is extremely sensitive. How you request relevant data has impact.

If your letter is intended to prompt action, specify what needs to be done and by when. The recipient needs to understand why the action should take place. A request for the completion of a contract is easy to convey. Correcting an error, however, may require an explanation of the origin of the error and the responsibility for the error. Asking the recipient to submit a proposal for a competitive bid might require that the letter be accompanied by a set of standards, expectations, and technical details.

Process: Formatting the Letter

Letter formats vary only slightly. Typically, a company will have standardized formats for all letters sent on company letterhead. These might be in the form of templates that are used for routine messages. Again, letterhead and formats may be available for both physical and electronic letters.

Two common reference formats used by administrative assistants are *The Gregg Reference Manual* (Sabin, 2000) and the *How 10: A Handbook for Office Workers* (Clark and Clark, 2003), which illustrate many formats. The most popular format today is the block format. On company letterhead, the first item is the date, followed by a complete internal address, a salutation, each paragraph separated by a blank line without indentation, a closing, the writer's signature, typed name, and title. Following this information, the typist's initials, a listing of all those who received copies (indicated with a CC: for "courtesy copy" or XC: for photocopy—no new abbreviation has emerged for electronic copies), and an indication of enclosures or attachments. Some letters (and memos) now include a code for the letter's location in electronic storage at the bottom of the page.

Letters rarely exceed two pages in length; the ideal letter is only one page, with three or four paragraphs. In the first paragraph, include a positive greeting and express the purpose of the letter. In the middle one or two paragraphs, discuss the details. In the last paragraph, summarize and close the letter. If the letter has grown beyond a page and nearly filled a second page, consider creating an attachment that includes the details, then reduce the body of the letter to a brief summary of three or four main points.

Individuals writing to a company may use a variation of the block format that places their home address in the upper, right-hand corner of the page, and then proceed with the block form for the remainder of the letter. With the advent of personal computing, many have created their own letterheads. When doing so, they might include more information than contained in the traditional business letter—address, date, and a phone number. A common feature in the personal letterhead is a personal Web address and one or more e-mail addresses. Clip art and draw programs have made the creation of personal **logos** easy as well. When such a letter is being sent to a business, bank, or government agency, the professionalism and apparent attention to detail convey a nonverbal message that the writer is serious about the concerns expressed in the letter.

Nonverbal messages present in the personal letterhead contribute to professional advancement too. If applying for a position, your skill in making a first impression begins at the top of the page and continues throughout your letter and resume. You might not want to send a flamboyant, colorful, and cryptic letterhead to an accounting firm, but a software firm that makes children's games might be very impressed.

Products: Types of Letters

Letters are used for the same tasks as memos. The difference is that the letter is used for external business communication or formal internal communication. When an account manager wins a huge account, the company president might send a formal letter of congratulations. After a class-action lawsuit regarding a wide array of potentially unethical practices, the head of the auditing division might receive a formal letter announcing the terms of his dismissal. Companies often use letters that they send through the U.S. mail or other bona fide carriers because they can establish a verifiable date sent and received. Certified mail provides an independent verification of delivery, and a return receipt provides a level of legal protection. In many circumstances, letters sent by fax have the same legal weight, especially for notification of termination of an account, acceptance of a contract, or arrival of a delivery. Electronic signatures became legally binding in 1999 (the appropriate provisions of the Electronic Signatures in Global and National Commerce Act became effective October 1, 2000). The major uses for letters are to request information, to request action, or to convey information.

Letters that Request Information

Request letters should be civil and polite, direct and businesslike. Requests for unusual information not commonly distributed by a company usually require some explanation. A college placement officer, for instance, may write all of the employers in a region and request information about new employment projections. The placement officer should explain the reasons for needing this information, even if the casual reader might think that the reasons are obvious. If the officer is planning a career fair, information about job opportunities will help justify the size and coverage of the fair. The officer may want to share information about the graduates being helped. For example, graduates of a community college may intend to stay in the area. Graduates of a four-year college or graduate program may be more open to being recruited for placement in other parts of the country. Personnel managers contacted by the placement officer should be given this information; it can affect their responses and their recruiting strategies. Local companies may have a number of technical positions available but few managerial or executive training opportunities. National and international companies may have few openings locally but many in other regions. Offering information creates a reciprocal expectation of information in return, just as being polite usually engenders politeness in return. See Figure 3.9 for an example of a letter requesting information.

Letters that Request Action

A letter in which you can request action other than the exchange of information involves asking someone to engage in something that they probably had not planned. A regulatory agency may ask the management of an industrial plant to investigate complaints by local residents that a foul odor is emanating from the factory. This letter would be the first step in an investigation. For the recipient, it may signal a potential crisis that must be carefully managed and successfully negotiated.

The request that a company investigate itself is among the more extreme forms requested. Requests can range from considering a product to demands to fulfill an obligation. Table 3.1 includes a list of possible requests. This list is not comprehensive, but it illustrates the kinds of actions that might be requested. See Figure 3.10 for an example of a letter that requests action.

Letters that Convey Information

The letter is an excellent means for providing information. The corporate letterhead and signature are evidence that should inspire confidence in the information. The

FIGURE 3.9
...

Letter Requesting Information

> **CERTIFIED CONTAINMENT, INCORPORATED**
>
> A Division of *SHG General*   800.555.1234
> Suite 1100, One SHG Boulevard
> Dayton, Ohio 45439
>
> October 12, 2004
>
> Paul Accurat
> Senior Auditing Manager
> Accurat and Markof, CPA
> 450 North Westwind Road
> Chicago, IL 60600
>
> Dear Mr. Accurat:
>
> A firm that you recently audited has bid on a contract with our company. We have concerns related to the consequences and implications of the audit findings. Could you please explain how the firm received an audit in which their books for the previous year were "closed" with "recommendation regarding standard practice"? We are unclear about the implications of this auditor's letter.
>
> Thank you for your attention to this matter.
>
> Sincerely,
>
> *Jefferson Davies*
>
> Jefferson Davies
> Contracting Agent
>
> JD/lpm

TABLE 3.1
...

The Kinds of Actions Requested Through Memos and Letters

- Arrange a meeting.
- Participate in a task force, workshop, town meeting, etc.
- Fill the accompanied order for a product or service.
- Submit an invoice or pay an invoice.
- Prepare a bid for product or service.
- Meet with sales representatives.
- Try a sample.
- Persuade a potential customer.
- Comply with a previous request.
- Comply with a contract.
- Terminate an arrangement.

FIGURE 3.10
...

Letter Requesting Action

TEXAS GAS SERVICE
Serving Local Communities Since 1922

October 12, 2004

Dear Customer:

We are required by law to read your gas meter at least once a year. While we do appreciate your regularly sending us the readings for the two apartments in your duplex, we must ask that you make an arrangement with our local meter reader to provide him with access to the meters. Please call the representative at the number below and schedule a time for this very important meter reading. If you have any questions, call customer service at (800) 555.2341.

Thank you for your attention to this matter.

Sincerely,

Gas Service

kind of information may dictate the form and style of the letter. Information can be classified according to several types: good news, bad news, requested data, and a confirmation of some other action. Each of these types requires a tone and approach specific to the information. See Figure 3.11 on page 90 for an example of a letter that conveys information.

FIGURE 3.11

...

Information Letter

SHG FINANCIAL AND ANNUITY MANAGEMENT SERVICES, INC.

Suite 1200, One SHG Boulevard   800.555.3214
Dayton, Ohio 45439

Dear Fellow Stockholders:

Over the past several years, many instances of malfeasance by major American corporations have been reported in the national news media. Unfortunately, some of those found to be acting improperly have been in the area of financial and annuity services. Because all of those in this field are often tarred with the same brush when one bad apple is discovered, I am writing to assure you that all of us at SHG Financial and Annuity Management Services, Inc. (SHG-FAMS) are appalled by the unconscionable actions of those few. Furthermore, I want to assure you that not only does SHG-FAMS condemn such practices, but we have taken steps since the very inauguration of our company in 1940 to make sure that these reprehensible actions cannot take place here.

The Securities and Exchange Commission has recently taken steps to require corporations to follow certain guidelines as a means of avoiding future incidents of this nature. Please understand that integrity and customer safety and security have been our trademarks since our inception over sixty years ago. Like that of our parent company, SHG General, our reputation for high ethical standards is recognized throughout the industry. Indeed, we have been considered by our clients, colleagues, and competitors alike as the model to emulate in regards this important principle. And, because maintaining your trust is so important to us, I personally want to assure you that I, the board of directors, and every employee of this company are aware of your concerns. More importantly, every one of us will continue to adhere to the high standards that have been our watchword from day one.

We appreciate your confidence in SHG and SHG-FAMS. We will not let you down. If you should ever have a question about our performance, please feel free to contact me personally via letter or my email (shershalceo@shg-fams.com).

Sincerely,

Hershel Perle Simon

Hershel Perle Simon
President and Chief Executive Officer
SHG Financial and Annuity Management Services, Inc.

Good News Letters Good news is easy to share. Acceptance of a proposal or contract, notification of acceptance from a college, selection for a position, notice of a promotion, completion of a project—these are good news. In a letter that contains good news, happiness, joy, congratulatory comments, or pleasure should be expressed in a manner appropriate to the occasion. A letter conveying good news should never leave the recipient in an ambiguous state wondering whether the news really was so good. Direct, appropriate language should be your guide. Overstatement and exaggeration can sour the pleasure. Saying that we are "truly excited about your retirement" may express everyone's feelings, but it can send the wrong message. Instead, saying that we are "proud that you have served the company for thirty years" and that "you will be hard to replace" is undoubtedly the best way to get the message across. See Figure 3.12 for an example of this type of letter.

Bad News Letters The traditional approach for writing letters containing bad news has been to soften the blow with praise. In the first paragraph of a bad news letter, the author often lauds the applicant (in the case of a rejection) or the employee (in the case of a layoff or dismissal). Praise supposedly helps to diminish the unpleasant emotions that the news evokes. However, most people who receive this kind of letter read the indirect, often bureaucratic, language as trying to accomplish two things. First, that it is intended to make the sender feel better about what is being done. Second, the style shifts responsibility for the decision to a nameless office or vague entity.

There is one caveat. When the information is really bad news, such as someone being fired, most efforts at softening the blow have a hollow quality. Praising an employee

FIGURE 3.12
...

Good News Letter

CERTIFIED CONTAINMENT, INCORPORATED

A Division of **SHG General**   800.555.1234
Suite 1100, One SHG Boulevard
Dayton, Ohio 45439

October 12, 2004

J. J.'s Office Cleaning
Suite 3000
100 Park Suites
Shelby, MN 01234

Dear Mr. Johns:

We are very pleased to inform you that we have completed our review of your proposed contract for services to our company and have decided to accept your bid. Please contact me when you receive this letter and we will discuss the contract. We can also discuss at that time technical matters regarding building access and security.

Many staff members are eager for you to begin, as they have been dissatisfied with our previous service. We know that your work will meet our very high expectations.

I look forward to discussing the contract details. Again, congratulations.

Sincerely,

Jefferson Davies

Jefferson Davies
Contracting Agent

JD/lpm

---

who is being fired can have serious consequences if the employee files a legal challenge. Offering more justification than the reason for firing can also cause trouble. Typically, an employee is dismissed for violating a single rule. This may be the last of a series of violations, but it is the given reason. **Sandbagging** the letter to the fired employee or the memorandum to supervisors can have negative consequences. You might be asked to explain why the employee was not terminated earlier or given a chance to improve his or her performance (and given suggestions as to how this might be done). Just as problematic, the multiple reasons used to shore up the defense may not be as sound as the single cause, leading the employee to charge that you are being discriminatory because others do the same things but are not fired.

There are practical reasons for taking care when sending bad news. You may want a losing bidder to participate in the next round. The facts about the rejected bid can be accompanied with a suggestion that additional contracts will be offered for bid soon. You may even recommend that a conversation about these upcoming contracts would be appropriate, although you must be even-handed and not give the company an unfair advantage. In some circumstances such as the awarding of government contracts, this kind of discussion might be considered illegal. Still, if your company wants to establish business relationship with the contractor, even a rejected bid can be a starting point.

From the rejected applicant's perspective, receiving bad news provides an opportunity for maintaining the business relationship. If your proposal, bid, or application for employment is rejected, you can take the opportunity to send a note of thanks for having been considered. The applicant who helps the rejecting party feel better about the rejection earns good will and improves his or her chances in the next round (there always is a next round). For an example of a bad news letter, see Figure 3.13.

Transmittal Letters   Letters often accompany transmitted reports and proposals. These letters can be matter-of-fact, or they can be used as opportunities to inform recipients about other services that you provide and to inquire about other needs that they might have. However, be sure that your offer is aimed at the right audience. A transmittal letter accompanying a final report that will be filed by the legal department is probably a waste of time and effort since it is unlikely to provide an opportunity to address other services that you offer. See Figure 3.14 on page 94.

INSIGHT BOX 3.3
···

Bad News Letters

There is absolutely nothing wrong with a straightforward: "I reviewed your application and have decided that another candidate was more appropriate for us at this time." Similarly, in the case of a dismissal, straightforward wording is sufficient. From an immediate supervisor who requires additional authority from his or her supervisors: "I have reviewed your work history, and because of your actions, I have recommended that your employment be terminated. The department head is in agreement with my recommendation." These are harsh and brief, but they are honest. A fully empowered manager might say: "Effective today [date], your employment with [company] is terminated." If a reason is added, it is usually generic rather than specific: for poor work performance, excessive absence, stealing, sexual harassment, and so forth. Specifics would only be provided only with legal counsel and through legal channels.

FIGURE 3.13
...

Bad News Letter

CERTIFIED CONTAINMENT,
INCORPORATED

A Division of *SHG General*   800.555.1234
Suite 1100, One SHG Boulevard
Dayton, Ohio 45439

October 12, 2004

Daniel Davis
3751 East Fourth Street
Shelby, MN 01234

Dear Mr. Davis:

For the last 12 years, your work has met and exceeded the standards we have for publication support. As a consequence of your skill and attention to detail, we have been able to meet virtually every deadline for booklets, fliers, promotional advertising campaigns, and the many other printed materials that we have asked you to prepare. We are certain that your dedication has contributed to our significant growth over the past decade. Unfortunately, after much discussion, we have decided to undertake a fundamental change in how we conduct this portion of our business.

Our decision to discontinue contracting routine services externally was a hard one, but the need to cut costs has become a major corporate mandate. We think that it is time for change, and we are bringing several new faces to our staff who will undertake the role you have served on a contractual basis for these many years. However, in the near future we may have special projects that will require your services. You will be first on our list of vendors.

Again, thank you for the many years of service you have provided us. We know that you will continue to do well, and we wish the best for you.

Sincerely,

Jefferson Davies

Jefferson Davies
Contracting Agent

JD/lpm

Confirmation Letter Because letters have a formal and official character, they frequently serve to confirm a decision, the completion of a task, the acceptance of a position, and so on. The more official the letter, the less friendly material or relationship building should be included. The letter accepting an appointment can include inquiries about minor details and statements of anticipation and eagerness to join the team. Such a letter might be necessary before an employment contract will be sent or forwarded for completion, and your cordial response will be appreciated. See Figure 3.15 on page 95 for an example of a letter of confirmation.

FIGURE 3.14
...

Letter Accompanying Transmittal

**CERTIFIED CONTAINMENT,
INCORPORATED**

A Division of *SHG General*   800.555.1234
Suite 1100, One SHG Boulevard
Dayton, Ohio 45439

October 25, 2004

Robert Johns
J. J.'s Office Cleaning
Suite 3000
100 Park Suites
Shelby, MN 01234

Dear Mr. Johns:

I have enclosed the final contract for your signatures. Senior management agreed to all of the changes you requested, and the changes have been included. We have discussed the wording on the phone, and no word changes have been made since. If you find everything in order, please sign and return the contract to me within two weeks. I will have your access cards ready when you bring the contract back. Please be sure to have your signature and that of Ms. Jaspers notarized.

We look forward to your beginning your service according to the agreement.

Sincerely,

Jefferson Davies

Jefferson Davies
Contracting Agent

JD/lpm

SECTION SUMMARY

Business letters are written, formal communications with those outside the sender's organization. Finding the appropriate tone for this kind of document involves identifying your purpose, identifying your audience, characterizing the message, and specifying your desired results. Letters are used to request information, to request action, or to inform. Letters that inform can carry bad or good news, accompany transmitted reports and proposals, or confirm a decision, the completion of a task, or some similar action.

CHALLENGE PROBLEM FOR REVIEW

What is your opinion about good and bad news letters? Find some examples from your own experience. Letters of rejection from your college applications or job applications as well as letters of acceptance or job appointment are excellent personal examples you might use. Read them closely and compare their approaches to delivering the news. What would you change about the bad news letters? What would you change about the good news letters?

FIGURE 3.15
...

Letter Confirming Receipt or Acceptance

J. J.'s Office Cleaning
Suite 3000, 100 Park Suites, Shelby, MN 01234

October 28, 2004

Jefferson Davies
Contracting Agent
Certified Containment, Inc.
Springfield, MN 01256

Dear Mr. Davies:

Just a note to let you know that we received the contracts. Our attorney is checking them one last time. She says that she will have them ready for us to sign as early as tomorrow.

I will deliver them as soon as Sharon and I sign them. Will we need to sign for the gate and door access cards? If so, you might need to hold Sharon's, because she is starting a short vacation this Friday. She will return in a week. However, if I can sign for both cards, that would be very helpful.

Sincerely,

Robert Johns

Robert Johns
Owner and Manager

RJ:sj

CHAPTER SUMMARY
...

In this chapter, you have learned to use memoranda for communicating with those inside the organization and letters for communicating with those outside the organization. You have also learned several strategies for setting the proper tone for your message.

CHECKLIST: FORMATTING MEMOS
...

Use this list in your prewriting and revising of memos:

Format:
_____ Four major headings (TO, FROM, DATE, RE)
_____ Body single spaced, double spacing between paragraphs
_____ Typist's initials and copy notations, if appropriate

This memo's primary purpose is to (check one):
_____ Inform or remind
_____ Provide a record
_____ Serve as a report

A memo that informs or reminds:

_____ Is directed at a clearly defined audience
_____ Uses persuasive organization and other persuasive techniques
_____ Uses an appropriate tone
  • Courteous and relaxed for informative memos
  • Polite but firm for reminders

A memo that provides a record:

_____ Is directed at a broad secondary audience
_____ Provides full, exact details and background
_____ Uses a semiformal tone, neither casual nor stiff

A memo that conveys a report or itself serves as a report:

_____ Is directed at a broad secondary audience
_____ Provides sufficient information for the secondary audience
_____ Uses headings to clarify its main points
_____ Uses a semiformal tone, neither casual nor stiff
_____ Uses only a minimum of jargon

CHECKLIST: FORMATTING LETTERS
...

Use this list in your prewriting and revising of letters:

Format:

_____ Letterhead contains identifying information
_____ Heading is internal address with date and salutation
_____ Body is single spaced, double spacing between paragraphs
_____ Close includes proper gratitude and signature line
_____ Typist's initials and copy notations are added, if appropriate

This letter's primary purpose is to (check one):

_____ Request information
_____ Request action
_____ Inform about good news
_____ Inform about bad news
_____ Inform of a transmittal
_____ Confirm a receipt or completed action

A letter that informs or reminds:

_____ Is directed at a clearly defined audience
_____ Uses persuasive organization and other persuasive techniques
_____ Uses an appropriate tone
  • Courteous and relaxed for informative memos
  • Polite but firm for reminders

A letter that requests an action:

_____ Is directed at a specific audience
_____ Provides full, exact details and background
_____ Uses a semiformal tone, neither casual nor stiff

A letter that transmits or provides a confirmation:

_____ Is directed at a specific audience
_____ Provides sufficient information for the receipt and acts as a record
_____ Uses a semiformal tone, neither casual nor stiff

EXERCISES

...

Prewriting Exercises

1. Define tone. Gather several memos or letters you have written that illustrate different tones you have used.
2. Read and analyze the letter to fellow shareholders shown in Figure 3.16 on page 98. In your analysis, determine the purpose and effect of the letter. Is it successful?

Writing Exercises

1. Choose a sample memo in this chapter and analyze it. What is the writer's purpose? Who is the audience? Characterize the message and its tone.
2. Write a memo to your instructor intended both to inform and to create a record.
3. Chose an event reported this week in a local or national newspaper or a news magazine. Write a series of letters based on this event:
   1. requesting information
   2. requesting action
   3. informing two different audiences
      a. for whom it is good news
      b. for whom it is bad news

   Explain how what you did in each letter is different from the others and what you expect to accomplish with these different approaches and techniques.

FIGURE 3.16
...

Letter to Fellow Shareholders

Neuberger Berman Management Inc.
605 Third Avenue
New York, NY 10158-0180

NEUBERGER | BERMAN

A Lehman Brothers Company

Dear Fellow Shareholder:

By now you have surely seen the disturbing reports that some mutual fund companies allowed improper after-hours trading and market timing of their mutual fund shares. I am taking this opportunity to assure you that Neuberger Berman does not condone—and in fact strongly condemns—such practices.

We are pleased to assure you that the types of abusive trading arrangements and practices alleged to have taken place at other firms have not taken place at Neuberger Berman. In our 64 years of investment management, we have built a reputation for high ethical standards in our business with clients, competitors and colleagues. Our founder, Roy Neuberger, began our mutual fund family in 1950 so that all investors could participate on an equal footing. The idea of providing a few privileged investors with unfair trading advantages—as some firms apparently have done—is simply incompatible with our basic principles.

You can rest assured that we will continue to do everything within our power to maintain the integrity of our firm and fairness to all our clients. We already follow stringent procedures to prevent after-hours trading. Our mutual fund Board of Directors—which is comprised of 18 Trustees, 15 of whom are independent—is committed to following not only the letter of the law, but the spirit of the law as well.

As recent news reports have noted, new regulations have been proposed by the SEC to combat industry abuses. We welcome any changes that will lead all firms in the mutual fund industry to treat all investors by the same rules of fair play.

The last few years have been challenging for investors, but I am pleased to report that all of our equity mutual funds have performed well this year. Although past performance is not indicative of future returns, it's nice to see that investment success can go hand-in-hand with responsibility.

In closing, we remain deeply aware of the trust you have placed in us and we will continue to strive to earn it every day. If you have any questions or comments, please do not hesitate to write to me personally.

Sincerely,

Peter Sundman
Chairman of The Board
Neuberger Berman Equity Funds

_____

_____

_____

_____

_____

_____

_____

_____

_____

IN-BOX EXERCISE

...

Auto-Widgets International, Inc., "A-WII" operates several auto parts manufacturing and assembly plants. Your division ships millions of parts to several automakers every year. The unit you manage completes a final assembly of the dashboard components for several popular automobiles. They send materials to other automakers in North and Central America.

IN-BOX

ITEM 1: SHANNON, HEAD RECEIVING CLERK FOR A-WII'S MAJOR CLIENT'S OTTAWA ASSEMBLY PLANT. We are desperate for the clock assemblies we ordered last month. I was told they should arrive Thursday, and they do not even show up on the shipper's tracking system. We have only a two-day supply. You might want to overnight the order.

Your Response

Check one: ☐ Memorandum ☐ E-mail ☐ Letter ☐ Note ☐ Other

To: _____

_____

_____

_____

_____

_____

_____

_____

_____

_____

_____

_____

_____

_____

_____

_____

_____

_____

_____

_____

_____

ITEM 2: E-MAIL FROM ASHLEY, PACKAGING AND SHIPPING MANAGER.

I tried to fill another order for six thousand more clock assemblies for the X model. What are they doing up their. We only have about a thousand in inventory. I went ahead and put them on a pallet for shipping, and its ready to go. They also use these in their lift-back Y model, and we have not scheduled any more assemblies. Those clocks come from Japan, and I know it can take weeks for them to get to us. You better order some and schedule the assembly run.

Your Response

Check one: ☐ Memorandum ☐ E-mail ☐ Letter ☐ Note ☐ Other

To: _____

_____

_____

_____

_____

_____

_____

_____

_____

_____

_____

_____

_____

_____

_____

_____

_____

_____

ITEM 3: HANDWRITTEN NOTE FROM JASON, LINE 1 ASSEMBLY
FOREMAN. Ashley over in shipping told me she shipped the last of our slim-line LCD in-dash clock assemblies to Ottawa and that it was a partial order. I thought they just sent a complete order of six thousand five days ago. What's up?

Your Response

Check one: ☐ Memorandum ☐ E-mail ☐ Letter ☐ Note ☐ Other

To: _____

_____

_____

_____

_____

_____

_____

_____

_____

_____

_____

_____

_____

_____

_____

_____

_____

_____

_____

_____

_____

_____

_____

_____

_____

_____

_____

_____

_____

_____

ITEM 4: MEMORANDUM FROM HEATHER, QUALITY CONTROL. This is to inform you that a quality control check of PN65503 found in the clock assembly for all our LCD dashboard clocks PN numbers 43300 through 45100 revealed a failure rate that is unacceptable (3 percent). This is the hour and day "set" button. Do not ship these assemblies.

Your Response

Check one: ☐ Memorandum   ☐ E-mail   ☐ Letter   ☐ Note   ☐ Other

To: _____

_____

_____

_____

_____

_____

_____

_____

_____

_____

_____

_____

_____

_____

_____

_____

_____

_____

_____

_____

_____

_____

_____

_____

ITEM 5: E-MAIL MARKED "URGENT" FROM KATHY, MAINTENANCE SUPERVISOR. As part of our routine maintenance of a clock assembly unit, we checked the equipment that holds clock assemblies while the clock face is snapped into place and found that the front and back plates can be misaligned if the operator pulls the lever too quickly. This started when a spring that provides resistance broke. We don't know how many clocks were assembled with this not working.

Your Response

Check one: ☐ Memorandum   ☐ E-mail   ☐ Letter   ☐ Note   ☐ Other

To: _____

_____

_____

_____

_____

_____

_____

_____

_____

_____

_____

_____

_____

_____

_____

_____

_____

_____

_____

_____

_____

_____

_____

_____

_____

_____

_____

ITEM 6: E-MAIL FROM ASTRID, A CLIENT'S SUPPLY AND PURCHASING MANAGER. We are pleased to have received six thousand dashboard clock assemblies in 10 containers this Thursday. Unfortunately, we did not order them, and I think they are for a model assembled in our Ottawa plant. Please do not bill us, and please let me know where they are to be sent. I assume you plan to cover shipping.

Your Response

Check one: ☐ Memorandum   ☐ E-mail   ☐ Letter   ☐ Note   ☐ Other

To: _____

_____

_____

_____

_____

_____

_____

_____

_____

_____

_____

_____

_____

_____

_____

_____

_____

_____

_____

_____

_____

_____

_____

_____

_____

_____

KEY TERMS

...

Administrative control (p. 73)

Bureaucratic style (p. 85)

Jargon (p. 85)

Logos (p. 87)

Memorandum or memo (p. 71)

Memorandum of understanding (p. 82)

Paradigm (p. 71)

Sandbagging (p. 92)

REFERENCES

...

Clark, James, and Lyn Clark. (2003). *How 10: A Handbook for Office Workers*, 10th edition. Cincinnati, OH: South-Western College Publishing.

Sabin, William. (2000). *The Gregg Reference Manual*, 9th edition. New York: Glencoe/McGraw-Hill.

CHAPTER 4
...
PREPARING *the* ANALYTIC REPORT

LEARNING OUTCOMES
...

Upon completion of this chapter, you will be able to accomplish the following tasks:

1. Define the types of analytic reports.

2. Know the uses of the different types of analytic reports.

3. Understand the strategies for preparing an analytical report.

4. Differentiate between external and internal analytic report strategies.

5. Arrange an analytic report.

6. Identify criteria, establish report protocols, and collect and organize data for an analytic report.

7. Use the tools for analysis necessary for writing an analytic report.

8. Prepare a problem-focused analytic report.

9. Prepare an organizational analytic report.

"Wentworth, could I take another look at that reorganization plan?"

The term *analyze* originates in the Greek word meaning to break up or to separate into parts. In formal rhetoric, "to analyze" means to separate the examined item into its constituent parts—or smaller components—in order to gain a more complete grasp of the item. An **analytic report** exemplifies this meaning. The report provides a description and account of the parts or elements of the studied item as well as the relationships among the elements. Analysis depends on evidence, as analytic reports are rich with information. Building on the analysis undertaken in the report, the author supplies a comprehensive picture of the whole.

The **case study** is the educational or training equivalent of an analytic report. Case studies are popular in management and business administration schools. They provide a real-world feel for learning business principles and the best management practices. Some consulting processes result in a deliverable product called a business case. The **business case** is an analytic report covering a problem or opportunity and a recommended response. It begins with an analysis of a situation within the context established by the consulting agreement. Unlike an instructional case study that has composite or representative details, the business case involves actual details of a real situation. A formally prepared business case may be the final report provided by a consultant.

The case study model derives from an important, ubiquitous practice of collecting and analyzing information. Managers use the kind of information gathered and analyzed in the analytic report to guide the decision-making processes and the human resources within their jurisdiction. Analytic reports include data collection, conformance, analysis, and presentation. Each of these four activities is central to effective management. A good manager understands what is involved in each step and that all four are generally necessary for success.

The strategies for preparing an analytic report are described in detail next, as are a number of the common variations of analytic reports. Analytic reports can be prepared as part of a consultation, a strategic plan or reorganization effort, an analysis of a critical problem or in determining the productivity of a business unit. They can accompa-

INSIGHT BOX 4.1

...

Simulations

Case studies are a flexible means of delivering a diverse array of focal topics and are popular among students and instructors alike. Topics can range from comprehensive organizational cases to critical incidents and from highly focused, single-case personnel issues to industry-wide globalization challenges. The kind of experience gained with a case study provides the first step toward the more complex experiences found in internships and eventually full employment. Like the simulators used by airline pilots, a simulated case can crash (with no real damage). The pilot can start again and hone critical skills while learning from mistakes and miscalculations. The case study in business school and similar learning environments has proven to be a durable, life-like simulator.

ny proposed solutions or they can be submitted to others who are responsible for devising a solution.

Analytic Reports: Types and Uses

Analytic reports focus on problems or organizational structures.

Every analytic report begins with a clear definition of the task to be accomplished. Usually, the person or office interested in an analysis makes an assignment or enters a consulting contract for the report. For instance, the head of a business unit may commission a report on the effectiveness of a recently implemented manufacturing procedure. Another report may be needed to provide an analysis of a major system failure, such as the breakdown of a delivery system or a dramatic increase in customer complaints. When a project has not been finished on time, analysis can reveal the causes of the failure. An important initial step for a manager is to determine whether the scope of an assigned task is appropriate. For example, a request from the vice president of engineering to determine why manufacturing is not producing sufficient product to meet demand may be inappropriate if it is already known that frequent design changes are disrupting production productivity. An astute manager will address discrepancies immediately without wasting resources on the wrong assignment. An analytic report is the mechanism for any situation that requires a balanced, unbiased assessment of circumstances. These reports take two forms: the *problem-focused report* and the *organizational report*.

Problem-Focused Analytic Report

Not all business problems require an investigation and a report before a solution is found. As problems become more complex, and as they increase in size and impact, a systematic analysis can be useful. At some point, a report becomes necessary to inform and guide those involved. Specific problems can be solved with **problem-focused analytic reports**. The problem can be anything—an increase in accidents, a decline in productivity, a drop in sales. The report can be used to address a more positive challenge, such as how to move a successful regional division to the national level or how to globalize. This kind of analytic report is usually solicited or commissioned by the organizational unit most likely to benefit from the report. It begins with a directive that establishes its intent and scope.

Uses of Problem-Focused Analytic Reports

Problem-focused analytic reports can be used to define or clarify problems and to explore solutions. In clarifying a problem, you focus on the elements of the problem. These elements can include suspected causes, short- and long-term consequences, costs, and so forth. The report is a record of the analysis or research conducted while exploring the problem. An important goal of making such a report can be as narrow as simply trying to cope with the specific problem or as broad as informing and educating others in order to prevent similar and repeated occurrences. The particular use of the report depends upon what is requested.

Types of Problem-Focused Analytic Reports

Classifying problem-focused analytic reports might seem unnecessary, but a problem may have a characteristic that is more apparent when categorized. For instance, some problems are chronic and persistent; others are unique or transitory occurrences. Some center on a specific event, called a *critical incident*. Other problems arise from the structure of the department or unit, while others arise because of the personalities involved. There are at least three broad types of problem-focused analytic reports:

1. formal structural
2. chronological
3. critical incident

Formal Structural The **formal-structural analytic report** closely parallels an organizational analytic report, but rather than providing a comprehensive review of an organization, the report is focused upon a narrow problem that plagues either the formal processes or the organizational structure. For example, one of the authors of this book recently had a problem with his laptop computer. Having an extended service contract, he called the service department of the computer company. This call was made on a Sunday. He had a two-day service-call guarantee, so when he had not been contacted by Tuesday, he called to discover that the order had been submitted but that through some oversight, the work order had not been "authorized." Authorization was merely a technical term, but it meant that the part would be shipped to the service contractor. During this call, he informed the service agent that he was leaving for a short business trip and that the service must be delayed until he returned. Upon his return a week later, he found that the local service contractor had left several messages, but had returned the needed part to the company because he could not contact the professor. Because of this lack of communication between the service department and the local contractor, the entire process had to be repeated. As minor as this problem is, if it occurs often, it can prove disastrous for a company that promotes its service contracts as unequaled by any other manufacturer.

The process that involved another level of approval for the service call is a point of failure. The failure was magnified when the service contractor received only part of the first service order—the authorization procedure did not transmit the entire request (that is, the fact that the customer was unavailable for a specified period). The missing instructions to wait for the customer to return caused this error. If the approval process exists for quality control, it does not have to occur as an intervention between the request for service and the actual work order to the contractor. If the approval process exists for another purpose, then the problem represents one of the costs against the benefit of the procedure.

An analytic report on this authorization procedure would require research to tabulate the frequency of the particular problem and the circumstances when it is most likely to occur. Frequently it is helpful to create a flow chart of the process in order to uncover gaps, redundancies, or unnecessary steps in the process under investigation. The report writer should determine the role of the authorization process that comes between the problem and the service call. The impact on customer loyalty, potential losses, and an increase in costs due to the inefficiencies of repeated shipping of the replacement part would be assessed. The report should include an analysis of alternative processes or a restructuring of the existing process. The goal is to correct the problem, so several recommendations can be made in a recommendation section of the report. If the manager has the authority, he or she may include a conclusion with respect to what changes are to be made and their effective date(s).

Chronological The approach of the **chronological analytic report** to problem-focused analysis begins with a thorough but concise chronological account of the problem's history. The presumption of this approach is that the chronology—the time line of events—will reveal particular elements of both the organization and the context of work. Both of these factors can contribute to the existence of the problem. Your report might include documenting how market factors, changes in vendors or personnel, or other relevant events have had an impact on the existence, frequency, and intensity of the problem. Not all problems are internal to the corporation. In a study of problems with sales in a particular region, for instance, you might trace the history of the problem from its inception to the present and show how demographic changes in the region are linked to the declining sales. You might find that the unit within a company that must deal with the problems may not be the unit that caused the problem.

Whatever the source of the problem, it can be viewed as an opportunity for change. Analysis of the history of the problem can eliminate possible causes of the problem, including those in the organization. The chronological approach is particularly useful for balancing the analysis between internal and external elements. In contrast, the formal-structural approach often presumes an internal nature to the problem.

The chronological approach also can be used in exploring a problem or a potentially threatening change that may affect a large sector of an industry or even an entire industry. These reports may be commissioned by a task force composed of members of an industry coalition or by a governmental agency. The airline industry, through trade groups like the Air Transport Association, might commission a consulting firm to prepare a report on recent changes in business and personal travel patterns. For instance, they might want to know how travel patterns have changed under Homeland Security measures and increased airport security.

The current status of an industry may be one kind of problem, but an analysis of recent changes might serve to predict even more threatening potential shifts in travel habits. This kind of analytic report makes the most sense to a reader when presented as an analysis of changes over time (that is, chronological). The chronological approach provides an extraordinarily versatile method of organizing a variety of factors and showing their interaction. As it reveals patterns that may indicate coming trends, chronological approach helps managers anticipate and avoid problems.

Critical Incident A **critical incident analysis** follows a pattern similar to either the formal-structural or the chronological report, but it has the distinct feature of focusing on a single event; the incident is viewed as critical to the function of a unit or even to the corporation itself. This kind of analytic report should be focused on an analysis of the event and responses to it. Consider these examples. An airline accident can result in the grounding of all aircraft of the type involved in the accident. Some years ago, a Concorde supersonic transport crashed during take-off. The suspected cause was a piece of debris from another aircraft being thrown into the engine by the Concorde's tires. The fatal crash resulted in a grounding of the entire Concorde fleet. This was a critical incident of the first order—lives were at stake, so all precautions had to be applied. Eventually, the Concorde was retired completely from service: Was the eventual retirement a consequence of the accident? More recently, a piece of insulation dislodged and damaged the wing of the space shuttle *Columbia*, resulting in the death of all on board during re-entry. The shuttle fleet was immediately grounded during a complete and thorough investigation of the critical incident. Both of these incidents require extensive specialized and technical analysis. Even if the specific cause is known and clearly understood, there are hundreds of ramifications of the incidents that must be explored. A couple of closer-to-home examples will help illustrate the mechanisms of the critical incident analysis.

British Airways Concorde

NEWSCAST

Consider a college that has an unexpected rate of accepted first-year students registering for an upcoming term. Most schools anticipate that only a portion of those accepted will actually attend. That percentage is relatively stable from year to year. What happens if 25 percent more students chose to attend? Great news? Not if there are beds for only the usual number and enough room in the classes to add only 10 percent more. If the college is to benefit from the growth, costly plans must be implemented. It can take several years to build a residence hall, and what if the increase was a fluke? Adding faculty may also mean that more classrooms are needed. The critical incident—the unexpected increase in first-year attendees—must be thoroughly and expeditiously analyzed to guide decisions about financial commitments.

Unexpected increases or declines in sales may have a similar impact. Sales may be easier to handle if the production, storage, and delivery processes are flexible enough to increase and decrease according to the up-and-down curves of demand. However, there may be points at which production or handling volume cannot grow until another production line is added or until more handling personnel are in place. When an unexpected increase in demand occurs, managers and the corporate leadership may not be able to wait to see if the change is permanent. By the time the nature of the trend becomes evident, it might be too late to make adjustments, and someone else captures the customers. A critical incident report would be used to explain the increase and to determine whether it indicates a future trend or a single event.

Whether positive or negative, the analytic report must be used productively. The organization must move forward, accepting the change signaled by the incident and finding ways to improve protection of passengers, the projected needs of students, or the purchasing trends of customers. Table 4.1 summarizes the types of problem-focused analytic reports.

Organizational Analytic Report

The **organizational analytic report** is used to offer a comprehensive review and analysis of a "business unit," essentially everything from a single department to the entire corporate structure. It can be focused on a single process or function such as the use of information technology or employment demographics. Any strategic planning process undertaken by a business or a nonprofit institution must include a comprehensive organizational analysis. In long-range planning, one utilizes **needs assessment** to determine how to assign financial and human resources through a defined period. This needs assessment is a class of organizational analytic reporting.

Some organizations maintain a unit that systematically collects data and makes analytic reports. This might be the function of an internal auditor in a business, or, as is common in universities, the office of institutional research. In an organizational analytic report you might identify problems in much the same way as in a problem-focused report, but your primary goal is more descriptive than solution oriented.

Uses of Organizational Analytic Reports

Organizational analytic reports serve multiple functions. The report can guide significant organizational change. For instance, a modestly sized company could be poised to grow significantly within a market sector because of a new product. Preparation for that growth is crucial if the company is to succeed in capturing and holding its projected market share. Is the company ready for dramatic growth? While production capacity may be a known quantity, the human resource department might not have the capacity to increase

TABLE 4.1

Types of Problem-Focused Analytic Reports

Formal Structural	A specific problem within an organization is focused on its processes and procedures or its organizational structure.
Chronological	The time line of events is used to analyze the development and evolution of a problem, identifying the root causes of the problem, and the conditions that led to it becoming a challenge to the organization.
Critical Incident	The focus is on a catastrophic or transforming event that resulted in a problem or on a challenge that had damaging consequences or had productive consequences.

staffing rapidly. Recruitment and training of staff could be a major issue. An organizational analysis would be the appropriate process to identify those strengths, capacities, opportunities, and challenges that would support or undermine corporate growth.

Another use occurs frequently in our current economic condition. A merger or a corporate takeover requires a thorough understanding of the organizational structures and processes of the companies involved. In a merger, plans for combining offices and departments, possibly relocating personnel in a new structure, and melding divergent corporate cultures require a careful assessment of the existing structures. The merger plan should be founded on a comprehensive organizational analytic report. Determinations must be made concerning which units might remain independent business units, reorganized into new units, or disbanded. These decisions require a solid grounding in how the units worked before and how they are expected to work after the merger.

A third common use of the organizational analytic report is to secure capital. Investors, brokers, and economists examine more than financial reports when they assess the viability of a company. In the late 1990s, initial public offerings (IPOs) ruled the New York Stock Exchange and NASDAQ. Astute investors watched for opportunities by reviewing the reports made by the companies and by watching both the market analysts who monitored the market for the companies' goods and also the brokers who monitored the habits of the investors. Unbiased organizational analyses are critical in this mix.

Types of Organizational Analytic Reports

While there may be innumerable variations of organizational analytic reports, there are really only two types: internally produced reports and externally produced reports. An internally produced organizational analytic report is researched, prepared, and written by an internal team or, though rarely, by an individual. The team might include members of an office who regularly prepare this kind of report, such as a corporate research department or an auditor's office or a task force composed of members of different departments. Often an executive body—the primary audience for such a report—will develop the charge to the team to prepare a report following specific parameters. In a large corporation, any number of contributors might be involved.

The external organizational analytic report represents a more exciting opportunity for writers of analytic reports. A company may contract with a consulting firm for an analysis of organizational structure, personnel, infrastructure, efficiency, productivity, and so forth. Over the last decade, many organizations have engaged in *technology transfer analyses* to determine how best to move the organization from one level of information technology to another. Some companies have analyzed the transition from desktops and mainframes to integrated networks and wide area networks and now have made similar transitions to Web- and Internet-based information technology services. Each of these transitions required a detailed assessment of existing technologies, costs estimates for new technology, support personnel, and staff training (and in some cases, even customer training). Organizational analytic reports were used to facilitate these transitions and in many cases would have been prepared by the vendors or by a technology consultant. A consultant can bring skills and expertise to the preparation process that the organization may not have. Furthermore, the consultant provides an independent point of view, as was the case with Professor Gale's work with Pacific Bell mentioned earlier. The independence of the consultant ensures an objectivity that the organizational culture may not otherwise allow. Organizational analytic reports are often commissioned to identify "gaps" that must be overcome to achieve certification or accreditation. For example, companies that want to achieve ISO certification or achieve some level of the Capability Maturity Model will probably commission a study to identify what it is that they still must do in order to be deemed in compliance. The Capability Maturity Model (CMM) is the standard set by the Software Engineering Institute, similar to ISO 9001. CMM defines the standard for continuous improvement in software, and it defines five levels of the maturity of software development (Paulk et al., 1995).

There are occasions when external consultants work closely with internal staff members to prepare what should be called a joint external-internal report. The external label seems to validate the report in ways typical of the external report. However, the utilization of internal staff helps save costs and often includes highly skilled staff such as accountants and other specialists familiar with the material being analyzed. These types of reports are summarized in Table 4.2.

SECTION SUMMARY

There are two primary kinds of analytic reports: problem focused and organizational. Problem-focused reports are used when dealing with a specific problem within a company or industry. The types of problem-focused reports are formal structural, chronological, and critical incident. The organizational report is used for a comprehensive review and analysis of a business unit. Organizational reports are produced either internally or externally.

CHALLENGE PROBLEM FOR REVIEW

Analyze today's main stories on the front page of your local newspaper (or the front page of a national daily paper). Identify which of these stories would call for one of the problem-focused approaches. Explain why you would choose one of the methods over another. Would one or more of the stories call for an organizational strategy? Why?

Strategies for Analytic Reports

KEY CONCEPT 4.2
...

Each type of analytic report is structured by approaches defined by systems theory, human resources, decision methods, or strategic planning. Reports are prepared by external agents or by internal task forces.

Strategies for Analysis

Four common strategies are utilized in preparing analytic reports: (1) organizational or systems; (2) human resource; (3) decision systems; and (4) strategic planning. These strategies prescribe the types of data that will be collected, focus the emphasis of the report, and address the organization's needs. In addition to these four strategies, there may be specialized analytic reports that are derivatives of these basic approaches. However, even specialized reporting in industries that focus on manufacturing, engineering, logistics, distribution, and so forth, can easily be fit into one or more of these basic strategic approaches.

TABLE 4.2
...

Types of Organizational Analytic Reports

Internally Prepared	An internal unit in the organization charged with analyzing and reporting on an activity within the organization or an opportunity outside the organization.
Externally Prepared	An external agent commissioned by officers of an organization to achieve an objective, balanced, and honest report.
Joint External-Internal	An external consultant utilizing internal resources to collect data and information. Typically, the external consultant undertakes the analysis and report preparation.

Organizational or Systems Approach

A **systems approach** is used in an analysis in which the units within an organization are viewed as a system. Systems have processes, structures, resources, and even cultures. They may be organized according to units or processes such as communications, distribution, manufacturing, production, assembly, resource management, and sales. A systems strategy might focus on relationships and interactions (inputs, process, and outputs) between and among different subsystems of the organization. Often, this strategy examines processes as if they each processed some·form of information. The report shows how information flows through the overall organizational system. Products and services are treated as information being communicated from one point to another. Another tactic involves analyzing the efficiency and productivity of each subsystem. This activity is useful for determining how many personnel are required to make the system work, the financial and time costs entailed in creating each product of the system or subsystem, and the waste produced (lost materials or time). For instance, some corporations, especially high technology companies such as Hewlett-Packard, Lexmark, and IBM, measure their effectiveness in bringing a new product to market by measuring the time it took for the idea to move from conception and design through testing and to production. The time frame from design to delivery is an indicator of responsiveness to market demands and new technologies. Another approach is the customer-supplier model recommended by ISO and many quality management theorists. In this model, each organization supplies something to the organization next in the process flow. The supplier organization must determine what its internal customers need and provide it. The receiving organization (customer) must insist that the internal supplier is meeting its expectations.

Human Resource Approach

The **human resource approach** utilizes knowledge about existing personnel to develop a comprehensive analysis of an organization. Information about personnel may be acquired from existing data or by conducting an assessment of personnel. This kind of analytic report can be the first step in a comprehensive assessment and evaluation of the existing workforce. It should include job and skills analyses. A **job analysis** is a detailed description of the workplace activities of individual employees. It can include a detailed description of the activities required to complete each task assigned to an individual or a group responsible for a specific task or tasks. Organizational specialists use a variety of tools to conduct job analyses. Another source that might be drawn upon would be job and position descriptions held by the human resources department, which also retains the original application of individual employees. Unfortunately, updated information about the employee may be inconsistent. For instance, if the employee completes additional training—especially outside of work—the human resources department may not place that information in the individual's file.

Normally, specialized training provided by the company or contracted by the company for the individual or team is recorded in employee files. Nonetheless, the initiation of an organizational analytic report is an excellent opportunity to make employee files current. In effect, the assessment of employee skills provides the material needed for the organizational report. In developing a comprehensive picture of the work and the worker, an organizational analysis based on the human resource approach is the best method for planning organizational change and for assessing organizational capabilities. A prospective customer may require a company to provide a detailed analysis of its workforce, facilities, and capital to ensure that the company will be able to meet the customer's needs. Such an analysis may call for the number and educational credentials of managers, engineers, shop floor personnel, and support staff.

Besides providing analyses of available staff, available skills, and the processes and procedures currently being used by the staff, this approach can also reveal underutilized processes, procedures, or personnel, and even equipment. As a result, this kind of analysis produces the groundwork for systematic and effective organizational transformation.

Decision Systems Approach

With the information age has come an inundation of knowledge about how we conduct work, how we interact with each other, how information flows from one place to another, how we make decisions, and how we fail at each of these endeavors. The ease with which we follow the trails made by the information flow and the decisions which accompany that flow has made the **decision systems approach** a useful method for producing insights. A decision systems approach to organizational analysis is a methodology involving the decision-making processes as they apply in an organization. To prepare such a report, an analyst must examine the organizational system as if it were an information system based upon *decision processes*. Each decision process may involve actions such as approval to initiate or to continue a project, the modification or realignment of a plan or strategy, and specific linkages between information and action. A thorough decision systems analysis includes every type of decision made in an organization. This ranges from decisions based on quality control (whether to accept or reject a finished product) to decisions about employment and staffing, to decisions about when to act and what production goals or market targets should be set, and to the broadest strategic decisions made by the corporate leadership.

This approach is so important for business and government that the specialized area of study called **decision sciences** has emerged in recent years. Decision scientists examine psychological, sociological, technological, and organizational factors that influence the decision-making process. Broadly speaking, decision science can be applied to any human endeavor that involves making a judgment or selecting a course of action. An early technological innovation associated with decision science is called the expert systems. An **expert system** is a computer program that analyzes a data set and makes an assessment. For instance, a medical expert system can process information about a set of symptoms and make a diagnosis of the most likely disease syndrome. Large credit corporations utilize expert systems to make decisions about the creditworthiness of applicants. The military employs a wide array of expert systems to support numerous military decisions. These decisions can range from placement of supplies to the targeting of enemy resources. Decision science is used to determine how vast amounts of information can be organized into a strategy for success.

A decision systems approach to organizational analysis results in a report in which the means by which the organization makes its business decisions is described. This includes all decisions. The report can be focused upon individual decision processes or on all decision processes. If management seeks to empower line employees with specific decision-making powers, it must first understand where those decisions are made currently. In the Harley-Davidson example used earlier, leadership chose to empower its engine manufacturing personnel. They were given the responsibility of deciding what type of equipment to purchase and use for things such as boring the piston cavities in the engine block. Prior to this shift in organizational philosophy, upper-level management, many of whom had never worked with this equipment, made the decisions. Although the managers were nervous, success came through the re-emergence of Harley-Davidson as a leading manufacturer of motorcycles. Of course, many other changes took place as well. However, for such a change to be effective, those individuals guiding the change must know how things occur before as well as how they occur after the transformation. This cannot be done without some form of decision systems analysis.

Another example is the facilities capacity decision-making processes at a major telecommunications corporation. In this case, decisions being made in one organization, based on one set of criteria, were being overturned by the next organization in the overall process, based on a conflicting set of criteria. In order to achieve the corporate goal, a third organization was engaged to restore the decisions of the first organization. Identifying and eliminating this kind of internally inconsistent decision making can increase both effectiveness and efficiency.

Strategic Planning Approach

A strategic plan is a statement of an organization's goals for a specified period—often presented as a two-to-five-year or five-to-ten-year plan. The purpose of a **strategic planning approach** to organizational analytic reports is to create a foundation for preparing or modifying a strategic plan. In this approach, the plan is organized into short- and long-term goals, with specific time frames for each goal. *Strategic* planning differs from *tactical* planning by focusing on goals and related objectives rather than on the methods (tactics) used to accomplish an objective.

The first step in the development of a strategic plan is an examination of internal strengths and weaknesses and an assessment of external opportunities and threats. Members of the organization, often representatives from every level of an organization, determine the direction that the organization should head. Following this decision, the committee creates a draft identifying goals and objectives. Finally, a needs assessment is conducted to determine what resources are necessary to achieve the objectives and reach the goals.

A report based on strategic methods can be used to analyze or monitor a current plan and make recommendations for adjustment, modification, or a complete revision of the plan. In fact, a strategic planning approach to organizational analytic reports can be limited to any step in the process (that is, subsets or series of briefer reports may be used to modify an existing strategic plan). An organization might prepare a new strategic plan before a previous plan has been fully executed.

Once a strategic planning process has begun, it becomes a continuous process of assessment, evaluation, and re-evaluation. A strategic planning approach should focus on those components relevant to a strategic plan. An analysis of the effectiveness of specific organizational units in terms of their progress toward a defined goal might be required. This may involve an evaluation of the effectiveness of an existing strategic plan.

Strategies for developing an organizational report can overlap, and one approach may provide the overall guiding strategy while elements of other approaches are used to complete the analysis. For instance, a strategic planning approach can be used to evaluate a current strategic plan, yet the decision systems approach might focus on possible weaknesses in the organization. Table 4.3 summarizes strategic approaches to analytic reports.

TABLE 4.3
...

Strategic Approaches for Analytic Reports

Organization or Systems	An approach that views the organization as a system of interacting processes and entities and relies on the analysis of all parts of the system, including processes, resources, people, subunits, and cultures to develop an analysis of how the system succeeds or fails.
Human Resource	An approach that addresses the personnel required to complete a given task or to reach a particular goal. A job analysis of those involved in the area of interest is required.
Decision Systems	An approach in which decision makers collect, interpret, and use information to make decisions to engage in a particular type of work, market, or service.
Strategic Planning	An approach that is focused on the organization's goals and objectives and the time frame established to achieve each objective. Tools to verify meeting goals and evidence of success in reaching objectives are used to analyze an organization from the strategic planning perspective.

Internal Versus External Analytic Reports

Internal authors can prepare reports or these can be outsourced to a management consulting firm. In some cases, a consultant may work with an internal team to collect information, and then the consultant prepares the report for submission. Occasionally, internal individuals may participate in the preparation of the final report.

Commissioning Internal Reports

Internal reports may be less costly than external reports, and they can be included as the routine work of a department or team. For these reasons, internal analytic reports often require a less detailed charge. The company may have preset formats, time frames that match the time frames of other reporting cycles, and a budget that provides for costs. However, an internally prepared analytic report must reflect the same professionalism as an external report.

Directions should be very specific for any report that is not part of the routine work of the staff. The directive is issued as a memorandum from the commissioning party (the board of directors, the CEO, or perhaps an internal auditing group). It contains the specifics of the task (what is to be analyzed, the purpose of the analysis, and the time line). It identifies who will participate in the collection and analysis of data, who will prepare the report, how preparation costs will be charged (including personnel time costs), and who is responsible for submitting the interim progress reports and the final report. Often hierarchies of the company or organization will be observed. A vice president might have the final overview and submission requirement for a report being submitted by the president and CEO to the governing board. Materials submitted to an outside accrediting or authorizing agency frequently are submitted through a specific officer of the company. This may be a comptroller, vice president, or public relations officer.

Commissioning External Reports

The decision to outsource an analytic report may be routine for companies that regularly commission consultants for this kind of work, or it may be a difficult decision for a company that maintains an image of self-reliance. Some company heads are reluctant to have outsiders peeking into their secrets. Even for the most cautious, there are valid reasons for seeking an outside contractor to conduct an analysis:

- *Objectivity*. Sometimes a third party can be more objective than internal contributors. The U.S. Senate and Congress constantly engage in party warfare over cost and revenue projections. Democrats favor their specialists and Republicans favor theirs. If the president offers a projection, the Congress turns to the Congressional Budget Office. In this arena, there may be no objective analysts! Beyond the political sphere, for most corporate-level, government agencies, and nonprofit organizations, though,

INSIGHT BOX 4.2
...

ISO Certification

In many businesses, especially those engaged in international commerce, International Standards Organization (ISO) certification is required. Because the application process is so strictly detailed and the three-year ISO certification vital, most companies look for outside help in preparing the application. There are for-profit companies that conduct pre-ISO audits, analytical evaluations of a company's readiness to meet ISO requirements.

there are separate industry or professional associations that act as objective third parties and establish standards of confidentiality and professionalism.

- *Expertise.* For one reason or another, the expertise to undertake an analysis may not be available within the company. The internal report author might have other tasks and duties that are distractions. An external consultant should be able to offer undivided and undistracted attention to the task.

- *Insufficient human resources.* Even if a company has the necessary expertise, the employees may be occupied with other tasks, located at distant offices, or otherwise unable to conduct the analysis. The internal human resources may not be sufficient to complete a comprehensive analysis: Not only may there be too few specialized experts available, but the workers responsible for the day-to-day processes may not be available. Outsourcing resolves these problems immediately because a consultant brings the necessary resources to a project.

- *Legal or accreditation requirements.* Under certain circumstances, local, state, or federal law may require that an outside agent do a report. Many accrediting processes require an external report. Hospitals, pharmaceutical labs, schools, and similar kinds of organizations that depend upon the public trust have strict policies and procedures for oversight of the business activity. In nonprofit accreditation procedures, the outside or external reviewer is often mandated for reasons of objectivity and impartiality.

- *External threats and opportunities.* In preparing a strategic plan, the step of determining the existing strengths and weaknesses can require an outsider to force all constituents to make meaningful contributions to the process. The external consultant would serve first as a moderator and then as an analyst. The external agent then prepares a series of smaller reports. In the end, however, the constituents must own the strategic plan, so an internal task force would be the best choice to prepare a final report.

Once a decision has been made to outsource an analytic report, a bidding process may follow. A "request for proposals" (RFP) is sent to a number of consulting groups. The RFP must be carefully crafted. Indeed, there are groups that specialize in preparing RFPs. The reason for using such a service is to be sure that the company gets what it needs. Another solution is to prepare a "request for information" (RFI). The RFI can be a fishing expedition. Management may admit, "We do not know if this task can be done," so an RFI is sent to likely vendors. The consulting vendors return a brief statement claiming that they can do the job and that they would be willing to bid on it. They may suggest a price range, schedule, and other related details about doing the job. An RFP can then be prepared by reviewing a number of RFIs.

RFX = RFP and RFI

In addition to RFPs and RFIs, there are a variety of other requests that may be made to external entities. For example, a request for a quote is designated an RFQ. Given that individual companies may have their own terminology for some of these requests, the designation RFX (where the "X" is a variable) is sometimes used as a catchall template.

The RFP must be detailed and specific about the scope of work, the time frame, the costs, and any details that may make the task difficult. After a contractor wins the bid, a specific contract for work is prepared in which both parties agree to what is expected. The details included may be as specific as the formatting of the proposal, how many copies to submit, and so on. This contract is far more specific than the charge prepared for an internal analytic report.

SECTION SUMMARY

The strategies or approaches for analytical reports include organizational systems, human resources, decision systems, and strategic planning. Each of these approaches focuses on a specific strategic element. Organizational-systems approaches analyze the subsystems of an organization. Human resources are evaluated and analyzed in the human resource approach. Decision systems approach examines the expert systems and decision processes involved in corporate decision-making processes. The strategic planning approach looks at the established goals and objectives and the success the organization experiences in reaching them. The reports are written either by internal staff or by external consultants. Outsourcing the report involves several possible advantages.

CHALLENGE PROBLEM FOR REVIEW

In the Key Concept 4.1 Challenge Problem you were asked to analyze today's main stories on the front page of your local newspaper (or the front page of a national daily paper). Given your analysis, determine which would be best approached through an organizational, human resource, decision systems, or strategic planning approach. Explain why you would choose one of the approaches over the others for each.

Organizing the Analytic Report

KEY CONCEPT 4.3
...

Analytic reports follow consistent and predictable organizational formats. The commission that authorizes the report prescribes these elements.

Preparation of an organizational analytic report is usually the responsibility of the team. The team should select the type of report that is most appropriate and the strategy that will be its guide. Once these two elements have been selected, steps are undertaken to organize the report and the work to be done in preparing the report. These steps include articulating the criteria for analysis, establishing protocols for formatting the report, collecting and organizing data, and employing appropriate analytic tools.

Identifying the Criteria for Analysis

The first step in preparing an analytic report is to establish the criteria that you will use in your analysis. The number of parties involved in identifying the criteria makes this ingredient critical in report preparation. Any information can be relevant to the report. Accordingly, a method of selecting relevant data and excluding irrelevant data must be in place to keep the team focused. Those who commission a report must never be surprised by the content or direction of the report. A properly designed charter for the report indicates the purpose of the report.

Many types of information, including performance standards, quality assessments, strategic goals and objectives, and other measurable factors, can be chosen to serve this purpose. The charter or commission for the analysis will specify, or at least suggest, the criteria required. This charter is in the form of an executive memo to the team or group assigned to prepare the report. If outsourcing is involved, the contract, whatever form it takes, should specify either the criteria or a clear means of developing the criteria. Occasionally, there are cases in which new criteria emerge in the process of collecting and organizing data or even during a statistical analysis of quantitative data. There should be a procedure for approval by the commissioning group for any change in criteria after the report is underway.

If the report is expected to take several months to complete, the report authors should offer regular updates on the progress of the report at predetermined intervals with agreed-upon report criteria, reporting schedules, methods of reporting (normally memos), and submission deadlines. If the report is part of a regular and ongoing institutional process, regular updates are necessary only if immediate adjustments are needed. If abrupt changes occur in an important factor—like productivity or waste, for instance—information about this change will be critical to ongoing managerial and executive decisions. If an expansion is being planned and evidence suggesting major difficulties appears during the process of collecting data, then the report authors must provide notification of the pending problem to all concerned.

What kinds of information can be used for establishing analytic criteria? While selection of report criteria arises from the objective of an analytic report, there are common factors. The criteria easiest to identify are those deriving from a strategic plan. These include: growth of market share; improvements in efficiency, productivity, and quality; development and marketing of new products or services; changes in globalization of the workforce. Some of these criteria may require clarification, but they are usually identified in the strategic plan itself.

Performance standards represent another criteria. Objectives and goals are often set at the beginning of a work period or business cycle. These cycles typically reflect monthly or quarterly targets for production, worker productivity, waste reduction, quality improvements, and so forth. Performance expectations and standards are often easily measured and quantified for comparisons with the performance of other business units.

Quality assessment is another type of criterion. *Quality* is defined as the level of productivity, waste, customer satisfaction, cost, and/or overall competitiveness. Quality may also mean conformance to specified standards.

The key point to keep in mind is that criteria selected for the basis of an analytic report must be easily understood. If they are unusual, they must be defined and described. In any case, this should be done *from the very beginning of the project*. On occasion, a new issue may emerge during data collection. Developing a criterion relevant to this new area of concern would be appropriate. As indicated, the group commissioning the report should approve the addition of a criterion. If approval cannot be sought due to time constraints or the availability of the group, the report must include an explanation to make clear that this is an additional element so that there is no confusion as to why it has been included.

Establishing Report Protocols

Several formats can serve for the report protocol. **Report protocol** is both the contents and form of the report, the method for making adjustments (like adding a criteria or discussion section), and the means of delivery. The four basic formats are formal, informal, consultant, and executive summary.

The Formal Report Format

A formal protocol specifies who will serve as resource for various kinds of data, who receives the drafts and final versions of the report, the degree of confidentiality, and any related special concern the commissioning party may have. A formal report is composed according to traditional report formatting schemes as illustrated in Figure 4.1 on page 122. The most common components include cover page; a separate title page; table of contents; list of figures; an executive summary; the main text of the proposal, including

FIGURE 4.1
...

Formal Report Format

Elements of a Formal Report

Front Matter

Cover Page (sometimes called a half-title page); includes name and author
Communication of Project (sometimes called letter of transmittal)
Title Page; includes name of report, authors, date, etc.
Table of Contents
List of Figures, Charts, and Illustrations
Letter or Memorandum; authorizes report
Executive Summary

Text

Introduction
    Purpose
    Background
    Methods
Body (may be divided into chapters or sections)
    Evidence, data
    Analysis
    Discussion
Conclusions
    Recommendations

End Matter

Figures, if not included in narrative or appendixes
Sources and Bibliography
Appendixes (often supporting letters, evidence, etc.)

an introduction, the body, and a conclusion; bibliography; and appendixes. The body may also be further divided into chapters or sections. Government agencies commonly commission the most detailed and exhaustive of these kinds of reports. The *Warren Commission Report* on the assassination of President John F. Kennedy is among the best-known formal analytic reports. The commission reported its findings in a multivolume, nine-hundred-page report. The regular accreditation process for colleges and universities involves a detailed self-study followed by a comprehensive formal report. Health-care organizations—including hospitals, elder care homes, and rehabilitation centers—regularly submit self-reports and undergo frequent accreditation visits. Organizations that monitor the status of an area of social, political, or commercial concern publish formal annual reports on subjects such as poverty, the voting habits of Americans, or the trends in home construction and home buying. These reports often involve in-depth research as well as the integration of information that other groups have collected. Figure 4.1 lists the most common elements of a formal report.

Formal reports do not require a broad scope. A company can conduct a fairly focused analysis of something as narrowly defined as purchasing procedures, employment practices, or quality assurance processes. The controlling idea in choosing to prepare a formal report is your audience. Even when the analysis is expected to remain in-house, a report that will be made to the company president, CEO, or the board of directors should be formally presented.

The Informal Report Format

E-mail is not a good medium for submitting reports. Still, people use it. We do not mean that attaching the report in an e-mail is inappropriate. Some lengthy reports are submitted via e-mail. Nevertheless, a brief update is all that e-mail should be expected to include.

Simply spacing a column over to a point in one's own e-mail screen does not ensure alignment on someone else's screen. Keep this rule in mind: What looks good on your screen may be automatically rearranged by your or the recipient's e-mail system. Worse than that, what looks and sounds good in your e-mail will look very good when someone unscrupulously copies it and forwards it without crediting you. Be aware, then, that by informal, we do not mean careless.

An informal report may be a brief update in an e-mail with data attached in a spreadsheet or database file. For large companies, this information can be linked through an intranet, and your e-mail serves to notify the recipient that the analysis is available. This may be a good format for interim reports. An informal report of any length can be sent as an attachment. Again, caution is advised. A word-processed document prepared on a desktop computer does not always look the same on another, identical machine. People personalize their computers. The result is that the recipient might print your report with the alignment of tables and charts completely askew. To avoid this problem, use one of the document formatting systems that produces an uneditable copy (portable document format, or pdf, solves this problem; see Chapter 8 for a discussion of how to use this tool).

Why is this concern for preparation and formatting so important? We do not want you to mistake informality for other forms of interaction. E-mail is informal, as is the use of "we" and "you." Informal reports mean that there are no cover pages, tables of contents, outlines, complex headings, and possibly even no sources. There may be up to five or six very clear headings, but not so many as to require a table of contents. Graphs might be inserted from a spreadsheet program (like Microsoft Excel) without an effort to make them stylistically consistent.

What conditions warrant an informal report? Usually a supervisor, a quality team, or you have decided that an analysis of a specific problem should be undertaken. The executive leadership may be trying to determine whether a formal, external analysis is necessary. The quality team needs an analysis of data on complaints for several areas covering several business cycles. You want your staff to understand the increasing costs associated with writing too many unsolicited reports. These informal reports should be completed accurately and professionally, but they do not require publication beyond the immediate group. They are also brief enough not to require extensive formatting.

The Consultant Format

This format is listed as a separate format because of some unusual characteristics it can have. For instance, the consulting firm's logo will be somewhere on every page of the report, even on any purposefully inserted blank pages when pagination is involved. Not only are the client's expectations represented in the report, but the report may reflect the expectations of others as well, such as vendors and consultants. One company with which we have some experience prepared an analysis of the transition costs for information technology for a state agency. From the report's point of view, the entire information technology system that had been analyzed sounded as if it were about to crash. The only solution presented was the continued involvement of the consulting company that conducted the survey and analysis. Perhaps the initial charter left too much unsaid in the directions that had been given. The formal report had all the right components in the right place, but the slant was definitely biased in favor of additional contracts for the consultants and their partner vendors.

Does every consulting firm undertake analytic reports in this fashion? No, but you must be aware that some do. The demise of the Arthur Andersen accounting firm and the problems encountered by brokerage firms like Merrill Lynch and other companies that served both the client(s) and the consulting firm(s) at the expense of the customer are unfortunate examples of this misuse of public trust. These recent corporate ethics failures shook everyone's confidence in externally hired consultants. This is why executives who decide to outsource need to be careful to dictate the criteria for analysis and the scope of the report.

The Executive Summary Format

Can you say it in one page? Two? Formal reports often have a single-page summary at the beginning of the report. Many call this an executive summary because it is meant for top-level executives who do not have time to read the entire report. These executives treat the report as supporting evidence for the claims in the executive summary. Because of the quantity of material that must be digested on a daily basis, the president of the United States has an entire staff devoted to reading reports, analyzing them (sometimes doing independent research in the process), and summarizing them. Similarly, in large corporations a good executive assigns trusted staff members to read and study reports and confirm summaries, although the executive reads crucial reports. There simply is not time for one person to consume thousands of pages a day.

The summary plays another role: It serves as a preview of the report contents. Lengthy reports are enhanced by summaries at the beginning of each section to alert the reader about what is to be analyzed, reported, claimed, or proposed in the coming section.

Sometimes a regular reporting process is used to keep executives and board members informed. This involves executive summaries at designated intervals. You may find yourself preparing a detailed monthly report for your supervisor—who studies the report very carefully—and an executive summary report that your supervisor submits to higher levels that is separate from the complete report. The ability to write these abbreviated reports is a valuable skill.

Collecting and Organizing Data

Setting a strategy and determining a format requires only a brief discussion with your team. If you are to write the report yourself, you can decide these items on your own, but you might ask coworkers for data and additional information sources. This may be an important element in an investigation regarding a critical incident in which you are restricted from some kinds of information.

Prior to beginning the analytic processes that precede your report, you should prepare a time line and a specific work schedule. When working with a team, be sure that the schedule indicates when portions of the work are due, when data needs to be collected and properly processed, and so on. This activity is like any other project and requires that you employ the same project management skills: delegate responsibility, assign duties, establish time frames, define the means of submitting work, and record the process. All members, even of a self-managed team without a designated leader, should agree on the process and schedule.

Any information can be considered data. Alternatively, *data* may be considered isolated facts or impressions, whereas *information* is a set of data organized analytically to convey meaning and understanding. Some data can be quantified, some merely recorded in narrative form. Reports regarding critical incidents, formal processes, and even the entire organization, can include a wide variety of information. The data can include transcribed interviews, work observations, personnel evaluations with both descriptive and quantitative information, and other forms of data. It is important to collect the information systematically. If the collected data includes large volumes of descriptive narratives, one means of analyzing the data is to look for trends and to code them for how often the trends occur. If the report involves investigating an accident in a plant, you might look for what is missing from the descriptions as well as what employees might have noticed or even reported that anticipates the accident.

Once data is in numeric or quantitative form, you need to organize the data to fit the report. Mere collected numbers, charts, graphs, and other forms of data are not sufficient for making a sound argument. The data requires analysis, **conformance**, and presentation. This process takes time and may require the skills of someone familiar with numerical analysis. Typically, this is the work of a statistician, accountant, or information manager. If the quantitative analysis you require exceeds your skills or experience, you must recognize this need for assistance. For the most part, the kinds of analysis that will be necessary should be within the range of skills that one learns in a basic statistics course.

There are four distinct phases to working with numbers and quantifiable data. The first phase is the collecting data phase. This can be ongoing or focused on a single point in time. The second phase involves analyzing the data. The third phase is selection of the meaningful outcomes of the analysis. The fourth phase is determining the best way to present your results. Some outcomes make more sense reported in charts, some in graphs, and a few in tables. The data and the analysis determine the presentation method. (See Chapters 9 and 10 for more discussion and information about analyzing and presenting data.)

Nonquantitative data goes through similar phases. Phase One is collecting and organizing the information into meaningful groupings—summarizing the observations but being clear that they are not numeric. Phase Two is preparing an analytic review. For instance, describe whether the staff noticed the danger after the fact or that they actually foresaw the problem. Written, pictorial (photographic), and other forms of recorded information can serve as supporting evidence, but you do not need to quote every instance. Phase Three is determining how best to present the nonquantitative information. This phase is critical. At times a sampling of customer statements, staff recollections, and so forth, will illustrate your point. To present your analysis in a convincing and meaningful manner is the goal of mastering the information.

The kind of evidence needed to support conclusions in the report determines the types of data to be collected and organized. Do not arrive at a conclusion and then seek the evidence to support it. The process of developing an argument can dictate the kind of evidence needed just as much as the evidence determines the conclusions. Sometimes, one type of evidence leads to another.

Tools for Analysis

Several general tools can be used to organize your argument and to prepare the report's conclusions and recommendations. These include tools to analyze evidence, tools to identify solutions, the ability to recognize resources, and models or examples that support your conclusions and recommendations by illustrating them at work in other situations.

Findings

Findings is a term common in legal and governmental proceedings. A city building and zoning board will review the claims and requests for approval of a building permit by reaching findings. Findings are a blend of ordinances with the supporting evidence and community claims made by citizens for or against the project. The board then announces what it has discovered and board members vote on granting permits based on these findings. In a jury trial, the judge may ask the jury, after deliberating a complaint against the defendant, "What have you found?" The term *findings* is perhaps the simplest way to express the analytical process of taking various types of data, policies, procedures, and other information and forming a conclusion. Mathematical processes render results, but we still ask students to compute problems and give the answers they "find." Similarly, the analytic report has a set of findings. Some report authors actually use this language; most will say that in the course of their investigation they "found the following to be true . . . ." The point is simple: During the course of the report, an author makes a clear and unequivocal statement of the findings that led to the conclusion. Arriving at the findings means that accepted methodology was employed to analyze the evidence.

Solutions

Solutions are not requested in every report, but at some level the reason for the analytic report is to move toward a goal. Solutions are part of the process if problems are impeding the progress. In fact, some analytic reports focus on the consequences of selecting one solution over another. The tool is being able to match solutions to problems. Part of the analysis must show the linkage between a particular solution and the specific nature of the problem. In the response to the service for the laptop computer problem described at the beginning of the chapter, lack of authorization was the impediment to success. In the communication between the service representative and the service contractor, something was lost. Adding another layer of oversight was not what was needed.

Resources

Success can be too much of a good thing. Consider the college that had an unexpected jump in freshman enrollment. The trend cannot be followed for several years to see if it will last; failure to act may itself prevent the trend from continuing. If there are no rooms available for the students, they will not come back—there will be no second year of the trend. Solutions must be identified quickly if the college is to exploit this opportunity. This is equally true of a small company that must respond to an expected demand for its product. The company cannot survive if it responds to orders too slowly. Again, solutions that match the company's resources with its opportunities are required.

Analogies

An excellent tool for supporting the analysis of findings, the offered solution, and the utilization of resources is the use of a model or example that illustrates the same problem solved elsewhere. Reasoning by analogy can create possible fallacies. For example, to communicate findings that one organization had too many people with one critical but limited, skill set, and not enough with others, the analogy was to a thoroughbred horse farm staffed entirely with jockeys (there may be a few thoroughbreds at work, too). Nevertheless, in an analytic report, a parallel analogy can be persuasive, especially if the proposed analysis or solution is a novel one. Good analogies can be supported with evidence as well. The entire report cannot rest on the validity of the analogy, but the insight required for making one can. Analogies, as well as all of the other tools of reasoning discussed in Chapter 2, can be a significant support tool in an analytic report.

SECTION SUMMARY

Organizing an analytical report involves identifying the criteria, establishing protocols, and collecting and organizing data. Analysis must be based on criteria that focus and guide the report. Those who ask for the report will set specific guidelines or protocols that govern to whom the report is sent, what format is has, and time frames for the report. All such reports begin with carefully collected and analyzed data. Tools used in analysis include findings, solutions, resources, and analogies.

CHALLENGE PROBLEM FOR REVIEW

People commonly receive analytic reports from stock market firms and from companies in the form of annual reports. Another place for an analytic report would be in a church or similar organization that reports to its membership. These can be annual reports or special reports, such as the report of a building committee. Examine a few of these (they are available on the Web) for clarity of language and their purposes. Do you notice any trends?

CHAPTER SUMMARY
...

Analytical reports are used when there are problems within an organization or for a comprehensive review of an organizational unit or department. To be a successful analytic report writer, you must develop a strategy for preparing the report and be aware of the elements that can be utilized in organizing the report.

CHECKLIST: ORGANIZING YOUR WRITING
...

Is this report a problem-focused analytic report? What type is it?
_____ Formal Structural
_____ Chronological
_____ Critical Incident

Is this report an organizational analytic report? What type is it?
_____ Internally Prepared Reports
_____ Externally Prepared Reports
_____ Joint External-Internal Reports

Which strategy makes the most sense for this analytic report?
_____ Organizational Systems Approach
_____ Human Resource Approach
_____ Decision Systems Approach
_____ Strategic Planning Approach

Is it an (check one):
_____ Internal analytic report
_____ External analytic report

EXERCISES
...

Prewriting Exercises

1. Select a story about a current event in a specific business or government sector (airline industry, pharmaceuticals, government waste, etc.) and explain which approach (formal structural, chronological, or critical incident) you would use in writing an analytic report about this event and why you would use this approach.
2. Write an RFP for an analysis of the event chosen for Item 1. Discuss which strategy you want employed.
3. Explain why you chose the particular strategy in Item 2.
4. Explain why you might want or not want to use each of the other three strategies.
5. Create an outline for the analytic report in Item 1.

Writing Exercises

1. Write a one-page executive summary report of this chapter.
2. Write a one-paragraph executive summary of a *Wall Street Journal* or *Business Week* article.

IN-BOX EXERCISE

...

IN-BOX

In this assignment, the SHG General unit you now manage in Auto-Widgets International completes a final assembly of the dashboard components for several popular automobiles.

ITEM 1: MEMORANDUM FROM MAURICE RICHARDS, PLANT GENERAL MANAGER.

TO: Division Managers
DATE: Friday [two days ago]
RE: Increasing accident rates

The corporate human resources department has determined that an unusually high number of accidents have been reported for the last quarter at our plant. Their report also identifies an upward trend for the past year. I have noted that waste is up, primarily in rejected components and damaged final assemblies. Our productivity is up as well, but I wonder if the productivity, waste, and accidents are somehow interrelated.

   I want each division to complete a report of the number of accidents, level of quality rejections, and changes in productivity. Please try to determine whether these factors are related or merely a coincidence. The preliminary reports will be discussed at our managers' meeting in two weeks.

Your Response

Check one: ☐ Memorandum ☐ E-mail ☐ Letter ☐ Note ☐ Other

To: _____

_____

_____

_____

_____

_____

_____

_____

_____

_____

_____

_____

_____

_____

_____

_____

_____

_____

_____

ITEM 2: TYPED NOTE FROM KIM, YOUR ADMINISTRATIVE ASSISTANT.

I saw the Maurice Richard's memorandum, and I thought you might want the names of your main staff and the line supervisors. They all really know their stuff, and you can count on them to get the information you need for the report. You already know Pat, our secretarial support.

Davendra, Human Resources staff assigned to our division.

Daphne, Shift 1 Supervisor.

Dick, Shift 2 Supervisor.

Erin, Quality Control Specialist.

Alyssa, Training Specialist.

Heather, Safety/Compliance Officer.

Your Response

Check one: ☐ Memorandum ☐ E-mail ☐ Letter ☐ Note ☐ Other

To:
_____

_____

_____

_____

_____

_____

_____

_____

_____

_____

_____

_____

_____

_____

_____

_____

_____

_____

_____

_____

_____

_____

KEY TERMS

...

REFERENCES

...

Paulk, M.C., C.V. Weber, B. Curtis, and M.B. Chrissis (1995). *The Capability Maturity Model: Guidelines for Improving Software Process*, Boston: Addison-Wesley.

CHAPTER 5

...

ASSESSMENT *and* RECOMMENDATION REPORTS

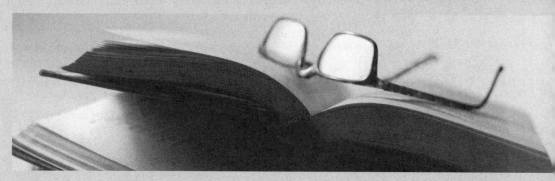

LEARNING OUTCOMES

...

Upon completion of this chapter, you will be able to accomplish the following tasks:

1. Describe the key elements of persuasive writing.

2. Distinguish approaches that consider the communicator, audience, and message factors in persuasive communications.

3. Explain why assessment reports are central to a manager's tasks.

4. Describe the key elements of analytic writing that serve the purpose of persuading the reader.

5. Determine how different types of reports influence initial assessments.

6. Describe the format of a solicited recommendation report.

7. Describe the format of an unsolicited recommendation report.

8. Outline the strategies required for each type of recommendation report.

9. Describe the format and major characteristics of an evaluation report.

10. Outline the strategies for an evaluation report.

11. Describe the format and major characteristics of a feasibility report.

12. Outline the strategies for a feasibility report.

"On the one hand, eliminating the middleman would result in lower costs, increased sales, and greater consumer satisfaction; on the other hand, we're the middleman."

Reports rank high on the list of common writing responsibilities for managers. Whether it is a recommendation for a marketing approach, an analysis of a car for the company car pool, or the feasibility of changing the price structure for the corporate cafeteria, the same basic format provides a solid foundation for building a convincing argument for the conclusions of the report. Skills with this type of writing are useful in the management of staff, customers, clients, other managers, supervisors, and even investors.

In fact, an effective persuasive writing style is invaluable. The ability to persuade starts with an effective interpersonal style. Usually that style is expressed in a mix of oral and nonverbal communication. At some point, however, successful managers need to inject a friendly, confident, and supportive style into their written communications.

Basic strategies inform the three most common types of persuasive reports (recommendation, evaluation, and feasibility). In the broadest sense, some form of assessment is followed by a recommendation in all of these reports. While many types of reports, including evaluation, feasibility, and progress reports, may incorporate recommendations, the recommendation report is focused entirely on the recommendation and the explanation for the recommendation. There are two kinds of recommendation reports: solicited and unsolicited.

In an evaluation report, the emphasis is on the analysis of information. Several different approaches can be taken when evaluating products, projects, or personnel.

Feasibility reports are common in companies that conduct research and development, do construction, or execute campaigns. In these reports, questions like the following—Should a project be expanded and Should the company enter a new market—are addressed. Although the feasibility report incorporates much of the same material as recommendation and evaluation reports, the emphasis is different. A definite recommendation must be made, as in a recommendation report, and the situation must be analyzed, as in an evaluation report, but the emphasis in a feasibility report is on a project's likelihood of success and the reasons for that conclusion.

You should be able to formulate a strategy for writing a successful report that persuades others to accept your recommendation. You should be able to select the appropriate stylistic elements and format for writing a report to recommend an action, evaluate a project, or analyze the feasibility of a proposed course of action. Many companies have specified formats for reports, often called *report templates*. If your company does, it is important to know it and to use it. These prescribed formats normally do not limit persuasive writing, but they structure the content and format for the data to be discussed.

Strategies for Persuasive Report Writing

KEY CONCEPT 5.1

Managers prepare reports using an appropriate style of persuasive writing.

Most writing reflects an effort to convince the reader. You want to convince someone that you are the right person for a job or that your service is the best available. You try to persuade the recipient of the accuracy of a report or the time-critical nature of an impending opportunity. You try to open a new market, satisfy an existing customer, or speed a shipment from a vendor. In almost every case, some element of persuasion guides your word choice and the tone of your message.

Reports that make assessments and offer recommendations depend heavily upon your persuasive skills. Since the reports are meant to convey an assessment of a product, service, procedure, or plan of action, they must persuade the reader to adopt the point of view advocated in the report. Recommendation reports go a step further. In them you must persuade the reader to accept the particular course of action advanced in the report. Several strategic approaches for persuasive writing are effective for assessment and recommendation reports.

Techniques used in advertising are typically distinguished as **central route persuasion** and **peripheral route persuasion** (Petty and Cacioppo, 1986). Since you are trying to sell your point of view, these two approaches may be helpful. The peripheral route is seldom used in report writing; it involves using indirect strategies for changing the behavior of an intended audience (mostly purchasing and voting behavior). Peripheral route arguments should not be confused with indirect organizational patterns common in many business letters. The peripheral route approach may contain many of fallacies discussed in Chapter 2. These help strengthen the emotional response to the conclusions being offered. They can be helpful in changing perceptual and emotional elements associated with your efforts to influence others. A political party may use scare tactics to persuade elderly voters that the opposition candidate is out to strip away social security benefits. Unfortunately, sometimes, managerial reports are written to obfuscate or mislead. For instance, the manager responsible for software development in a company may write a negative evaluation of a software-outsourcing firm, when in fact that firm can provide superior software at a lower cost. The reason is that the manager perceives a loss of status if the work is outsourced.

Other peripheral techniques include distracting or logically unconnected elements as in using beautiful female models to create associations with brand names. The presumption is that the audience will identify with the models and not pay attention to the quality of the product. The success of this approach is quite limited when applied to assessment and recommendation reports, although, brand identification may have value when it draws attention to important reputation concerns such as a reputation for high quality and dependable service. You should be aware that peripheral route presentations often contain distorted information. Still, in choosing the peripheral route, writers should understand that their audience may be aware of their tactics and as a result may reject the message out of hand. While effective with uninformed or unobservant audiences, it is usually best to avoid this approach.

The substitution of superficial glitz in place of substance derives from the fact that today many business reports are not written documents, but are PowerPoint presentations. It once was a criticism of a presentation's analytic depth to say that it was only "**vugraph** deep"; that is, there was nothing to support the vugraph's summary view. Today, people seem inclined to accept a vugraph level of presentation without question.

The "central route" strategy is used to address specific issues by utilizing authoritative information, reasoning, and analysis. Because the reports that you make should be businesslike and professional, they must be grounded in this direct approach. Depending on your audience and message, occasionally you may wish to cushion a blow with some indirectness. A bad news assessment might be delineated with some indirect tactics to help minimize the impact, but the crucial points must be offered in clear and well-founded terms. Figure 5.1 on page 136 illustrates this approach.

As you learn how to develop an effective strategy for assessment and recommendation reports, you need to keep the central route versus peripheral route tactic in mind. Use this distinction as a guide for determining critical issues that require complete analysis and those that may be helpful but are not directly appropriate to the analysis. For instance, an ethical report writer does not cloud the core of the report with innuendo and propaganda. In fact, imagine a gauge that links propaganda included in the

FIGURE 5.1
...

Analytic Report that Includes Bad News and a Solution

ANNOUNCEMENT

All Staff

We have launched a requirements management initiative within our company. The purpose of this initiative is to ensure that we fully satisfy requirements associated with our development commitments. In the past, we have used a variety of techniques and tools with somewhat "spotty" results. For Release 5.0, we must clearly define, plan, control, and ultimately fulfill our development objectives in as efficient and effective a manner as we can. To that end, **we are focusing on establishing our requirements management process implementation** as defined at a high level in Document 10000601, a document that I encourage you all to read.

Integral to improving our requirements management process are tools that allow us to achieve greater efficiency. **We have selected a premier requirements management tool in Telelogic's DOORS suite.** This is the one used for the past three years by one of our divisions and cited by our ISO 9001 registrar, TUV, for its powerful capabilities. We have already loaded a number of requirements "modules" from customers, our design organization, and Engineering into this tool and plan to complete the migration and generation of other requirements sets into DOORS during the Release 5.0 time frame.

There are a number of DOORS implementation details to be resolved (e.g., numbering conventions, change management process, tracing rules, level definitions, access rights. etc.). To expedite closure on these items, **I have appointed a Requirements Management Process Team to establish appropriate instructions (G. Smith, M. Jones, B. Lyons, M. Brown, and U. Grey).** These instructions are a prerequisite to developing DOORS training materials. Our goal is to get these items addressed within the next month.

In the meantime, our design organization is preparing the Release 5.0 Feature Description Documents (FDDs). These form a basis for Engineering's development plans—our new product introduction (NPI) representatives are already developing work packages to detail these plans. Given the importance of requirements-driven development plans, **I expect each project to write and approve development requirements prior to commencing implementation.** Requirements may be needed at one or more levels of detail, depending on the nature of the project. Please work with NPI to define these as deliverables in the work packages.

In the past, we have used the Functional Specification to capture both requirements and design material, typically toward the END of the development phase. This practice is no longer acceptable. In fact, the Functional Specification document template was made obsolete several months ago and replaced with the Hardware Requirements Specification Template (Document No. 10000598) and the Hardware Design Specification Template (Document No. 10000590). The intent was for the 598 document to capture requirements (only) ahead of design and the 590 document to capture design (only). (Note that Software has been using database tools for capturing their requirements, so there is no 598 equivalent for them; they do, however, have a Software Design Specification, Document No. 10000585.)

Going forward, **I expect hardware requirements to be entered and traced directly into DOORS** instead of into a Word document, just as Software has been doing. Please now use the 598 template only as a guide in planning what a requirements deliverable should contain. **Special attention should be made of the test matrix** in the back of the document—it is essential that appropriate requirements be designated by the design engineers for Manufacturing Test development. (Our Operations

FIGURE 5.1
...

continued

staff need this information as early in the development phase as possible to plan their tests given our current outsourcing issues.) **The Requirements Management Process Team will resolve how best to do all this using DOORS.**

Finally, please be aware that we are required to plan our overall development activity as prescribed in the Design and Development Process, Document No. 10002413. Though I wanted to highlight the current requirements management activity focus here, **there are other factors to consider in planning Release 5.0, such as design reviews, verification, validation, and associated records and metrics.** Please read 2413 too!

Stay tuned for further announcements.

Thanks,

VP Engineering

report to the suspicion with which the report will be read: As the propaganda increases, so does the suspicion of the reader.

To prepare a successful assessment or recommendation report, you must coordinate three strategic elements: the communicator, the audience, and the message. Communicator factors include the writer's position, reputation, skill, and level of authority. Audience factors include cultural and social elements, the audience's opinions and roles in the decision-making process, and the attitudes that they hold regarding the message and the communicator. The components of the message include the structure of the message, how the message matches the expectations of the audience, reasoning techniques, sources of evidence, and clarity. Business writers are encouraged to make sure that they include the "three C's" to make their writing comprehensive, clear, and concise.

Communicator Strategies for Persuasive Writing

In an assessment report, you are offering your knowledge or discovered information to your audience so that they can make an informed decision. In making a recommendation, you want the audience to accept your assessment and to follow your recommended course of action. Your basic objective is to persuade the audience to follow your recommendation. If the assessment will result in major costs to the company or potential upheaval for the organization, who you are and how you have analyzed the situation becomes relevant to the report's reception. When offering recommendations about which piece of office equipment to buy, your personal character may not be relevant. See Figure 5.2 on page 138 for an example of this type of recommendation.

The first step in developing a specific report-writing strategy is to define your role as the communicator. The following questions will help you choose your tone.

- *What is your objective?* Is the report routine or required for your position, or is this a special opportunity for you to prove yourself? Routine reports do not need dramatic delivery or alarmist language. Alternately, the discovery of a potential biohazard in the workplace with significant corporate liability requires writing with an emphasis that sets off an alarm. Even in this case, this can be done without histrionics that might distract from your message. An analysis of quarterly figures that reads like a warning of doom may actually bring the

FIGURE 5.2
...

Example of Persuasive and Analytical Recommendation

EXECUTIVE SUMMARY

Logo Wireless International Inc. has requested the professional services of TSG Inc. in support of its network risk analysis and contingency planning initiatives. Logo Wireless International Inc. has an immediate need to develop plans to recover from possible personnel and infrastructure losses. A critical business requirement has been brought to the forefront of Logo Wireless International Inc.'s mission: to put in place comprehensive plans that will reduce, if not eliminate, the threat of losing its core business, technology, personnel, and infrastructure.

This proposal outlines the necessary steps involved in developing such a plan. TSG proposes a phased approach to analyzing the critical assets and need of Logo Wireless's business requirements and processes.

TSG is an industry leader in business continuity and disaster recovery planning and has significant experience in the assessment, design, implementation, and management of data center environments and disaster recovery contingency planning.

TSG demonstrates this capability through three primary characteristics:
1. Experience
2. Collaboration
3. Commitment to Knowledge Transfer

Experience—TSG's business continuity and disaster recovery consultants managed by Dave Deare have performed risk assessments and developed and implemented plans for clients on five continents. This environment has allowed our staff to become proficient with current technologies and related methodologies. Many of these methodologies and technologies are applicable to the Logo Wireless International Inc. project. Dave Deare's team have performed risk assessments and developed plans for the following customers: AT&T, NT&T, Wal-Mart, SWIFT, Telefonica, Saudi Arabia Telephone, VISA, Telefort, Telia, Telstra, Alestra, Genuity, and AAPT.

Collaboration—Our company has a proven track record in our ability to interface and collaborate effectively with clients and contractors. We have a willingness to go the extra mile and be responsive to Logo Wireless International Inc.'s needs. We are a known entity that has a track record of starting projects quickly, engaging fully, and completing them on time. This experience lowers the risk of the project for Logo Wireless International Inc.

Commitment to Knowledge Transfer—The collective knowledge of our consultants and engineers is one of TSG's most valuable assets and one that we make a concerted effort to share with our clients on every engagement. Each TSG consultant is a full-time employee and has ready access to the combined expertise of other highly qualified engineers and consultants. While no single individual can be an expert on every core technology, the TSG organization as a whole represents a dynamic "knowledge store," offering technical experience in nearly all Internet-working disciplines. Knowledge transfer to resident technical staff is an integral element of the value that TSG strives to bring to its clients on every assignment.

TSG offers a balance of high-level technical engineering and consulting skills coupled with real-world experience, and a consulting methodology, company culture, and systems infrastructure that ensure the full engagement of this expertise on every project. TSG routinely provides on-the-job knowledge transfer as an inherent element of our consulting engagements. TSG firmly believes that prolonging "client dependency" serves neither TSG nor our clients, and unless instructed not to provide knowledge transfer, we do so as a natural course of business. It is, in our view, an integral component of the value purchased when clients select TSG as a consulting partner.

wrong level of attention to you as the communicator, especially if it appears to be reactionary or overstated.

- *Do you have any personal investment in the outcome?* That is, are you partial to one choice, and will the decision have a positive or negative impact on you? If you cannot hide your personal anxiety about the outcome of the report that you are writing, it may be best to address that anxiety at the very beginning. If the reader detects that you are concerned that the result may be detrimental to your position or that the outcome may greatly influence your chance for promotion, then the entire message may become suspect.

- *How will the audience view you?* Do you currently have a reputation for being knowledgeable, thorough, and fair? Sometimes, for internal reports, the reader knows you and does not need to be convinced that you know what you are doing. In some reports, you have to establish your credibility through the report itself. If you need to establish credibility, qualifying phrases like, "I believe," "It may be the case that . . . ," and "Some think . . . ," can divert attention from you as the originator of the idea or analysis that you are offering and add an element of uncertainty. Instead, phrases such as "In our last experience with this product, we found . . .," "Our research and development staff have tested this and discovered . . .," or "A competitor uses this product and has been able to save . . ." will convey a sense of assurance that you speak with authority. Indeed, you can turn to authoritative sources and demonstrate your own credibility by managing the evidence effectively.

With each of these issues, the author's credibility is the main theme. The report preparer must avoid any taint of personal investment in the outcome and must express an appropriate level of urgency for a decision or action. Personal issues or over- or underreactions diminish your credibility substantially. A powerful tool for establishing credibility involves examining both sides of an argument or offering alternative interpretations of an assessment. Once the differing views are explored, a focused analysis concerning why one interpretation is more accurate than the others is effective. Likewise, if alternative points of view appear misrepresented, a loss of credibility results.

Audience Strategies for Persuasive Writing

After defining your role as communicator, the next important step is to devise a strategy for shaping the message to the audience. Again, key questions can help organize your approach.

- *Who is your audience?* If the audience includes individuals who may be gatekeepers of information, you need to address their concerns. In some cases, these gatekeepers are looking for certain elements in a report. If these elements are missing, the report may come back to you for more information or it may be ignored.

  If the audience members are decision makers, are they supervisors or individuals who have higher positions than the author? The approach to addressing this group should be different from that used in addressing a potential client. The level of respect shown to the readers will be the same, but in some corporate structures, all reports are considered "mere" recommendations until they reach the ultimate decision maker. You may say to a potential client, "If you want the highest level of functionality and security in your software, you will have little alternative but to select our software, because we have the highest rating. . . ." "You must select" is not appropriate in addressing a supervisor. In this latter case, a more appropriate tone would be, "Since we have identified security as a top priority. . . because of their holding the highest security rating, our best choice would be. . . ."

- *What does the audience already know?* The audience already knows you—as a vendor, client, subordinate, or manager of a department, for example. They have an image of you that affects the message that you are trying to communicate. Readers may also have ideas about the situation that you are addressing. You must be aware of these potential prejudices. They can create bias both by encouraging the audience to consider itself an authority (which it may well be) and by discounting your counterefforts.

  While you should not be defensive about what you have to offer, you can present information in a way that anticipates challenges and inquiries. This "preemptive strike" is called **inoculation** (McGuire, 1964). In effect, you are providing a vaccine against disagreement. This is achieved by addressing the points of difference during the narrative of your analysis. Inoculation serves several crucial purposes. First, it shows that you have explored options and given them serious consideration. Second, it provides readers who were unaware of the objections information about the objections—and even the means of defeating those objections. Third, the inoculation enhances your position or the view that you are trying to convey by improving your credibility.

- *Is this good or bad news for the audience?* Good news is easy to report and to receive. You state the news without excessive elaboration. Be aware, though, that good news can have a "Pollyanna" effect: People may be so pleased with the basic positive message that they ignore potential negatives. A realistic balance is best. Presenting bad news, an assessment of a negative trend, or a negative evaluation of a popular option requires more care for it may not be well received at first reading. Still, most decision makers like to have this information up front, even if it makes much of the remainder of the report unsavory. Managers need to be ahead of the market and prepared for any looming disaster.

Every piece of bad news can have a positive perspective. Bad news can have good results because it allows the company to anticipate problems and head them off. To emphasize this possibility, bad news can be countered in your conclusion with the suggestion or recommendation of a forthcoming opportunity that arises from the circumstance. Bad news about a decision that might have disastrous consequences—perhaps for making a commitment to a product that ultimately will not meet the real need—can actually save the company financial and personnel resources, as well as the cost of recovery from an error. When you need to report bad news, look for, but do not dwell on, the positive side.

Yet another kind of bad news is the conclusion that a reader's pet project is in trouble. While the messenger should not be held responsible for the message, a wise approach is to be alert to your reader's potential emotional and personal commitment. There are ways to suggest with sensitivity that someone's plan is unsatisfactory. Your strategy must be responsive to office politics and your fellow workers.

- *Will the recommended decision or action be easy or hard to make?* Reducing the work force by 20 percent will be difficult, especially if there are few employees close to retirement and the turnover rate is low. Selecting one of several candidates for a promotion will be an easier task, but still there may be a potential for hard feelings and so on. For the message to lead to a decision and action, the audience must include the key decision makers. The more complicated and interdependent a decision is to make, the more supporting argument will be needed to clarify what is being decided. However, extremely difficult decisions (such as a significant reduction in the work force) may not need much supporting argument (the company is losing money and has no prospects for a turnaround in sales). Such decisions need resolve, not argument.

Message Strategies for Persuasive Writing

Your message strategy rests on the distinction between **direct** and **indirect messages**. Direct messages have a strong impact and reflect a confident author. The direct approach includes active language. In the direct approach, the recommendation is at the beginning. This placement can involve a clear statement of the key elements of the recommendation. Some writers include a brief summary of the recommendation in the introduction to the report. The analysis follows the recommendation as a supporting narrative. Reasons, evidence, and logic are used to provide support. The analysis thus follows one of the methods described in Chapter 2 and avoids the fallacies outlined in that chapter. In a report written using the direct approach, you conclude with a restatement of the recommendation.

The indirect approach may divert attention from the author and distract decision makers. The language used in the indirect approach is often passive (though not necessarily so). Statements like "The choice of Brand Y will be a good one" not only obscure the source of the assessment, they do not address the reader as a decision maker. Note the difference in this alternative stated in a direct manner: "We recommend that the executive board select Brand Y as the company's standard materials source." The direct, active approach always has a real actor undertaking real actions. *Real actors* are a person or group of people, such as a department, team, or committee. The structure of the indirect approach is a presentation of the reasoning, evidence, and analysis in a manner that appears to the reader to be the same, step-wise manner undertaken in the actual preparation of the assessment or recommendation. Therefore, the resulting assessment is revealed at the end of the report.

When should the indirect approach be used? Current convention favors the direct rather than indirect method. It avoids confrontation. We recommend that you avoid the indirect method in almost every circumstance. The indirect approach may be used if you want to get a decision other than the one supported by the relevant facts; that is, when it is in your interest to have a decision made contrary to the best interest of the company. We do not recommend this use of the indirect approach, but you need to be able to recognize it.

Furthermore, for truly dramatic effect, an indirect approach can be used to inoculate the audience against any perceived negative baggage that the message or the communicator may have. If you have low credibility or know of bias against you, or if the message is particularly unsavory, this approach is reasonable. Passive voice can be used to separate the bias toward you from your analysis. An appeal to external or independent authorities also separates you from the message. However, to counter bias, using active language increases credibility. Rather than saying "three current users were consulted" (which is the passive voice), you might say, "I consulted three current users of this equipment" or "I found research demonstrating this manufacturing process to be more efficient because . . . ." These active statements can be included in the indirect approach, and they can help lead readers through the steps of the analysis to take ownership of the recommendation. Additionally, effective use of the indirect approach requires the knowledge that the reader has a high level of patience (it is usually a longer approach) and requires care to avoid making the report appear intentionally obscure, even if it is.

SECTION SUMMARY

There are two kinds of persuasive reports: (1) those meant to convince a reader to adopt a point of view and (2) those meant to convince a reader to accept a course of action. Common techniques include the "central route" and the "peripheral route" strategies. Normally, the central route is most appropriate and effective in managerial writing. Elements to be coordinated are: (1) the communicator, (2) the audience, and (3) the message.

CHALLENGE PROBLEM FOR REVIEW

Select several editorial opinions from your local newspaper or from a national paper such as the *New York Times*. Identify which of these encourages a point of view and which encourages action. Assess the reasonableness the persuasion. Which seems to be most important: the audience or the message?

The Recommendation Report

KEY CONCEPT 5.2
...

The recommendation report is the standard format of managerial persuasive writing. Recommendations flow from an accurate assessment of conditions and options.

There are two general types of recommendation reports: solicited and unsolicited. A **solicited recommendation report** is a response to a request by corporate management for a report on any aspect of the company's affairs. Commonly, the request dictates, or at least suggests, the purpose of the report. Most important, of course, is the role that the report will have in a decision-making process. These reports can be written by internal or external authors.

Unsolicited recommendation reports are generated for a number of reasons. Typically, they differ from the solicited report in that they arise when an employee recognizes a new opportunity, a new risk, or a procedural or managerial oversight that needs to be brought to the attention of higher management. The recommendation of a potential vendor may have the look and feel of a recommendation report, but normally it serves the interest of the vendor and not the company. If your company is considering a change in its information technology structure, then an assessment made by a potential vender—such as AT&T, IBM, Lucent, Cisco Systems, Dell, or a similar organization—should be reviewed with caution.

The Solicited Recommendation Report

Recommendation reports may be described by several different names, some of which are specific to the type of product made by the company or the type of recommendation being made. If prepared by a committee or task force, the report may be called a committee report or task force report.

Consider this example. Universities, schools, and academic programs undergo a regular evaluation and accreditation process in which large amounts of data are collected to validate the effectiveness of the school. The final step involves a committee with members drawn from outside the school who evaluate the data and make an accreditation recommendation. This committee makes recommendations only about accreditation. These recommendations are either for or against accreditation, and many required or recommended changes can be attached. The accrediting agency—usually constituted of representatives from other institutions that have the same accreditation—then awards or denies accreditation or grants a conditional status.

Such a narrowly focused activity is not unusual. External auditors of a company's finances regularly review the financial dealings of the company and make a report to the board of trustees and eventually the stockholders. This review is usually highly focused on accounting practices. Another external type of report may develop from a management consultant who reviews the entire corporate system and makes recommendations for changes in management style, financial procedures, and even manufacturing practices. Often, contracted consultants have more specific tasks, such as finding ways to improve customer service, employee diversity, or employee morale.

In writing a recommendation report, your approach should be straightforward. Elaborate, persuasive language is not needed, since the writer has been asked for definite recommendations, but the report should show how the recommendations are in line with the criteria considered. The format should be as follows:

- An introduction describing your "charge" or job to evaluate.
- A statement detailing the criteria considered.
- An explanation of the options ("finalists") for your recommendations.
- Conclusions and recommendations.

Since solicited recommendation reports are directed toward an audience that already has expressed an interest in the findings, we can assume that the readers are open to the recommendations—if the recommendations are consistent with the criteria agreed upon by both the solicitor and the writer. The writer's job, then, is to present the information logically and methodically.

A recommendation report might be requested to evaluate the publishing of an in-house corporate newsletter. Assume that our fictional company SHG General publishes a biweekly employee newsletter that correlates with the company pay period. The newsletter is an important communication tool for management. Historically, the material has been typed, taken to an outside printer where it is typeset, proofread, and printed. As the manager for the department responsible for this project, you are asked to take a look at desktop publishing as a possibility for automating this process.

Your report needs to contain a definite conclusion: Should SHG General outsource its printing or should it publish the newsletter in-house? If both of the options appear to have advantages and meet specified criteria, then the criteria themselves need to be weighed. Is initial cost the most significant criterion? It could be, if the audience considers a payback period longer than one year to be excessive. What about personnel and training time? If the departmental budget does not permit overtime or part-time help, then these criteria might assume significant roles.

When developing a recommendation report, your first questions should be about the criteria that are to be used for arriving at your recommendations. If the audience soliciting the report has not established definite criteria, you will have to develop some that will be accepted without much argument. In this particular example, SHG General would probably suggest the criteria illustrated in Table 5.1.

You have to determine whether the long-term cost savings, time savings, and other advantages of in-house publishing are enough to offset the increased cost of employee time for training and for operating equipment. The explanation for your recommendation is simple since there are only two candidates: in-house or outsourced publishing. A shared discussion of each option's advantages and disadvantages will prove a simple way to reach a conclusion and make a recommendation. If several items are under consideration, however, you might want to consider the major criteria and list the best options in each category before concluding with a specific recommendation and explanation for your selection. Figure 5.3 on page 144 illustrates a portion of a typical solicited recommendation report.

TABLE 5.1
...

Sample Criteria

• Cost, including payback period
• Time savings
• Employee time required
• Advantages (less lead time for publication; more professional-looking product; training time, etc.)

FIGURE 5.3
···

A Solicited Recommendation Report

SHG GENERAL   **Providing Quality Services Worldwide**

Suite 1000, One SHG Boulevard   800.555.4321
Dayton, Ohio 45439

DATE: January 10, 2004
TO: Lawrence Accurat
           Vice President, Administration
FROM: Marcia Stein *MS*
           Manager, Data Processing
RE: Recommendation for Office Software Integration,
           Summary Recommendation

Background

At our January 2nd Executive Committee meeting, you asked that I provide a recommendation for an integrated office software program that meets SHG General's current and anticipated future needs. You indicated that the Executive Committee would then establish a policy that requires any user who prefers another program to justify that position based specifically on a unique set of circumstances. As you know, our requirements are minimal, and we need only to integrate databases, spreadsheets, and document preparation for our operations.

Criteria

At our meeting January 2nd, the Executive Committee indicated that the spreadsheet program I recommended must meet the following criteria:

- Intel/Windows compatibility and cross-platform data retrieval (including MAC files)
- Conversion capabilities for Lotus Format (archived data)
- Comprehensive integration capabilities for office functions

Recommendations

I found only two programs that meet our criteria: WordPerfect Office 12 and Microsoft Office 2004. The current configurations of these two office products even make them compatible with each other. I recommend that we ask vendors to bid on an integrated and networked solution. I believe that we can get competitive pricing, which will include some basic training for the transition of staff to the new format.

The Unsolicited Recommendation Report

An unsolicited recommendation report is volunteered. It is not requested and it may be that no one is interested in reading it. If it addresses a problem resulting from a manager's action or inaction, you must be careful not to accuse specific people of incompetence, unless your intent is to prove it.

What if you feel that a serious morale problem exists in your department because the personnel evaluation process is too subjective? The form used is not quantitative and lends itself to staff assumptions about managerial favoritism. Suppose you and several colleagues have developed an evaluation tool that you feel is more accurate in assessing employee accomplishments. Because the primary and secondary audiences for an unsolicited recommendation report such as this may not be favorably disposed toward considering it and may even feel defensive about their part in developing what you perceive as a problem, the best approach may be indirect rather than direct.

Instead of focusing on the inadequacies of the present instrument, you can discuss the benefits and advantages of using a more quantitative tool for evaluation. Carefully choose the criteria used to justify your recommendation. Since this report will include persuasive techniques, remember that the audience has not asked for the report or agreed upon the criteria. Therefore, criteria cannot be so biased that readers will not accept them as the basis for selection. The problem of personal evaluation is a widespread one and central to the work of managing people. The topic is so old and worn that bringing it up could alienate many experienced managers. Most managers have gone down the path of trying to quantify performance only to find it leads to difficult choices between relying on what little can be measured or assessing important behaviors that cannot be quantified. Unfortunately, it strikes at the heart of managerial duties.

The appropriate use of diction is always important. In this case, your audience will be upper-level managers, so your diction should be formal. You might discuss "SHG General employees" rather than "all of us working here."

The organization of an unsolicited recommendation report begins with an introduction to the problem and specific documented examples. This provides evidence that there is a problem.

A statement outlining possible solutions should follow. Your organizational strategy might be to list solutions from least expensive to most expensive, from least likely to most likely, or perhaps solutions from departmental to companywide. You need to discuss both the advantages and disadvantages of these possible solutions.

INSIGHT BOX 5.1
...

Stereotypes

There is a cliché that the corporate world is a "dog-eat-dog" world, that people trying to climb the corporate ladder of success are willing to do anything to get to the top. Another stereotype is that management always tries to shift the blame for any problem that occurs.

Popular culture is filled with examples reflecting these clichés. Theatrical productions such as *The Merchant of Venice* and *Glengarry Glen Ross* and novels (and the films made from them) such as *Wall Street* and *Nine-to-Five* all include stereotyped businesspeople and situations that are readily accepted. These are also the subjects of Scott Adams' extremely popular *Dilbert* comic strips. There is even a book of business cartoons that have been published in *The New Yorker*. One of these cartoons, by Michael Maslin, depicts a boardroom meeting in which the chairman suggests that the purpose of the meeting is to place the blame on someone else (p. 32).

Admittedly, these stereotypes do not apply to all businesspeople or corporations. There are many examples of successful businesspeople who are loved by their colleagues and who contribute to their communities. There is enough truth in the stereotypes, though, that they can serve as cautionary examples to keep in mind while composing your unsolicited report.

The final portion of your unsolicited recommendation report consists of a conclusion. Here the problem needs to be restated and recommendations provided. It is important not to dictate what action must be taken, since management did not ask for an opinion in the first place. Figure 5.4 illustrates a portion of an unsolicited recommendation report.

A Checklist for the Solicited Recommendation Report

_____ Does your introduction indicate your "charge" (the job that you have been given of recommending a product or course of action)?

FIGURE 5.4
...

An Unsolicited Recommendation Report

SHG GENERAL   **Providing Quality Services Worldwide**

Suite 1000, One SHG Boulevard   800.555.4321
Dayton, Ohio 45439

DATE: March 15, 2004
TO: Lawrence Accurat
           Vice President, Administration
FROM: Peter Harris *PH*
           Chairman, SHG General Minority Employees Caucus
RE: A Recommendation to Increase Minority Retention,
           Summary Recommendation

Background

Despite Mr. Richman's explicit affirmative action statement, a number of us are very concerned about SHG General's inability to boost its recruitment and retention of minority employees. Although we do not have precise figures, it would appear that African-American and Latin-American workers rarely stay more than a couple of months at SHG General. We would like to help you rectify this situation and thus help the company meet its affirmative action goals. We also would like to suggest a way to save the company money while achieving these good-faith goals.

Why Do Minority Employees Leave SHG General?

While we are sure that there are many reasons why minority employees leave SHG General, there is one reason that we can correct. SHG General's plants are more than thirty miles from any major minority population center. The bus connections are so poor that it takes the average worker more than 90 minutes to reach the plants and even longer to come home in the evening. Our own recent poll of minority workers (see attached) suggests that workers would be happy to contribute a sum of money equivalent to their bus fare through payroll deduction to pay for a van that could establish a morning pickup schedule through the major minority neighborhoods and then provide a ride home in the evening.

We recommend the van pool option to help retain these valuable employees. We have included figures (see attached) that indicate that such a van pool would boost productivity by reducing employee absences. It would boost company profits by increasing minority employee retention, thus reducing the amount of money that would have to be spent for recruitment. It would serve as a positive public relations gesture for SHG General, a definite example of the company's willingness to "reach out" to the minority community. I look forward to the chance to talk with you about this project after you have had a chance to examine our figures.

_____ Do you indicate the criteria that you used to arrive at your recommendation?

_____ A solicited recommendation report must include a definite recommendation as part of its conclusion. Do you make that recommendation clearly so that the reader knows precisely who or what you are recommending?

_____ Do you explain your recommendation and why you eliminated all but one solution?

A Checklist for the Unsolicited Recommendation Report

_____ Does your introduction establish that there is a problem to be solved?

_____ Do you have a clear organizational pattern for examining possible solutions?

_____ Do you examine all possible solutions and show why all but one are inadequate, ineffective, or at least inferior to the one that you have chosen?

_____ Do you propose a definite next step, an action for your readers to take?

SECTION SUMMARY

Recommendation reports are solicited or unsolicited. Management requests solicited reports. The recommended format for solicited reports is: an introduction; a detailing of criteria; an explanation of possible solutions; conclusions and recommendations. Management does not request unsolicited reports. The format for unsolicited reports is the same as that for solicited reports. Because these reports are unsolicited, your diction should be formal and nonthreatening.

CHALLENGE PROBLEM FOR REVIEW

Television commercials are, in effect, recommendation reports. Select a few of your favorites and analyze how they are effective or ineffective in making recommendations.

The Evaluation Report

Evaluation reports are used to address the extent to which an evaluated item meets specific criteria.

All reports share certain characteristics. The differences between the kinds of report writing are the author's intent, the material utilized in the evaluation, and the audience. An evaluation report is a specialized form of a recommendation report.

As with any kind of writing, part of your prewriting preparation is to determine what is required (i.e., what is the subject and how is it to be treated?). Normally, your assignment makes this clear. For example, the manufacturing division might ask you to evaluate a new product that the company has created. Product evaluations are very valuable. The magazine _Consumer Reports_ is a popular monthly journal consisting entirely of product evaluations. Given your assignment, you will want to develop guidelines that help keep you within your audience's range of comprehension and purpose. A product evaluation for marketing will be focused on different elements than will an evaluation intended for the manufacturing division, even though there are elements that fit both evaluations. The language that you use in the evaluation differs too, depending on the division for which the report is being written. Technical data needed by the manufacturing division may be appropriate for the marketing division as well, but it is likely that the marketing division will need the data to be expressed in nontechnical language. A humorous yet insightful guideline is: For engineering, use tables of data; for marketing, draw pictures.

There are three major areas for which an evaluation report might be requested: products (including services), projects, and personnel. Note that there are several applications for the results in each of these areas, even though the fundamentals of the report remain the same. For instance, if you are evaluating a product, your rationale may be to determine whether the company should purchase a product, whether it should create a product (which might involve competition with another product already on the market), whether the product currently being produced should be modified to make it better or less expensive to produce or sell, whether the product has outlived its market potential, and so forth. In any case, the following are the kinds of questions that you would ask to guide yourself in designing and executing your evaluation.

Products

1. Purchasing considerations
   a. What is the purpose of the product?
   b. What company needs does the product fulfill?
   c. How efficient is the product in fulfilling those needs?
   d. What is the cost of the product?
   e. Do the company's needs justify obtaining the product at that cost?
   f. What warranties are available from the supplier and/or the manufacturer? What do they cover?
   g. Are the supplier and manufacturer reliable? Are they likely to remain viable for the life of the product?
   h. Can the company service the product? At what cost? If not, who can, are they reliable, and what will the cost of the repairs be?
   i. Are replacement parts readily available?
   j. What is the life of the product?
   k. Could the company produce as good a product less expensively?
   l. Are there any alternative products that should be considered?
2. Production considerations
   a. What is the product's function?
   b. Does the product fulfill its function as effectively and efficiently as possible?
   c. How much does it cost to produce the product?
   d. Is manufacturing the product cost effective?
   e. Is there an established market for the product?
   f. How competitive is the product in terms of selling price?
   g. How competitive is the product in terms of quality?
   h. Does it, or can it, make a profit?
   i. What does the future look like in terms of a continued market, production costs, and competition?

Projects

1. Was the project completed on schedule?
2. Was the project completed within the budget allotted?
3. Was the work performed efficiently?
4. How well did the personnel involved perform?
5. Was the project or process effective?
6. Were the expected results obtained?
7. Should any changes be initiated?
8. Would it be more cost effective to outsource similar projects in the future?

Personnel

1. What is the job description?
2. How well does the employee perform each aspect of the job individually and overall in fulfilling the duties outlined in the job description? Are there areas in which the employee excels? Are there areas in which the employee is deficient?
3. Is some merit recognition in order? Should the employee be promoted?
4. Is the employee willing to work at improving areas of deficiency? Should the employee be retained or perhaps moved to another division within the company?
5. What might the employee do to improve job performance?
6. Has the employee improved since the last evaluation?
7. Is the employee cooperative?
8. Does the employee work well with peers?
9. Does the employee comply with company regulations?
10. Does the employee show initiative?

Your next prewriting step is to collect pertinent data. The nature of your evaluation determines what kind of data is to be collected, but you will be conducting tests to establish the answers to a series of questions. For instance, as just suggested, you might ask what the cost of a product is, how long the item will last, what its characteristics are, and so forth. You would start with an evaluation of the company's needs. If the transportation department is considering buying tires for the company's fleet of vans, you could compare and contrast the tires that are on the market that would fit the vehicles. Are all-weather tires required or are regular tires sufficient (this would involve knowing where, when, and how often the vans are driven, what they carry, and so on)? The performance records of the tires would be evaluated relevant to the company's needs. How do the tires perform in snow, do they tend to hydroplane in rain, what is their heat index, how well do they grip the road in braking, what is the length of the warranty and what does it cover, and what is the average mileage for each tire? These are the kinds of questions that you collect data to answer. The initial cost of the tires would be a factor, but the availability of replacements and whether the supplier gives you a reduced rate based on the number of tires that you order are considerations too.

Having collected this information, you can create an outline to present the material. The introduction should make a reference to the assignment. This will explain what product, person, concept, or system was evaluated and the purpose of the evaluation. Next comes the data. Conclusions and recommendations follow.

Organizing an Evaluation Report

The evaluation report should contain the following sections:

1. A short summary of evaluation (a summary of conclusions is optional)
2. Background information
3. Project guidelines, including criteria examined and methods employed
4. Presentation of your data
5. Results of your evaluation
6. Conclusions and recommendations

A Checklist for the Evaluation Report

_____ Do you understand the assignment? What is to be evaluated and why?
_____ Establish the idea or concept that will serve as your organizing principle.
_____ Determine your criteria (cost, number, performance record, resources, availability of parts, availability of personnel, outlook for company's future need, outlook for future projected costs, and availability of resources).

_____ Collect your data (discuss the pertinence, completeness, and accuracy of the data).
_____ Evaluate data according to the established criteria.
_____ Draw conclusions.
_____ Make recommendations based on the conclusions.
_____ Make sure that your format is correct.

SECTION SUMMARY

Evaluation reports are used to determine whether a product, program, or person meets certain criteria. The challenges are to define the criteria carefully and to apply them systematically.

CHALLENGE PROBLEM FOR REVIEW

Surely, you have been on the receiving end of an employee evaluation. Reflect on that (it even could be the evaluation of a project for another class) and write your own version of what should have been said—for both the positive and the negative elements.

Feasibility Reports

KEY CONCEPT 5.4
...

A feasibility report is an assessment of the likelihood that a specific course of action will be successful for achieving a goal. The report has all of the elements of a recommendation report, but it differs in that it is focused on "what if" scenarios.

Any major change in corporate strategy requires information and analysis. Should the company enter a new market, open a new plant, or even change the name or nature of a once popular product? **Feasibility reports** provide managers with the information necessary to make an informed decision. The report should contain a conclusion based on the research within it and not on the writer's assertions or feelings. In today's marketplace, high-quality feasibility reports are critical for long-term success. In many cases, a decision about a course of action may be based on a comparison of two profitable options. In the 1990s, companies sometimes closed plants that were profitable, just not profitable enough! The resulting loss (or outsourcing to foreign countries) of jobs in part led to the financial depression at the end of the century. *Feasibility can mean that it is more profitable not to act.*

Establishing the Report's Criteria and Scope

A feasibility study must have a clearly defined purpose, scope, and criteria. What does management want? If SHG General's top management is contemplating opening a new plant to produce an innovative product, it may specify that the feasibility study be limited to operations criteria including start-up costs, retooling expenses, distribution costs compared to the current facility, and initial hiring and training costs. On a smaller scale, a marketing department might do a similar study to define a marketing campaign and predict the public's response.

Like a proposal writer who must analyze the report's audience and determine which details should be emphasized, a feasibility report author must analyze the audience before beginning to write. What types of information do the readers require, and what specific criteria do they want used to evaluate the feasibility of the project under scrutiny? Are the readers managers from technical departments who want technical details or are they concerned with financial information? What do the managers want to accomplish with the report?

After establishing the feasibility report's objectives and the criteria to be used for evaluating options and reaching a conclusion, your next task is to evaluate all of the elements to be considered in determining a project's feasibility. Given the task of producing a feasibility report on an employee-paid van for car pooling to an outlying plant, you might consider the following factors:

1. Number of employees willing to use the van pool
2. Initial cost of the van
3. Operating cost of the van
4. Commuting distances for employees
5. Times for the different shifts
6. Data on another plant's successful or unsuccessful van pool
7. Job level of the employees (after-hours committee meetings for managers might create time conflicts)
8. Data from recent employee attitude polls
9. A national study comparing absenteeism among commuting employees driving their own vehicles and those employees using company-sponsored van pools

After making a list of possible material, you should review the criteria that management has established for the report to see if all of the elements listed are appropriate. If management has indicated that the van pool is to be used only by hourly workers, for example, a national study that included a high percentage of managers would be irrelevant. Similarly, if the commuting distances for the company's other plant are 50 percent shorter than national averages, the national data might be irrelevant.

Once this list has been trimmed to items that are consistent with desired criteria, your next step is to write a detailed outline. From the outline, you will be able to discern which items need more research (all major sources of information should be consulted) and which do not appear to fit into the report. The amount of research required has lately become an issue. Extensive research can be costly in both dollars and employee time. Unfortunately, few rules of thumb can guide a manager who wants to set limits on time spent on research. Common sense should be the guide. One criterion that helps is to ask whether the research conducted demonstrates or supports the main arguments. Once a point has been proven, additional research should be needed only as a response to challenges and related inquiries.

The organizational structure of a feasibility report should be clearly defined in the outline. There needs to be an introduction in which the purpose and scope of the study are stated. The report's body should contain the facts presented in an organized way. The organizing principle can vary depending upon the type of project being analyzed, but you need to link each paragraph and each section together with a transition.

The conclusion in a feasibility report follows from the facts presented in the main body. If all the facts suggest that a new plant would be too expensive to be successful, the conclusion should not dismiss these facts and indicate that the plant must be built because of other considerations that have not been discussed previously. It is crucial that the feasibility report present a clear analysis or definite recommendation according to its charge.

A Checklist for the Feasibility Report

_____ Who is the audience for this report?

_____ What are the report's objectives?

_____ What criteria should be used to determine the feasibility of a project or product?

_____ What should be emphasized in this report? Does the audience want financial information? Technical information? Does it want a combination of both types of information?

_____ Have you utilized all major sources of information before drawing your conclusions?

SECTION SUMMARY

A feasibility report is used to determine whether a specific course of action should be undertaken. Objectives must be defined that guide the decision to follow one course or another, and a conclusion and recommendation based on appropriate evidence must be presented.

CHALLENGE PROBLEM FOR REVIEW

Feasibility reports can easily suffer from bias of the analyst making the report, and it can be either pro or con. What kinds of actions can the recipient take to avoid or diminish this bias? What are some of the clues you would look for as you root out such bias?

CHAPTER SUMMARY

...

Persuasive reports are meant to convince a reader to adopt a point of view or to accept a course of action. They may be solicited or unsolicited and are used to evaluate the performance of products, programs, and personnel or to determine the feasibility of undertaking a specific course of action.

EXERCISES

...

Prewriting Exercises

1. Given the courses that you have taken and your work experience, list the qualities that you think you need to possess in order to be successful in your chosen career field.

2. Evaluate your performance in writing reports and make a list of recommendations about how you can improve your performance.

3. Examine a report on a product in *Consumer Reports* and outline it as an evaluation report for potential users of the product.

4. Examine an article in *Money Magazine* or the *Wall Street Journal* about money market funds or a similar investment that interests you and list the items that should be extracted for an evaluation report that would be based on the evidence that you find. Your audience would be others interested in the investment opportunity.

Writing Exercises

1. Write an evaluation report that justifies either your staying in your hometown or moving to another city in order to pursue your career goal. The audience for your report is a family member.

2. Write an unsolicited recommendation report in memo form indicating a change that should be made at work or school. The audience should be the various stakeholders in such a change.

3. Interview a manager at work or at school who frequently writes recommendation reports. Discover the most common primary and secondary audiences for these reports. How do the

two distinct audiences affect the manager's choice of words and strategy when writing the reports?

4. Would you include the element of increased employee morale in the unsolicited recommendation report in Figure 5.4? Why or why not?

5. Find out what the Hawthorne Effect is. Given the nature of the Hawthorne Effect, how would you address a response from Peter Harris (Figure 5.4) regarding the possible duration of the positive outcomes that you list in your unsolicited recommendation report?

6. Pick a piece of popular literature (a novel, motion picture, or magazine cartoon) that contains a stereotypical business or businessperson. From the point of view of coaching someone, write an unsolicited report to that person recommending how the situation or person in the artwork can be dealt with. Among your considerations can be evidence from your source regarding the accuracy of the stereotype, whether it is positive or negative.

Classic and Contemporary Forms   Part One

IN-BOX EXERCISE

...

You have been asked to assess the customer service unit of the A-WII electronics manufacturing and sales division. You are aware that there have been complaints about service being unresponsive and inaccurate. That is all you have been told. You are expected to improve the quality of service provided by the unit.

IN-BOX

ITEM 1: A MEMORANDUM FROM MR. EVERETT, YOUR SUPERVISOR.
Glad to have you on board. By Wednesday I would like to hear your preliminary recommendations for how to analyze our service problem. I know you are good, and you have been successful in your last assignments. So, I am looking forward to a draft recommendation. I will schedule a meeting at 1:00 P.M. for us to discuss it. You do not need to get the draft to me before that morning.

Your Response

Check one: ☐ Memorandum   ☐ E-mail   ☐ Letter   ☐ Note   ☐ Other

To: _____

_____

_____

_____

_____

_____

_____

_____

_____

_____

_____

_____

_____

_____

_____

_____

_____

_____

_____

_____

_____

_____

_____

_____

_____

_____

_____

**ITEM 2: E-MAIL FROM EVAN, EVENING SUPERVISOR FOR THE CUS-
TOMER SERVICE CALL CENTER.** I want to welcome you to the shop! I also wanted to let
you know that the flu has caused staff problems for the last six weeks, and it looks like we are about to
come out of the woods (sorry about the pun!). The call wait time should be back down to fifteen minutes by the time you get back.

Your Response

Check one: ☐ Memorandum   ☐ E-mail   ☐ Letter   ☐ Note   ☐ Other

To: _____

_____

_____

_____

_____

_____

_____

_____

_____

_____

_____

_____

_____

_____

_____

_____

_____

_____

ITEM 3: E-MAIL FROM ESTER, EVENING SUPERVISOR OF THE TECHNI-CAL ASSISTANCE UNIT. I know this will not make your day, but I have been complaining to your predecessor about the customer service people simply dumping non-technical questions on us for about three months. We have more than 25 percent of our calls as transfers from customer service that have not been properly screened. We pay these technicians too much to have them be telling customers how to plug in their DVD players.

Your Response

Check one: ☐ Memorandum   ☐ E-mail   ☐ Letter   ☐ Note   ☐ Other

To: _____

_____

_____

_____

_____

_____

_____

_____

_____

_____

_____

_____

_____

_____

_____

_____

_____

_____

_____

_____

_____

_____

_____

_____

_____

ITEM 4: MEMORANDUM FROM ETHAN, QUALITY CONTROL SUPERVISOR.

Welcome to Customer Satisfaction services. Mr. Everett wanted me to supply you with six months of data about performance and quality in your unit. I opened those files to you. Pat has the codes for access. It is a bunch of data that has not been analyzed. Just a warning!

Your Response

Check one: ☐ Memorandum ☐ E-mail ☐ Letter ☐ Note ☐ Other

To: _____

_____

_____

_____

_____

_____

_____

_____

_____

_____

_____

_____

_____

_____

_____

_____

_____

_____

_____

_____

_____

_____

_____

_____

_____

_____

_____

ITEM 5: E-MAIL MARKED "URGENT" FROM ETHEL, IT MAINTENANCE SUPERVISOR. We will be taking the customer tracking system down again for another upgrade. The software supplier has guaranteed a fix that should reduce the lost connection rate for the call center.

Your Response

Check one: ☐ Memorandum ☐ E-mail ☐ Letter ☐ Note ☐ Other

To: _____

_____

_____

_____

_____

_____

_____

_____

_____

_____

_____

_____

_____

_____

_____

_____

_____

_____

_____

_____

_____

_____

_____

_____

_____

_____

_____

_____

_____

_____

_____

_____

ITEM 6: E-MAIL FROM EZEKIEL (ZEKE), A SERVICE REPRESENTATIVE. I have been complaining for months about the static on my telephone line. Now that you are here, maybe you can get someone to fix it.

Your Response

Check one: ☐ Memorandum   ☐ E-mail   ☐ Letter   ☐ Note   ☐ Other

To: _____

_____

_____

_____

_____

_____

_____

_____

_____

_____

_____

_____

_____

_____

_____

_____

_____

_____

_____

_____

_____

_____

_____

_____

_____

_____

_____

_____

_____

_____

_____

_____

ITEM 7: 245 E-MAILS FROM UPSET CUSTOMERS. These e-mails are arranged by date. They have been printed and are in a folder on your desk with a note "Thought you might want to look at these" signed "Kim."

Your Response

Check one: ☐ Memorandum   ☐ E-mail   ☐ Letter   ☐ Note   ☐ Other

To: _____

_____

_____

_____

_____

_____

_____

_____

_____

_____

_____

_____

_____

_____

_____

_____

_____

_____

_____

_____

_____

_____

_____

_____

_____

_____

_____

_____

_____

_____

KEY TERMS

...

Central route persuasion (p. 135)

Direct message (p. 141)

Feasibility report (p. 150)

Indirect messages (p. 141)

Inoculation (p. 140)

Peripheral route persuasion (p. 135)

Solicited recommendation report (p. 142)

Unsolicited recommendation report (p. 142)

Vugraph (p. 135)

REFERENCES

...

McGuire, W. (1964). "Inducing Resistance to Persuasion: Some Contemporary Approaches." In L. Berkowitz (ed.), *Advances in Experimental Social Psychology* 1. New York: Academic Press, pp.191–229.

McGuire, W. (1961). "The Effectiveness of Supportive and Reputational Defenses in Immunizing and Restoring Beliefs Against Persuasion," *Sociometry* 24: 184–197.

Petty, R.E., and J.T. Cacioppo. (1986). *Communication and Persuasion: Central and Peripheral Routes to Attitude Change.* New York: Springer-Verlag.

CHAPTER 6

...

FORMATTING *the* PROPOSAL

LEARNING OUTCOMES

...

Upon completion of this chapter, you will be able to accomplish the following tasks:

1. Recognize the crucial role played by proposals in corporate settings.

2. Demonstrate why and how management/marketing strategies must be considered for a proposal to be successful.

3. Identify the parts of a needs analysis.

4. Apply a checklist of the key elements of a sales proposal when formulating a proposal outline.

5. Identify the request for proposal, unsolicited proposals, and solicited proposals, and describe how they differ in content and form with respect to the intended audience.

6. Understand and comply or respond to a request for proposal or bid invitation.

7. Write key elements of a sales proposal and prepare an outline of the proposal.

8. Identify the special elements of government and foundation proposals.

9. Write a proposal using appropriate language and format for a specified audience.

10. Evaluate the effectiveness of a proposal.

"This CD player costs less than players selling for twice as much."

An old vision of the manager's role in corporate success was limited to the enforcement of company policy and supervision of employees. Over a decade ago, this supervisory view of managers gave way to the philosophy of managers as leaders, as key players in shaping the corporate mission, and as entrepreneurs. Today, managers must be prepared to find new ways of doing business, new methods of increasing productivity, and of recruiting and retaining high-quality employees. Because managers are now expected to take the initiative and become entrepreneurs, they must promote and expand their business units. One way to do this is to use the proposal as a key tool in the process of expanding business, increasing service, or improving employee satisfaction. Even small businesses expect to be approached by vendors with specific proposals. Typically, letters of agreement, sales agreements, and binding contracts are preceded by detailed proposals. Successful bids for government contracts require detailed and thorough proposals. In this chapter, we examine the proposal and various strategies for preparing and writing proposals.

What Is a Proposal?

KEY CONCEPT 6.1

Formal proposals represent a major means of acquiring new and renewed business, internal support for ideas, and external financial support.

The Importance of Proposals

Proposals are a part of everyone's life, whether they are a marriage proposal, a legislator's proposal to raise the minimum wage, or a professor's proposal for research funds to study a new type of virus. The person making the proposal must tailor the format and style to a specific audience—the "target" audience. Understanding the audience becomes an imperative for the proposal writer, and this understanding must guide even the prewriting stages.

A **proposal** offers for consideration a course of action that requires approval. A man proposes marriage to his girlfriend; a "yes" from her means that she agrees to share her life and her financial resources with him. Knowing his audience well, the man paints a rosy picture of what married life will be like. He carefully selects his words to maximize his chances of obtaining approval. If, for example, he has purchased a new home next door to the home of his former girlfriend, he probably would avoid mentioning this proximity in his proposal. He might, however, disclose that he knows that the neighbors have been very friendly in the past.

A legislator seeking to raise the minimum wage would certainly emphasize the beneficial effects for the lowest paid of the nation's workforce. Still, he would probably not mention any detrimental effects on the small businesses that will have to pay the increased wages. Finally, the professor who wants the National Science Foundation

(NSF) to fund a research program to study a newly discovered virus will carefully follow the NSF proposal guidelines. She must meet all deadlines and supply all budget information according to the NSF's precise instructions. For this kind of proposal, the professor must identify and document the value of her research, especially with respect to immediate and future benefits to humanity.

Proposals can take a variety of forms, but each must be geared to its audience in a language and format that enhances its chances of being approved. A proposal is a plan offering to solve a particular problem, and it generally requires a sum of money to be provided for implementing that plan. In the early 1820s, Charles Babbage convinced the British government that it should pay him fifteen-hundred pounds to develop a mechanical calculating device. The device, he promised, could produce accurate navigation tables. Since the government desperately needed accurate tables for its navy and Babbage needed the funding for his project, this was a perfect match! In 1828, the Duke of Wellington viewed a model of the "Difference Engine" and ordered that Babbage receive three-thousand pounds to continue his work. In 1854, a Swedish printer, Charles Scheutz, finally used Babbage's plans to create a working machine that would print accurate navigation tables. As the history of the difference engine illustrates, proposals can have an odd life from the first inspiration to fulfillment, since Babbage's engines are considered the beginning of modern computers (Swade, 2001).

Major Types of Proposals

Proposals are closely related to recommendation reports. Often an employee is asked to study a problem and recommend a solution. Generally, this type of report is internal. Sometimes, companies contract consultants to prepare recommendation reports and these may include specific proposals. Sales associates and managers write external proposals (such as sales proposals) based on their perception of a customer's needs. Frequently, sales representatives reply to a formal **request for proposal** or **RFP** (see Chapter 4) from a customer. If the good or service is a commodity well understood in the industry, a request for quote (a price-only RFP) may be used. In an RFP, the customer specifies needs and objectives. Individuals and organizations (both for-profit and nonprofit) often submit proposals requesting funding from philanthropic foundations or from the government. These proposals are considered *solicited* because they are responses to an invitation for proposals, an announcement of a grant program, or an RFP. If a fund-seeker sends a proposal that has not been developed in response to an announcement, the proposal is *unsolicited*. There are differences in format and style between these types of proposals, but the key elements are the same.

In writing a proposal, there are essential topics that you must address. These include:

1. *Need*. You must address the needs, goals, or expectations of the organization to which the proposal is being made. Certainly, your need to secure the contract is paramount, but this is of little concern to the organization being solicited. Even internal proposals must convince the recipient that the proposed action is in his or her best interest. Sometimes your proposal may be related to a goal rather than a need. For instance, a proposed new plant may be potentially more profitable than the current plant, and the change makes sense even if the older plant is profitable. This is an argument used by those who wish to replace existing sports stadiums—even though the old stadium makes profits, a new stadium will make even greater profits. The proposal may address a profit motive rather than a critical need. In fact, the prior decision-making process that led to current conditions may be a point of focus in convincing others to make a change: "When you chose this approach, you made the right decision. Now the situation is ripe for the same kind of aggressive decision."

2. *Ability.* You are trying to convince decision makers that you have the "right stuff" to accomplish your proposed actions. Many contracts are determined by whether or not the proposing agent already has or can organize the resources to fulfill the contract. Sometimes, RFPs will even specify the weight that this factor will be given. Even if not specifically required, your proposal should include a clear statement of how technical expertise, equipment, personnel, time, and materials will be available for completing the proposed action in a timely and successful manner.

3. *Methods/Procedures.* In those sections of the proposal relating to the plan of operation, you should offer detailed accounts of how the proposed activity will be managed. Many proposals include a flow chart of activities with specified start and completion times, personnel assignments, and contacts for each phase of the project. Large proposals may include the means of communication between the proposer and the client and even a procedure for making complaints. Often a proposal for a large-scale project is developed in two stages: In the first, the initial bid is made and critical requirements are addressed; in the second, a complete and detailed description of the methods and procedures to be followed during the execution of the contract is offered.

4. *Accountability.* The results of a project may seem obvious on first glance, but business activities do not necessarily have a clear moment of completion. Many are ongoing processes or procedures, and many have a formally recognized completion element such as a sign-off or acceptance procedure that initiates billing (submitting the invoice) and payment. When constructing an office building, for instance, the owner anticipates discovering problems (minor problems, one hopes) months after the work has been completed and the final payment has been made. Most contractors retain responsibility for correcting these problems and may be called back to the site to make corrections. This responsibility continues for a time period specified in the contract and is always a component of a proposal. Software installations often require that maintenance continue until the software is upgraded with the next version. For example, Electronic Data Systems (EDS) employs thousands of teams to install and service software applications. In some instances, EDS employees have offices on site in a client's office building. Depending upon the type of work that you propose, your responsibility for the work may end on delivery or it may continue as defined in the contract or service agreement. Thus, a high-quality proposal has detailed methods of measuring and reporting results and monitoring the correction of errors and problems. Typically, the contract secured through the proposal provides legal mechanisms for accountability, including penalties for lateness and sometimes rewards for early delivery.

5. *Costs.* In most proposals, costs are described in a separate budget section that includes an itemized listing of material costs, projected personnel costs, all related equipment and overhead costs, and even the projected profit. Some budgets include profit as a percentage added to each item cost; some include a separate percentage. The detail required for a proposal varies from one type of proposal to another, within each type, and from one client to another. For example, Federal Acquisiton Regulations (FAR) include comprehensive and detailed requirements for presenting and tracking costs for federal projects. Cost Accounting System (CAS) requirements are designed to make it clear to both parties what costs are acceptable so that specified profits can be properly calculated and verified.

6. *Business Terms and Conditions* ("T's and C's"). The legal relationship for a transaction must be spelled out, including such issues as when ownership passes, insurance, liability, penalties and incentives, when payment is due (initial payment, progress payments at specified times or upon completion of defined events), and so forth. Some specifications for T's and C's can run several pages. These terms and conditions are typically found in business proposals, but federal and state grants and contracts have equivalents.

The different ways in which this information can be presented will be clearer after we look at each of the major types of proposals. Each type has the same kinds of requirements. Nevertheless, there are few industry-wide standards or guidelines for proposals and each organization may have its own preferences. Some preferences are standardized; others allow wide variation in the format that can be accepted. Each, though, has certain questions that must be answered and issues that must be addressed. Unfortunately, at times the requesting organization is not fully aware of what should be expected of the proposer. This is especially true for a company that has begun a new venture, is adding new technology, or is otherwise entering unfamiliar territory. So, while fixed guidelines are uncommon, the key points just described do have variations that reflect the type of proposal being written. Table 6.1 on page 168 illustrates the differences between various types of proposals and the key features in each. Sometimes an RFP is preceded by a **request for information (RFI)** to ask potential suppliers how they would approach solving a problem. The RFI is also used to gather preliminary information about the suppliers and vendors. A refined RFP can then be issued, based on an analysis of the responses to the RFI.

SECTION SUMMARY

A proposal is a tool utilized to expand business, garner support for ideas, and/or solicit financial support. In a formal proposal, a course of action is suggested and approval

INSIGHT BOX 6.1
...

Simple Errors Can Be Costly

 A course-management system is a method for delivering Web-based course services. Recently, the managers of a popular course-management system (CMS) were eager to be included in what is called the "state price contract" for the state of Kentucky. The contract prices are negotiated for all state-supported educational institutions. The negotiation saves money for the CMS company and sets a competitive price for institutional purchasers who want to adopt the course-management system. The state finance office that receives these proposals requires that two separate packages be sent: (1) one that includes the narrative description; and (2) another that includes the financial statements. Someone at the popular CMS company sent the two parts in the same envelope; this action disqualified the proposal. The CMS company had to wait another year to be placed on the price contract, and each institution using the system had to negotiate separately. Since these programs cost fifty- to one-hundred thousand dollars per installation, the cost and time impact can be great if one is forced to change or delay a change for any period of time.

TABLE 6.1
...

Types of Proposals

Component	Internal		External			
	Policy	Exploratory or Venture	RFP	Unsolicited	Nonprofit Competitive	Nonprofit Unsolicited
Need	Relates to procedural improvement and efficiency or compliance with law	Must be specific to corporate mission (usually profit or productivity)	Is reflected in the reason for RFP being issued	Must be a point of persuasion in the proposal in order to convince the recipient to undertake the activity	Is defined by the agency or philanthropy	Is usually defined by the applicant in terms of agency mission
Ability to complete the contract or project	Is assumed unless change requires new personnel	Depends on assignment of resources critical to being effective	Must be shown	Must be shown	Requires proof	Requires proof
Method	Internal changes typically follow preestablished methods	Often new ventures require new personnel or the rearrangement of existing resources	States how the activity is to occur; the proposal must show that the applicant has a full grasp of details	Must demonstrate efficiency and timeliness	Will probably be compared to others seeking a grant or gift	If the proposal receives review, then how the activity will be accomplished is critical to acceptance
Accountability	Assignments of responsibility follow organizational structure	Monitoring progress of risky ventures is often critical to the corporate commitment	Must show how the client's needs will be met and how the vendor can ensure success	Should focus on ensuring the client's improved success	Must follow strict expectations for demonstrating how the goals of the proposal are met	Must follow strict expectations for demonstrating how the goals of the proposal are met
Budget	Can be easily overlooked in policy changes, but should be carefully described	For internal ventures will be closely scrutinized	Makes the proposal competitive, as other vendors will also submit proposals	Is central to convincing the client to accept a proposal that they did not request	Follows strict guidelines for what can be funded and what cannot be funded	Follows strict guidelines for what can be funded and what cannot be funded

Note: Some internal proposals can be unsolicited, but the term typically refers to proposals that come from external sources.

of the action is requested. The intended audience determines the particular format to be used. All proposals must address the needs of the organization being solicited, one's ability to meet those needs, the methods and procedures to be used, performance accountability, a detailing of costs, and the business terms and conditions.

CHALLENGE PROBLEM FOR REVIEW

Locate several published RFPs (these can be found in newspapers that publish "news of record" and on Web sites for the state and federal government finance and accounting offices). These RFPs will serve as samples for the chapter. If you were the person responsible for developing a response to one of the requests you have located, what strategy would you follow to make your proposal? List five steps that would result in a successful proposal.

The Sales Proposal

The sales proposal includes elements that are designed and intended to persuade a client to decide in favor of the proposed product or service commitment.

The sales proposal is among the most common types of proposals. Sales can involve a product, a service, or both. Whether the salesperson is selling telecommunications, computers, accounting services, or janitorial supplies, there are common elements. These include a needs analysis, a price quotation, and product information. The needs analysis, though, is the key ingredient to a successful sales proposal.

The Critical Role of Needs Analysis

Sales proposals are usually written after at least one meeting with a potential customer. Following a meeting with potential customer Bill Coffey of Paul Sawyier Art Gallery, Inc., and performing a needs analysis, Barbara Martin, an account executive with Web Associates, wrote the following assessment for future reference in preparing her sales proposal:

> *Paul Sawyier Art Gallery sells a wide range of art and office decor for professional offices. The Gallery currently sells to decorators and others responsible for professional interiors in a ten-state region, with some sales of special art (primarily Paul Sawyier prints) nationwide. The company currently consists of the owner and eight employees (three sales associates, two office personnel, three distribution personnel). They currently use a networked personal computer system to manage inventory and accounts. The stations in the network are about a year and a half old and are quite functional for current operations. The office personnel prepare reasonably professional-looking sales brochures for mailing to regular clients, and the sales associates visit larger clients and interior design shows. Orders are placed by mail or fax. Mr. Coffey remains cautious about Internet-based sales and art promotion. His primary concern is the value for the investment, and his secondary concern is Web-site maintenance.*

Sawyier Gallery does over three million dollars in sales a year. Recent integration of office procedures, inventory, and shipping resulted in free time for office and shipping staff, as well as Mr. Coffey himself. Consequently, his staff can prepare and send more brochures to potential customers, and Coffey has been able to devote more time to new clients. The current level of business represents a 15 percent growth that resulted from integrating the office. Coffey has learned that investment in automation can increase business. Thus, he is willing to explore other innovative ways to increase his business.

Furthermore, Coffey foresees a growing competitive problem with other direct sales outlets. In addition to the prints to which he owns the rights, he also distributes fine prints from several dozen print makers. Some of these print makers have direct sales; all sell to distributors nationally and internationally. Sawyier Gallery attracts customers on the basis of prints from many sources being available at one place. One order can be placed for prints from a variety of sources and framing can be specified (large framing orders are subcontracted). Coffey is not willing to disclose the profit margin at Sawyier Gallery, since he considers this proprietary information. He does offer, however, that at similar operations the margin is generally in the neighborhood of 30 percent and that he does better than this. However, competition can undercut his pricing, though few can match the comprehensive service provided by Sawyier Gallery.

Coffey's sales associates do not utilize information technology other than fax machines (and one does use a portable fax for orders). They all carry sample prints, frames, and large sales books complete with price listings and photos of the most popular prints.

Coffey has complained about the cost of maintaining these books. He wishes that there were a way to minimize their cost and streamline the process of updating them.

Coffey has several general goals for the future. He would like to increase his business by at least 10 percent a year for the next several years. He would also like the business to grow to a point where he can hire a general manager and no longer be involved on a daily basis. He has several other business ventures that he wants to explore, but at present his time is completely occupied by the gallery business.

Barbara Martin believes that Web Associates can help Coffey meet his goals and increase the business at Paul Sawyier Art Gallery even more than he projects. Web-based sales can begin modestly with a simple Web page for advertising, phone contacts, and name familiarity. At the high end, Sawyier Gallery could have thumbnails of all of the prints to which they have rights or can secure rights and could create interactive pages on which customers could review and modify their decorating theme and view frames and prints that match or complement their chosen theme. The process can be done securely so that only sales associates and decorator clients can design the schemes and show them to the customer both online and with color printouts. The range of options will allow Sawyier Gallery to operate at a level that is comfortable but expandable.

For Martin's proposal to be successful, she needs to provide Coffey with detailed costs in terms of both financial and personnel resources. From her sense of his views, and in order to be convincing, she believes that her projections for Internet sales need to be conservative and with well-documented similar successes. Her plan is to propose a solution that is midway between a fully interactive commercial site and a mere home page with phone numbers and a few pictures. She believes that the success of the site will encourage Coffey to expand his presence on the Web as the level of success increases. Also, Web Associates focuses on clients in his exact situation. They provide a full range of services that can be added as the sales volume increases. Martin only needs to convince Coffey and his staff that even a modest investment will bring worthwhile results.

The Elements of a Sales Proposal

As Barbara Martin begins planning her sales proposal, she has in mind her company's standard format, which consists of the following elements:

1. Title Page
2. Letter of Transmittal
3. Table of Contents
4. Executive Summary
5. Customer's Objectives
6. Customer's Present Operations and Equipment
7. Proposed System
8. Benefits of the Proposed Activity or Solution
9. Investment Required for the Proposed Activity or Solution (Budget)
10. Implementation and Training Schedule
11. Reference Page

Title Page

An effective **title page** is used to identify certain key elements: the date, the customer's organization, the name and title of the person to whom the proposal is being presented, and the salesperson's name and organization, (phone numbers, and Web and e-mail addresses may be included here or with an attached business card). Sometimes a nondisclosure statement is added, since the information is proprietary. Ornate title pages usually do more harm than good; some customers interpret fancy covers as an indication of flash without substance. Figure 6.1 is an example of a title page for this account executive's proposal.

FIGURE 6.1
...

A Sample Title Page for a Sales Proposal

WEB-BASED SALES AND MARKETING FOR

Paul Sawyier Art Gallery, Inc.

PREPARED BY

• • •

Barbara Martin

Account Executive

Web Associates

• • •

Submitted to Mr. Bill Coffey

December 12, 2005

Letter of Transmittal

The **letter of transmittal** is a letter or memorandum that "hands over" or transmits the sales proposal to a potential customer. In this letter, you should thank the decision maker for his or her cooperation and also recognize other individuals who provided information for the proposal. Martin must ask for Paul Sawyier Art Gallery's contract in this letter. Asking for acceptance of the proposal is a must in proposal transmittal letters. To communicate her expectation of a decision, Martin suggests in her letter (Figure 6.2 on page 172) a follow-up meeting to discuss a contract and an implementation schedule. She is "assuming" that Sawyier Gallery will approve the proposal, obviously the right solution to help the company achieve its objectives. Coffey's agreement to another meeting with Martin will indicate a high level of interest in the proposal.

While a letter of transmittal should be no longer than one page, it can have a significant psychological impact. The letter sets the tone for the how the reader will view the actual proposal that follows. Barbara has been careful to focus on the potential for growth and sales productivity described by her potential customer. She has also stated, in quantitative terms, that the proposed interactive home page for the Paul Sawyier Art Gallery will provide a very specific benefit—a 15 percent increase in sales and a 10 percent savings in time. This wording needs to be reviewed by an attorney. If not worded properly, the language could be interpreted as a guarantee of the increase in sales and the decrease in time. If the objectives are not met, Coffey might sue to recover the shortfalls from Web Associates. The law allows margin for "puffing" in sales, so properly worded inducements can be used without legal liability. This is the bait that will propel the reader to approach the proposal with a positive attitude.

Finally, the letter of transmittal in a sales proposal should establish a sense of urgency. Martin wants the Paul Sawyier Art Gallery, Inc.'s owner and staff to make a decision immediately and not simply to treat the proposal as information to be filed in the event

FIGURE 6.2
...

A Letter of Transmittal for a Sales Proposal

Web Associates

700 Skyline Drive, Jefferson, MN 90007, E-mail @email.com, 888-123-4567

December 12, 2005

Mr. Bill Coffey
Paul Sawyier Art Gallery, Inc.
100 North Fifth Avenue
Shelby, MN 92007

Dear Mr. Coffey:

I am delighted that Paul Sawyier Art Gallery has decided to consider our proposal for Web-based Marketing and Sales. A great many businesses have found that Web-based sales increase sales promotion and productivity as they substantially boost revenue. In fact, you will find documented evidence in the attached proposal that a Web-based solution can increase your company's annual sales volume by 15 percent and free 10 percent of your staff time for additional promotion.

Your staff has both been generous with their time and provided me with detailed information about how your office presently operates. They understand your desire to streamline operations and increase your sales in the future. I would like to thank your staff for being so helpful and candid in their assessment of Sawyier Gallery's present status and future needs. In order for Sawyier Gallery to achieve these goals, it is essential that the Web-based marketing plan be implemented as soon as possible.

After you and your staff have had a chance to review this proposal, let's get together and discuss a contract and when the implementation should begin. Because of the flood of orders we've had within the past month, the calendars for our training specialists and installers are filling rapidly; I know how important thorough training of your staff is to both you and the staff. I will call you later this week to set our next meeting.

Sincerely,

Barbara Martin

Barbara Martin
Account Executive

Attachments

---

that they eventually decide to pursue Web-based sales. By establishing that Sawyier Gallery will lose money if it delays and that it is easier to lead than to catch up, Martin has put some pressure on her readers.

Table of Contents

The **table of contents** is a tool to help the reader locate information. It should contain page numbers. While novice writers sometimes pad their proposals with sales brochures and technical specifications, this practice can be self-defeating. Some readers refuse to read a document that appears too imposing. Always be alert to this ABCD rule of managerial writing: Authority, Brevity, Clarity, and Directness. Miscellaneous materials are better located at the end of the proposal as appendixes. In the table of contents in Figure 6.3, each appendix is clearly described in its title.

Executive Summary

Not all busy executives read an entire proposal. Instead, they read the executive summary and then skim through the parts of the proposal of interest to them. The **executive summary** (sometimes called an abstract) distills the complete proposal into one or two pages, but it provides enough information for the decision maker to be well-informed in presenting the proposal to a board of directors.

The summary should include a brief overview of all of the major points included in the proposal, expressed quantitatively whenever possible. Problems associated with present operations should be identified, a brief analysis of the present and proposed systems provided, the benefits of purchasing the new system indicated, and the amount of investment required specified, in that order. The implementation schedule should also be discussed briefly.

The reader has a clear guide to the complete proposal, and there will be no great surprises buried in the closing pages of the proposal. Figure 6.4 on page 174 provides an excerpt from Martin's executive summary.

FIGURE 6.3
...

Sample Table of Contents and Appendixes for a Sales Proposal

The appendixes should be printed on a separate page. Also, the table of contents reflects the customization of the topics to fit the proposal. A proposal should always reflect the specific interests and guidelines of the receiving organization.

FIGURE 6.4
...

An Excerpt from an Executive Summary

EXECUTIVE SUMMARY

We propose to develop, maintain, and upgrade a Web site for Paul Sawyier Art Gallery, Inc., that will provide a Web-based marketing presence and sales vehicle for the gallery. Initially, within two months of the agreement, the Web page will begin with basic information, allow ordering online, and provide a few samples of available work. Other growth, especially additional images on the site, will occur as the gallery personnel become more comfortable with the site and how it creates sales activity. Each expansion will follow the proposed plan for action outlined in detail in the proposal. Projected sales volume increase is 15 percent for the first twelve months of operation. Projected costs for each development, training, and continuing maintenance and full-service hosting are outlined as follows:

Initial Development: $5,500.00

Hosting and Maintenance: $6,000.00 (per annum; $500.00 monthly)

Staff Training: $3,000.00 ($75.00 per hour, 40 hours projected)

Client's Objectives

The client's objectives section must be a totally accurate statement taken directly from a client's own words. As you prepare a proposal, you can find the objectives either indirectly through company literature or more directly through an interview with the client. You cannot determine these without some investigation though. The statement of each objective in the proposal should be expressed in clear, measurable terms so that it can be compared and contrasted with the company's present performance. Before a final proposal is made, confirm these objectives with the RFP or directly with the client.

Writing a sales proposal requires psychological insight. Stating the client's quantified objectives in his or her own words provides this section of the proposal with the credibility that is needed for acceptance. This section contains the premises on which the rest of the sales proposal is built. If the potential client accepts this section as valid, then the section describing how each quantified objective will be achieved at considerable cost savings will likely also be regarded as sound. The Sawyier Gallery's quantified objectives are illustrated in Figure 6.5.

Client's Present Operations and Equipment

This section must include an analysis of the client's existing operations as they relate to the proposed venture. In it, you should describe the client's problems and explain why the present equipment/system does not meet the client's quantified objectives for the future.

Proposed System

This section is based on your analysis of the client's present operations and equipment. It is here that you demonstrate that your proposed system will meet the client's objectives. To establish the proposal's credibility, it is absolutely essential that in this section the client's point-of-view is presented accurately. In some cases, the client's present condition and needs are spelled out in an RFP (discussed in the next section in greater detail), in which case the proposal is a paragraph-by-paragraph response to the requirements written by the potential customer. In Figure 6.6, part of the analysis section describing Sawyier Gallery's present system is illustrated. This section of the proposal

FIGURE 6.5
...

Objectives for the Sawyier Gallery

Sawyier Gallery: Its Objectives

As president and owner of the Sawyier Gallery Corporation, Bill Coffey has indicated that his company has the following objectives for the coming fiscal year:

- To increase Sawyier Gallery's net revenue by at least 15 percent in the coming year

- To increase the number of client contacts produced by Sawyier Gallery by 25 percent

- To improve Sawyier Gallery's ratio of sales per employee

- To reduce fixed costs by at least 15 percent by making the office run more efficiently

FIGURE 6.6
...

An Excerpt from the Analysis Section of a Sales Proposal

Sawyier Gallery's Present Situation and Web Associates' Proposed Solution

Paul Sawyier Art Gallery, Inc. (PSAG), has an annual gross income in excess of three million dollars. However, its work force is composed of only nine people: three sales associates, two office personnel, three shippers, and the owner/president. Sales involve clients who are primarily decorators of professional office spaces, office buildings, and others involved in office furniture. A small portion of sales is to resellers, and a small portion of sales is to home decorators. More than half of the prints are prepared from paintings or rights owned by the gallery, and the rest are from print makers worldwide. The gallery does about 40 percent of the framing, and the rest is contracted. Web Associates proposes to develop, install, and maintain a Web-based sales and marketing system that will expand the reach of PSAG to national and potentially international markets. The system will begin with online pricing, ordering, and phone contact information, and Web Associates will build into the system the potential for live, interactive design and selection processes.

is a good place to introduce charts and graphs that compare the existing system to the proposed system.

Benefits of the Proposed Activity or Solution

The benefits section of the document should emphasize the desirable outcomes for the client that will follow from approving the proposal. Both short-range and long-range benefits are examined. In the early meetings with Martin, Bill Coffey, the gallery's president, stated several short-range objectives, including increased sales and decreased costs. What additional benefits could the system provide after the first year? Martin could state that by adding a Web page now, Sawyier Gallery will enjoy strategic advantages over its competition, including the ability of the sales associates to make design and decoration changes from home, on the road, or from their customers' offices. With appropriate computer software, Sawyier Gallery would be able to create superior color-integrated design presentations. This might open new doors for the gallery. For example, home shoppers could locate high-quality art prints that match their home decor, personal tastes, or special interests.

The benefits section is a place to talk about intangible costs (sometimes called *soft dollars*) as well as tangible costs (*hard dollars*). Intangible costs represent the time that the company will save expressed in terms of the money this time represents. These dollars are termed soft since they are not actually dollars in Sawyier Gallery's bank account. Nevertheless, they represent a real savings because the staff can use this time to increase productivity. Tangible costs are the actual costs of salaries, equipment, supplies, and so on.

Investment Required for the Proposed Activity or Solution (Budget)

Generally, you do not use the term "price" in sales proposals since it can carry negative connotations. Instead, the word "investment" suggests that money used to purchase the proposed solution will yield a good return on the dollar. Indeed, in this section, you indicate estimates of how soon the payback period for the system will begin and how much money will be saved on an annual basis and over time. If three sales associates could produce the sales volume of four and because they earn salary plus commission, then the salary of one sales associate has been removed, increasing the profit margin. On the other hand, since Coffey is also involved in sales, he may be able to discontinue his sales duties and move on to the other ventures that he has been considering. After the up-front costs of converting the sales books to electronic media, the updating process will only involve electronic input and transmission and ongoing costs associated with the software (maintenance, upgrades, back-up, and restoration).

Implementation and Training Schedule

This is a critical section in a proposal. It is usually divided into three key portions: installation, training, and service. Installation is putting the physical components of the system in place. In the case of the functioning Web page, developing and launching the Web site can be complex. This is what Martin and her associates do best, and this is the skill they are trying to sell to Coffey. Most products—heavy or light equipment, information technology, communication equipment, and so on—require on-site facility inspections prior to installation as well as extensive testing afterwards to ensure that the entire system is working as planned. This section may require disclaimers to protect the vender should conditions result in a difficult installation. All of the necessary issues pertaining to responsibility can be stipulated in a contract.

Training has become an important factor in most sales proposals involving high-technology products. In this proposal section, you must specify how much (if any) training will be provided without cost and the projected expenses for specified additional training. The training location should be identified too, as well as the materials that will be available for training, such as videos, computer tutorials, or other electronic media. If advanced classes at a later date are a possibility, this should be mentioned, including where they would be taught and who could take them.

Service can be a major selling point in any proposal. It has made several companies into corporate giants—Dell Computers is a major example. Dell made a significant effort to use service as a means of distinguishing themselves from other computer manufacturers. What service and maintenance does your company offer as a standard part of a contract? Do you provide or sell a service contract? What about call-in service? Can some problems be handled over the phone? Is twenty-four-hour, on-site service available? These issues could be deciding factors as to whether a proposal will be approved or disapproved.

Reference Page

If references have been made, even to interviews and company documents, a page should be provided that lists the sources and references used. Cost comparisons, sample documents, articles, books, reports and other materials used to support the argument of the proposal would be listed here. If included in the proposal, these materials would become an appendix.

SECTION SUMMARY

The sales proposal is used to convince a client to purchase a product or a service. It is composed of eleven elements: title page; letter of transmittal; table of contents; executive summary; client's objectives; client's present operations and equipment, the proposed system; benefits of the proposed activity or solution; investment required for the proposed activity or solution; implementation and training schedule; and reference page.

CHALLENGE PROBLEM FOR REVIEW

Given the perception that commerce on the Internet crashed at the end of the Internet "Stock Bubble," develop a convincing argument for a small business like Sawyier Gallery to invest in the resources needed to develop a meaningful presence on the Web. What are the pros and cons of such a business move?

Solicited and Unsolicited Proposals

Requests for proposals originate from a variety of sources, including both public and private sectors. They can be required for government contracts, foundation support, and for profit or nonprofit projects.

KEY CONCEPT 6.3
...

The RFP and the Solicited Proposal

In this section, the concept of the RFP is examined in more detail. An RFP is the main method used to publicize a **solicited proposal**. Often companies issue a RFP to make explicit the questions that a sales proposal must address and what format must be used. Although the RFP differs from company to company, generally it contains the following sections:

- Background Information (who is making the request and why)
- Instructions for Preparing Proposals and Submitting Completed Proposals
- Overview of the Current System
- Mandatory Vendor Requirements
- General Vendor Questions
- Specific System Requirements
- Information Technology System Requirements
- Exhibits

For evaluation purposes, each RFP will reflect the different values given to each component of the various guidelines. If the Paul Sawyier Art Gallery becomes so successful with its Web venture that Coffey decides to purchase a large, multiuser computer system to do all of the accounting and record keeping, he might list the following criteria in an RFP with these corresponding values or "weights" assigned to each criteria:

20%   Ability of the system to satisfy Sawyier Gallery's requirements as defined by this request for proposal

15%   Reliability of the proposed solution, i.e., hardware reliability and hardware/software warranties

15% Hardware and software maintenance availability
20% Initial and recurring costs of proposed solution
5%   Local representation of hardware vendor
10% Overall vendor qualifications, i.e., financial performance, positive perform-
     ance record, commitment to enhancing product line, experience with similar
     systems
10% Quality and ease of use of software packages and related documentation
5%   Local system installations

In writing a proposal to match the requirements of this RFP, the writer must emphasize those areas that carry the most weight. If the proposed system is expensive in comparison to local competitors, the proposal must emphasize the superior quality of software and the ability of the system to meet the RFP requirements better than the competition can.

Figure 6.7 represents a typical RFP checklist that must be answered in a sales proposal. Note how specific this checklist is. It requires answers that are just as precise in order to keep the proposal in the running for the contract.

The Unsolicited Proposal

An **unsolicited proposal** is simply a proposal that is initiated by someone other than a contracting or funding organization. Suppose SHG General has serious problems recruiting minority employees in its technical areas. The affirmative action officers are frantic because they realize that the company could lose key government contracts if its management does not show greater effort in this area.

Bill Wilson is a technical trainer in SHG General's Training Department and also a good friend of Ralph Morrison in the Affirmative Action Office. Over lunch he listens to his friend's problem and suggests a possible solution. Why not offer an apprentice program in conjunction with a local high school that has a high percentage of minority students? He knows that the school is looking for new vocational programs and SHG

FIGURE 6.7
...

An RFP Checklist

When submitting your proposal, be certain to include the following:

____ Specific equipment types, technical specifications, and attachments

____ Activity, installation, and service plans

____ Specific costs for each line item

____ Specific costs to be charged for each group of employees

____ Expertise of responsible parties

____ Projected time frame for repair and/or replacement

____ Evidence of similar successful installation

____ Proposal following provided outline with separate budget

____ Contact person, phone numbers(s), e-mail, and fax number(s)

Note: RFPs will often specify method and time frame for payment, penalties for delays, and so forth.

General has plenty of surplus materials and equipment. What is needed, though, is some budgeted time to teach a class and then maybe some funds for part-time student employment and full-time summer employment.

Wilson and Morrison agree that the best way to get the program approved is to write a proposal for increased minority recruiting. They would submit the proposal to training manager Jane Wright with a request that she forward it to Mary Worth, director of personnel. Morrison will use his political clout to talk with company president Frank Richman and impress upon him the importance of this project. Richman will bring up the subject with Worth's boss, Vice President of Administration/Finance Lawrence Campion so that, when the idea becomes a formal proposal and works its way up the organizational ladder to this level, it will meet with support.

To be funded, though, the proposal has to be persuasive and well written. Wright and Morrison begin the prewriting process by considering what kind of evidence will improve the proposal's chances of approval. What may appear to be a simple proposal will actually be complicated and require several careful steps. To manage the steps successfully, they make a list of tasks that have to be accomplished prior to the writing of the proposal:

1. Morrison will discuss their concern with President Richman explaining how SHG General may not be in complete compliance with its government agreement to increase minority representation. Morrison will itemize the dire consequences that could occur—including listing which current government contracts are in danger—if demonstrable action was not taken immediately.
2. Morrison will ask his long-time coworker Bill Bartell in employment for a series of job descriptions for entry-level positions. These will include detailed listings of entry-level skill requirements, which Morrison will share with Jane Wright.
3. Wright will write a series of proposed training classes that will meet the skill requirements found in Bartell's job listings.
4. Wright agrees to call the principal at the local high school and discuss the proposed apprenticeship program. She will find out whether the principal will write a letter to Bartell indicating the school's interest and possible support for the program.
5. Morrison will then ask Bartell to provide him with an analysis of costs for benefits if students are hired in part-time and full-time positions at minimum wage rates.
6. Wright in turn will ask Bartell for a breakdown of how much the costs (salary and benefits) will be on an hourly basis so that she can budget for her own project time.
7. Morrison finally will agree to talk with Jack Marks (service manager) and his friend John Benjamin (Plant 3 manager). He will ask Marks if there is any older equipment that can be borrowed for the project. He will ask Benjamin if Plant 3 has any spare equipment that can be loaned to the project.

Notice how an unsolicited proposal that is generated internally takes special attention to be written with managerial expertise. Rather than simply writing the proposal and sending it to a manager who might ignore it, Wright and Morrison plan their strategy to ensure the proposal's success. Knowing their audience (the managers who ultimately decide upon the proposal), Wright and Morrison anticipate and answer any criticism before it can cripple the project.

Worth, director of personnel, represents the proposal's first real hurdle. As a "big picture" person, Mary likes to concentrate on the macrocosm and not really concern herself with small details. She delegates details to her staff. Wright and Morrison decide to keep the proposal focused on the major issues and place all of the specific details in appendixes. Victor Alvarez, the vice president of manufacturing, is known for his lack of interest in targeted recruitment and his frugality. Morrison is determined to show that not funding this proposal will cost more than funding it, since government contracts valued at a million dollars will be lost.

Unlike Alvarez, Lawrence Campion (vice president of administration and finance) does not have any particular bias, but he is known as a detail-oriented individual. If the proposal fails to address details such as Wright's exact cost (including benefits) and which particular jobs the students will be trained to handle, Campion will focus on these points. Moreover, he will refuse to examine anything else about the proposal until he is satisfied about these issues.

In preparing their proposal, Wright and Morrison are working within the system by drawing on their personal and professional relationships to gain the information that they need to develop a successful proposal. Much of the work occurs before they even begin to write the final proposal. After gathering their information, they have to be careful to use an appropriate proposal format that will cause the managers who are the document's intended audience to respect the authors.

Format for an Unsolicited Internal Proposal

An unsolicited proposal, especially an unsolicited internal proposal, typically has no predetermined guidelines. Thus, in comparison to highly prescribed RFP components, you will have somewhat more freedom in style and format in composing these proposals. They also will be less formal than a government-solicited proposal. Nevertheless, the general format for an unsolicited internal proposal should contain the following sections:

1. Cover Letter or Memorandum
2. Executive Summary or Abstract
3. Title Page
4. Table of Contents
5. The Problem
6. Proposed Solution
7. Budget
8. Implementation Schedule (time table)
9. Conclusions

Cover Letter or Memorandum

A cover letter or memorandum should be addressed to the decision maker who heads the writer's area. Even though this person usually is not the one who will make the final decision, it can be a political disaster if he or she is bypassed. The cover letter should indicate why the proposal is important and whet the reader's appetite to read the proposal. It should not summarize everything in the proposal.

Executive Summary or Abstract

Executive summaries are extremely important for this kind of proposal. Often, chief financial officers (CFOs) review the proposal for financial soundness and devote little attention to the activity details. They will, however, need to have a clear thumbnail sketch of the activity. Given that executives generally do not read proposals cover to cover, the document must address the areas of responsibility and the corporate interests of the top executives who read it.

Title Page

The title page needs to identify the authors, the name of the project or proposal, date, and other relevant items. On short proposals, the title page information and the table of contents can be combined.

Table of Contents

Any proposal over four or five pages long needs a table of contents. The contents should be organized in a systematic manner and flow logically from problem to solution. An internal proposal can draw upon internal company materials and place them in appendixes or make reference to them if they are readily available (in policy manuals or other contracts). Wright and Morrison should refer to the requirements of the government contracts that are in jeopardy due to the lack of affirmative action progress. Still, they do not need to duplicate the contracts in the proposal itself. On the other hand, they may need to inform the readers about where the contracts are located in case more details about the contract stipulations are needed. This information should be placed in the body of the proposal at the appropriate place in the narrative.

The Problem

In this section, you explain why this proposal was written. For example, Wright will describe (with Morrison's help and materials) what can happen if SHG General's affirmative action problems are not solved. Provide quantitative data whenever possible. Losses of contracts and other penalties, as well as loss of competitiveness, can be quantified in financial terms that have a strong impact on the reader.

Proposed Solution

In this section, you use charts, graphs, other visual aids, and whatever else is appropriate to make clear what needs to be done to solve the problem facing the company. You should offer alternative solutions and, if appropriate, reasons explaining why this solution should be embraced. This section should include a discussion of how funds will be expended— both a budgetary summary and a procedural summary—and who has budgetary authority over the funds.

Budget

If the budget is complex, a detailed budget page should be prepared and placed here or as the first appendix. Figure 6.8 illustrates a sample budget

Implementation Schedule (time table)

This section must include a project schedule showing beginning and ending dates for each stage of the project. With this schedule, Wright and Morrison should indicate targets for

FIGURE 6.8
...

Sample Budget Items

For a sales proposal, personnel, benefits, and overhead may be collapsed into a single fee. Charges that may vary depending on need are also listed, such as travel and training. Nonprofit proposals can have all these details required to be specified.

Items to include in a budget:

- Personnel
- Benefits
- Overhead
- Equipment
- Furniture
- Software

- Travel
- Consultants
- Refurbishing
- Training
- Trainers

permanently hiring a minimum number of apprentices. In this way, they can quantify success as well as the individual cost of each recruit. Figure 6.9 illustrates a sample schedule.

Conclusions

In the conclusion, the authors should emphasize how the solution will work and how much money the company will save. They should focus on why the selected personnel who intend to participate in the project are the right people to handle this project. Finally, corporate commitment should be emphasized as well. At this point, the proposal's authors can suggest that this program will have many hidden benefits, including an improved corporate image both locally and in the view of the government. Local goodwill and more government contracts are excellent benefits.

Grant Writing and Solicited Government and Foundation Proposals

Knowing how to locate the federal agencies and private foundations that offer funding for projects and then being able to write a proposal that secures these funds requires grant writing skills. More and more nonprofit organizations and scientific institutions are hiring specialists whose sole function is to write proposals for competitive funds. Where do you learn about funding sources?

There are numerous sources of information on funding agencies. The Internet is the most easily accessed resource for locating funding agencies. Many private, state, and federal agencies maintain online and downloadable RFPs and application forms. For a physical browsing method, the *Catalog of Federal Domestic Assistance* is an excellent place to locate agencies that might fund a particular project. This directory indicates application procedures, examples of previously funded projects, and criteria for selecting proposals. It is indexed by topic so that you can quickly locate which government agency is interested in particular kinds of projects.

Private funding sources are more difficult to identify, although there are several directories that a researcher can use, including *The Foundation Directory*, the *Foundation Grants Index*, and the *Taft Foundation Reporter*. These directories provide detailed sample grants and information on areas of interest, previous grants, and private foundations' officers.

The description of a foundation in the *Taft Foundation Reporter* is typical of the information that grant proposal writers need. For example, it includes the names, addresses, and phone numbers of key contacts within the Harder Foundation (an example of a foundation not found on the Web). Before a grant proposal is written, a proposal writer usually contacts someone within a foundation to learn more details about proposal format or a foundation's interests. Often, **preproposals**, brief descriptions of pro-

FIGURE 6.9
...

Sample Schedule

Month 1:	Site preparation
	Application development
Month 2:	Begin installation
	Convert database
	Train key personnel
Month 3:	Trial period begins
Month 4:	Correct system for errors found in trial period
Month 6:	Test system for continued integrity

posed activities, are encouraged. Some agencies and private donors require prepoposals and regularly announce invitations to submit them.

The Harder Foundation description lists application procedures along with an analysis of previous grants, areas of interest, and sample grants. By studying this listing, a grant writer for a local environmental organization might decide that the Harder Foundation is the perfect target for a proposal to save a local lagoon from real estate company executives who want to build a country club on the site.

Format for a Proposal Seeking Foundation Support

While some foundations prefer a particular format, the general outline that follows should prove adequate for proposals to almost any funding group.

- Letter of Transmittal
- Cover Sheet
- Summary
- Background
- Goals: What the Organization Hopes to Achieve
- Procedures and Activities: How the Organization Plans to Achieve Its Goals
- Evaluation: How the Organization Will Know if It Succeeds
- Budget: What this Project Will Cost
- Conclusion
- Appendixes

The top official in the organization seeking the grant should sign the *letter of transmittal*. This letter emphasizes the group's support for this project and its willingness to discuss it at greater length with the foundation. Often, this section includes a discussion of why the organization is being solicited for funds, including how you came to know about the organization.

The *cover sheet* should be simple and include the organization's name and the writer's name, title, and telephone number in case additional information is needed. Many inexperienced grant writers use fancy folders in the mistaken belief that this improves the proposal's chances for funding. This probably does not work with most fifth grade teachers, and it certainly does not work with experienced grant evaluators. However, a crisp, professional appearance invites the decision maker to read it by letting him or her know that you are a professional. A good working title for the project helps catch readers' attention. "Project Boost: A Plan for Implementing a Home Reading Program" is catchy because the concept of boosting children's performance creates a word picture.

In the *summary*, you must cover all of the key sections found in the proposal itself, including specifically what problem or problems will be addressed, why the organization offering this proposal is the one best qualified to handle this problem, how the organization will handle this problem and evaluate success, and what all of this will cost.

The *background* section is the beginning of your actual proposal. In it you should cover your organization's experience and history, together with a description of the problem that needs to be addressed. This section should be followed by a description of what the organization's objectives are for solving the problem(s) and how it hopes to achieve this result.

An organization to aid homeless children might describe the problem it wants to address in these terms:

> A recent survey by the Los Angeles Times *estimated that over 10,000 people in the Los Angeles area are homeless; this survey quoted Dr. Wilimena Williams, president of the California Pediatric Association, who indicated that approximately 35 percent of these individuals are children suffering from serious malnutrition.*

We believe that funding of this proposal will enable it to provide these 3,500 children with two hot meals a day that will meet all minimum nutritional requirements.

This statement also establishes the organization's goal of providing children with meals in order to meet nutritional needs. *Goals* often address specific problems or opportunities. After a description of the proposing organization's background and the nature of the problem to be addressed, the proposal should contain an explanation of the project and its methodology. This is accomplished with a section describing how the organization will proceed to carry out the project. Following the explanation of the *procedures and activities*, there should be a definition of how the project will be evaluated. This would include quantifiable results and objective methods to determine whether or not the project has been a success. The sections on methodology and *evaluation* should be followed with a *budget* that explains what portion of the total expenses your organization will cover. Many foundations expect some degree of expense sharing whether it is 90/10 or even 50/50 between the funding group and the organization.

Finally, every proposal needs a *conclusion* that addresses the prospects for future funding. Will the foundation need to continue to support this project indefinitely or is there a plan for the project to become self-supporting? The appendixes provide the place to put supporting figures and graphs that have not been directly included in the narrative. For example, the appendixes may include supporting letters and related evidence, detailed data tables, or details concerning how costs were determined.

SECTION SUMMARY

There are two categories of proposals: solicited and unsolicited. These may be intended for either internal or external sources. Internal proposals include a cover letter or memorandum, an executive summary, a table of contents, a definition of the problem, a proposed solution, a budget, an implementation schedule, and a conclusion. For grants, proposal formats are similar to those of other proposals: a letter of transmittal, a cover sheet, a summary, a background description, the organization goals, how the organization plans to achieve its goals, how success will be determined, costs, conclusions, and appendixes.

CHALLENGE PROBLEM FOR REVIEW

Most people in academe presume that federal funding sources and private nonprofit funding sources support research and community service types of activity. However, in a brief search of the sources, you will be surprised to discover that there are many entities that exist to support research and development that is intended to lead to commercially successful inventions, applications, and marketable services. Locate several of these and determine how they accept and fund proposals, where they publish or otherwise promote their successful ventures, and what it takes to participate.

CHAPTER SUMMARY

...

Proposals offer a strategic tool for selling products or services. Whether solicited or unsolicited, correct, logical proposal formatting is crucial and contains specific necessary elements. Grant proposals are similar to other proposals and are designed to obtain funding for particular projects.

CHECKLIST: FORMATTING THE PROPOSAL

...

Solicited

_____ Background Information (who is making the request and why)
_____ Instructions for Preparing Proposals and Submitting Completed Proposals
_____ Overview of the Current System
_____ Mandatory Vendor Requirements
_____ General Vendor Questions
_____ Specific System Requirements
_____ Information Technology System Requirements
_____ Exhibits

Unsolicited

_____ Cover Letter or Memorandum
_____ Executive Summary or Abstract
_____ Title Page
_____ Table of Contents
_____ The Problem
_____ Proposed Solution
_____ Budget
_____ Implementation Schedule (Timetable)
_____ Conclusions

EXERCISES

...

Prewriting Exercises

Search the Internet for one examples of each of three kinds of RFPs: corporate, nonprofit foundation, and government (see the Challenge Problem for Section 6.1). Also, hundreds will appear when you place RFP in your favorite search engine. Examine them for their differences and similarities.

1. List the differences.
2. List the similarities.

Writing Exercises

1. Consider a local campus problem that could be solved by taking some action. This issue might be as simple as the quality of the snack bar food or as significant as the need to improve security in the dorms and parking lots. Develop a detailed list of facts that must be gathered, people who must be interviewed, and surveys that need to be written. Discuss the audience for this proposal. What action must you take to ensure approval from this audience?
2. Virtually every student is eligible for some kind of scholarship. Consult with a librarian and find a description of scholarships available nationally. Select a scholarship for which you meet the eligibility requirements and write an unsolicited proposal indicating why you should be awarded this particular scholarship.
3. Take a piece of equipment such as a computer with disk drives, a monitor, video adapter card, or printer, and discuss all of the specific criteria that you would need to establish in order to write an RFP for the equipment. How could such a document be "slanted" to ensure that a certain company would win the bid?

IN-BOX EXERCISE

...

You have just been given the job of purchasing manager for A-WII.

IN-BOX

ITEM 1: FRED, CHIEF MAINTENANCE ENGINEER. We have just been approved for a replacement of three block casting and boring lines. These lines each have several machines and will require that the vendor install the lines. Of course, we need to get the old lines removed. Management told me that you could do the RFP. I can meet next week to discuss it with you.

Your Response

Check one: ☐ Memorandum ☐ E-mail ☐ Letter ☐ Note ☐ Other

To: _____

_____

_____

_____

_____

_____

_____

_____

_____

_____

_____

_____

_____

_____

_____

_____

_____

_____

_____

_____

_____

_____

_____

_____

_____

ITEM 2: E-MAIL FROM NORM, LINE SUPERVISOR. I heard we were getting new machines in Lines 6, 7, and 8. Last time they changed the lines, it took three times longer than it was supposed to take, and half the crew ended up laid off for a month. If we do repeat that process, we might lose those guys that were here then. One of them threatened to quit if we don't plan better.

Your Response

Check one: ☐ Memorandum ☐ E-mail ☐ Letter ☐ Note ☐ Other

To: _____

_____

_____

_____

_____

_____

_____

_____

_____

_____

_____

_____

_____

_____

_____

_____

_____

_____

_____

_____

_____

_____

_____

_____

_____

_____

_____

_____

_____

ITEM 3: HANDWRITTEN NOTE FROM FROMME, LINE 3 TEAM LEADER.

If we install new machines, maybe the company should send us to be trained on them while they are installing them rather than after. Last time I almost had to quit and get a new job.

Your Response

Check one: ☐ Memorandum   ☐ E-mail   ☐ Letter   ☐ Note   ☐ Other

To: _____

_____

_____

_____

_____

_____

_____

_____

_____

_____

_____

_____

_____

_____

_____

_____

_____

_____

_____

_____

_____

_____

_____

_____

_____

_____

_____

_____

_____

_____

_____

ITEM 4: E-MAIL FROM FRITZ, HUMAN RESOURCES. Fred informed me that new lines would be installed in 6, 7, and 8. Will there be any new skills required or any new workers to hire? You should know that if they have any specialties, company procedures take about two months to get the processing done. We would need to get this done on a proper schedule (it was really screwed up last time). Oh, by the way, welcome aboard!

Your Response

Check one: ☐ Memorandum   ☐ E-mail   ☐ Letter   ☐ Note   ☐ Other

To: _____

_____

_____

_____

_____

_____

_____

_____

_____

_____

_____

_____

_____

_____

_____

_____

_____

_____

_____

_____

_____

_____

_____

_____

_____

_____

KEY TERMS
...

Executive summary (p. 173)

Letter of transmittal (p. 171)

Preproposal (p. 182)

Proposal (p. 164)

Request for information (RFI) (p. 167)

Request for proposal (RFP) (p. 165)

Solicited proposal (p. 177)

Table of contents (p. 172)

Title page (p. 170)

Unsolicited proposal (p. 178)

REFERENCES
...

Davenport, G., trans. (1976). *Herakleitos and Diogenes.* San Francisco: Grey Fox Press.

Swade, D. (2001). *Charles Babbage and the Quest to Build the First Computer.* New York: Penguin.

Catalog of Federal Domestic Assistance. Online at http://12.46.245.173/cfda.html.

The Foundation Directory. Online at http://www.fconline.fdncenter.org/.

Taft Group. *Taft Foundation Reporter.* Detroit, Michigan and Washington, DC: Taft Corp., 1980–1990.

CHAPTER 7
...
WRITING *to* GUIDE PEOPLE

LEARNING OUTCOMES
...

Upon completion of this chapter, you will be able to accomplish the following tasks:

1. Determine when written directions are more appropriate than oral directions and when oral directions should be given.

2. Recognize the different writing strategies involved when management is focused on processes or goals.

3. Employ writing to strengthen group and team-building processes.

4. Understand how delegation requires both responsibility and authority and how each can be assigned through a written directive.

5. Use written directions to create a means of monitoring progress and establishing a schedule for feedback and completion of a task.

6. Use writing to reward success.

7. Encourage a coached employee through written feedback and guidance.

8. Use writing to establish reflection on work and goals.

9. Distinguish between formative and summative evaluations and the reasons each would be used in a work setting.

10. Develop measurable objectives that can be used to establish evidence of achieving specific goals.

11. Write a fair, accurate, and fact-focused evaluation.

"Oh, hiring's O.K., but firing provides a real sense of closure."

You may be surprised at both the amount and the kinds of writing required once you are on the job. We have approached writing as a task focused on work; that is, on managerial products rather than on managing workers. In this chapter, we examine one of the most important roles of the manager: directing people through communication. A managerial priority is to guide others to accomplish organizational goals. Although there are different ways of expressing this fundamental aspect of management, managers accomplish their work-related goals by guiding others to complete tasks, and writing is a primary tool for accomplishing this priority.

For today's workforce, the primary role of managing people has blurred, and the changes in the workplace over the last two decades have encouraged more active involvement by managers in direct production activities. (We even have terms for executives who engage in the daily minutia of a business; the most polite is "micromanager.") Simultaneously, both line and staff employees have been encouraged to take more active roles in self-management. In many corporations, the self-directed team concept has empowered workers at all levels. Some companies, like W. L. Gore & Associates, Inc., the creators of Gore-Tex, have only two officers (as required by law), a president or CEO and a secretary/treasurer. In fact, Bill Gore's philosophy offers guidelines for the ultimate "flat" organization. Being an associate is a natural commitment to four basic principles established by Gore. These principles are (Gore, 2004):

Principles

Fairness Everyone will try to be fair. Everyone will sincerely strive to be fair with each other, our suppliers, our customers, and all persons with whom we carry out transactions.

Freedom Everyone will allow, help, and encourage other Associates to grow in knowledge, skill, scope of responsibility, and range of activities.

Commitment Everyone will make his or her own commitments—and keep them.

Waterline Everyone will consult with other Associates before taking actions that might be "below the waterline" and cause serious damage to the Enterprise.

We all would be fortunate to be employed as an associate in a corporation with this kind of ethical standard. W. L. Gore may be the flattest organization in the world, which means that it relies heavily on the core elements of effective management—guidance and coaching. Nevertheless, imagine you have just been employed by W. L. Gore, reported for your first day at work, and were told only the four basic principles. What would you do? Where would you start? As a practical matter, managers have to provide sufficient guidance to orient and initiate even the most empowered, enthusiastic, and self-motivated employees.

How you manage your subordinates depends more upon your individual talents than the prescriptions of your employer. Your company may have established guidelines that you must follow, even prescribed forms for evaluation. However, the methods that you use to direct, guide, coach, and evaluate others can be personalized within even the most extremely restrictive formats. Writing is a tool that you can use to encourage your subordinates. Moreover, effective writing complements effective verbal management.

In this chapter, you will learn about a variety of written communication tools. You will learn about strategies and formats that include giving specific directions to guide the actions of others in a given task, identifying opportunities for coaching and developing the skills of others, and knowing how to write a meaningful and productive evaluation of an employee.

Using Written Communication to Direct Others

Often, the performance of others is directed through written instructions. These instructions convey the authority to act, the expectations for the action, and the means of verifying the successful completion of a task.

The quickest route to assigning a task may be verbal. Just as writing is preceded by prewriting, most complex tasks involve planning sessions and even preplanning phases. The simplest tasks have logistic components. Consider what it takes to convene a planning session for a new corporate initiative. Questions arise. Who should come? Where should we meet? When is the best time to schedule the meeting (the more people involved, the more difficult it will be to find a common time)? Staff members can make arrangements, but who decides the priority level of the planning meeting for the initiative? In many organizations, these questions cross into territorial gray areas.

Simply shouting orders to a crowd does not ensure the completion of a task. Such an approach works only in a fully regimented workplace. Some organizing thought must precede giving directions and some means of controlling the interpretation of the directions must be involved. When oral directions are used, it may be appropriate or even necessary to follow up with written confirmation. Likewise, written directions are enhanced by oral confirmation. Important meetings should be followed by a written account of assigned tasks and then by a follow-up telephone conversation to confirm that the written account was correct. For the effective and productive management of others, writing must not be considered an independent or isolated function; it is an integral part of the management process.

Written Versus Oral Directions

The decision to initiate a set of instructions will itself influence whether the first directions are given orally or in writing. An initial discussion, in both formal and informal meetings, is most effective. Imagine receiving a large set of written instructions without warning. Would you simply read the instructions and begin working on the task? If you receive a task list every Monday, you would expect the instructions and would proceed without concern. Still, what if the unexpected set of instructions represents a complete shift in job duties? You would immediately contact your supervisor for clarification. The written instructions, without regard to the form in which they arrived—e-mail, interoffice memorandum, even a letter—would seem formal or official and threatening.

Sometimes the first contact about an activity is written. A new CEO might distribute a letter announcing a new corporate philosophy. This letter may not be very specific, but it would promise details to follow. Another instance might be when a new procedure is implemented and detailed instructions for the procedure are being conveyed. Even this kind of instruction should not come without some form of advance notice.

Emergencies may require a written directive. The shipping slowdown in West Coast ports during 2002 caused many crises due to lack of product and material availability. Frantic store managers and parts vendors needed directions (and solutions) urgently. What would you have done in this situation? If you had hundreds of local store managers around the country, a call to each one may not have been feasible (unless you already had in place an automatic recorded message capability). An e-mail with specific instructions (e.g., what kind of written notice should be placed on the shelf where customers expect to find the season's hot toy) would have been the quickest and most efficient method of communication.

Other than special circumstances like this, it would be rare for a manager to communicate critical instructions in writing without a preparatory communication. When you are communicating with half a dozen subordinates, for instance, a brief discussion warning about forthcoming events almost always precedes any written communication. Communicating with larger numbers of employees may require a preliminary group meeting or an e-mail announcing the forthcoming changes.

In fact, surprises are often taken one of two ways. Employees may think: (1) "This is actually a bad news message, and the manager is out to trip me up," or (2) "The manager is dumping this on us without warning—more evidence that the manager does not know how to manage!" No one ever gets an unexpected package with a fifty-page instruction booklet for a new procedure the day before the procedure is to be implemented and says, "Oh, what a pleasant surprise!"

The decision about where to begin and whether to use written or oral directions rests with the manager and depends on common sense. Effective management involves a stream of communication at all levels: written, oral, nonverbal, formal, informal, official, and unofficial. Even for unpleasant news, managers should not avoid direct communication. Letting employees learn from the press of a pending plant closure does not serve anyone's interest.

Here are a few simple questions to ask as you decide between written and oral forms:

1. Who (i.e., how many employees and what level) needs to know?
2. How soon do they need to know?
3. Which is more important, a brief statement or comprehensive detail?
4. Can notification of an event or change be separated from its details?
5. How will a written notice be interpreted?
6. Will oral instructions be too complicated to ensure that everyone gets the complete message?
7. If I provide the directions orally, will I have an opportunity to provide a follow-up confirmation before the activity begins?
8. If I provide detailed instructions in writing, will I have an opportunity to contact everyone verbally and confirm their understanding of the instructions?
9. How geographically dispersed are the people who need to know? It may not be possible to talk to each person who needs to know if the organization is, let's say, three thousand people in nine countries.

Although written instructions can be highly detailed, details can obscure clarity and minimize urgency; spoken instructions can be obscured by the audiences' memory. Both means of communication should be cross-checked with each other.

Writing Strategies

Clarity of directions ranks with appropriateness of directions when you consider how to guide others. The beginning point with these two elements is your expectation of what will happen when the directions are delivered. Will the recipient place a high priority on completing the assigned task? Will there be permanent change in performance or will the action be effective for only one event or a short period of time? Instructions must be clear, they must be appropriate, and they must achieve the desired result.

Using writing to direct others requires every bit of your managerial skill. To be successful, your message must reflect sensitivity to the work context and corporate culture, especially the *microculture* of the recipient group. Your message must reflect the extent to which the recipients embrace the task or goal, and you must demonstrate an awareness of the extent to which the task is already understood. For instance, if the written message provides extensive details and the recipient is already fully aware of the details, then he or she may feel insulted. If a specific step has been overlooked or ignored, most employees would rather be told something explicitly about that missing step—not be given a review of the entire process. Yet, if you as manager want to remind everyone of the process, then address the placement of the missing step in the context of the process. You might write something like this:

> *Everyone,*
>
> *There have been instances when the notification of supervisors during the recording and ordering of service for clients has been insufficient. This notification is important for supervisors who must track resource allocation. When the notification is omitted, the supervisor must manually retrieve the work order. This results in lost time and inefficient service. Just for a reminder, here are the steps:*
>
> 1. *Respond to the customer service call.*
>
> 2. *Request a complete account of the customer's problem.*
>
> 3. *If you cannot resolve the problem, order a service call:*
>   a. *Place the customer number and call number in the service call queue.*
>   b. *Copy the service order number to the supervisor.*
>   c. *Call the customer with details of the service call, giving the service order number, expected time of the service call, and a number to call back for additional problems.*
>
> 4. *Use the service call number to track progress in the service log tracking system.*

In this example, the manager is able to identify a problem, offer a reason for compliance, and review the original steps for handling a customer need. The detailed but brief message (easily sent as a printed memo or an e-mail) is an example of the type of strategy-based tools employed when writing to direct others. This strategy addresses a process. Other approaches include goal-oriented and team-building strategies. Regardless of the type of strategy, keep in mind that every communication with subordinates is an opportunity to guide or direct them toward improved and effective work performance. Three core strategies are: process-oriented management, goal-directed management, and team-building leadership.

Process-Oriented Management

In this strategy, **process-oriented management**, writing is one tool among many designed to reinforce and strengthen appropriate processes. It may not be appropriate for every type of work, especially for workers who have professional responsibilities and fairly high-level skills in defined job tasks. Writing instructions that address the management of processes must be restricted to writing and clarifying instructions. A common challenge to writers of instructions is to write instructions for a physical task such as tying shoelaces. We have great difficulty converting an almost automatic manual skill into a verbal instruction. As for tying shoelaces, parents struggle with small children to model the skill, then help one step at a time, and finally, go buy Velcro-buckled shoes. Some core skills may not be addressed easily in writing. Imagine designing a showroom layout of mannequins wearing formal and semiformal attire in which, rather than showing the placement of the mannequins with notes about which outfit to wear, you have to explain the details of each dress element: how to buckle a belt, how to put the arms through the garments, and how to tie shoelaces. What might be a one-room plan with the layout could easily turn into a multipage document.

Some writers overdirect their readers with that kind of microdetail. When you ask an engineer to develop plans for wiring a conference room with complete multimedia capabilities, you do not send along an electrical wiring textbook. You might show where in the room you want the projector and where you want the computer connections. Most likely, you will communicate these expectations in a face-to-face walk-through of the room and in a written follow-up. Processes are best managed when based on a shared understanding, and these meetings build a common ground for communication about the project.

What kinds of tasks are appropriate for this kind of process description and instruction? For the most part, the administrative aspect of any project will be clearer when approached as a process. By administrative, we mean those aspects that require managerial controls: when and where to submit the report, what the report format is, how to record a completed step, who needs to be informed and at which stage of the procedure, and so on. In addition, roles and responsibilities generally need to be assigned to functional organizations so that each unit understands its part in the overall process. For example, will engineering or manufacturing keep the official design records? These are not skill-based activities. In general, writing that pertains to how to complete a work task is *technical* writing, not *managerial* writing. Too many managers want to be technical experts when they need to trust the technical experts to do their jobs. Table 7.1 offers a comparison of technical writing and managerial writing in terms of providing instructions.

Many managers become successful because they are good at the work they oversee. They want to maintain their performance excellence and encourage others to follow their example. This is rarely achieved when a manager directs employees as if they are completely uninformed about how to do their job.

Too often functional areas or organizational divisions of a company will write instructions for themselves based on unconfirmed assumptions about how other divisions will support them. If processes are left in this unconnected state between functional silos in an organization, work will flow inefficiently or perhaps not at all. Written procedures targeted at the hand-offs between organizational units are frequently the most troublesome areas to be addressed.

Goal-Directed Management

One means of breaking the technical-expertise urge is to shift from a process-based strategy to one based on goal direction. We are all called upon to give our subordinates specific process instructions. These instructions are most successful when accompanied by an explanation of the desired outcome or goal. In the service call directions presented on page 197, the writer makes it clear that failing to notify the supervisor results in additional work. While the big picture of the **goal-directed strategy** may imply **management by objectives (MBO)**, anyone can lead others by establishing goals and objectives.

TABLE 7.1
...

Technical Versus Managerial Instructions

Technical Writing	Managerial Instructions
Instructions for using the new copy machine.	Guidelines for what can and cannot be copied.
Descriptions of how the calibrations of the cutters on a paper-cutting machine are to be set.	Directive to place in the work order for any paper cutting that requires tolerances for size variances.
Instructions with illustrations for partial assembly of a lamp prior to packaging, with the packaging instructions as well.	A requirement for all employees in the packaging area to check for inclusion of the instructions on final assembly of the lamp.
Step-by-step description of the proper method of installing an engine on the automobile assembly line.	Expectations that each assembly worker will initial the paperwork that tracks the automobile during assembly.

Sometimes, goals can sound more like cheerleading than achievable ends. Consider improved safety. Suppose you address employees with a memorandum containing this directive: "We must work more safely and reduce our accident rates." Why is this not helpful? The goal of improved safety is a vague goal, even when attached to a reduction of accidents. How will the accident rate be reduced? By working more safely! What does it mean to work more safely?

Here is how vague encouragement can be converted into direct action:

> *Eye injuries have risen slightly over the past six months. All employees must wear goggles when on the assembly floor. (Remember: Goggles are mandatory equipment!) Assembly workers are reminded that their safety record is factored into their team and group bonuses.*

In order to be reached, specific goals (reduced eye injuries and increased bonuses) depend on actions. A more explicit safety campaign might involve a chart of accidents, targets for reducing the accident rate, and specific actions that contribute to the accident-rate reduction. We cannot expect line workers to respond well to the plea, "We must reduce our accident rate," with a systematic, coordinated safety program of their own making, unless they are empowered to develop a safety program. People participate in programs in which they have some form of ownership. The best goal and objective writing accomplishes this kind of employee buy-in. To help focus your writing of goals as a means of directing others, then, consider the problem of vague, nonspecific encouragement in comparison with specific targets and specified means of reaching those targets. Table 7.2 lists and compares vague versus specific goals.

Also, having goggles available to wear supports the wearing of goggles on the assembly floor. Someone needs to be given the task of determining what goggles to buy, and someone must place an order and take receipt of and deliver the goggles to an identified area where assembly personnel know to look for them. If not specified, purchasing may wait for a requisition from manufacturing, while manufacturing is waiting for the goggles to appear, based on an order placed by human resources. Even while using a goal-directed strategy, the use of process-oriented instructions prevents these gaps in expectations. Sometimes, these strategies are used most effectively in combination.

Team-Building Leadership

A highly desirable strategy for corporate management is the use of self-directed and self-managed teams. With both types of teams, the team members collectively have the skills required to complete the assigned or chosen task. A **self-directed team** is given a project and

TABLE 7.2
...

Comparison of Vague Versus Specific Goals

Vague Directives	Specific Objectives
Work Harder!	Increase productivity by reducing downtime on the assembly line by 20 percent.
Improve Quality!	Increase the quality control checks by 20 percent in order to reduce defective merchandise.
Reduce Waste!	Monitor procedures for employees using shortcuts that increase error-based waste.
Increase Profits!	Reduce waste and reduce merchandise defects in order to generate more profit.
Be Happy!	Take at least one extra day off each month.

develops its own organization and distribution of work. A **self-managed team** goes a bit further. The team accepts responsibility for management tasks such as performance assessment and project selection. A self-managed team may be entrepreneurial, seeking projects that match its expertise. Self-directed teams tend to be restricted to an assigned task or series of related tasks, and other corporate administrators do the managerial work of personnel assessment and work assignments. Self-managed teams may seek additional experts without consulting the corporate hierarchy. Their work is entirely project and goal driven.

Manufacturers like Toyota Motor Manufacturing utilize the team concept extensively. However, the team in an assembly plant is different from a team in a design company. The assembly plant team works toward specific, shared productivity goals but has little freedom in how the specific procedures are completed during assembly and manufacturing. Still, the team may work to make recommendations that can be tested for improved productivity. This is the essence of the Toyota Quality Circles. **Quality Circles** are special groups within the Toyota organization composed of team members, team leaders, and group leaders. The Quality Circle explores ways to improve quality and productivity in a plant. Team members make recommendations, and the Quality Circle members devise a plan to test the recommendation. If successful, the recommendation can be used throughout the assembly plant, possibly throughout the company. The question for this text is, how can we use writing to encourage teamwork and the benefits that teams bring, both to the Quality Circle and to any other kind of team?

Be aware that some managers proclaim that they want the staff to think of themselves as a team and that teamwork is the best way to meet the goals of the group. After such a proclamation, they demand that their professional staff answer the phone, get coffee, and bring baked goods for visitors—because "we are all team players." Leadership does not mean dictatorship. Likewise, the declaration of team membership alone does not make a team. Finally, a work team is not necessarily a social team.

What writing tools encourage team membership? For a team to develop, certain elements must be present. They include the foundation of mutual respect among team members, the empowerment of team members with the authority to complete their tasks, and the support of acts of leadership even from employees on the lowest rung of the organizational chart. Written communication can play a major role in the team-building process. An idea from the secretary that speeds work throughout the group can be recognized by the manager and shared with the entire group. Support of the employee's initiative should be made known to all team members. An e-mail to all involved can promote favorable, healthy feelings, especially when accompanied by a letter of recognition sent to the employee and copied to the employee's personnel file.

Managers develop team membership and participation through a number of basic communication activities. Most communication that includes direct contact can be reinforced though follow-up notes, e-mails, and, to recognize especially important contributions, letters of commendation. The following membership-building elements can be included as a part of or as the entire content of written communications:

- Comments supporting the ideas of another.
- Praise of ideas, actions, and suggestions that build and revise rather than reject completely.
- Encouragement that leads to further support by other team members of a contribution.
- Efforts to focus attention on the current problem or issue rather than side issues and distractions.
- Praise for successes of the group and of members of the group.
- Praise for efforts that ultimately did not work out but that brought the team together in a common cause.

The contribution of written communication to the success of a team should not be underestimated. Written communications establish a permanent record of the team's activity and progress. In fact, the act of recording the group's activity enhances the recorder as a member of the team and is thus a form of leadership (the team leader must first be an effective team member). Writing can provide guidance, affirm team goals, offer reinforcement for team participation, focus team activity, remind team members of the importance of fair and equitable participation, and many other membership-building activities. The successful use of writing as a means of directing team interaction requires a writer who can sustain a positive outlook even while criticizing a discontented team member.

The concepts of empowerment in the workplace, self-directed and self-managed teams, and participative management have been around for years. Some people challenge such concepts as just another way to manipulate employees and to get more work done without corresponding compensation. The clerk who offers a suggestion may not be happy with a letter of commendation, but may want money for his or her efforts, especially if the idea is a good one and saves money for the organization. Although increased cynicism to these concepts is apparent in some organizations, it is by no means universal.

Management Tools for Written Directions

It may be helpful to review a few key management tasks that are used to direct others. Delegating authority, assigning specific tasks, monitoring and sustaining progress, establishing time frames and feedback, and recognizing success are daily activities that require managerial writing. The role of clarity and directness is critical in each of these activities. For example, if you plan to delegate authority, you must be clear and to the point: "Kathy, I am authorizing you to investigate last quarter's extraordinarily high complaint ratio. You have the authority to conduct an investigation of the complaints, but if you need additional resources, please ask me. Please develop a report that analyzes the complaints and at least two options for correcting the problems that have caused them." Clarity empowers the delegate to do the work required. Lack of clarity, as in a note that says, "Kathy, check out last quarter's complaint ratio," may lead to a misunderstanding. Kathy could respond with "Wow, I didn't realize it was that high" and not even know that she had been assigned a job to complete.

Delegating Authority

As the leaders of a unit with specific productivity or service goals, managers have clearly defined authority to complete work tasks and assign work activity. At every level of an organization, each unit head is technically assigned all of the duties of the unit. He or she delegates duties, authority, and responsibility to the next lower organizational level. The number of trained and educated managers who do not grasp this idea is amazing. Therefore, although this key fundamental of good management has been addressed in other courses and through job experiences, the following examination of the importance of writing for effective delegation should be quite useful.

How does this simple idea of **delegation** go astray? People tend to delegate responsibility for an action without providing the authority to do the task completely. Another major error involves hiding the identity of the delegating agent ("You are being assigned . . . ") without indicating who is making the assignment. Combine these poor practices and you get: "You are assigned the responsibility for investigating the complaints from last quarter." Such a message fails to indicate what you are investigating, the authority under which you will act, the extent of power you will have while undertaking the investigation, who is to receive the results of the investigation, and the form for reporting those results.

Every delegation of authority requires identification of the extent of power or authority being delegated, the delegating agent, and the extent of accountability the delegate will have. Delegation also requires four additional elements that must be clearly communicated: tasks, monitoring, time frame, and completion. Before these elements are addressed, you must indicate that *you* are *delegating authority* to a *subordinate* (or a team) to perform certain *activities*. You identify the authority, the tasks, and the responsibility. You also inform others that this task has been delegated to a person or group and that they are expected to consider these delegates as if they were you. Failure to respond to a delegate would be equivalent to failing to respond to you. Supporting them is the same as supporting you.

Assigning Specific Tasks

Assigning specific tasks is another action that can be mishandled. There may be a preliminary discussion of what is to be done and what is expected of the subordinate or team. A written list of assigned tasks leaves nothing to be assumed or overlooked.

The assignment might look something like this:

Memorandum

To: Kathy
From: Richard
Date: January 15
Re: Investigating Customer Complaints

Within the next thirty days, please investigate the increased number of complaints received during the previous quarter. To do so, you should examine:

1. *Where the complaints were generated*

2. *What products were involved*

3. *Which plant had the most problems with quality*

4. *Which sales representatives were affected*

5. *Whether complaints were addressed in the manner prescribed by customer service*

6. *Any factor that would cause an increase in complaints*

If you need a data analyst, please contact me so that I can assign one to you.

In this example, the subsets of a systematic analysis of a potentially damaging problem are defined (other directions may be highly detailed as well as specific). This list also includes a possible additional resource person. Sometimes activities require additional personnel or other resources, such as a travel budget. In most cases, projects like this one will draw on corporate accounts for travel and do not need special accounts. If this were an external consulting firm, a specific account number would be identified in this communication for all related expenses and charges. Additional resources must accompany assignments that are not intrinsic to the assigned individual's normal duties.

Monitoring Progress

As with analytic reports (see Chapter 4), delegated activities require a schedule of interim reports and a final report. Similarly, an action that takes place over a few weeks may require a more informal report system (such as an e-mail detailing the progress made) and for more extensive and long-term projects, regular interim reports provide for monitoring progress.

Establishing Time Frame and Feedback

This element is easy to do but is sometimes forgotten. You might direct a department head to talk with several employees about a problem on the assembly line. They may recommend a change. Either you or their supervisor should give them prompt feedback about their idea, just as your immediate subordinate will report the recommendation to you. Feedback flows both up and down the corporate hierarchy as well as sideways, from unit to unit. Regular and thorough feedback establishes trust and respect for all concerned. As a manager, you should include a written confirmation that feedback is expected by a given time and identify other parties to whom the report should be sent (a copy or notice of that report should be available to the line employees).

Recognizing Success

Have you ever written a paper for a professor and then wondered what became of it? Imagine preparing a significant report and not hearing back from your supervisor. You might wonder: Did I do it correctly? Was it too long? Did I make some other mistake? Anyone whom you have asked to do a task reacts in the same way. Not only should you respond, "I received your report" or "Thanks for talking with those employees," but you should include, "When I finish reviewing the report, I will get back with you" or "I will consider these ideas." This brief message should include a time frame: "I will review the report, meet with [the report preparer] on Friday, and make a decision by the end of the month." Sometimes an employee asks for a change in an assignment, but not for a specific decision date. The decision and its timing is up to you. If an employee wants to be assigned a different task, then you must say, "I will consider this and let you know in five days [or however long] from today." If you cannot develop the answer in that time frame, then, in five days, tell the employee that you are still working on a solution.

Some recognition of the work done, the quality of the work, or the success of the activity should be included in your feedback. If you want to encourage the employee to continue doing good work, recognition of the success—even if it is only verbal praise—is appropriate and mandatory.

SECTION SUMMARY

Writing can be used to direct others to act in predetermined ways and to complete specified tasks. The first step is deciding whether the instructions should be given verbally or in writing. This decision requires knowledge of the work contexts and the receptiveness of the addressees. Writing strategies differ according to whether the management is focused on how processes are to be employed or on specific goals that all employees share. When a manager writes an instruction, the delegation of authority must be clear. The recipient of the instruction must know the extent of responsibility and authority entailed. There should be a clear set of guidelines for how the work will be monitored as well as how and when the manager should be informed about the progress.

CHALLENGE PROBLEM FOR REVIEW

Self-directed and self-managed teams tend to be spontaneous and more or less free flowing. Creative solutions often emerge in the interactions between team members. It seems that writing may be particularly difficult during these sessions and efforts to keep track of ideas and assignments may be pushed to "after-the-fact" summaries. Identify one or two skills that you think you might want to develop to aid in your successful participation in self-directed teamwork. How can these skills help foster spontaneity and creativity?

Coaching with Written Communication

Most coaching of an employee occurs in one-on-one circumstances, but writing can be a powerful tool for affirming and reinforcing lessons.

Coaching Begins in Conversation

Mentoring is a management task that managers can look upon with pleasure. It includes direct **coaching** of a management trainee, and coaching can take many forms. In addition to coaching the trainee in accomplishing relevant tasks, the mentor serves as a role model. (Anyone who knows a skill should be able to coach others in using that skill.) A senior executive may identify a promising junior executive and work with that employee in an advisory role that is outside the executive's regular assignment. Some companies assign new executives and managers to senior executives to help acclimate the new person. Coaching can occur within a team of assembly workers with peers coaching peers in new tasks. Mentoring always includes more than the procedures for completing tasks, though. Typically, we learn the ropes from experienced employees. There are frequently unwritten rules, codes of conduct, or valuable pieces of information that are passed informally on to new employees through the coaching process. When the coaching begins to include being a role model, we refer to the activity as mentoring.

A more formal coaching process begins with the first level of supervision. An employee acquiring assembly and manufacturing skills is engaged in **training**. An experienced worker can coach (or train) a new employee on the tasks required in the job; this is referred to as OJT for on-the-job training. Training is related to learning a trade or skill; mentoring relates more to administrative and the organizational cultural processes. The process of mentoring involves a well-informed and experienced person helping a less experienced or less knowledgeable individual. That help can be in the form of modeling appropriate behavior, providing constructive criticism concerning how an assignment was completed, providing insight into corporate culture, or guiding the individual to improved self-management. Mentoring means that contact occurs regularly and usually in person. Typically, the contact is one-to-one. The coached employee is encouraged to share every concern with the coach, and the coach is expected to be frank but supportive.

Mentoring depends upon discussion and open communication, which can involve writing. There are two major domains of writing in mentoring: (1) writing that strengthens the relationship of coach (mentor) and coached (trainee); and (2) encouraging the coached person to develop a habit of self-reflection and self-recognition. E-mail and short notes can include encouragement in the form of praise and guidance that helps refine and focus efforts. Normally, people do not change unless they see a reason to do so. In effective mentoring, a mentor can employ writing as a means of building the coached person's identity.

As you learn these aspects of managerial writing, much of the writing will be from the point of view of the mentor, because, as a manager, you will be in that position. At the same time, be aware that you will be in the role of the protégé for much of your career. Especially in the beginning of your career, you need to understand the intent underlying these procedures. This understanding establishes the basis for taking advantage of the lessons being shared. If a task is designed to reinforce your self-awareness and you recognize that principle, you can pay particular attention to the process involved to see how it works. You can also enhance the intended outcome by focusing on your self-awareness.

Writing to Guide and Encourage

In the casual conversations that you have in your mentor's office, you may feel tempted to agree with whatever your mentor says. One way to break this pattern is for the mentor to ask for several written scenarios. These might begin, "I am required to dismiss an employee, how should I go about doing it?" Another scenario could be, "I must inform three of four candidates for a promotion that they will not get the promotion. What steps should I follow?" With a written set of directions (such as, speak to them in person, follow-up with a written bad news note), the mentor can review the steps and make recommendations about how to be more sensitive and how to encourage those who did not get the promotions by telling them that there will be other opportunities.

In the process just described, the mentor coaches the trainee to do the writing. Another exercise can arise when the mentor is working on a draft letter to a client or a contractor. As long as no confidences are violated, the mentor can ask the trainee to review the letter and make recommendations for improving it. The mentor can employ several models for guiding the employee. First, and logically, continuous improvement in our writing skills is good for all, and working from examples is always a good approach. Second, the tone of letters to clients is exceptionally critical. The difference between how we address a client and a contractor is just as important. Both the client and the contractor may be bound by contracts, but the client holds the power to simply choose someone else in the future. The reverse is true with the contractor. There is no need to threaten a contractor with nonrenewal; this is an assumed possibility in all contractual relationships. Understanding power and seeing how it is manifested in writing may be a central task of any coaching relationship.

In addition to helping improve the trainee's writing, a mentor can guide by modeling communication as a management tool. After a meeting, the mentor might write, "I enjoyed our brief session today. Be sure to work on praising your staff as I suggested. Remember, though, too much praise is as damaging as none at all. Also remember that several of those staff I worked with only a few years ago are going to think you are praising them because I told you to. Being and appearing authentic will always be the challenge. Good luck!" While this praise may be delivered nicely in a verbal manner as well, the written note can be part of a permanent record for the trainee. Thus, this note offers reinforcement and reminds the recipient of the most important facts of the meeting. It also continues to strengthen the coaching even as it reinforces the personal nature of the suggestion.

Writing to Force Reflection and Self-Awareness

Directing an employee to write as a means of self-discovery might be perceived as odd by the employee, but as the mentor, you are not required to reveal your larger goal. Effective participation occurs when assignments are small, concrete steps. They can be part of a larger plan or they can arise spontaneously in the course of a session focused on one coachable action. The main types of mentoring assignments involve maintaining a schedule, building a reminder file, collecting samples of written reports and follow-up messages, keeping a journal or work diary, keeping personal notes during a meeting, and preparing a to-do list.

So, what written formats are pertinent? The following list offers several options, but it is not comprehensive. A creative mentor can find other ways to incorporate writing into the mentoring relationship.

- *Schedules.* If you have one, keep your personal data assistant (PDA) as current as possible. This involves more than keeping an appointment calendar. Work is more than meetings, and realistic work schedules serve a valuable purpose. Good managers have a regular schedule for routine items and scheduled time for the nonroutine. The work of preparing a schedule and learning to modify the schedule to fit realistic time expectations is a challenge. Duties grow and transform; patterns we followed last year require modification. A written schedule provides the mentor with an opportunity to gain insight into the coached individual's self-perception. Likewise, it is concrete evidence of how work is perceived and balanced. With this information, the mentor can redirect perceptions and help make them more realistic.
- *Meeting notes.* Meeting notes have been entered into court evidence in many circumstances. Consequently, you should be very cautious about what you record and the language that you use. In an environment or industry that tends to have litigation, a mentor can provide training to a protégé by examining the way that the individual takes notes. Imagine what tobacco company executives have experienced as a consequence of damaging memoranda that eventually became public. Did they really target minorities and the homeless? Did they really try to enhance the chemicals in cigarettes? What we write today has the potential to

make us look like complete fools ten years from now. Can these disasters be avoided? Certainly they can be, but this requires careful coaching.

Another purpose of meeting notes is that they illustrate whether or not the note-taker was focused on the same main points as others and whether or not the note-taker detected the nuances of important comments. Following the action is one thing; hearing what was not said or catching subtle implications is another. After a meeting, the mentor can review the meeting notes and have the note-taker summarize the meeting from the notes themselves. This exercise of notes and summaries aids the coaching of the protégé toward effective listening. Listening is one of those crucial management skills that few managers practice well!

- *Goals and objectives.* Writing goals and objectives for oneself is a precursor to writing them for others. A common mentoring task involves asking the coached individual to state a specific goal. A **goal** is a general statement of direction. Instead of talking about goals, have your mentee put a goal in writing and bring it to the next meeting. The goal can be for the week or month. It can be for work or even for the coaching relationship. An assignment can be to write a goal statement for a team or another employee. This might be: "Improve customer relations." This goal statement indicates the direction that a unit or company wants to head. An **objective** is the measurable statement of a goal: "Improve customer relations by reducing complaints by 20 percent." This objective provides measurable interpretation of customer relations, which can lead to improved customer relations. Most objectives contain specific time frames or due dates, and a goal can have several objectives: "Reduce customer complaints by 5 percent each quarter to reach a 20 percent reduction by the end of the year." Another customer relations' objective might be to increase the number of callbacks to the customer checking on customer needs. "Call each client every three weeks to maintain contact and anticipate areas of customer needs" is compatible with the preceding goal, and it is specific and quantifiable.

  There is, however, no general consensus on the definitions of goal, objective, mission, vision, and so forth. These definitions tend to be organizationally or even situationally specific. The manager needs to determine the terminology used in his or her organization.

  Composing goals and objectives requires practice and patience. An experienced coach helps too. Generally speaking, the strategy for solving a problem or addressing an opportunity is derived from a goal. The goal statement provides a mission and offers a long-term direction. Objectives, derived from goals, establish specific outcomes. Objectives need to address specific questions: When should it be done? How will anyone know it is done? How will accountability for completion be provided? Who is responsible for the task? Not every objective needs to have this kind of detail in its actual statement, but the accountability and responsibility should be clear, as well as the means of verifying completion.

- *Journals.* Managers benefit by written records. Keeping a **journal** or **work diary** is probably less frequent in this era of electronically connected work, but the value of making a personal record, even a brief one, has not lessened. A work diary can take many forms, and it will be useful only if the form is comfortable for the individual. It should also be compatible with the individual's work. Some records require more detail than others. In many jobs, a clear record of activity is required either by the company or by the government. Professionals (lawyers, physicians, therapists, etc.) must keep records of their work in order to charge the client or patient and to provide a record for the client or insurance company as well as to trace the patients' progress to determine which treatments work.

Design engineers and scientists keep journals to support applications for patents. Entries in lab books or other forms of journals are used as evidence of when a discovery or invention was made and may resolve competing claims for a patent from more than one researcher.

Another reason for keeping a journal includes personal reflections on work. Many people keep personal journals, but they often leave work-related activities out of these journal. For managerial development, a personal diary is a record of insights into reactions, feelings, and frustrations, as well as failures and achievements. Furthermore, a journal can become a valuable asset as one progresses up the organizational hierarchy. In the mentoring experience, a journal can be used for something as simple as summarizing a coaching session or as complex as reflecting on an ethical issue. A final hint: Keeping a journal is most beneficial if you refer to it and reflect on what you have written. Keep in mind the potential legal concerns should your record be subpoenaed. What you write in a personal record at work can be used as evidence in court.

- *Portfolio of sample writing.* Keeping a **writing portfolio** is an extension of keeping a journal and the exercise of this practice is an amplification of the benefits of keeping a journal. The preparation of a writing portfolio is a means of conducting a comprehensive review of activity over a period of time. Your portfolio should contain examples of ineffective as well as effective written work. The person collecting examples for a portfolio can be directed to include memos, proposals, and requests that did not produce the desired results. These are as informative as those that were successful. Our best work gets us jobs, promotion, recognition. However, our mistakes and missteps are the places where learning occurs.

SECTION SUMMARY

Employee mentoring requires intensive conversation and, generally, face-to-face work. The mentor may teach through example, showing the protégé the steps taken in complex managerial activity. Writing may be a small component of this activity, but insofar as the coach must also be a mentor for the role of writing, it is important to utilize writing as part of the process. Writing can also be a means of providing reinforcement for the protégé. In a coaching situation, writing provides the coached employee an opportunity to engage in self-reflection. For self-reflection, the employee can articulate and reconsider goals, reflect on ethical dilemmas, and even keep a work diary of experiences for later reflection. Keeping a journal extends the efficacy of this experience by allowing the protégé to consider numerous examples of successful and unsuccessful writing projects over an extended period.

CHALLENGE PROBLEM FOR REVIEW

You may have been in the trainee role at some time in the past. This could have occurred at work where a supervisor has tried to teach you a skill or at school where a teacher has tried to guide you through an important exercise. Pick a skill, procedure, or knowledge base that you were less successful at learning than you wanted to be. Put yourself in the place of that mentor and devise a schedule of tasks that will help the trainee master a desired skill, procedure, or concept.

Preparing and Communicating and Employee Evaluation

Evaluation provides tools for both guidance and discipline. Evaluations are used to set goals and objectives and to establish a record of employee performance.

Types of Evaluation

Assessment and evaluation represent a hot topic in management, in both for-profit and not-for-profit environments. **Assessment** is the collection of data about a particular project, event, process, team, or individual. **Evaluation** is the act of using the data collected through assessment to make a judgment about how well the project, event, process, team, or individual is progressing toward a desired end. In this section, you will learn about evaluation in the context of managing work (rather than in the context of making a decision). In Chapter 5, you learned strategies for making an assessment and a recommendation about a particular action. You also read a brief discussion about making recommendations about personnel. The list of points in Chapter 5 for an assessment illustrates the similarities among types of assessment and recommendation reports. Employee assessment and evaluation require more than a brief checklist.

If you have taken a human resources course or an industrial/organizational psychology course, you probably examined legal and managerial issues related to assessment and evaluation. Most companies and large organizations have highly codified methods of conducting evaluations. These can be extremely specific about what evidence to collect and when, when to conduct observations, and how to code and report the evaluation. Typically, these performance evaluations are closely linked to pay and promotion. Consequently, the process of conducting an evaluation becomes anxiety laden. The more the process is tightly packed into a brief period as opposed to spreading it throughout the year, the more anxiety one can expect. One of the first objectives of a manager is to relieve this anxiety, because anxiety can disrupt performance.

Specialists distinguish between formative and summative evaluation. The evaluation techniques commonly applied in business and management usually can be employed for either type of evaluation.

Formative Evaluations

Formative evaluation is the use of evaluation to develop employee skills and knowledge while improving employee performance. The mentoring process discussed earlier involves an ongoing, informal, formative process of evaluation, guidance, and reappraisal. The general goal of formative evaluation is to identify areas of needed improvement and to measure or otherwise judge the degree of improvement needed. Even informal sessions with a supervisor, when the supervisor suggests a needed improvement, are considered formative evaluations.

Formative evaluation, then, ranges from informal contact between a supervisor and an employee to a highly formalized process. The highly formalized process can be conducted in the work setting, in an office discussion, or in an assessment center. The process of improving skills, knowledge, and interpersonal relations is the rationale behind formative evaluation.

Formative evaluations can be comprehensive or focused. A *comprehensive formative evaluation* requires a thorough assessment of the individual being evaluated. Techniques might include observation of work performance, review of products delivered or services rendered, performance of work-related instruments (writing tests, programming tests, in-box assessments), interviews, and self-reports. For many skilled and professional positions, specialized tests are regularly incorporated into formative evaluations. *Focused formative evaluations* address a single area of concern or performance. For instance, an evaluator may focus on an administrative assistant's ability to complete mass mailings on time or a welder's ability to assemble and weld a specific component in a prescribed time.

Employee development requires formative evaluation. For a corporation to develop employee skills and knowledge, the management must know the existing level of skills and have a target level to be achieved. If resources are to be expended in an effort to improve performance through additional training, the executives of a company must be assured that the resources will be spent appropriately. After the training, the management also should have comparative evidence demonstrating whether the employees improved.

Formative evaluations are used for individuals to improve skills and, eventually, progress through promotion. Some companies utilize a system called *pay-for-skills* in which an employee is financially rewarded for acquiring a new skill. Cross-trained employees (employees who can do several jobs) are valuable because they reduce the costs of training replacement employees or temporary employees when someone is sick or absent for an extended leave (such as family leave or National Guard duty). If several employees are capable of doing each other's jobs, the company needs to hire and train an employee for the least demanding position when an absence occurs. Pay-for-skill was developed for this purpose. Usually, companies require a defined amount of continuous training and skill acquisition. Employees must engage in a minimum amount of formative evaluation and personal development in order to keep current. Many people undertake these kinds of development programs to enhance their opportunities in the future.

Summative Evaluations

Summative evaluation is the evaluation that many people dread. **Summative evaluation** offers a summary of performance for a previous period, often six or twelve months, and is almost universally linked to salary increases. This, however, is generally not true for union employees, where compensation is usually fixed by contract. In these cases, the summative evaluation is really a binary decision: Retain the employee or do not retain. This kind of evaluation employs the same tools as a formative evaluation, and often the two forms are blended. Although it is not necessary to separate the summative and formative processes, few people being evaluated notice the distinction. Next year's salary increase or annual bonus may hinge on a positive annual evaluation. Annual evaluations are perceived as being conducted to judge and then place a value on past performance. A manager may offer a thorough evaluation that combines both recognition of strengths and identification of weaknesses, but the employee may hear only the negatives in the judgment when trying to calculate an anticipated increase. This concern makes discussion of formative and developmental issues problematic. When required to combine these two formats in a single evaluation, managers should separate the processes, perhaps conducting the summative evaluation and then requiring the employee to prepare a set of goals for the coming year. Because the goals are prepared in the context of a summative evaluation, the employee expects that, if the goals are reached, a better evaluation will follow.

Common Workplace Evaluation Methods

Techniques of assessment and evaluation can focus on personal ability, work behavior, and work outcome. Ultimately, most organizations are interested in the outcomes, but simply measuring outcomes does not reveal other important details about productivity and efficiency, and it does not indicate who is responsible for good or bad outcomes. Outcomes are often the easiest factor to track, and they are usually evident in the annual balance sheets. Most employee evaluations focus on the person's work performance.

Among the more common methods, a form of graded or ranked graphic rating scale is a simple and easy-to-complete evaluation system. The **graphic rating scale** is a set of statements that the evaluator marks on a scale such as "meets expectations," "does not meet expectations," or "exceeds expectations." Other forms may use a ranking from 1 to 5 or some other numerical spread or they may have a range from "poor" to "average" to "good." Ironically, while projecting a sense of concrete accuracy, this type of scale is very subjective. Who establishes the expectation level? Our experience is that the evaluators using them have no quantifiable or shared concept of what it means to meet expectations, what the midpoint of 3 or 4 is on a numeric scale, and especially what kind of performance is rated "average" as opposed to "good." Even worse, the employee being evaluated has no sense of what the scales mean either. Of course, when the evaluator and the employee establish clear goals in advance, the concept of expectations is shared and equally understood—especially when established in writing. The major obstacle to this approach is the breadth of most jobs, especially in salaried and professional fields. If the list of goals runs to several pages, the sheer quantity of goals overwhelms the clarity. This unfortunate fact is the chief problem with management by objectives (MBO). While MBO might work for lower levels of management, it rapidly unravels as the scope of responsibility increases. Figure 7.1 illustrates a graphic rating scale.

Many graphic rating scales are accompanied by brief summarizing comments or short descriptive narratives. The best of these address specific performance issues of which the evaluator (typically the person writing these summaries) has direct knowledge. Direct knowledge comes from observation or qualified data (monthly production reports and so on). They should not include hearsay or personal feelings.

Another means of developing an assessment and evaluation is to use supervisory observations. Observations can be incidental or systematic. Usually, a supervisor has a checklist based on work being done with expected time lines or scales indicating proficiency. At regular intervals, the supervisor observes the worker and records the observations using the form or taking notes of the observed actions. These can be converted into a broader rating system or placed in the evaluation.

Another means gaining in popularity is to base evaluations on customer feedback. Customers can be external (that is, they buy products or services from the company) or internal (fellow employees who rely on the work of the person being evaluated in order to accomplish their own work).

There are as many methods of conducting supervisory evaluations as there are supervisors. Herein lies the problem: Supervisory evaluation differs from one supervisor to the next. A valuable exercise is for managers to meet periodically to discuss how they grade employees. Everyone rates the same sample and, in the meeting, the group determines why there are differences in the results (perhaps because of varying expectations). This practice promotes uniformity within the unit. It may be helpful to share with employees selected samples or definitions of what each rating category represents.

FIGURE 7.1

A Graphic Rating Scale

Employee Name: _____

Title: _____

Supervisor: _____

Date of Evaluation: _____

Attribute	Low				High
1. Observes timeliness.	①	②	③	④	⑤
2. Participates in group activity.	①	②	③	④	⑤
3. Keeps workplace clean and organized.	①	②	③	④	⑤
4. Follows procedures and adheres to guidelines.	①	②	③	④	⑤
5. Maintains appropriate personal grooming.	①	②	③	④	⑤

INSIGHT BOX 7.1

Focusing Expectations Using Discussion Exercises

The discussion exercise helps keep expectations focused and within a commonly accepted range. It also helps pinpoint potential problems. The Missouri Southern State University English department faculty members were asked to grade a set of student papers. The grades ranged from A to F on the same papers. Upon discussion, it was found that this was acceptable because the professors were stressing different things in their classes so their expectations related to specific elements differed. One instructor lowered a paper's letter grade for each misspelled word; other professors lowered grades only for massive numbers of misspellings. As long as everyone knew what was being stressed, there was a reasonable level of agreement and some common ground was established. The results were a lot closer in the same kind of exercise a year later.

The easiest way to avoid subjective and sometimes personal judgments found in both ratings scales and supervisor observations is to utilize assessment and evaluations methods that are grounded in specific work activities. Some approaches select representative work behaviors and observe these in the workplace. These are called **critical events** (or **critical incidents**) and are part of a comprehensive system known as **behaviorally anchored rating scales (BARS)**. A team of qualified human resource professionals identifies several critical incidents and defines levels of performance for each incident. For instance, contributions to a team project could be scaled from the top rating of "(5) fully participates by supporting the suggestions of others, seeking group consensus, and helping keep the group focused" to the bottom rating of "(1) engages in disruptive behavior, sidetracks the group with irrelevant suggestions, and occasionally exhibits combative attitudes." The BARS system uses either highly detailed scales with phrases like these or a few descriptors associated with a critical incident. For example, a frequent critical incident item is offering help. This can be scaled as: (5) frequently volunteers aid to other employees; (4) regularly aids others in his or her own group; (3) is willing to help, but must be asked; (2) offers aid only when directed to do so; (1) rarely offers help to others. This scale addresses only how frequently aid is offered. BARS scales are focused on a single aspect of behavior. It might be that an employee never offers to aid others, but when asked to do so gives good help and support. That behavior can be judged in several ways: from how easily help is rendered, to how good the help is, to the quality of interpersonal skills exhibited when help is being offered. Figure 7.2 on page 212 illustrates a BARS scale.

You may have had a teacher who appeared unconcerned and aloof when asked for help, but once helping began, was a superb teacher. Although we imagine that all good qualities go hand in hand, frequently they can and should be separated. Once identified, weaknesses such as being distracted or aloof can be developed into something else. If the teacher is told that something is wrong with his or her one-on-one sessions with students in need, how does the teacher know that the problem is the personal attribute of aloofness rather than his or her teaching skills? BARS types of systems allow discrete and focused attention on areas of needed development. Although BARS systems can be difficult to develop and validate (that is, to prove that they do fit the jobs being evaluated), they provide solid evidence for both summative and formative evaluations.

Evaluators use common graphic rating scales that are accompanied by brief summarizing comments or short descriptive narratives to summarize an impression of the

FIGURE 7.2
...

A Behaviorally Anchored Rating System (BARS) Scale

Employee Name: _____

Title: _____

Supervisor: _____

Date of Evaluation: _____

Regarding following procedures and adhering to guidelines, the employee:

_____ Frequently takes shortcuts.

_____ Misses a critical step on rare occasions.

_____ Follows the required steps but does not always check tracking form.

_____ Completes every step but may on occasion overlook a safety or quality guideline.

_____ Always completes every step without any shortcuts and complies with all safety and quality guidelines.

Biased Evaluation

In an exercise at San Diego State University, another problem was discovered. The faculty graded a set of papers. A year later they graded the same papers. The results were reversed. Papers that had been awarded A's the first time received C's and vise versa. It was discovered that there was an unintentional bias. The fictitious names of the essay writers were randomly assigned in the first grading: Mary, Nancy, Betty, Heather, Brittany, and Brandy. In the second grading, the names that had received A's were placed on the essays that had received C's and so on. It seems that the graders (evaluators) felt that Mary, Nancy, and Betty were serious students, as suggested by their "solid" names. Heather, Brittany, and Brandy were subconsciously perceived as being less academic and more party oriented. The graders rated the essays according to their own perceptions rather than the quality of the writing. To avoid this kind of unfair influence, some professors decided to cover the names on the essays until after the grade was determined.

In some kinds of tests, managers may be able to employ blind evaluation—a number might be used instead of the employees' names—but that option does not happen often. Our point is simple: Managers must be aware of potential problems like this and work to neutralize extraneous influences.

Evaluation Instrument

If you are charged with developing an evaluation instrument that will be used by more than one supervisor per employee, consider including a leveling factor. This negates the extreme effect of any one evaluator. The effect is seen in gymnastics and figure skating, where a judge can determine the outcome of a competition by rating one competitor higher or lower than deserved. By dropping the highest score and the lowest score, this bias is somewhat controlled.

Consider this example: Ten supervisors and fellow employees evaluate Bill on a five-point scale. The responses are:

Excellent =	5	Bill received 0
	4	Bill received 5
	3	Bill received 4
	2	Bill received 0
Poorest =	1	Bill received 1

Without leveling, the results are:
$$(4 \times 5) + (3 \times 4) + (1 \times 1) = 33 \div 10 = 3.3$$
Compare this to a leveled result:
$$(4 \times 4) + (3 \times 4) + (1 \times 0) = 28 \div 8 = 3.5$$

Here the highest (one of the 4s) and the lowest (1) scores have been dropped. Unfortunately, without the one out-of-line rating (the 1), the result would have been $(4 \times 5) + (3 \times 4) + (1 \times 0) = 32 \div 9 = 3.56$. This example also illustrates how averaging can be very misleading.

worker. These impressions are derived from the evaluators' interview or a more casual office discussion with the worker. Supervisor observations may utilize rating scales, but they add the direct observation of the work environment. The most systematic form of observation in the work environment is the BARS system that involves observations in the actual workplace based on agreed-upon events that represent or reflect work performance. They often conclude with some form of interview or discussion about observed and rated performance. They may also include brief descriptive narratives that are meant to summarize the scope of work and its effectiveness.

Another class of evaluation involves simulated work environments to observe a worker's or an applicant's ability to perform. This process is called an assessment center, and it is a tool used in a wide variety of work environments. An **assessment center** is a specialized environment in which an assessor observes an employee or job applicant participating in carefully designed and controlled activities. The center concept was conceived to help employees identify areas of strength and weakness, then enter training programs to remedy their weakness and develop their strengths. It is also used to screen potential employees, prepare an employee development plan, or select candidates for promotion. The assessment center is not a place, but rather a process. Assessment centers are professionally designed, and assessors—the personnel who conduct the centers—are professionally trained. Oftentimes, respected people in the position being assessed are added to the professional staff on a rotational assignment basis in order to provide a real-world dimension to the assessment. Activities of the assessment center include in-basket assign-ments, scheduling exercises, problem-solving activities, discussion groups, manufactur-ing simulations, and other simulations of work processes. The assessment center process provides insight into an individual's ability to use interpersonal skills when working with others, as well as revealing leadership potential. The detailed insights can form the basis for training and development programs that can be individualized for the employee. Assessment centers are used to train and select school principles and superintendents, police officers, corporate officers, manufacturing team leaders, and group leaders. While assessment centers are expensive, proponents argue that it is better to spend employee costs on initial screening rather than on frequent replacement and training.

Other methods for assessing and evaluating employees abound in the workplace. The methods used by your employer will be extremely important to your success as both manager and employee. Know these methods and use them to your advantage. Furthermore, these evaluation systems can require quite a bit of written narrative. Written elements must be clear and unbiased. They must reflect and describe observed behaviors and events. For the most part, the writing is carefully prescribed responses based on the items being evaluated.

Developing Measurable Goals

We have defined a goal as a general statement of direction, yet, evaluators emphasize the need to develop measurable goals. Progress toward an outcome is measurable. In the strictest technical sense, objectives are the measurable derivatives of a goal and one must learn to prepare easily measured objectives. Say that your goal is to improve profits. Your objective would be to improve them by at least a predetermined minimum percentage or quantity. A profit improvement of 1 or 2 percent may be adequate in one instance. In another, you may set the industry average as your minimum target. Your goal and its objec-tive could be quite similar. The goal may be "To meet or exceed the industry average for profit on an annual basis." Your objective would be, "In the forthcoming fiscal year, to match the projected 3 percent growth of industry profits."

That was not so difficult, was it? Now apply this formulation to human performance. Measurable goals (and their derived objectives) must be something that anyone can under-stand. This means that not only do your written statements involve numbers, but also that those numbers are countable quantities. Rankings are numbers that are not necessarily countable. Productivity is a countable outcome: How many products, deliveries, service calls, or customer orders are generated per employee hour? An increase in productivity is a measurable change that supports a measurable goal. These elements must be recognized and the quantifiable evidence must be included in your written evaluations.

Clearly, some goals can be measured and some cannot. A cannot-be-measured goal might be, "Recruit more minorities." Having more minorities on the staff does not mean that the increase in minority staff members was the result of the goal. The goal "Improve quality" is not measurable in this form either. What is quality? Is it fewer mistakes? Fewer complaints? Less waste? Even the laudable goal of improving quality requires definition before objectives can be derived from it.

In your writing, you must address these issues in clear, straightforward statements. The less vague and more concrete the goal statement, the easier it is to create realistic and meaningful objectives. Goals are not arbitrary. They serve a meaningful purpose for the organization. Ford Motor Company's slogan, "Quality is Job One," illustrates how a goal serves a purpose. Ford already achieved a relatively high-quality standard in the wake of an increasing import market. The import market was strong partly because of the per-ceived higher quality of imported automobiles. Ford needed to convince the public that it had recovered its standards of high quality. The slogan focuses on the goal of highest quality for both employees and customers. However, the resolve to "improve quality" is an incomplete measurement for employees. Specific objectives have to be developed and spelled out in detail in your writing.

In a countering parallel move, Toyota insists that its top of the line automobile, the Lexus, will always be made in Japan because of the high quality of Japanese workmanship. Based on a sampling of the percentage of parts that failed, the American standard has been found to be approximately five-hundred failures per millions parts. The Japanese standard is fifteen failures per million. This has lead Toyota to adopt more heavy robotics for spot-welding on its production lines. Toyota is now moving toward the concept of global or universal production lines, which means the parts will be of equivalent quality whether the model is a Camry produced in Georgetown, Kentucky, or a Celica assembled in Cincinnati, Ohio.

Specific objectives require a thorough understanding of the current level of performance. If you want to improve quality, then the definition of quality must be translated into every employee's work circumstance and job description. Quality can be measured as reducing waste in the stamping mill, paint shop, or parts supply. It may mean reducing assembly-line errors. It might also mean altering design so that the automobile is more durable and has a longer life. What is important is that you specify the essential component of the goal. Each of these objectives can have a specific target measurement if we know the level of performance at the starting point. To reduce waste to 1 percent of raw materials, for instance, means that waste must already be above 1 percent. Another approach targets a decrease in waste: We want to reduce waste by 5 percent. The reduction is easily calculated using the measure of waste and decreasing that measure by 5 percent. This means that if waste is measured at the quality control rejection rate of a finished door panel of ten panels per thousand, then a 5 percent reduction occurs when the rejection rate is nine and one-half panels per thousand. Because people are responsible for the actions that create door panels, they may also be capable of reaching the objective. Once goals and objectives are determined, they should be committed to paper for the employee and the supervisor to indicate their agreement with signatures.

It is important to be aware that the organization will usually get what it measures. Therefore, if the organization wants to reduce waste by 5 percent, the shop floor may well deliver on that goal, while reducing output by 10 percent or more. Slowing down the line and reworking material previously thrown away can reduce waste. For this reason, it is usually important to have an internally consistent set of goals that will lead to the overall outcome the organization wants. Structuring this set of goals and derivative objectives is a key managerial task.

Finally, be aware of problems inherent in establishing goals and objectives that require changes that are not under the control of the worker or work group. Material defects can cause waste or quality issues later. Are workers trained to identify defects in their raw materials? If not, how can they be held accountable for the defects? A reasonable way to develop goals is to collaborate with employees to write clearly understood and mutually accepted goal and objective statements. The problem here, however, is that employees, knowing that achieving goals will impact compensation, may lobby hard to make the goals and objectives easier to attain. In some cases, the debate over setting goals and objectives may continue unresolved through the rating period, leaving the manager and the employee in the tough situation of having to report performance for compensation determination without ever having agreed on the basis for the assessment.

Collaborative Goal Development

Individual goals for improvement in work performance must always be relevant to the organization's goals for profit or service (in not-for-profit organizations). The best method for developing individual goals is through collaboration. Collaboration is a requisite within a team or work group, but collaboration between a supervisor and an employee is also imperative. Collaborative teams can create shared goals and individual members can propose personal goals and objectives within the framework of the team goals. Supervisors typically work from predetermined goals and objectives for the unit and work with individual employees in defining individual goals.

What strategies might one employ to prepare collaborative goals? An effective approach involves the most participants and includes relevant data. Brainstorming is a good place to begin. A team or group meets in a work session with an agenda to define shared goals and to develop possible individual work goals. Individual goals are presented as generic goals that an employee can adopt and modify. In some cases, especially where a team is composed of professionals, individual goals may be drawn directly from the team goals and objectives. The collaborative process may also be part of the project planning. For instance, a design team for an automobile includes engineers, assembly specialists, market analysts, and others. The plan for a new model should have a clear schedule of due dates. Each specialist has the objective of completing work by the due date with a minimum of errors. A goal can be included to make adjustments to changes in the model within a defined time period. For the evaluation, the degree of timeliness for these modifications can be tracked. The main reason for tracking how long it takes to make alterations is for future model development. If it always takes the interior design team seventy-two hours to make alterations, why set a time frame of forty-eight hours? Unfortunately, many have had a bad experience with this approach. When those doing the work realize that the company is measuring for the purpose of setting performance goals, they slow down. The net result is that current performance suffers rather than future performance being enhanced. Instead, the role of defined objectives becomes one of improved planning in the next cycle. Careful planning reduces the down time of other team members as they wait for an update. Well-established and well-written objectives have an impact on the individual, the work team, and eventually the success of the company.

Collaborative goal development produces high levels of ownership. If you believe that the objectives are personal and not merely assigned by supervisors or influenced by other external factors, your level of commitment to the outcome will be high. Supervisors should develop methods of using employee input in goal development even for the shared or given goals that typically flow from the top as orders or mandates. When there is a set of mandated objectives, one means of gaining employee commitment is to involve them in interpreting the goals for their own work settings. When there is a need to decrease waste, a supervisor can ask for suggestions from employees about how to do this. Simply dictating that waste must be reduced may not produce the commitment needed to reach the objective.

Self-Evaluation

At some point in the evaluation process, most approaches require some form of self-appraisal or self-evaluation. Typically, self-evaluation involves the preparation of the next cycle of goals and objectives. Not only is this inescapable, but it is a common method used by supervisors to gain participation and commitment, especially when the results are put in writing.

What should you be able to accomplish by asking an employee to prepare a self-evaluation? Often, a required self-evaluation sets expectations through a prescribed formula of stating accomplishments, assessing how well the goals in the previous cycle were met, and stating objectives for the next cycle. It is rare that the instructions for self-evaluation prohibit the individual from adding comments and reflections. A required self-evaluation provides an excellent opportunity for an employee to inform and continue to remind supervisors of the employee's life ambitions as well as recent successes. In preparing a self-evaluation that involves a restrictive, preset form, encourage the employee to add a page or two of the employee's own thoughts. If no directions are given whatsoever, then address the following items:

- State your personal and professional long-term goals.
- Identify the strengths that you have acquired through time and practiced recently.
- List your accomplishments since the last self-report (as a matter of making a record).

- Identify the goals and objectives of the last cycle and indicate the extent to which you achieved and exceeded these objectives.
- Analyze current and anticipated opportunities that you expect in your work.
- Use the analysis of opportunities to formulate achievable objectives that exploit the anticipated opportunities and challenges.

Self-evaluation is an opportunity for self-reflection. There may be some aspects of your performance that you would like to improve. These can be woven into the self-evaluation as targeted objectives or personal goals. People tend to overstate their abilities and set potentially impossible goals and objectives for themselves unless it is clear that attainment of these goals and objectives will affect compensation. When compensation plays a role, the goals and objectives can suddenly become ridiculously easy to achieve. In a self-appraisal, it is sometimes difficult to see anything but the positive. It is not necessary to report your negatives to anyone, but this process will help you to find ways to address them. For example, it may be possible to claim sufficient organizational budget to support a training class by raising the issue in this way. Analysis of why a goal or objective was not met may also help understand what is needed to meet it if it appears on the next plan.

Evaluation Reports

An evaluation is a report. You must follow a defined strategy in preparing it, even in cases in which the mechanism includes specified codes and forms to be submitted. Forms should have places for comments and you must decide when to comment, when not to comment, and what to include in your comment. Just as the assessment and evaluation process is aimed at providing guidance for an employee and establishing a basis for retention, recognition, and promotion, the objectives of the evaluation process are related to your work as a supervisor.

The guiding strategy for this kind of writing, whether it is a few comments added to a form or a formal, multipage report on the fitness of an employee, is that the writing and the evaluation should make a difference. When you have finished the report, ask yourself if it will result in an improvement. If you cannot answer why the report is being completed, it may be time to question the process itself. Too often reports are filed without any anticipation of the consequences. What power does a poor performance report or a reprimand have if the recipients file it away? People who do not like their workplace typically believe that performance is neither rewarded nor punished and that dismissals come for reasons other than performance. Although this may be more perception than reality, it can be a strong perception. A manager must find a way to make evaluations be valuable and meaningful exercises.

Copy to the Evaluated Individual

The report probably has the greatest effect for the individual being evaluated. The degree of effectiveness requires a sincere effort to communicate honestly and fairly throughout the process. A copy of the evaluation with a cover note praising the employee's achievements as well as reinforcing the plan of development should be given to the employee. *Constructive criticism* offered in a reasonable way to help the employee see where and how job performance can be improved is a managerial strategy tool that benefits the employee and the employer. If you are recommending promotion or merit pay, the employee will be glad to see the support you have given. Such a report can lead to even better performance by the employee. *If you are recommending termination or some other punitive action, consult your corporate policy or legal representative before writing your report on the employee.*

An evaluation is seldom the single basis for termination. However, the evaluation is the part of the process that is used to state expectations for improvements in performance. If the evaluation results in potentially bad news, you must be clear about the consequences and the acceptable remedies. Do not hint at dire consequences; you might discover that in most instances vague comments (and threats) can be evidence of harassment. If the penalty for failing to meet expected objectives is termination, demotion, or transfer, you need to state that explicitly.

If you are recommending a promotion or placement in a promotion queue, be sure that you do not make promises that are beyond your control. A recommendation on your part may not carry the weight that you would like. Worse, the employee may not know the extent of your authority to promote individuals and award merit pay. Your credibility rides on the promises that you make and that you keep. Many evaluation processes require that you get the concurrence of your supervisor before informing the employee of his or her evaluation.

Copy to the Supervisory Hierarchy

We cannot stress enough the care and strategic considerations for the employee and the supervisory chain that you must exercise when writing evaluations. A negative evaluation can be couched in humane terms, but it must not be sugarcoated to the extent that the employee does not realize that there is a problem or that there are suggestions as to how to improve his or her performance. For example, if your secretary does not finish typing assignments in a timely manner, you can suggest that the "employee needs to concentrate on time management" or "task prioritizing" during the coming evaluation period.

If it is possible that the employee may need to be fired, a detailed record of poor performance and recommended actions for improvement must be established (part of the critical reason for careful writing). When you are unsure about what *can* be written and what *must* be written, consult with the human resources manager or corporate legal counsel. Usually, you will not be alone with this; most companies and organizations have established guidelines that managers and supervisors are expected to follow.

Here are some guidelines to use as rules of thumb:

- Report what you can defend.
- Be sure to maintain a written record of activities, observations, and meetings.
- Do not sandbag. If a disciplinary action is recommended, it must be based on appropriate grounds, not on a series or collection of items that may each be sufficient for a disciplinary action (why was no action taken earlier?).
- Use reasoning tools to show the link between your assessment and recommended actions. A development plan is expected to increase productivity or performance, not make someone feel good about themselves.
- Your actions as a supervisor have an impact on you just as much as they have an impact on those who report to you.

An evaluation report sent up the chain of command can be formative or summative, since an evaluation can perform either or both tasks. When evaluations are for an entire group, a set of actions should be enumerated to indicate efforts to improve performance. These actions should be collected and reported in either a regular report or a special report.

A proposed employee development plan will require the allocation of financial and human resources. The allocation of these resources requires authorization. Development funds usually fall into the category of expenditures that can be delayed in times of economic distress. They may come and go in the annual budgets of companies as well as in nonprofit organizations. In government agencies, annual funding cycles show marked differences in the area of employee development from one budget cycle to the next. This is one of the main reasons that government agencies have difficulty keeping long-term professional staff. Employee development is often among the first "luxuries" to be cut.

Reporting a plan for employee development may be the first step in obtaining the funds for the activities. Those in the supervisory chain of command need to know that you have devised an effective and productive human resource development plan in addition to the individual recommendations that you have made.

SECTION SUMMARY

Management involves guiding people to accomplish work-related tasks and reaching shared organizational goals. In addition, a manager must also be able to assess and evaluate the performance of individual workers as well as teams of workers. Formative evaluation is the process of identifying places for improvement, while summative evaluation focuses on cyclic goals and performance standards. The most common method used to evaluate employees is a graphic rating scale, although other scales and systems are available, including the BARS system and the assessment center. The ability to write clear, measurable objectives that are derived from specific goals is important for meaningful evaluation as well as self-evaluation. Managers must take care in the words they use and the behaviors they document in reporting an evaluation both to the employees and to the supervisors.

CHALLENGE PROBLEM FOR REVIEW

The concept of setting objectives for achievement has become suspect in its application. Too often employees have subverted the process by working to reduce the level of difficulty of the objectives so that achieving the highest evaluation is less demanding. The net effect, summed over the workforce of a large organization, can devastate performance. More recently, companies have moved toward profit-sharing programs to get employees aligned with the goals and objectives of the company. Without this dimension, MBO can be a problem. What other solutions do you think might be attempted?

CHAPTER SUMMARY
...

There are several methods of guiding others through writing. In some cases, such as in giving directions, writing can be either the primary means or an auxiliary means to verbal directions. Management style may also dictate approaches that focus on process or on goals. Writing also can be used to strengthen group and team participation. Employees who are given directions to accomplish a task must know the extent of their authority, when the task should be completed, and how to give feedback regarding the task.

Writing serves as a means of reinforcing the mentoring role that some managers have. Trainees benefit from direct contact with a mentor, but the mentor can use writing to extend a coaching session and to recognize the quality of work being done by the protégé. Establishing writing goals and objectives and maintaining a record of the coaching experience are additional roles for writing in coaching.

Assessments and evaluations are core activities of a manager; they require careful writing. Managers often produce written records, and these records serve as a foundation for the formative and summative evaluation processes. Employee development depends on an understanding of the current performance level of an employee and the target level of performance. Working with subordinates to develop meaningful goals and objectives also requires carefully articulated and recorded goals and objectives and a means of measuring those goals, all of which can be put into writing that involves careful application of suitable strategies.

CHECKLIST: ORGANIZING YOUR WRITING FOR A GENERAL EVALUATION REPORT
...

_____ What is the job description?
_____ How well does the employee perform the duties outlined in the job description? You should address each aspect of the job individually and rate the overall performance. Are there areas in which the employee excels? Are there areas in which the employee is deficient?

_____ Has the employee improved since the last evaluation?
_____ Is some sort of merit recognition in order?
_____ Should the employee be promoted?
_____ s the employee willing to work at improving areas of deficiency?
_____ Should the employee be retained or moved to another division within the company?
_____ What might the employee do to improve job performance?
_____ Is the employee cooperative?
_____ Does the employee work well with peers?
_____ Does the employee comply with company regulations?
_____ Does the employee show initiative?

EXERCISES
...

Prewriting Exercises
1. List a set of objectives or goals for you to accomplish in terms of the material presented in this class. Be specific and comprehensive.
2. Collect examples from work or school of written documents (memos, notices, reports, proposals, etc.) that are well-written and examples of documents that are poorly written. Explain the elements in the well-written documents that led you to judge them well-written. Rewrite the poorly written documents to improve them.

Writing Exercises
1. Compose a sample memo that might be used as a general template for a follow-up after verbally assigning a task to an employee whom you are supervising.
2. If you have been mentored, describe your experience in terms of what approaches, procedures, or processes were successful (and why they were successful) and which were not successful (and why they were not successful).
3. Evaluate your own skills and weaknesses.
4. Compare and contrast your skills and weaknesses with the skills needed for the job that you intend to seek (this may require research into the skills needed for that particular job).
5. Put into practice the good news/bad news strategies delineated in Chapter 5 and write both a good news version and a bad news version of the cover letter for your analysis of how well your job search for the position in Item 6.

_____

_____

_____

_____

_____

_____

_____

_____

_____

_____

_____

_____

_____

_____

_____

_____

_____

_____

_____

_____

_____

_____

_____

_____

_____

IN-BOX EXERCISE

...

IN-BOX

SHG General regularly partakes of the services of Wilder Investing, a multifaceted financial firm that provides financial planning, life insurance, brokerage, and a variety of other personal and professional consulting services. As a manager within the personal division of SHG, your focus is on business planning.

ITEM 1: E-MAIL FROM GINGER HUGHES, YOUR IMMEDIATE SUPERVISOR.

Since your department has been in operation for only about a year, and you have quite a number of new employees and trainee-level staff, I would like you to develop a mentoring program for your employees. You may want to be a mentor yourself, but be sure to assign all your senior staff to some mentoring duties. The division, and especially your department, is poised to expand rapidly; we need to have everyone ready to take on the mission.

Your Response

Check one: ☐ Memorandum ☐ E-mail ☐ Letter ☐ Note ☐ Other

To: _____

_____

_____

_____

_____

_____

_____

_____

_____

_____

_____

_____

_____

_____

_____

_____

_____

_____

_____

_____

_____

_____

_____

_____

_____

ITEM 2: PERLEY, TEAM LEADER FOR SMALL BUSINESS FINANCIAL CONSULTING, WILDER INVESTING. Glad you have been appointed! I think everyone has been on their own for a few weeks but it seems like months. I hope you can straighten things out.

Your Response

Check one: ☐ Memorandum ☐ E-mail ☐ Letter ☐ Note ☐ Other

To: _____

_____

_____

_____

_____

_____

_____

_____

_____

_____

_____

_____

_____

_____

_____

_____

_____

_____

_____

_____

_____

_____

_____

_____

_____

_____

_____

_____

_____

ITEM 3: E-MAIL FROM SIMON, OFFICE SYSTEMS COORDINATOR. I know I have only been here for a month, but I have a had a number of instances where it seems that the "old-timers" can't answer my questions about specific benefits, procedures, and investing options. I need to meet with you at your earliest convenience.

Your Response

Check one: ☐ Memorandum   ☐ E-mail   ☐ Letter   ☐ Note   ☐ Other

To: _____

_____

_____

_____

_____

_____

_____

_____

_____

_____

_____

_____

_____

_____

_____

_____

_____

_____

_____

_____

_____

_____

_____

_____

_____

_____

_____

_____

_____

_____

ITEM 4: MEMORANDUM (ON PAPER!) FROM GRACE, ACCOUNTS COORDINATOR.

TO: You

RE: Account Procedures

For each account you manage or for which you are assigned time, you must record the time on the appropriate time sheets. We have been charged by Wilder Investing on two different accounts from the same form. This is only one problem we have been facing with records for accounts. The problem appears to be in-house, not with Wilder. Until everyone complies with the time charges, we cannot track the other missing information. Please comply.

Your Response

Check one: ☐ Memorandum   ☐ E-mail   ☐ Letter   ☐ Note   ☐ Other

To: _____

_____

_____

_____

_____

_____

_____

_____

_____

_____

_____

_____

_____

_____

_____

_____

_____

_____

_____

_____

_____

_____

_____

ITEM 5: E-MAIL FROM SIMON, OFFICE SYSTEMS COORDINATOR. One of my systems people asked me about our policy related to cost-sharing for additional/higher levels of life insurance. That raised some questions in my mind regarding financial planning. Because I am new to the company, I do not know who to contact for this information.

Your Response

Check one: ☐ Memorandum   ☐ E-mail   ☐ Letter   ☐ Note   ☐ Other

To: _____

_____

_____

_____

_____

_____

_____

_____

_____

_____

_____

_____

_____

_____

_____

_____

_____

_____

_____

_____

_____

_____

_____

_____

_____

_____

_____

KEY TERMS
...

Assessment (p. 208)

Assessment center (p. 213)

Behaviorally anchored rating scale, (BARS) (p. 211)

Coaching (p. 203)

Critical events (critical incidents) (p. 211)

Delegation (p. 201)

Employee development (p. 209)

Evaluation (p. 208)

Formative evaluation (p. 208)

Goal (p. 206)

Goal-directed strategy (p. 198)

Graphic rating scale (p. 209)

Journal (see Work diary)

Management by objectives (MBO) (p. 198)

Mentoring (p. 203)

Process-oriented management (p. 197)

Objective (p. 206)

Quality circles (p. 200)

Self-directed team (p. 199)

Self-managed team (p. 200)

Summative evaluation (p. 209)

Training (p. 204)

Work diary (p. 206)

Writing portfolio (p. 207)

REFERENCES
...

W. L. Gore & Associates. (2004). "About: Culture." http://www.gore.com/about/culture.html (accessed July 30, 2004).

PART 2
...

ESSENTIAL TOOLS *for* MANAGERIAL WRITING

CHAPTER 8

OPTIMIZING *the* ELECTRONICALLY INTEGRATED WORKPLACE

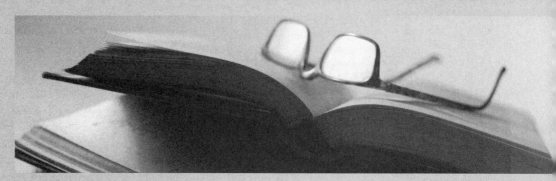

LEARNING OUTCOMES
...

Upon completion of this chapter, you will be able to accomplish the following tasks:

1. Identify and select the appropriate means of delivering information and communicating using electronic media for a particular task.

2. Know the basic terminology of the electronically connected office.

3. Discuss the range of basic issues unique to communication that takes place in the electronically connected workplace.

4. Name and identify basic tools that facilitate electronically based communication.

5. Know how to use essential writing-enhancing utilities.

6. Recognize and avoid critical problems that can accompany the tools of the electronic office.

7. Know and be able to use the basic protocols of electronically facilitated communication.

8. Recognize and evaluate effective means of communicating via the Internet and the World Wide Web and know the common forms of Internet-based communication.

9. Identify and employ strategies appropriate to electronic communication.

10. Recognize efficient uses of electronic communication tools.

"No, Thursday's out. How about never—is never good for you?"

Typewriters have joined the collection of obsolete office tools that can be traced all the way back to quill pens and clay tablets. Like the quill pen, a typewriter is now rarely seen in a modern office. Eventually, even word processing tools may be challenged by voice-to-text software. The standard office now includes a personal computer with word processing, spreadsheet, and database software; a personal organizer; and office scheduling programs. In most circumstances, the office computer is connected to a private **local area network** (**LAN**) and to the Internet.

Replacement of one tool with another frequently means expansion of possibilities and potential. Electronic spreadsheet programs that almost any well-informed manager can manipulate and use have replaced ledger sheets. Database management programs have replaced index card files (a relic even in libraries). These programs produce highly shareable and integrated data. If we look back only a short time ago, the office of the early 1970s was filled with IBM Selectric Typewriters, Rolodex business-card files, Dictaphone machines, reel-to-reel tape recorders, and other pieces of office equipment that today's manager might think belong in museums and antique stores. In the 1970s, fax machines were just coming of age and Teletype was the standard for critical instant-information broadcast. In 1970, the network that was to become the Internet had its first birthday.

The telecommunications revolution joined the computer revolution in the 1970s, and together they transformed the modern office—composed of banks of typewriters and oversized calculators—into the fast-paced, ear-to-the-cell-phone world of e-everything in the new millennium. We now move from place to place and carry our virtual office with us. We are never out of touch.

After three decades of modernizing telecommunications and office machines, the business world is reaping the benefits of increased productivity and efficiency. This ever-changing world of electronic gadgetry requires special strategies. In fact, the pace of activity requires that the strategies for communication become a matter of reflex-like habit. Errors become ever more difficult to retract. The failure to plan and implement an effective writing strategy based on reasoning can result in serious errors. Before the electronic revolution, an assistant may have checked as he or she typed a letter or reviewed grammar and style before sending a message to a wide audience. More and more, managers use the quick tools of today's office to write and type their own work and even mail it automatically.

The automated, electronically wired, high-technology office must be carefully navigated. In addition to using these tools within the office environment for intracompany communications, many people have a growing list of contacts with whom they maintain informal, and even formal, communication links. In this chapter, you will see some of these changes and how they affect management-level writing.

Strategies for Managing Communication in the Integrated Office

Written communication now occurs in every imaginable medium. Each means of communicating has advantages and disadvantages with associated communication errors.

The range of methods for conveying a written message has multiplied dramatically with the revolution in information technology (IT), including both telecommunications and computing technology. While the potential for effective communication increases with each innovation, few innovations completely replace previous methods. Consider one of the most common business tools today, the portfolio. Often made of fine leather, today's portfolio—a notebook-like, hand-carried folder—may hold the best of miniaturized technology, typically a calculator and an electronic **personal data assistant** (**PDA**). Traditionally, these are placed on the left side of the portfolio among its many organizer pockets. On the right side, there is the ubiquitous, lined notepad. Although we may not have imagined an improvement on the notepad—especially since it fits so comfortably beside the other high-tech tools—improvements are on the way. For several hundred dollars, one can buy a portfolio with a special component that the user places below the notepad page on which he or she is writing. This cardboard-like material senses the pressure of the writer's pen or pencil (or a special stylus). The program learns the owner's handwriting and converts it to text. The text can be uploaded to a computer for storage and further processing. Unlike the PalmPilot type of PDA, this newer technology allows the writer to keep the original paper copy as well as the converted electronic text. The new technology is composed of PC tablets, laptop notepads, and tablet laptops, laptop computers with screens that double as writing tablets.

We are unlikely to see a single method of communication replaced by another. In fact, we should anticipate that the example of the integration of the notepad and the computer will be a model of communication technology. However, this does not mean that strategies for managing office communications can stay the same. As the time from conception to printed copy to transmission shrinks, the potential for errors increases. Common errors of grammar and style may be forgivable, but rarely are they separated from the impression that they leave with the receiver of the message. A central part of the strategy for office communications and informal corporate communications must be one of habitual review and revision prior to hitting the "send" button. In fact, one associate of the authors leaves the address field blank until he has completed and reviewed his message. If he accidentally hits "send," the message has nowhere to go!

Basic Electronic Media Strategies

You might wonder why an entire chapter is devoted to a discussion of items that are in reality variations of memos, letters, and reports. In fact, electronic media is merely the medium by which these conventional writing products are transmitted to their audience.

E-mail, the most common contemporary form of technology-mediated written communication, provides the paradigm for this transformation as well. Once considered an offspring of e-mail, the **instant message (IM)** has taken on a life of its own. Faxes, teleconferences, **online forums** with live **chat rooms**, and **asynchronous communication** have expanded the number of means by which we communicate. Each of these has its weaknesses and strengths. As a manager, you must be able to negotiate these effectively and to take advantage of all of the functionality of the technology.

E-Mail Strategies

The effect of e-mail on personnel, on the formal contact with customer or client, and on informal communications with business associates cannot be underestimated. Many managers complain of the vast number of e-mail messages that they must review and for which they must formulate responses. Upper-level managers may receive several hundred messages a day. Recently, a newly appointed university president returned from her interview to find over 1,500 e-mail messages awaiting her. Inundated, some CEOs simply turn their e-mail over to an assistant or remove themselves from the system completely. An analogy of e-mail to the medieval introduction of gunpowder has been made: The gun made it possible for peasants to kill knights. Before its introduction, knights fought knights, and serfs fought serfs. Before e-mail, paper messages filtered through a predefined hierarchy. In the twenty-first century, customers, clients, staff, and line workers all can e-mail top managment. Even if the policy requires that communicants follow the hierarchy, policy and protocol may be breached. Also, when followed appropriately, the "cc:" and "copy to" options result in e-mail being sent directly to a supervisor without the benefit of preview and buffering by a secretary or administrative assistant.

It is important to keep in mind the various purposes of the memorandum (of which e-mail is one form). The traditional purposes of the memo and types of letters are described in the Table 8.1.

The problems generated by e-mail abound. First, a vast number of messages must be reviewed. Second, responses require time and effort that increase workloads. Third, responses need to be appropriate to the original sender. (It is the nature of most e-mail to sound like a telegraphed message, with much shorthand being used and many message

TABLE 8.1
...

Purposes of Memos and Types of Letters Review

Five Basic Purposes of Memos
1. To Inform
2. To Create a Record
3. To Transmit a Report
4. To Request an Action
5. To Transmit a Memorandum of Understanding

Three Basic Types of Letters
1. Letters that Request Information
2. Letters that Request Action
3. Letters that Inform (offer good news or bad news or "transmit" a document)

elements missing.) Often, the recipient must decipher more than the surface meaning of the message. Sometimes the effort to decipher may result in misinterpretation. Fourth, tracking the results is perhaps the greatest weakness—follow-up techniques require integrating the message into other software (like a reminder or calendar program). Fifth, decisions about who else needs to be informed and at what point in an e-mail exchange other recipients need to be included always pose a challenge. Simply copying every communication to a supervisor only inundates the supervisor. If a general manager has five plant managers with each of them responding to twenty e-mail messages a day and copying the general manager, then the general manager receives an additional 100 messages per day. Should he or she answer or acknowledge each one?

With all this, what approach or approaches can you take? Following a systematic approach works best. Begin by developing a reasonable tactic for reviewing incoming e-mail first, then follow a strategy for responses that is most appropriate for your work activity. Consider the following strategies:

Organize the E-Mail Every recipient of e-mail should develop a simple, efficient means of reviewing incoming messages.

Most people check their e-mail the first thing each morning. Excellent time managers check their voice mail while the computer is booting up and loading their e-mail messages. Sometimes, a voice-mail message might be answerable by way of an e-mail. Some callers followup an unanswered call with an e-mail.

While the two systems are not commonly linked, a fully integrated workplace now includes message software that lists both e-mail and voice mail. Some can convert the voice to text and the text (e-mail) to voice. A common error that people make is to start down the list of new e-mails and answer each one as it is opened and read.

A smarter approach is to use the e-mail program's filing system and place each e-mail in an appropriate folder. Most programs allow the user to establish filters that automatically place an e-mail in the appropriate folder. This allows the user to recognize patterns and identify groups in the e-mail. How often have you responded to an e-mail only to open the next e-mail from the same person that either asks another question, says to ignore the first e-mail, or completely reverses the earlier message (making your answer or response wrong)? Organize the e-mail messages into folders that reflect who sent them.

Read the Messages in Groups Read the last e-mail from a person first, but read them all before you respond.

If you have three messages from one person, read them all before you respond, in reverse order. Why? The sender may have found the answer before you had a chance to respond. This will save you three or four lengthy paragraphs that merely duplicate work that has already been completed. As you review the message group, identify what the sender wants. Are you to undertake an action, confirm receipt, or provide information? Is the message a response to one of your e-mails or to others' initiatives?

Some priority of response may also be established at this time. If the sender cannot continue with an activity until you respond, then you should place this action at the top of the list. If the sender is simply keeping you informed about the progress of an activity, then a response can be delayed.

Respond to Messages Systematically Just as you review messages in a systematic manner, whether you read from last to earliest or follow your own strategy, you must also respond in a systematic manner.

This becomes especially important if you have grouped several messages in order to prepare one response. Be sure to inform the recipient that your e-mail response covers several e-mail messages. E-mail programs can be set to include the entire series of communication from the first e-mail to the most recent message, but it only does so for messages that are replies from one to another. If you have grouped the messages, the inclusion of those messages not in the reply chain is important. The recipient may not realize that you are responding to all of the messages unless you explicitly say so.

This careful response requires that you pay attention to who received the original messages and copies of replies. If you are asking for more information prior to making a complete response, you may want to communicate only with the originator. If you are making a complete or final response, then take care to involve everyone who was originally contacted. With communication occurring with such fluidity, people can become upset (and even suspicious) if they get dropped from the loop.

Organize Your Sent Messages The greatest challenge in mastering e-mail is that of systematic and meaningful follow-up.

E-mail programs have the capacity for reminders, calendars, auto-replies, and tickler files. However, few people take advantage of these functions. Add-on software for managing business contacts is fairly inexpensive, and this software can also be used to track projects. Complex projects involving large numbers of people can be managed with more sophisticated software, but at some level, the management of projects and participants may need to be assigned to a specific person. Nevertheless, for normal daily or routine activities, you should activate the reminder and calendar systems in your e-mail and addressbook software.

Instant Message (IM) Strategies

America Online (AOL) and Netscape pioneered the availability of **instant messages** or **IMs**. ICQ, Yahoo!, and others offered instant messaging earlier, but AOL and Netscape brought the communication technique to a broad public. Although IMs remain atypical for the workplace, many employees engage this free software through a connection provided across the Internet by a partnership between AOL and Netscape. Employees can communicate instantly without using the phone, and they can maintain multiple discussions simultaneously. Working parents can tell when their children or spouses are online and can communicate quick messages. Because instant messages must be typed, they tend to be short.

A common instant message panel

The value of this communication tool to employers has yet to be realized. The IM program maintains **buddy lists** that can show who is online, who is available, who is away from their desks, and other critical messages that are time savers. An employee can modify the "I'm away from my computer" message with specific whereabouts. The message "I am in a meeting" can be useful. Employed effectively, IM could become an important scheduling tool for telephone calls and netconferencing.

As yet underdeveloped in the workplace, this simple dialogue tool could soon become a useful aspect of office communication. Several hints for how to manage the tool may help us get ready for this innovation. First, being short and direct is the key to effective IM use. Any time you find yourself beginning to type long IM messages, it is time, instead, for an e-mail or a phone call. In fact, IM can be used to notify the recipient that you are trying to call or are about to send an important e-mail message. If the long discussion persists, it may be appropriate to move the conversation to a meeting or teleconferencing format.

Security appears to be the major concern for instant messaging. IM does not have the same level of protection or audit trail that e-mail has. Once the security issue is solved to the satisfaction of information technology administrators, then IM will become widely used.

Conference Tools Strategies: Chat Room and Discussion Pages

Some offices create **discussion forums** (also called **threaded discussions** and **discussion boards**) for important topics that are in initial development stages. These are placed on a

Here is a typical discussion thread from a discussion board.

These discussion forums, secure server on an internal Internet (**intranet**), **wide area network** (**WAN**), through dedicated telecommunication lines, or a **virtual private network** (**VPN**), a secure network that is distributed through the Internet. Intranets, WANS, and VPNs are accessible only to authorized personnel.

These discussion forums, or discussion pages as they are often called, allow simultaneous and extended discussions of critical topics. The simultaneous discussion pages are called chat rooms, and Internet-based meetings take advantage of the instant chat or message and often occur in tandem with **teleconferences**. Other tools that can be used at the same time include the computer-based **whiteboard**, on which each participant can mark on the text or graphics being viewed. Each participant has his or her own color marker, and typed discussion or live teleconference accompanies the activity.

A chat room used for instructional purposes.

These tools are currently underutilized, but when used, they enhance communication among project team members or employees without requiring them to be in the same location. Soon, these tools will be more effectively and widely exploited for cost savings and clarity of communication, especially as broadband connections become more readily available. Even so, today they remain fairly clumsy and depend on sometimes temperamental technology.

The person responsible for leading a conference based on chat rooms or discussion threads and online-shared whiteboards must focus on planning how to manage messages and the several media involved. Sometimes, limitations can speed communication by reducing the potential for confusion. If more than five people use a chat room or a whiteboard, communication can bog down. Tracking who is speaking or who is marking on the workspace becomes complicated. As a result, the medium becomes the focus of activity rather than the instrument for communicating a message. People in different locations can also become easily distracted. To avoid this, specify the particular purpose of the discussion and keep the activity focused. Be sure to give participants sufficient time to make and develop their points, and maintain a record of each suggestion, each agreement, and any assignments for follow-up that the participants may have. This kind of meeting should be followed with a clear memo, perhaps electronic, in which the process, the consensus that was reached, and the specifics of assignments are reviewed and summarized. Seek a reply from each participant to record that he or she agrees with the items reported in the memo. Be sure that future assignments developed in the meeting include continued tracking of the progress of whatever was recommended and whatever agreements were reached.

Whatever mechanism enters the workplace, you must keep in mind that it is there to facilitate work, not to become the work itself. Treat the activity and its outcomes as you would any other meeting or conference. Do not presume that everyone comes away from the conference with the same understanding of what happened and what agreements had been reached. Use e-mail, memos, or letters—whichever is most appropriate to your participants—to establish closure.

Strategies for Routine Office Communication

How often are office communication channels used to announce the birth of puppies or a pending yard sale at an employee's home? Such messages are clutter in an uncontrolled e-mail system, and they can clog even the most powerful system. This clutter gets mingled with crucial corporate announcements and related messages and has led corporations to find alternative methods for employees to use the electronic tools available to them for social announcements. Consider the following strategies to separate corporate and noncorporate messages while continuing to provide employees much-needed social communication.

Newsletters and Company Bulletins

Give space in newsletters and company bulletins, even online bulletins, to social information. If the space is not provided, then employees usually create their own equivalent, typically through the e-mail system. Even if this requires preparation costs, the savings in extraneous communication costs can be great. The human relations value gained by enabling communication that is secondary to the corporate mission may be difficult to document, and its positive effect on worker loyalty may not be measurable, either. However, the inability to quantify does not mean that it is not desirable. In fact, more people may read the newsletter because it contains such information.

Announcements, Group Memoranda, and Postings

The bulletin board has gone electronic. Many companies include announcement pages on their private intranet. The cost of Web space is relatively low and, locked behind a password, this information is available only to employees. Another form of announcement is the group e-mail function. This is probably the most abused format. In addition to legitimate communication, anyone with an e-mail account can send mass mailings of jokes, devotional messages, e-mail scams, and so on. These should be controlled through policy and loss of privilege for the abuser. Unfortunately, **spam**, which now requires significant time to erase, is not in the control of the receiver.

Group memoranda need to be sent with caution. Some people read group and mass e-mail with care; others ignore them. Unfortunately, as mentioned, some managers like to send every notice and information item through group announcements. More conscientious managers reserve this practice for specifically important information. The result is that recipients learn the habits of their managers and alternately ignore or give the most cursory

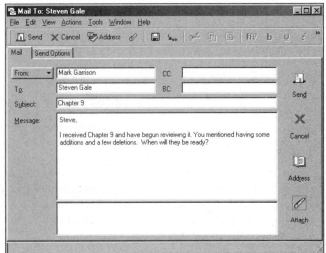

E-mail screen with partial text. Note the spelling error. Even the simple messages should be spell-checked before being sent.

review to some messages. The tendency for recipients to stereotype the sender's messages can be handled with careful attention to the **subject line** of the e-mail. While this line is important for a regular memo, it is much more critical for e-mail because of the physical e-mail format. When on paper, the subject line is physically linked to the body of the memo. In e-mail, the subject line may be all that the recipient views at first, and any further reading requires a mouse click or other minor action. The inherent consequence of this format is the tendency to ignore the message content.

Another aspect of the e-mail format, after the "subject line" feature, is that the equivalent of one page of text on a paper memo does not appear in the viewing area of an e-mail. The clarity and attention-getting first few lines determine the likelihood of whether a message will be ignored or read. Just to see the equivalent of a one-page memo in an e-mail requires the reader to scroll down. Again, this format makes the first few lines particularly crucial. Although the subject line should grab the attention of the reader, the first four or five lines must provide an encapsulated summary.

Success with office and contact communications requires you to be comfortable with a wide array of communication tools. These tools can quickly overwhelm the unprepared employee. Thus, the beginning of any strategy for effective office communications must be to become familiar and comfortable with the means of communication commonly used in your office.

SECTION SUMMARY

Because of the ease and quickness with which people can generate electronic communications, it is imperative to be able to handle large numbers of messages. Simple strategies to manage e-mail involve organizing incoming messages into groups so they can be read and responses sent quickly and systematically. This approach should be included in your strategies for working with routine forms of office communications as well.

CHALLENGE PROBLEM FOR REVIEW

Most people evolve their strategies for dealing with routine communication through a trial-and-error approach or even more "after-the-fact." What makes you sure that you will be different? It is also easy to assert that you won't make those mistakes, but this is clearly one of those "best-laid plans" situations. Many beginning managers, not to mention higher-level managers, cope with hundreds of e-mails every day. Do you have a plan? What is it?

Formatting Office Processes

Like memoranda, many office tools—both software and hardware—preset the physical format and look of transmitted documents. Because so much of the message is preformatted, the writer can focus on content.

KEY CONCEPT 8.2
...

E-Mail Format and Contact Management

Closely connected to the content, the format of e-mail requires some attention. While e-mail programs allow customization of the **interface** (how it looks and is configured on the screen), most people make only minor adjustments in the preset look of their e-mail messages. Indeed, it may be bad form to make your office e-mail overly personalized. Sometimes, customizing e-mail can result in making responses more difficult. Even a change as minor as using a large font that requires the receiver to enlarge the screen to read the message can be an unnecessary distraction. When inundated with numerous e-mail messages, even the slightest aggravation may be seen as a lack of consideration on the sender's part.

What are the common features of e-mail? E-mail programs have menu selections that allow attaching files, replying to the sender, replying to the sender and all recipients, forwarding the e-mail, and other controllable options. Some of these options can be set as default actions. When replying, should you always include a copy of the original e-mail? This choice depends on the amount of e-mail "traffic" to which a person is subject. In environments with low amounts of traffic, copying the reply may not be necessary. In high traffic environments, a copy provides a quick reminder of the context.

Should replies automatically include all recipients? This depends on the content of the message. A group e-mail (or memorandum) regarding preferred vacation dates does not require that the responder send a copy to everyone, while a query that is copied to all parties involved but directed at one person does mandate a copy to everyone. In essence, the rules that you follow in replying to a memorandum should apply with e-mail. Unfortunately, copying everyone for the sake of protection is all too easy with an e-mail. Because automatic replies are an important consideration with potential wide-ranging consequences, you must devise a strategy for handling this concern that is based on your situation. That strategy may well involve several different kinds or levels of response, but the process of devising your strategy will help you understand the need and rationale for each type of response. It will also make the application of your response easy and quick.

Electronic Address Books

Recently, many business tools have evolved that can be used to keep track of addresses and these tools are fairly uniform in structure and function. The key point to keep in mind when selecting an address-book program is the ease of maintaining, updating, and exporting data from one location to another. A fully integrated office software package includes an address-book feature that effortlessly imports contact information as it comes to the desktop. An e-mail contact list should automatically fill in known information in an address book. Conversely, inputting a name and address into an address book in order to send a letter should also generate a contact in the e-mail contact lists. With a few minutes of clerical time, you can arrange your lists according to a logical grouping. Often, critical fields that are missing are highlighted (if an e-mail address is missing, an alert message is produced) and inputting the information should be relatively easy.

Contact Tracking

The address book is a central feature for all organizational and self-management tools. The purpose of this tool is to help the user maintain a list of frequent contacts and crucial information. Of course, you must balance the time costs against the time required to create a listing with comprehensive information and the usefulness of that information. The more contacts that you must maintain, the more useful the tool will be. An important principle that guides the selection and use of an address book and contact manager program is "write once; read everywhere." This means that you should be able to input data about a contact only once and then view and utilize that data throughout your electronic office.

A number of Web sites like those of Netscape, Microsoft, Yahoo!, and Alta Vista incorporate features in their customizable Web pages (pages that anyone can set as their Internet browser home page) that provide services such as address books, calendars, reminders, and stock watch lists. These free tools allow customers to access this information no matter where they may be. Imagine being on a business trip and needing quick access to information, yet being in a place that is inconvenient for booting up your laptop. You can access this information from any computer with an Internet connection. To ensure security, address books and calendars require a password. Additionally, you might want to limit the types of information that you store on the Internet (for instance, you can load the phone number and address of the contact and leave sensitive information on your office computer). Many corporations use VPNs that provide these services to their employees with advanced security. These VPNs are Internet-based networks. In contrast, WANS use public switched–voice telephone service, or leased telecommunication lines to maintain a distance network. Unlike the LAN, these networks are not confined to a building or campus of buildings. They can be reached through any available Internet connection (VPN) or through a dial-in service (WAN).

Basic Formats for Word Processing

The single greatest impact of computer technology on writing remains word processing. Dramatic changes in the flow of work have occurred because of the ever-increasing power and sophistication of word-processing software. Early forms of the software enabled tremendous strides in office communication, and now major programs are tightly integrated with e-mail, Web authoring, desktop publishing, image development, electronic personal managers, universal address books, databases, spreadsheets, and presentation tools. The software is so entwined with the whole spectrum of computer programs used for managing communications that users must engage in systematic planning in order not to be overwhelmed by the complexity of the process. Fortunately, a consistent, intuitive, and simple file-naming rubric and a manageable habit of storage and back up will keep the computer from becoming an electronic version of the cluttered desk.

Word processing is an unfortunate term because it suggests that some magical process transforms words into sentences, paragraphs, and even best-selling novels. The truth is that bad writers using a word-processing program will still write poorly, although they will produce poorly written documents more quickly and voluminously. A good writer uses a word-processing program to write a rough draft of a document, to revise the document, and then to print it. The major advantage of word processing is that a document need only be written once. The revising stage is much more efficient because words, phrases, and even paragraphs can be added, changed, moved, or deleted without having to retype the entire document. Maybe if we called this "keyboarding" with functions (copy, paste, etc.) we could remove the connotation of magic from the notion.

A newer form of word processing bypasses the typing stage and converts speech into text. Considering the potential of poor writing that can be associated with typing-based programs, one can only imagine what will come of this method of generating printed words. In fact, speech-to-text programs accentuate the poor quality of badly written communications. It is important to remember that even if one masters the various tools and functions of the fully integrated word processor, that does not mean that the written product will be better. However, the product may look nicer, get to its destination quicker, reflect greater efficiency, and even promote the author. The easiest solution to poor writing is not a better software program; it is more practice and systematic revision habits. We stress that these writing tools are mechanical in nature and that a good writing strategy demands an essential step that is aided but separate from these tools. Good writing requires that you take the time and care to rewrite, to hone your product until it says (and communicates) exactly what you want to say in exactly the way you want to say it. With this word of caution, the following formatting guidelines can be used in the well-managed electronic office.

Basic Universal Features

Word-processing programs have preset defaults for every function. Changing them is a matter of style and sometimes the organization may dictate certain formats and styles. They may require that the font be a certain size and type, such as Times Roman 12 point. The basic features can be altered for the current document on which you are working, or they can be altered for all future documents. For most purposes, the effort to alter the default values is not productive and may result in wasted time.

Templates Templates are the backbone of the word processor, yet few users recognize their role. Every document begins with a document format that includes basic information about the font, spacing, tabs, paper size, and all of the features that give the printed page its look. For each of the common types of written communication used in an office, a template can be prepared. Reports, letters, memoranda, interoffice notes, all can have a preformatted template. These templates can be shared throughout an office and customized to each person and department. Templates can be used to specify what is to be reported and how the report will look. Those responsible for reporting can simply fill in the blanks, so to speak, without spending time designing the report. Those receiving the report become accustomed to where the information is located on the page and can more readily find what is of interest.

Styles Every major word-processing software program allows the user to establish default styles for documents. A style specifies particular font faces and sizes for each type of heading used. Styles also specify the indenting distance for paragraphs and the numbering system for sections of a report. Styles allow significant uniformity for large projects that may require several chapters and be worked on by several authors and word-processing personnel. Styles can be utilized for standardizing the format for page numbering and creating headers and footers. Although there is considerable latitude for choosing style components, normally, you would expect to do so only in special instances. You do not want to draw attention to the look of your style at the expense of the content. Additionally, people get used to standard styles and major deviations might frustrate them. Figure 8.1 illustrates the components of a style sheet.

Spell Check and Auto Correct This feature is a true joy for those who are spelling challenged. Perhaps the best innovation for spelling has been the appearance of the jagged underline that informs the typist that a word may be misspelled. Specialized terms, unusual words, and jargon can easily be added to the program's dictionary when needed. However, many writers disable the auto-correct feature because it frequently "corrects" specialized words and usages. Nevertheless, the alert feature is useful because it signals a misspelling as soon as it occurs. A jagged underline of a different color indicates grammar problems, while the more powerful programs have a "correct-as-you-go" grammar feature. Serious writers view this feature with great skepticism. This is because the process is slow even on extremely fast machines and the changes made in grammar may change

FIGURE 8.1
...

Sample Style Formatting

Body Text = Times Roman 12

Body Text 2= Times Roman 10

Body Text Indent = .5 inches

Body Text Indent 2 = 1.0 inches

Default Paragraph Font = Times Roman 12

Hyperlink (URL) = underline

Header = (Text defined as header would be here)

Footer = (Text defined as footer would be here)

Heading 1 = Centered Bold Helvetica 14

Heading 2 = Centered Bold Helvetica 12

Heading 3 = Flush Left Bold Helvetica 12

Heading 4 = Flush Left Italic Helvetica 12

the meaning as well. You must consider each correction carefully before accepting it. If you do not, the result may be an upset supervisor or client.

Tables, Columns, and Text Boxes Not many years ago, we were happy that we could write and revise without constant retyping. Today we can place information in easy-to-read tables, develop charts, and make disconnected text boxes that appear to be more interesting than the core narrative. These features enable any proficient word processor to create the kind of good-looking newsletters and bulletins that used to require professional desktop publishing, and at one time required professional typesetting. As we fill our messages with boxes, tables, columns, and charts, keep in mind that no matter how fancy the formatting, the text must remain clear and easily followed or we will lose the reader.

Import/Export Any document prepared using a major word-processing program should be exportable to any other document format. Current versions of WordPerfect and Microsoft Word easily communicate with previous editions of the other program. This feature is critical because sending a document to someone at another company by attaching it to an e-mail requires that the recipient be able to read the document. Most e-mail programs have embedded viewers that will open and print the document.

The most popular format for sending messages to someone with an unknown word-processing program involves a program called Adobe Acrobat. This program creates a file that can be read on any computer that has the Acrobat Reader (a free program that can be downloaded from the Internet). The document format appears to the viewer exactly as it was prepared. This ability to exchange document formats is so widespread that people take it for granted. Not everyone realizes, though, how easy it is to convert word-processed documents into this Adobe format (called "pdf" for *portable document format*). People who do not use pdf files are surprised when the word-processed documents they send have paging and formatting that are different from their original documents. Often people format their documents with the space bar rather than tabs, and they will set new pages by adding lines until the text moves onto the next page. It might look fine on the screen, but when printed with someone else's computer and personalized word-processing software, all the alignments and paging shift. Special characters like bullets can also misprint, becoming asterisks or exclamation points. Of course, the strange text leaves an indelible impression.

Another method of sharing documents is either to convert the document to an extremely basic or generic word-processor format (ANSII or even DOS), in which much of the sophisticated coding and formatting disappear, or to convert it to a rich text format. Rich text format, or RTF, utilizes standard coding that can be read by any word processor and usually preserves most of the complex formatting in the original. However, RTF is only an intermediate solution for sharing documents because it loses the some of the more advanced formatting features. With a conversion to one of these file formats, layout and formatting information is lost or degraded in ways that prevent it from being recovered in the new file. (Always save the file in its original format!)

Another popular method has emerged with the use of HTML as a means of sending documents. HTML is the code used for the World Wide Web (HyperText Mark-up Language). Placing a document in HTML means that anyone with a Web browser can read it. Some e-mail programs utilize HTML format. Care must be taken not to create documents that require extra wide screens or other unusual formatting because the recipient may be forced to scroll or may not have the most current browser.

The most current word-processing programs have features that will convert a document prepared in the program into a pdf document or an HTML document. After generating one of these formats, you should open the result in a browser or in Acrobat Reader to make sure that it looks the way you expect it to look.

Outline   The outline feature of word processing can be manipulated in a number of interesting ways. It can be used to give each section of a report a unique number. From the automatically created outline, the program can generate a table of contents. Properly used, the page numbers in the table of contents change automatically as text is added or removed from chapters and sections. For large reports or frequently revised items, a template that utilizes the outline and table-of-contents features saves time and reduces errors. (If you have ever written a paper requiring an outline, revised the paper, and then forgotten to revise the outline with new page numbers, you know what a valuable tool this is.)

Advanced Common Features

Merge   Mass-produced, identical form letters should be a thing of the past. Even letters sent to hundreds of thousands of potential clients can be customized with name, salutation, address, and personalized information. However, people continue to underutilize word-processing technology because they do not recognize its power. An essential element of an address book that can help promote a business enterprise is the use of merge features to customize and individualize letters to large numbers of clients and contacts. Inserting names, addresses, and appropriate salutations is merely the beginning of what a clever merge master can accomplish. A set of paragraphs that focus attention on concerns relevant to each client's record of purchasing or level of participation can be merged to create highly individualized letters. If promotional offers are made on the basis of sales volume, why send that paragraph to a customer who buys regularly but who buys only a few at a time? With some planning, a sales executive can write half a dozen paragraphs and merge the appropriate paragraphs even as the addresses are merged in making the printed letter.

Index   Reports and manuals, especially employee manuals, are most useful if they have an index of important words and policies at the end of the manuscript. Indexes are prepared by making a list of the critical words and phrases. The index tool reads this list and locates every appearance of the word or phrase in the document. It generates a document with the page numbers listed that can be edited just as any other document can be. Sometimes authors want to remove an index reference or create one common reference for several versions of a word. The index tool is a powerful addition to the word processor.

Macro   A *macro* is a program that repeats a series of actions. If the company name is long, a macro can be created that inserts the company name when two keystrokes are combined. The tool is easy to use, and it typically requires only a few selections. One simply begins recording the macro, executes the series of commands (which are remembered by the macro program), and then saves the series of commands as a macro. After the macro is saved, it can be assigned to a keystroke combination such as the alternate key and a letter.

Macros can be complicated or simple. Macros can be used to execute basic computer commands as easily as they can insert a desired word sequence. They can search for words and replace them, locate the next instance of an event and give it a number, pause and wait for the operator to insert information, then save all files and turn off the computer. In fact, many now common features, such as search and replace and convert case were originally macros and still operate like a macro.

Graphics and Image Import   No matter how easy it is to import and place images, the quality of the material inserted still governs the finished product. Also, the composition of the page requires some skill. Doubtless, you are familiar with newsletters so cluttered with images, boxes, and columns that you can barely decipher the message. The importance of the project should dictate the extent to which you seek professional art and layout. The finer points of layout and page design still require practice and experience in order to produce effective, good-looking documents.

Publish to Web, Export to Presentation Tool   This option leads the writer through the steps required to publish a document on a Web site or to prepare a presentation for a formal meeting. Unfortunately, there are no **wizards** that make ugly products look good!

Despite what the term wizard implies, no amount of magic will convert poorly designed or overdesigned material into slick presentations or professional-looking Web pages. Table 8.2 summarizes basic and advanced word-processing features.

Important Office Strategies for Technology

The electronic office—whether it is a one-person office or a multinational office—must be organized in a manner that accepts and takes advantage of the continuous revolution in office communications. If the office is poorly planned and poorly organized, these additions will eclipse the communications themselves. These are strategies that should help you cope with the potential hazards and opportunities:

TABLE 8.2
...

Basic and Advanced Word-Processing Features

Basic Universal Features and Description	
1. Templates	Preformatted pages, letters, memoranda, invoices, and other business forms.
2. Styles	Preset headings for font size and shape, indentation style, outlining style, and other repetitive formatting.
3. Spell Check and Auto Correct	Feature that alerts typist to spelling errors and automatically corrects common errors.
4. Tables, Columns, Text Boxes	Simple tools that do not require special features for creating these elements in the manuscript.
5. Import/Export	Feature that allows any document to be exported to a specified file format, such as "save as" function for Microsoft Word to WordPerfect.
6. Outline	Automatically inserts outline with each "enter" keystroke.
Advanced Common Features and Description	
1. Merge	Feature that merges names and addresses, even entire paragraphs, into specified locations.
2. Index	Feature that creates an list of subjects, names, or other items by reading the marked items and collecting them at the end of the document.
3. Macro	Feature that allows the proficient user to "program" a sequence of steps that can be repeated with an assigned keystroke.
4. Graphics and Image Import	Feature that allows most programs to import some image file-types directly into the text; others make their own conversions.
5. Publish to Web, Export to Presentation Tool	Feature that allows the most powerful programs now to convert a document into a Web format, create a PowerPoint version, and can produce a pdf (Adobe's portable document format).

Standardize Software with Flexibility

In many offices, the purchasing agent or IT department helps standardize the software tools used throughout a corporation. Once a secretary, assistant, or manager becomes competent with a word-processing program, the basic skill is transferable from one poplular program to another. The person who masters WordPerfect can use Microsoft Word in a matter of hours. Both of these programs offer help functions that show how to use common features and even how the feature in one program is executed in the other. Desktop office database programs and spreadsheets are also interchangeable. However, larger spreadsheet and database programs require time for users to become familiar with them when moving from one to another, and image management programs have special differences.

The finished products in an office must all be in the same document format. Even if someone chooses to use WordPerfect to prepare reports in an office that has set a standard of Microsoft Word, the finished electronic document should be submitted in the Word format. Ideally, these final documents would be converted to pdf as discussed earlier. Art and photo software programs tend to offer numerous formats for producing the final image, since each file type for images has a different use. Standardization within an office should focus on the final document format for the files rather than on the program used to prepare it.

More critical than how a document is prepared is the issue of the various layout patterns (called styles in some programs, as discussed earlier) that can appear in the document. When an office sets a standard for a software program, style sheets and forms can be shared as well. The use of networks means that these styles, images (such as a logo), and even common contact information can be shared. A shared style for reports makes it easy for workers to contribute to a group-prepared report.

Use Electronic Images

Digital cameras make image work easy because a film-based photo must first be digitized in order to be used in an electronic communication. Also, logos and visual aids of various kinds can be converted to electronic media for the most effective and uniform application. To economize, a department can use a digital form of the company logo and place it in the letterhead rather than pay for the more-costly printed letterhead. Another department may follow, creating a similar—but not the same—letterhead. To encourage this economy, early in the process a standard format of the electronic logo and any other image should be prepared and made available to everyone.

Identify Shareable and Personal Data

The final area of office management that is of concern to everyone is the issue of the custodian of data and data privacy. Who is responsible for the electronic data? This issue must be carefully addressed and the responsible parties clearly informed. The cus-

INSIGHT BOX 8.1
...

So, Who Is the Expert?

 You need only surf the Web to discover that word-processing tools have made many people think that design and presentation are easy and that what they have done is good. If your ten- or eleven-year-old cousin can make your personal Web page look better than you can, then your efforts for the corporate site probably need help. Tools do not make the manager, yet many people have high opinions of their layout skills, just as they have high opinions of their writing skills. The best managerial writers know the limits of their own creative ability. They know what they can do and what requires specialized help.

todian of a set of data is responsible for preparing an archival back-up and for keeping the information secure. Inevitably, some of the information on a computer is personal. This, too, must be addressed in corporate policy. Personal data must be respected.

Other Concerns

The successful use of new and innovative electronic office resources does not guarantee that one will be successful as a manager or as a communicator. The difference between successful management of resources and successful management of communication lies in a full appreciation of the goals and objectives of the communication—not the means of communication. An effective strategy for managerial writing must be formulated on the basis of command of *all* available tools—electronic gadgetry, sophisticated office software, prewriting skills, rewriting skills, and other effective communication habits. An overreliance on one of these core skills will not generate an effective approach to communication.

Can anyone master the entire electronic office? While everyone can master the basic skills for using the technology found in the modern office, it is unlikely that everyone can completely know all the nuances of these technologies. Even if this is possible, it might be inefficient to do so. More than ever, the technologically sophisticated office continues to require that people work together. Fortunately, these technologies enable an increase in teamwork and sharing. For this reason, mastering all of the technology may not be productive. Effective managers delegate responsibilities to appropriate team members and empower those members to accomplish the assigned task without interference. You must know the abilities of your team and be willing to utilize those abilities. At the same time, you must be familiar enough with the applications and technologies being used to be able to make time and task delegations.

SECTION SUMMARY

Establishing simple and efficient formats can be a key to saving time that may be used effectively in revisions. Basic and advanced common features can be combined with office strategies that take into account personal concerns to produce a model office environment. An effective strategy for managerial writing must be formulated on the basis of mastery of all available tools—electronic gadgetry, sophisticated office software, prewriting skills, rewriting skills, and other effective communication habits.

CHALLENGE PROBLEM FOR REVIEW

Just what level of responsibility does a manager have for knowing formatting and processing features of common office suite software? Should the manager know all, or most of, the details of the frequently used common and advanced features? On the other hand, what checking should the proficient manager have others do? What will ensure that the manager gets appropriate proofreading from an assistant? Describe the strategy you plan to adopt for the production of important communications in your office.

Types of Office Communication: Where Will These Products Go?

Office communications methods are poised for a series of innovations that will require the vigilant attention of all involved communicators. Rapid changes can cripple an office if efforts to keep pace with these revolutions are not planned and approached calmly.

KEY CONCEPT 8.3
...

In this section, we ask you to consider the speed of change in office communications. Innovations occur rapidly and keeping an eye on the innovations makes sense. For the last few decades, the return of a manager from a training session has often been met with skepticism, as he or she would begin to implement the latest fad in employee motivation. In contrast to motivation and evaluation trends, infatuation with technology costs significant real dollars. Consequently, decisions about technology are made in a different fashion—sometimes on the whim of the CEO who thinks that he or she knows technology, sometimes in a well-considered, broad-based decision-making process. No matter how they come to pass, changes in writing and communication technology will continue to impact the workplace.

What's On the Horizon for These Features?

Broadband Internet Access

Several forces are driving the market for wider bandwidth for the Internet. First, people are using the Internet for communication and for sharing large files. E-commerce is flourishing, and the volume of sales increases dramatically with each holiday shopping season. In addition to MP3 music-compression technology, video delivery across the Internet is gaining popularity. Video delivery requires wider bandwidth than can be provided by the current modems found on most computers sold recently. This wider bandwidth can be achieved through telephone lines (with DSL), cable systems, and satellite. Broadband communications will improve as the ability to send video signals improves. The management of communication must follow corporate needs. In today's business world, customer service must be delivered via the Internet to an informed and skilled public. This method simply compounds the traditional-focused customer service tools.

Virtual Private Networks

A VPN is a network built on Internet connections rather than the technology used for LANs or WANs. A LAN traditionally employs secure wiring through an office, a building, or a set of neighboring buildings, although wireless versions are becoming increasingly popular. A WAN typically utilizes direct telephone dial-up into a LAN network housed in a corporate office and may connect two or more LANS. The VPN uses the common Internet backbone shared by all Web users. The VPN requires higher levels of security than other systems, and it enables corporate members to enter the network from anywhere in the world without having to make long-distance calls. Unlike the WAN and LAN that utilize cumbersome network software programs, the VPN uses Web-based software and encrypted communications available on new computers.

Another common use of the intranet LAN, the WAN, and the VPN has been to post critical reference materials, such as employee handbooks, organization charts, human resource forms, travel vouchers, and evaluation forms. The intranet is a safe place to provide access to all necessary paperwork and manuals for the company, save duplication costs, and provide the most current forms and regulations. Position announcements and job postings that are available to current employees can also be found on an organization's intranet. The use of this technology for delivery of critical information to employees and managers will only increase in the coming years.

Continuing Decentralization of the Office

Telecommuting, job sharing, home offices, e-commerce, and other forms of working in nontraditional venues continues to increase. Broadband and VPNs make this an attractive alternative to doing business in traditional, costly office spaces and expensive business trips. Already, the high-tech firm Sun Microsystems has half of its 35,000 employees working at home (Kallick, 2004).This trend has a direct impact on office communications. More information can be exchanged electronically, and more work is done asynchronously. **Asynchronous** work schedules mean that employees work at different times of the day and night and in different places. Effective and clear communication becomes especially important and requires more careful management under these conditions.

Virtual Office

A **virtual office** is the logical extension of the communication technology that expands beyond the walls of any office building. A person located away from a corporate head-quarters can now rent office space for very short periods and even contract for office support staff by the hour. Even office equipment can be shared with others who do not work for the same company. In such a building, there may be dozens of companies that need only minimal space and an office for occasional meetings. The next step is the virtual office. Employees may work cooperatively from different locations, usually communicating with one another through a variety of means, especially cell phones, teleconferencing tools, and E-mail. Individuals might be mobile and maintain no actual physical presence in the building. Instead, a person's office is a collection of hardware and software, including a laptop, cell phone, PDA, and other options that makes having a physical office building unnecessary. The employee communicates with the home office at will, often using their home as their office. In this context, a person may contract for the services of a support staff, including receptionist, typing, mailing, and reproduction support, and the availability of a meeting room or a teleconferencing facility. Skilled written communication is critical in this virtual setting.

Virtual Meeting Rooms

Broadband-supported, PC-based teleconferencing is a related emerging development that renders meeting rooms unnecessary. Forward-thinking entrepreneurs are hosting meetings in teleconferencing facilities strategically located in large cities nationwide. An extension of the virtual office, the entire teleconference activity can be contracted to a teleconferencing service. As the technology improves, these facilities will become more pervasive. Smart executives at companies with an increasing number of telecommuters (which translates into an increase in unused space) may find the opportunity to rent their corporate facilities to others during unused time. What this means in terms of communications is that as more of the process is contracted, the host (not the space and access provider) of the meeting will be required to ensure that everyone continues to be informed and have appropriate follow-up after the meeting is over. He or she cannot count on the administrative assistants who set up the meeting (unless that is part of the contract).

Dramatically Faster and Less Expensive Computing

The trend in computer sales is toward an ever less-expensive computer. Each new generation of computer comes equipped with an increasing number of **peripheral** devices. More and more customers and vendors are becoming electronically connected as a result of this inexpensive technology.

Powerful Online Instruction

Innovations such as the virtual office and the virtual meeting have given rise to the virtual classroom. Online education has the same asynchronous qualities as telecommuting work and virtual offices, and it can be used for everything from learning how to use a computer to basic cooking to ancient philosophy offered through a four-year university. Even graduate degrees can be earned online. Online instruction will have its effect on the office as well. Technical schools across the country provide training services for many kinds of technical skills that are necessary in the office. A new meaning of on-the-job training has emerged as a result of this online training and education. Technical and managerial writing can be taught in this manner as well.

Speech-to-Text or Voice-to-Text

This technology is in its infancy, and some traditionalists remain skeptical about its potential. Currently, the time required to make corrections to the text version of the document undermines any timesavings. Furthermore, few people can handle the process well enough on their first try to be able to do this without revising. However, in combination with increasingly smarter machines, this technology will soon enable good-quality, simple messages to be quickly and effectively created.

Improving Grammar Correction

Will future computers talk to each other and leave humans out of the picture completely? Already, there are a huge number of software applications that do so today, for things like updating inventories to the home office, moving billions of dollars between banks, or reporting the performance of a nation-

Person using speech-to-text software.

ASTRID GARRISON

wide telecommunications network. Luckily, they still require some human oversight. In fact, grammar will become even more critical as interpreter programs depend upon clear-cut rules. If you want to get a sense of how odd misinterpretations can become, ask a third grader to make a sentence using a dictionary definition of an unfamiliar word. In an anecdotal story, a child is asked to construct a sentence using a word that has the same meaning as "weight." After exploring the dictionary definition, he wrote, "Mommy said she gained too much plummet at Thanksgiving" (see Miller and Gildea, 1987).

Proceed with caution! If computers are to interpret speech to enable communication among humans, then these cautions apply. Using grammar and speech-to-text software must be done with the realization that they are not perfect.

SECTION SUMMARY

The future of the office will probably follow the traditional simple pattern: Rather than replace proven approaches to communication and office management, most of the changes will incorporate additional layers of activity. Some items, like the typewriter, will be replaced. However, the work once produced on typewriters must still be done. In fact, the tools that have replaced the typewriter generate more communication, not less. The easier it is to send a message, the more likely that message will need careful review, revision, and vigilance. The volume of messages in business today threatens effective communications. Volume needs to be reduced by good writing.

Preparing for the future requires knowledge of possible changes. Broadband Internet access together with virtual private networks may lead to further decentralization. Virtual offices and their equivalent will operate in a high-tech environment with contracted support services. The result will be a need for greater care in preparing communications.

CHALLENGE PROBLEM FOR REVIEW

Balancing fad against productive innovation threatens to be a major challenge for managers in the coming years. Have you ever purchased some type of technology or even a mechanical device that "underperformed"? What clues can you look for that will help with this problem? Formulate your plan as a recommendation to a business associate.

CHAPTER SUMMARY

...

Electronic communications are transforming the nature of the office. Taking advantage of these alterations and staying on the cutting edge of technology are requirements for success. The advantages inherent in the changes are almost beyond imagination, but so are the dangers. You will need to be aware of the significance of the changes and to develop strategies to accommodate for them.

EXERCISES

...

Prewriting Assignment

1. Create a document style for heads, subheads, body, and so forth.
2. Create groups in your e-mail program.
3. Program a calendar to reflect your schedule for the week.

Writing Exercises

1. Write a set of procedures to be used in your unit/department/work group to guard against system and individual computer failures by creating back-up procedures.
2. Examine the basic template in your word-processing program. Explain how you might alter some of the features depending on whether you are writing a letter for a business partner, a client, or a cover letter for a visually oriented person.
3. Create a cover letter to a varied group of clients and employ advanced common features to individualize letters to these clients. You can use your imagination in creating the clients to whom you are writing.
4. Create a wish list for your own virtual office. Explain what kinds of equipment you would purchase and why you are making that choice. This wish list should be composed in three versions: as a note to yourself; as a memo to the company-purchasing agent; and as a memo to your supervisor requesting authorization for these purchases.
5. Investigate recent office communications acquisitions in your department. Go online or visit a local supplier to determine what the next logical acquisition in this field would be. Describe that acquisition and explain why it is your choice.
6. Succinctly and clearly summarize strategies that you would have to employ in your writing to take advantage of the information presented in each of the three sections of this chapter.

_____

_____

_____

_____

_____

_____

_____

_____

_____

_____

_____

_____

_____

_____

_____

_____

_____

_____

_____

_____

_____

_____

_____

_____

IN-BOX EXERCISE

...

IN-BOX

As part of your corporate duties, you have been active in a large international professional association. The association offers a number of professional certifications, training and continuing education, and maintains professional registries. You work with the executive director, who works directly with the association. SHG General wants you to investigate the possibility of including some elements of the association's training seminars as part of the continuing education programs run by the company.

ITEM 1: AN E-MAIL TO YOU FROM HILDY, A PROFESSIONAL ASSOCIATION STAFF ASSISTANT (THE E-MAIL IS IN A RED, SCRIPT FONT). Quite a few people have been moved to the later split shift that starts at 1 P.M. and I am now by myself from 8 to 12. Sometimes, there is nobody to answer the phones at lunch and I don't get a break or lunch. These people have forgotten that we answer questions from European members who are just as important as Asian members. I can't get any work done answering the phone all the time, and my evaluation is going to suffer. Can you explain this to the executive director?

Your Response

Check one: ☐ Memorandum ☐ E-mail ☐ Letter ☐ Note ☐ Other

To: _____

_____

_____

_____

_____

_____

_____

_____

_____

_____

_____

_____

_____

_____

_____

_____

_____

_____

_____

_____

_____

_____

_____

_____

_____

ITEM 2: E-MAIL FROM CHUCK, THE SHG GENERAL OFFICE IT
SPECIALIST. I am having trouble with everyone using different office software. We now accept letters
of reference for special member status in the professional association, in electronic form. In fact, I think
we do not accept the reference letters in any form but electronic. Members use different formats, but the
association accepts files in only one format. I have tried to make everyone use that program, but quite a
few, including several very senior managers, claim that they need training or they prefer another program.
This needs to be fixed.

Your Response

Check one: ☐ Memorandum   ☐ E-mail   ☐ Letter   ☐ Note   ☐ Other

To: _____

_____

_____

_____

_____

_____

_____

_____

_____

_____

_____

_____

_____

_____

_____

_____

_____

_____

_____

_____

_____

_____

_____

ITEM 3: E-MAIL FROM MANDY, PROFESSIONAL ASSOCIATION SPECIAL EVENTS COORDINATOR. The Association International Conference organizing committee has a suggestion from two board members that we get everyone working the conference Blackberries for communication. They think that we will have better communication if we have them. The committee agrees with this recommendation. Can your company purchase thirty-five of them for us?

Your Response

Check one: ☐ Memorandum ☐ E-mail ☐ Letter ☐ Note ☐ Other

To: _____

_____

_____

_____

_____

_____

_____

_____

_____

_____

_____

_____

_____

_____

_____

_____

_____

_____

_____

_____

_____

_____

_____

_____

_____

_____

_____

_____

ITEM 4: AN E-MAIL IN A RED, SCRIPT FONT TO YOU FROM HILDY. Welcome to the office. We have all heard about you and are very pleased that you have volunteered to help us. The Association has been short-handed recently.

Signed, Tony, Stan, Oliver, Xena, Marcia, and Hildy

Your Response

Check one:　☐ Memorandum　☐ E-mail　☐ Letter　☐ Note　☐ Other

To: _____

_____

_____

_____

_____

_____

_____

_____

_____

_____

_____

_____

_____

_____

_____

_____

_____

_____

_____

_____

_____

_____

_____

_____

_____

_____

_____

_____

_____

_____

ITEM 5: MEMO TO YOU FROM VICTOR MARKOFF. President Richman is interested in the possibility of our becoming involved with a professional association. Please look into this and give me your opinion ASAP.

ATTACHMENT:

Copy of Memo to Victor Markoff from Frank Richman, President, SHG General

I think it might be useful for the company if we become more involved with a professional association. What do you think?

Your Response

Check one: ☐ Memorandum   ☐ E-mail   ☐ Letter   ☐ Note   ☐ Other

To: _____

_____

_____

_____

_____

_____

_____

_____

_____

_____

_____

_____

_____

_____

_____

_____

_____

_____

_____

_____

_____

_____

_____

_____

_____

KEY TERMS

...

Asynchronous (p. 248)

Asynchronous communication (p. 234)

Buddy lists (p. 236)

Chat rooms (p. 234)

Discussion forums (threaded discussions or discussion boards) (p. 236)

E-mail (p. 234)

Instant message (IM) (p. 236)

Interface (p. 239)

Intranet (p. 237)

Local area network (LAN) (p. 232)

Online forum (p. 234)

Peripheral (p. 249)

Personal data assistant (PDA) (p. 233)

Spam (p. 238)

Subject line (p. 238)

Teleconference (p. 237)

Virtual office (p. 249)

Virtual private network (p. 237)

Whiteboard (p. 237)

Wide area network (WAN) (p. 237)

Wizard (p. 244)

REFERENCES

...

Kallick, Rob. (July 18, 2004). "Employees Go the Distance." *Lexington Herald-Leader*, p. E-1.

Miller, George A. and Patricia M. Gildea. (1987). "How Children Learn Words." *Scientific American* 257, no. 3: 94 6p.

CHAPTER 9

...

MASTERING PRESENTATION TOOLS *for* CORPORATE COMMUNICATIONS

LEARNING OUTCOMES

...

Upon completion of this chapter, you will be able to accomplish the following tasks:

1. Formulate meaningful policies regarding how corporate information should be handled and made public.

2. Understand the importance of maintaining control over the release and dissemination of both good and bad news.

3. Determine when information should be released as a press release.

4. Use the basic components of a press release.

5. Write high-quality product announcements.

6. Assemble a press kit.

7. Use the basic methods for preparing presentations and recognize the limitations of any presentation tool.

8. Avoid common public presentation mistakes.

9. Make visual presentations more effective.

"Actually, I preferred 'Heaven' too, but then the marketing guys got a hold of it."

In today's competitive business climate, corporate communications have a major impact on a company's chances for success. Even modest-sized corporations and government agencies have directors responsible for public relations to handle the dissemination of information. A classic example occurred in 1988, when IBM was faced with lower-than-expected profits, almost for the first time in its history. In keeping with its policy of no employee layoffs, the company decided to shift thousands of workers from manufacturing to sales. Although some industry skeptics pointed out that many workers would quit and thus lower IBM's corporate payroll, the company's efficient corporate **communications department** issued multiple press releases emphasizing that not a single worker was terminated. The effect on the public was positive; IBM retained its public image of a giant that genuinely cared about its employees. Controlling information and its release to the general public is vital.

In this chapter, you will learn the standard means of releasing information to the public and the strategies that guide that release. The public image of a company or a government organization is crucial for many reasons. If that image is tarnished, the company can face serious consequences. Arthur Andersen, the consulting and auditing firm involved in the Enron scandal, was destroyed by loss of public confidence. Today, most companies have more social and public responsibility than the scandal-laden corporate giants that existed during the 1990s.

Often, government agencies refer to their communications department as their public information office. The directors of these offices regularly release information and news to local, regional, and national news agencies. Most local print and broadcast news organizations have several means of disseminating newsworthy items to their national networks. For example, when a university learns that one of its professors has been awarded a Fulbright Fellowship to Japan, its public information office will issue a press release describing the award and the professor's research goals. The effect of such an announcement is to heighten the public's positive perception of the university as a place where scholars perform research in the public interest. When public support is needed to persuade a governor not to cut a state-funded university's budget, the positive impact of dozens of such press releases can be substantial.

Indirect public support through a well-developed and cautiously maintained corporate image like IBM's that persists for decades or a direct information campaign that regularly strengthens the image of a public institution can have significant results—even if they are hard to quantify. These large organizations have specialists who dedicate time and energy to preparing news for public release. Why, then, would a manager who is not part of the public information team need to know how to prepare and disseminate news releases and similar communications?

In many circumstances, the information officer will ask the manager of a unit for which a press release is being prepared to provide most or all of the key information. Thus, the manager has an opportunity to make sure that the right material is shared. If you want it said, you may have to say it. If the news is the announcement of a new product, the manager of the unit that makes the new product is probably the best-informed person to describe the product and its features or qualities. Just like the members of the press who receive the news release from an organization, the information officer will appreciate the written material that is supplied. Editorial revisions as well as additions by other departments may be necessary, but well-prepared material is always welcome. It also assures you that the information is accurate and well-written.

Strategies for Disseminating Information

Sharing information about an organization is an important means of marketing a product, a service, and the organization itself. Well-delivered information strengthens the public image of the company or organization as well.

KEY CONCEPT 9.1
...

External communications with the public can be oral or written. The format for a **press release** or **news release** and other related methods of disseminating information are fairly standardized. However, the rules that various organizations follow in releasing information reveal a variety of approaches. Some organizations strive to share all relevant and newsworthy information. A company that shares everything has a corporate culture that is inclusive of the public interest, and most companies derive their profits and livelihood from the public in some way. In contrast, some companies and government organizations are extremely closed, keeping information to themselves and sharing only the most critical news when required. Indeed, some information may need to be restricted. The FBI, the CIA, and the Department of Homeland Security are government entities that have special powers to control information. They release news in carefully prescribed circumstances and with an objective of informing the public of crucial news. Both the open company and the closed company must be deliberate when considering why and how they share their information.

The careful and deliberate release of information follows from the prescribed strategic interests of the organization. Management must establish a consistent tone. The FBI is always serious, but Southwest Airlines is sometimes humorous. Herb Kelleher, Southwest Airlines' CEO, frequently uses humor in making important corporate announcements. Launching a charity campaign, he entered the boxing ring to arm-wrestle with the CEO of a competitor to establish a charity challenge. It also settled a law suit with such a challenge (Freiberg and Freiberg, 1998). When the Tampa Bay Buccaneers defeated the Oakland Raiders in Super Bowl XXXVII, California's Governor Gray Davis held a news conference to display the winning competitor's jersey and announced that he would be hanging it in the California state capitol as promised in a wager with Florida's Governor Jeb Bush (Emert, 2003). These kinds of acts, and the press releases that accompany them, help humanize large organizations.

Most organizations try to establish policies and procedures that govern the release of information externally. Strategies for when and how to release news begin with basic decisions about the control of information. Decisions must be made about the benefits of releasing the news.

Control of Information

Among the valid reasons for an organization to control the release of information is the fact that information can have damaging effects. Consideration of the consequences for the organization must precede the decision to release information and that decision must be made following an orderly set of procedures. The information may be proprietary and its premature or uncontrolled release could result in financial damage. A company wants to present a single image of itself and not speak with several voices. If for no reason other than to maintain this focus, an organization should control when and how information it possesses will be released.

Another reason for control is that mishandling corporate and public communications can be disastrous. A note on company stationery from an irate employee who takes a position on a political issue, a report addressing company concerns with meeting new government standards that is intended for selected industry experts only but that falls into the wrong hands, and a new-product announcement that inadvertently refers to a delay caused by quality-control problems are examples of harmful corporate communications. Every employee who uses corporate stationery for a private letter because it might carry more weight is probably committing a serious policy violation. Because the company has not made a decision to take a stand on that issue does not mean that an employee has the license to do so under the aegis of the company.

Consider these fictional examples. Bill Buhler works for SHG General as a marketing analyst. His major interest outside work is the environment, particularly the loss of irreplaceable flora and fauna caused by overdevelopment. When he learns that hearings are being held to determine the environmental impact of the ABC Corporation's plans to build a new manufacturing plant in a nearby canyon, Buhler writes a fiery letter. Using SHG General stationery and citing ABC's "terrible environmental record," he reports several allegations of the company's violation of Environmental Protection Agency policies. His primary source is a local environmentalist newsletter.

The letter stuns ABC's officials because, unknown to Buhler, they are negotiating with the SHG General sales department for a major contract that will increase SHG's new plant to full production. Since any company communication is assumed to be the official position of that company, ABC's executives feel that they have been stabbed in the back by SHG General's attempt to win public approval at their expense. They immediately break off negotiations and indicate that they are no longer interested in dealing with the company.

In another example, SHG General was contemplating a new computer system for its corporate headquarters and forty-two branch offices. Lakewood, the corporate officer charged with resolving the plan, was virtually convinced that a well-known local equipment provider and network services provider, A-Z Services, would be the most efficient and cost-effective way of linking company resources. One day Lakewood phoned the equipment and network company's headquarters because he had some final questions that needed addressing, and his local sales representative was not available. Because he happened to call at lunchtime and no marketing representatives were available, he was switched by a receptionist to the technical area where "someone can probably answer your questions." A young technician named I. M. Dumm indicated that in his opinion the network they were contemplating was "difficult to install and maintain" but "able to do the job if the company could provide good technical support."

Dumm was proud of his own expertise and felt good that he had been so honest; he felt that sales representatives often oversold the product. Lakewood, on the other hand, now had serious doubts about risking his own position by supporting a networking solution offered by the company. SHG opted for the safe solution of choosing a national provider. The young technician was fired when the sales representative discovered why the sale had been lost.

Information control is obviously important, as these two examples illustrate. Having a single source for public information makes control easier than coping with a misdirected call. Policies should be in place to help manage these kinds of situations as well as the common release of news of interest to the public. Although Buhler should not have used the company letterhead, he probably should have known about the negotiations. Dumm should have realized who was calling and the importance of the call. Was it his place to suggest that the network was difficult to manage? Was he aware that most networks are difficult to manage? These questions raise issues about the internal and external communications of the organizations involved. How much communication can be controlled, and how much of that control is the responsibility of the corporate public information officer?

Control of information is not always a negative issue. Unfortunately, those in the news media tend to jump at bad news and use good news as filler for when bad news is in short supply. Give the media plenty of good news to use. Major events like opening new plants, big contracts, corporate goodwill initiatives, environmental campaigns, and other contributions to the community should come from designated corporate officers.

Decision Strategies for Releasing News

Properly handled, press releases can be a valuable tool. In terms of the information that they release, as indicated previously, organizations are either open or closed. Open organizations freely share information and establish direct conduits to the news media, sending news, announcements, and reports of public interest through regular channels and on a regular basis. They may not hold press conferences on a daily basis, but they might have several communications a week with the local news agencies. Establishing rapport leads to positive benefits. For an announced press conference with releases provided, the press readily reports the news. At times they may even give the organization the benefit of the doubt and publish information that may have marginal news value.

Closed organizations communicate with the press only when necessary. This reticence can make them appear miserly with important information, but it may be from necessity. The extent of openness depends on the nature of the organization. A police department press officer makes formal statements and considers most information confidential until it is officially released, an action considered appropriate during an ongoing investigation. Imagine, in contrast to critical legal issues, the newspaper quoting an inside source concerning a local amusement park or the library board. In this context, citing an "inside source" suggests that something is being hidden from the public. Are children in danger? Has someone embezzled money at the library? The public expects to hear announcements of extended amusement hours or the donation of money for a new children's wing, not that safety has been compromised for the sake of profit. "Inside sources" just do not seem appropriate for these organizations. This kind of organization or for-profit corporation should operate with a strategy that is as open as possible.

Strategies for making information public should be based on the answers to a few simple questions. Of crucial decision-making importance, and probably before any of the guiding questions are asked, you must decide whether the information is newsworthy and to whom it is newsworthy. Once newsworthiness has been decided, the following questions should guide other decisions:

- Will release of the information benefit the company in the ways that we expect?
- Does the release of information create a sympathetic public?
- Does the release of information strengthen the company's community citizenship?
- Will the information damage the company if we leave it to others to discover?
- Is there harm in not releasing the information?
- Will the release of this information strengthen public trust in our organization?
- Are there regulations governing the release of this information?

These questions engender different responses depending upon whether the general approach is one of being open or closed. The focus of an open strategy approach is more on questions of trust, sympathy, and citizenship. The closed approach provides other benefits intended to manage the impact of privileged or damaging information being discovered by others.

The information being considered for release is the best guide to what gets shared and when. We would all like to tell everyone our good news and hope that no one finds out the bad news. The early twenty-first century corporate scandals concerning valuation of companies and the techniques used to make overextended companies appear profitable led to many revised reports. Because few companies benefit from announcing that last year's loss was worse than previously announced, these reports are mandated by both government and market agencies.

The information officer should have a clearly stated mission that reflects the corporate mission. That mission should guide how the qualifying questions are answered and the decision on how the news should be released (quietly or with fanfare).

Policies and Practices for Implementing Strategies

Typically, the responsibility for any official information released by an organization resides in one office. The information officer should make clear the role of the news office and the steps that employees should take to communicate information to his or her office for its further release.

The use of official logos and letterheads presents one area of great concern to many who have been charged with managing the process of releasing information. Most companies, government agencies, educational institutions, and not-for-profit organizations have a **corporate communications policy** relating to the use of letterheads or official stationery. A clear policy must be communicated to all employees concerning the use of logos and letterheads. The common practice is that press releases include the company logo or are placed on company letterhead. This is part of validating the official nature of the source. This is why the fictional actions of Bill Buhler would be misinterpreted. His use of letterhead stationery implies that his letter is the official stance of the company.

Professors often use university letterhead but universities have a policy that the practice is independent of the university's official public relations office. When professors write letters of reference for students applying for jobs or colleagues applying for grants or fellowships, the letterhead validates professors' affiliation with the university. The action is so thoroughly accepted that no one would confuse a letter of support for a student with the university's position. But, what if a professor writes a letter about a political campaign using letterhead? The policy is violated when the use of the letterhead conveys an inappropriate conception to the reader that the letter represents the official stance of the university. On the other hand, officers of the university, such as a dean, vice president, or president need to indicate when the expressed views are not those of the university. Even if not intended as such, these letters are treated as if they were news releases—if they can be shared, they will be; if they contain news, others will hear it.

News agencies should be told who the official source is for news from the organization. In fact, the information officer should establish credibility with these agencies. Developing rapport with the press is central to the job of the information officer. That rapport helps news agencies judge the truthfulness of the press release, its importance to the company, and the validity of claims made in the release (this could include claims of the impact of the news on the community, the long-term effects of a recent event, and so forth.) The press should not have to decide whether or not the information being released really is newsworthy.

Finally, the practice of disseminating information through a single source or point of contact allows the information officer to control the tone and the content of every official communication, whether it is a press release, a press conference, or a response to an inquiry from the press or public. When a manager gets a request from someone such as a reporter or nonemployee, the prudent course of action is to forward that request to the information officer. The actual response may be for the manager to answer the reporter or write a letter to the citizen under the direction of the information office. For some inquiries, the information officer may provide additional background details that can be included. Following this procedure ensures that the manager has spoken with appropriate authority.

SECTION SUMMARY

The release of information to the public serves several purposes: (1) it publicizes the work of the company; (2) it maintains an important element of control over the information; (3) it provides the public with a source for further information while establishing the company's willingness to share critical information. The basic strategy for releasing information depends on whether the company approaches its public role as a closed company or an open company. Open companies willingly share information as a method of generating goodwill, while closed companies or organizations operate more on a "need-to-know" basis. Either style requires clear guidelines for employees and officers of the company in order to avoid serious mistakes caused by misinformation.

CHALLENGE PROBLEM

What should happen to Bill Buhler, the employee whose environmental enthusiasm wrecked the deal for ABC and SHG? How much control should be exercised over employees, and where should the line be drawn between individual freedom of speech and corporate interests?

Formatting News for Press Releases

The format for press releases and similar information items follows a nearly universal formula. The press expects this format and depends upon it.

A nearly universal format for press releases makes preparing a release simple—merely applying the information to a template. Of course, like any other written communication, care must be taken to follow the steps of pre-writing, composing, and editing, just as if the news release were a formal proposal, formal letter, or term paper. Writing must be clear, sentences short, and paragraphs brief. Every official publication or release that belongs in the category of disseminating information to the public—including press releases, announcements of new appointments or retirements, general information announcements, and product announcements—must be placed on a company letterhead with a logo that clearly identifies the company, including address and contact information. A bold, large "News Release" or "News" and a bold, large title should head the announcement. Immediately below the title should be the statement "For immediate release" or "For release on [date]." Several standard methods are used to indicate the end of the communication. They are "—30—", —000—, "— ### —", or "— end —", to indicate the end. In addition, "—more—" or "—continued—" indicates that another page follows. On continuing pages, a **slug** is used with the page number. Figure 9.1 on page 266 illustrates all these components.

The content organization follows an inverted pyramid: The most important information comes first and, within each paragraph, the most important details lead the paragraph. We cannot emphasize enough how critical it is to use short, uncomplicated sentences. In fact, the more a news release reads like a newspaper, the better the reception by the news media will be.

Press Release

The simple press or news release is probably the most basic type of corporate communication with the public. News releases cover a variety of topics including the announcement of a new service, the breaking of ground for a new building, the hiring of new personnel, awards, or recognition received by a company employee or product, and, of course, company acquisitions and mergers. No matter what the subject, it is important to consider the company's goals and expectations.

A company needs to announce the official changing of its name for obvious reasons; it wants to avoid public confusion and reassure the public that the company is as strong as ever and that there is a practical reason for the name change. Figure 9.2 on page 267 illustrates a news release from SHG General announcing its official name change to SHG International.

Notice that this news release follows all of the basic writing guidelines associated with effective news writing by answering the key questions who, what, where, when,

FIGURE 9.1
...

Components of a Press or News Release

Press Release
(also News Release)

Title of Press Release
"For Immediate Release" or "For Release on Date x"

Identifying Information
  Logo
  Company address
  Information office contact name, phone number, e-mail address
  Current date

Body
  First paragraph, most important item
  Second paragraph, next most important item
  Third paragraph, next most important item
  Etc.

Mechanics
  Continuing pages have "—more—" or "—continued—"
  Last page indicated by:
  "— ### —" or
  "—000—" or
  "—30—" or
  "—end—"
  At the top of the page include a slug and the page number.

Other Items
  Attachments as needed or desired:
    Photos
    Biographies of new officers
    Technical descriptions of new products

---

why, and sometimes how. SHG General (*who*) has decided to change its name to SHG International (*what*). A news release should indicate *when* a change will take place; in this particular example, the change is effective the date of the news release. *Where* did this change take place? The news release indicates the board meeting took place at the Dayton, Ohio, corporate headquarters. Often a location placed in the dateline indicates the location of company headquarters or the location of the public relations office. The public's natural question is *Why?* and the news release answers this question by explaining that the new name will identify the company more closely with its international mission. As the quote of President Richman suggests "The new name will help align the corporate identity with the corporate mission."

The example in Figure 9.2 also illustrates some basic guidelines for the news release's physical appearance and format. Notice that it is titled News Release so that the news media will recognize its purpose at a glance. The release date is a critical piece of information because often the date will be some distance in the future. A company may provide the media with important information to ensure adequate coverage but request that it not be released prior to a certain date because of government requirements, a stockholder's meeting scheduled for the date of the announcement, or in an effort to

FIGURE 9.2
...

A News Release Indicating a Company Name Change

SHG INTERNATIONAL   **Providing Quality Services Worldwide**

Suite 1000, One SHG Boulevard   800.555.4321
Dayton, Ohio 45439

News Release

SHG General Announces Name Change

For immediate release
Dayton, Ohio, March 31, 2004

The governing board of SHG General has concluded its first quarter meeting at the headquarters in Dayton, Ohio, with a momentous change for the customers, employees, and stockholders of SHG. After decades of high-quality service and product development for its broad client base, SHG General will change its name to SHG International, Incorporated, on July 1, 2004. SHG has grown steadily over the past four decades through focused expansion into promising new markets throughout the world. The many divisions of SHG General have become successful SHG partners in the international arena, and this name change reflects the corporate goal of continued worldwide success.

Corporate headquarters will remain in Dayton and no change in leadership is anticipated. Said President Richman, "The new name will help align the corporate identity with the corporate mission."

For more information, contact Clarence House, chief information officer, at 1-800-555-4321. Additional press kit information is on the Web at www.shginternational.com.

—30—

---

keep the competition from learning the facts prior to the official release of the information. News people refer to this as an **embargoed release**.

Another important part of the news release format is the inclusion of the name and phone number for a key contact person. If a reporter wants additional information, the key contact person and phone number is easily accessible on the release sheet.

News releases seldom convey excitement, but they can be interesting. One technique to increase reader interest is to use quotes from key company personnel. In the SHG news release, the SHG president is quoted. In this case, the quote assures readers that the leadership is not being changed and the corporate mission will remain the same.

Every company wants good public relations, including public awareness and acceptance of its products. How can a company generate news when there is none? Figure 9.3 on page 268 is a news release announcing the eightieth anniversary of a soft drink company named Terry's Soda, Incorporated.

While many companies have been in business for eighty years, in the news release it is noted that "boutique soft drinks can thrive in a world of big-name giants." Anyone writing a news release must be able to interest the reader. Why should the reader care that a company is celebrating its eightieth birthday? Although most people have not heard of Big T sodas, the news release establishes credibility by describing the regional

FIGURE 9.3
...

A News Release Celebrating a Corporate Birthday

Big T Sodas

News Release

Terry's Soda Celebrates Eightieth Year

January 1, 2005

For immediate release

Terry's Soda, Inc., begins the celebration of eighty years of continuous service to the region as the acclaimed producer of the Big T soft drink line. Brothers Jim and Jeff Terry began producing the carbonated beverages from family recipes developed at the soda fountain of their drug store in Oklahoma City during the spring of 1925. Their popular flavors provided relief during the hot summers of the Great Depression. The brothers acquired their first small bottling plant at the height of the depression and put a half dozen unemployed people to work when no one else was creating jobs. This sense of community responsibility remains central to the Terry's Soda vision. Though they lease bottling capacity to major brands, they have never relinquished control of their popular soft drinks. The commitment to quality accounts for the continuity of success with a regionally recognized brand.

As other specialty drinks have become popular nationwide and demonstrated that "boutique" soft drinks can thrive in a world of big-name giants, Terry's Soda will mark its eightieth year with nationwide distribution agreements in major grocery store chains and international discount stores. The generations of people who have experienced the Big T— whether they grew up in the region or discovered a special flavor while visiting—will soon be able to find Big T in their local grocery.

Other celebration events will be announced throughout the year. Check our Web site at www.TerrySoda.com. For information, call Janet Terry at 1(800)123-4567 or e-mail jterry@terrysoda.com.

—- ### —-

soda and bottling company as a responsible citizen in the corporate world that has been able to survive and thrive against formidable competition.

The effect of this news release is to make the public aware of Terry's Soda and to provide the public with increased respect for a company that is successful and stable. The release also includes encouragement by suggesting that other celebratory events will follow throughout the year and that Terry's plans to expand. This news release epitomizes the point that every news release should have a definite purpose as well as a definite audience.

Checklist for Writing a News Release

Who?

_____ Who is the company making the news release?

_____ Who are the spokespeople making the announcement? (Names and phone numbers or e-mail addresses for contact should additional information be needed.)

_____ Who (including title) is being quoted?

What?

_____ What is happening that warrants news coverage?

_____ What are the key details that need to be presented?

_____ What is the significance of this news to the general public?

Where?

_____ Where will this news event take place?

_____ Where is the news release coming from? (Corporate headquarters?)

When?

_____ When will this news event take place?

_____ When is the release date of the news bulletin?

Why?

_____ Why is this story important?

How?

_____ How will the company accomplish what it says it will do?

Notice that most of these questions can be answered in a one- or two-paragraph news release. Also notice that the news release in Figure 9.3 is double spaced and contains a lot of white space on the page. Some local editors like to pencil in their own headlines and make changes in the news release. They appreciate the white space in which to make these changes.

News releases directed to different communities should be localized. Why should the residents of Phoenix, Arizona, care about a news release from Terry's Soda in Oklahoma City or SHG International in Dayton, Ohio? Both are announcing types of expansions. For an international company, an expansion of mission may require facilities including a new plant in another part of the world. If the expansion affected, for instance, Phoenix, that will mean a number of new jobs, then the news release should indicate approximately how many new jobs in the Phoenix area will result from this decision.

Product Announcements

Companies need to let their customers know about their new products. One company that has earned significant industry respect for its expertise in issuing new **product announcements** is IBM. On several occasions, IBM froze a particular market segment by announcing a forthcoming product. Customers were reluctant to purchase competing products because they might prove inferior to the market leader's forthcoming product. They thought, "If I wait just a few months, a new and faster machine will be introduced, and, if I buy now, I will be saddled with this slower competitor's machine."

The rapid flow of new machines and special offers can almost paralyze the consumer. A problem began in 1986 with what is the classic example. Rumors of a new IBM personal computer (the PS/2) depressed computer sales, including IBM's own personal computer sales. In an extraordinary move, the company issued an announcement that it would *not* be releasing a new computer that year. Sales immediately rose, and purchasing agents decided not to withhold their orders for new computers. True to its word, the computer giant waited until the following year to announce its PS/2 series of computers.

The computer industry has been plagued by new-product announcements for **vaporware** (products that do not appear on schedule or in some cases never appear). In the early days of microcomputers, some under-financed companies deliberately announced new products that did not exist, accepted orders and payments for these products, and then used the money for research and development funds to complete the product. Some computer periodicals still issue a vaporware award each year to the product whose announcement drew the most interest but never appeared.

Figure 9.4 illustrates a real-world example of a new-product announcement. The Segway is far from an ordinary new product and this release heralded the radical new product. The announcement has all the standard features of a news release, indicating the time and place of the announcement, why it is important to know about the product, and comments from Dean Kamen, CEO and inventor. The announcement also has other features that help build interest in the product. The announcement includes a listing of companies and organizations that will soon begin evaluating the Segway for use.

It is clear from the headline that this new-product announcement is directed toward a broad audience, even if the machine itself will initially be appealing to a specific market.

FIGURE 9.4
...

A New-Product Announcement, Courtesy Segway

Inventor Dean Kamen Introduces The Segway, the World's First Dynamic Self-Balancing Human Transporter

Provides Revolutionary Approach to Personal Transportation with Commercial, Consumer Application

MANCHESTER, NH, December 3, 2001—Segway LLC, the business founded by inventor and entrepreneur Dean Kamen to transform the way people work and live, today announced the much-anticipated debut of the Segway Human Transporter (HT), the first self-balancing, electric-powered transportation machine. With dimensions no larger than the average adult body and the ability to emulate human balance, the Segway HT uses the same space as a pedestrian, and can go wherever a person can walk. The Segway HT will allow people to go farther, move more quickly, and increase the amount they can carry anywhere they currently walk.

"The Segway HT is an enhancement to personal mobility that will allow people to make better use of their time," said Dean Kamen, Segway's chairman & CEO and the man with the technological vision behind the human transporter. "Ultimately, the Segway HT can make urban environments more livable by providing a solution to short-distance travel. If the Segway HT is widely adopted, it could help solve major urban problems, such as pollution, congestion, and livability."

The company will produce three distinct models: the i-series optimizes range and speed across a variety of terrain; the e-series is designed for business applications where it is necessary to carry cargo—up to 75 pounds in addition to the rider; the p-series will be ideal for densely populated areas, both indoors and out. The Segway HT's footprint is narrower than the average adult's shoulders and its length is no greater than a large shoe. And it's quiet—designed to emit only a barely audible harmonic hum.

FIGURE 9.4
...

Continued

Segway HT will first be introduced for commercial use. Initial applications include large scale manufacturing plants and warehousing operations, travel and tourism, public safety, corporate and campus transportation, mail, package and product delivery. Consumer availability is planned for late 2002.

Customers

Segway will soon begin evaluation with some of the world's leading corporations and service organizations.

Company	Usage Benefit
United States Postal Service	Improved work environment; productivity enhancement
Michelin North America, Inc.	Easy R&D facility and plant navigation
GE Plastics	Improved worker productivity/proximity
National Park Service (NPS)	Increased ranger mobility; environmentally friendly
City of Atlanta (Ambassador program)	Visitor education and improved navigation
Amazon.com	Distribution efficiency and improved logistics

According to Jack Hennessy, retired chairman of Credit Suisse First Boston Private Equity, "Dean is a uniquely talented engineer, passionate about using technology to solve important social problems. Human transportation is one of the biggest challenges facing cities around the world."

The "Magic" of Segway

Kamen's team developed a breakthrough technology the company has termed "Dynamic Stabilization," which is the essence of the Segway HT. Dynamic Stabilization enables Segway's self-balancing emulation to work seamlessly with the body's movements. Gyroscopes and tilt sensors in the Segway HT monitor a user's center of gravity about 100 times a second. When a person leans slightly forward, the Segway HT moves forward. When leaning back, the Segway HT moves back.

The Vision

"With over 80 percent of the world's population soon to be living in urban areas, we believe that the Segway HT can, over time, play a vital role in these areas," said Kamen. "In the past, every major advance in powered transportation technology has involved ways of going long distances faster from the horse and buggy to the car to the airplane. The Segway HT, on the other hand, addresses the problem of moving people and products relatively short distances more efficiently. . . a few miles rather than from town to town using very little energy in the process."

SEGWAY

The Segway© name is now copyrighted, though when this announcement was made, it was a trademark.

The technical terminology, "dynamic stabilization" is clearly defined, making the announcement understandable by any reader. Because new-product announcements may be read by a variety of different audiences, they should be stated in simple and clear language unless the preparer tailors a separate release to each audience. If marketed to a business audience such as the readers of *Business Week*, the release would have to be in plain language so that any business person could understand why it is important for a business to have these remarkable machines. How will the purchase of a Segway improve a company's productivity and efficiency?

The first paragraph of this announcement, coupled with the information appearing above it, provides the basics that every such announcement needs. The announcement is on the Web, so we know the means of contacting the company (a linked page has phone numbers for quick contact).

Although each paragraph in this release provides information about the Segway, there has to be an ordering principle to tie the announcement together. In other words, why are the aspects of the Segway discussed in the order in which they appear? Features should appear in descending order of importance beginning with the most significant features. This is a reasonable strategy because it places the most emphasis on the most important— and therefore most attractive—feature. Also, newspapers often cut the releases in order to shorten them. The editors expect the most important information to be first. The final paragraph offers the corporate vision that guides Segway, and this is perhaps the most general aspect of the information offered in the announcement.

We might contrast the Segway new-product announcement with one from another company unveiling a product for a different market. Figure 9.5 illustrates a new-product announcement from The Vermont Teddy Bear Company.

FIGURE 9.5

A New-Product Announcement Partnership Announcement

> The Vermont Teddy Bear Company
>
> **Elvis Presley Enterprises Authorizes 50th Anniversary Promotion Partnership Announced with Vermont Teddy Bear, Kroger, and Regional Bakers**
>
> MEMPHIS, Tenn., March 15 — In honor of 50 years of Rock and Roll, Elvis Presley Enterprises and its Licensee, The Vermont Teddy Bear Company are teaming up to celebrate the historical recording of Elvis Presley's first song. The Vermont Teddy Bear Company designed and imported a commemorative, limited edition Elvis Bear 2, which is licensed as an Official Elvis Presley Signature Item by Elvis Presley Enterprises. The one-of-a-kind teddy bear will be offered in more than 750 Kroger stores in six states free of charge with a minimum purchase.
>
> Fifty years ago Elvis Presley recorded *That's All Right* at the legendary Sun Studio in Memphis, Tennessee. The recording of Elvis Presley's first single is recognized as a major event in musical history, and is widely lauded as the "big bang" that helped launch the Rock 'n Roll Era, changing the course of music and popular culture.
>
> The 50th Anniversary promotion brings together The Vermont Teddy Bear Company, selected Kroger stores in several states, and a regional group of independent bakers. This event marks the second time Elvis Presley Enterprises has partnered with Vermont Teddy Bear Company and a bakery to offer these limited edition "Elvis Bears" as a premium. In August 2003 EPE authorized Klosterman Baking Company to offer the "Elvis Bear" in selected Kroger Stores. The promotion was one of the stores most successful to date.
>
> The bakers will offer an 8-inch Teeny Tiny Teddy Bear, Elvis Bear 2 designed and imported by The Vermont Teddy Bear Company, FREE with PURCHASE of selected products, exclusively through regional Kroger stores. The promotion,

FIGURE 9.5
...

Continued

beginning in April 2004, will feature a completely new design for the Elvis Bear. Each of the specially designed bears is a "one run, limited edition" never to be produced again.

Consumers will be asked to use their Kroger Plus Card, in one of the participating stores and purchase the selected products offered by the participating baker in that area. Once the minimum number of products is purchased, the consumer will receive the commemorative, limited edition Elvis Bear 2 free. The bears will be available in the store, for immediate delivery to the consumer.

The promotion will run for a limited time in Kroger stores March 29–April 24, 2004. The Elvis Bears 2 will be offered to consumers only while supplies last.

More than 750 Kroger stores Michigan, Ohio, Indiana, Kentucky, Tennessee and Mississippi will participate in the promotion. Major markets include Detroit, Columbus, Cincinnati, Dayton, Indianapolis, Louisville, Lexington, Nashville and Memphis.

The participating bakers and their products include: Perfection Bakeries (Michigan, Cities in Ohio and Indiana including Toledo and Columbus) Aunt Millies Brand, Klosterman Bakery (Ohio and Kentucky Cities including Cincinnati, Dayton and Northern Kentucky Region) Klosterman Brand, Lewis Bakeries (Indiana, Kentucky and Tennessee Cities including Indianapolis, Louisville, Lexington and Nashville) Healthy Life, Southern Country, Bunny, Hartford Farms Brands, Flowers Bakeries (Parts of Kentucky, Mississippi and Tennessee Cities including Memphis) Nature's Own Brand.

Note that this actual press release from The Vermont Teddy Bear Company does not have all the parts identified in the template. It does convey all the necessary information.

Source: Reprinted with permission. The Vermont Teddy Bear Company, March 15, 2004, http://ir.vtbearcompany.com/index.php?id=159 (accessed July 7, 2004).

The Vermont Teddy Bear Company's new-product announcement headline introduces a lead product in a series or family of products. In effect, the headline creates credibility for the product because it indicates the company's partnership with Elvis Presley Enterprises. Not only has a unique product been created to honor an anniversary, but other companies are involved in the promotion as well. The release describes how a prior Elvis Bear promotion was the most successful of its type of promotion for the Klosterman Bakery. To entice potential customers, the special "signature" bear will be a "one run, limited edition." Not only does the release indicate a dateline of Memphis (Elvis country), but it lists the Kroger stores that will be participating in the promotion. It is important to note that The Vermont Teddy Bear Company carries enough name recognition that it is unnecessary to address the quality with which the bear will be made.

Checklist for New-Product Announcements. Most, but not all, of these items will appear in a new-product announcement.

_____ Who is announcing this product? (What company?)
_____ Who can answer further questions? (The contact person)
_____ Who is the company spokesperson?
_____ When is the announcement?

_____ Where did the announcement take place?
_____ What is the product being announced?
_____ What features does it have?
_____ Why is it important?
_____ Why should the media carry this story?
_____ When is the product available?
_____ How much will the product cost?

Preparing the Press Kit

A **press kit** is the material made available at a press conference or when a press release is made. A pocket folder (for a small amount of material) or a bound package (for a large amount of material) contains the press release, pictures of the new executive or product, brief biographies if the announcement is about new appointments, and some technical information if the announcement involves a new product. It should include a list of contents, with the contents arranged in the inverse pyramid order that the press release follows. The most important information should be the first item in the list, and so on. Figure 9.6 lists the major elements of a press kit.

Preparing Profiles of Key Officers

Companies put together a press kit containing information on new products as well as profiles of the company and its major corporate officers. While these profiles may seem to be busy work and of little importance, they can be important because they provide

FIGURE 9.6
...

Components of a Press Kit

The press kit is usually a folder or binder with the company logo on the folder.

When opened, the first item in the right-hand side pocket should be the press release or other most critical information presented on a single page.

In the left side pocket, the first item should be a list of contents if the kit has more than just a few items in it. If it is an announcement of a new CEO or other top executive, include a photo.

The items should flow logically from the most important to the least important. These can include:

Calendar of events
Biography
Résumé
Quotes
Comments

Mechanics

Each item should have a page number on it, identifying its original place in the folder.

Other Items

If presented at the beginning of a long press conference, a notepad and pen or pencil are commonly included.

Include the business cards of the information officer(s) and other important contacts.

the reader with a sense of how well the company is managed. Profiles are usually brief, maybe three or four sentences, but they have to capture the person's major strengths, including education and experience. Figure 9.7 illustrates SHG Internationals' description of its key management personnel.

FIGURE 9.7
...

Key Management Profile

SHG INTERNATIONAL   **Providing Quality Services Worldwide**

Suite 1000, One SHG Boulevard   800.555.4321
Dayton, Ohio 45439

News Release

SHG International Introduces CEO and CFO

Dayton, Ohio, March 31, 2004
For immediate release

The Governing Board of SHG General announced the name change to SHG International following the March 31, 2004, board meeting. The Board is also pleased to state that SHG General President Frank Richman will continue as President and CEO of SHG International and that SHG General Vice President for Financial Affairs Catherine Osaku will become Chief Financial Officer of SHG International.

Frank Richman   Mr. Richman has been with SHG for twenty-five years and has been president for the past six years. He has served in supervisory and executive roles at all levels of the company throughout his twenty-five years. Born in the Midwest, Mr. Richman is a proud graduate of the University of Michigan in management and holds an MBA from the prestigious Wharton School. His wife and family reside in Dayton.

Catherine Osaku   Ms. Osaku has been with SHG since she joined the team developing the Tokyo office fifteen years ago. Born in California, she studied for several years in Japan. Her language skills and knowledge of Far East cultures have proven critical for the successes of SHG in the Asian market. Her education includes an engineering degree from California Polytechnic Institute and an MBA in finance from Stanford University. Ms. Osaku and her husband reside in Dayton with their seven-year-old twin sons.

—30—

Notice that few details of a person's life are included. In the case of the president, for example, his twenty-five years of experience with SHG is far more important than his impressive educational background, so that experience is listed first. Similarly, other positions he held outside SHG are not relevant because he has been with SHG such a long time. However, the fact that he has held numerous management and executive positions in SHG is important in establishing his strength of commitment and experience.

SHG's announcement of the CFO describes her educational background, but it also focuses on her cultural experience and technical competence. Note that she has an undergraduate engineering degree and a specialization in finance, which means she has a broad grasp of the workings of SHG. The announcement also humanizes the two corporate leaders by mentioning their spouses and children.

Sometimes companies issue corporate profiles that include both a brief description of the company and a description of the major officers. Figure 9.8 shows a brief corporate profile for Terry's Soda, Inc. This fact sheet includes a "pointer" for more information in the mention of the Web site. Today, most companies with extensive customer support have readily available public information on a Web site. Web site information can be changed quickly and can be economical, because the materials can be shared without printing and mailing costs.

Checklist for Corporate Profiles and Fact Sheets

_____ Where is the company located?

_____ Who are the key executive officers?

_____ What makes them qualified for their leadership positions?

_____ How many employees are there?

_____ How well is the company doing?

_____ What are the major products?

_____ What are the major markets?

What to Include

Every form for releasing information to the public must include identification of the organization releasing the information, the name of a contact person or office, and physical and electronic addresses. This information must be put in a format that readers will recognize immediately. Instructions concerning when the information can be used (immediately or at a certain date in the near future) must accompany the date of the actual release ("today's date"). These standard formatting issues were detailed earlier, but we want to emphasize that the formatting is as important as the content. The information is being released to inform the public; if these crucial formatting elements are missing, the media might ignore the message.

What content should be included? The first criterion is that the content should be newsworthy and to some extent urgent, time sensitive, or likely to be of high interest to

FIGURE 9.8
...

A Corporate Profile

Corporate Fact Sheet

Terry's Soda, Inc.

January 1, 2005
For immediate release

Founded: 1925

Corporate Office: Oklahoma City, Oklahoma

Production Facility/Bottling Plant: Edmond, Oklahoma

Annual Sales, Big T products: $9.5 million with 750,000 cases (twenty-four bottles per case)

Earnings from Bottling and Distribution, related products: $2.4 million

Employees: 17 full time

For more details, see our downloadable reports available at our Web site, www.TerrySoda.com.

the community. The final decision about *when* construction on a new office building will begin is not news if the fact that the building will be built has already been announced. Nevertheless, the public may have an interest in new information—when the building would start—if that had not been settled at the time of the earlier announcement. This is certainly important for the local media and the community officials who may be required to cope with the disruption of a new building. It may not be urgent, and if the start date is several months in advance, it may not be time sensitive. When the schedule for construction is set, it is newsworthy. Three weeks later, the news may be stale. The content of a news release must be timely and important to the reader.

If a building schedule is being announced in a news release, then the press kit might contain a set of the earlier news releases that had announced the decisions about location, expansion, and related information. The reasons for the new office building could rest on a growing local economy, efforts by the chamber of commerce to attract new business, or the appearance of other new businesses in the area. The press kit should include this information so that the media can enrich the story to suit their interests without having to undertake extensive and time-consuming research. Only one or two important relationships need to be included in the body of the press release. Otherwise, a simple announcement of a schedule for building might be overwhelmed by the secondary information.

The press kit can include architectural drawings, maps, and other graphic material ready for print in the paper or a weekly magazine and ready for display in a news telecast. Professionals, whether in-house or contracted, should prepare these graphics. Photos of the CEO, CFO, and other officers should be included in press kits when the release is being made by or about them.

Making judgments about what to include rests on the relevance of the information. To keep a press release short, the rule of thumb that separates news from information will be most helpful. The criterion might be: "If there is more information than the reporter will read or use, leave it out." Placing supporting information in the press kit will be helpful, but clogging the release with additional detail will not be.

What Not to Include

If the reason for the press release is not clear in the first paragraph, no amount of additional information or further details will encourage the reader to continue. The first thing to be excluded from the release is filler. **Filler**, any unnecessary additional material that does not add any newsworthy information, can be confusing and distracting. Making sense of the extra material requires time, and most reporters have little time to decipher something that is not significant. Even worse would be when the reader assumes that the information must be connected, yet cannot find the connection and so is confused. The intention is to clarify, not confuse. The worst-case scenario is when the filler information is perceived to be more interesting than the press announcement.

Suppose that there is an announcement that new hand-held computer technology will soon be available. In the press kit, the company has sales figures for the technology being superceded by the hand-held computer. What happens to the orders for the now obsolete PDA technology when the reporter headlines the story: "PDAs to be Obsolete by End of Year"?

Do not include non-news as if it were news. Including past press releases in a press kit works well if the contents indicate the prior release dates. Companies regularly post previous releases on their Web sites; most call the area "News" or "News Archive." A press kit should include URL links to the Web site and the archives of previous releases. A smart information officer includes links to stories written by local and national newspapers that make use of prior news releases. This encourages the media; it shows appreciation and enhances rapport.

Unless they are clearly separated, do not include more than a single news item in a simple press release. Every newsworthy item deserves its own release. To strengthen the effort to get all the news out, a covering press release can be used to indicate that the company is making "two important announcements today." This release would accompany both announcements. Each press release would also indicate "In the first of two important announcements . . ." and then "In a second announcement . . . ." At the end of the second announcement, the narrative should refer to the first announcement. This is critical. Later, someone may refer to the press release by its date and discover that there were two releases. Clarity must rule.

Finally, as noted earlier, insiders have a habit of using language that looks like alphabet soup to outsiders. Jargon, acronyms, and abbreviations aid communication among those who share knowledge of these specialized terms and shortcuts. On rare occasions, jargon may be used to emphasize a point, but only if it has immediate translation. At a news conference concerning the 2003 *Columbia* shuttle disaster, a NASA representative referred to FOD. Quickly, another representative translated: "foreign object damage." (NASA, 2003). Apparently FOD occurs frequently because of space debris and tiny extraterrestrial particles. It is an important class of damage to space vehicles. Normally, jargon results in highly convoluted and distracting questions that require clarification. Avoid jargon, acronyms, and abbreviations unless they represent a critical part of the message—then be sure to give necessary definitions.

SECTION SUMMARY

The press release follows a mechanical format that leaves no ambiguity for the recipient. Members of the media are always starved for time, so an easily followed release assures the information officer that the information will have the best chance of being published or announced in the media. Other than mechanical guidelines, the release follows the classic inverted pyramid style, with the most important information being given first. Press kits, product announcements, and personnel announcements follow the same strict patterns.

CHALLENGE PROBLEM FOR REVIEW

With 24-hour network news and instant information on the Internet, what changes might the press release yet face? Will standard printed media conventions give way to Web-based conventions? Will these migrate back to the printed releases? Look for examples on the Web and see if some companies no longer conform to the older, traditional conventions.

Making Effective Presentations

KEY CONCEPT 9.3
...

The use of electronic presentations has become pervasive in corporate and governmental meetings, from private and confidential board meetings to public press conferences.

Presentations have become universal elements of business and manager's meetings. The ability to prepare persuasive and informative electronic presentations is now considered as basic a skill as using a computer or sending an e-mail. Unfortunately, as critical as this skill may be, many people seem to forget every lesson they ever had in how to make a presentation. You must approach the presentation just as you would any other writing task. You must recognize the need for consistent strategy as a guide to effective presentations.

Many of us have been swept away by the new electronic technology, and we have forgotten that the four or five word lines that head each point of a presentation do not convey the entire message. Common presentation tools such as Microsoft's PowerPoint or Corel's Presentations are easy to use and quick to deploy. Instructors across the country have begun using these presentations in class and then placing them on the class Web page. Students find the material, print it out, study it, and then discover that the presentations are only superficial outlines that are of minimal help if relied upon exclusively when preparing for an examination. This is a useful lesson when applied to the workplace. Rarely in the corporate environment can an electronic presentation stand alone. Splashing a graph on the screen does not ensure that the viewer has absorbed the information in any usable detail. The best presenters learn that presentation software is merely an aid to constructing a complete package of information.

Graphics and presentation tools share a common thread: Clarity is more important than dazzle. The discussion of how to prepare graphic materials in Chapter 10 applies to the use of graphics in presentations, though it addresses broader issues of the preparation of graphic illustrations for any kind of written materials. A graph prepared for printed material may be an impossible item for an electronic presentation. Similarly, a graphic prepared for a presentation may not work well in print.

In this section, you will learn the basics of electronic presentations, common mistakes made in preparing them, and a few points about what makes a presentation effective.

Presentation Basics

Microsoft's PowerPoint presentation tool is used so commonly that one might think that it is the only such tool available. There are a number of others, some of which exhibit more power than Microsoft's. Corel Presentations and even Microsoft's Publisher have features that provide a competitive choice. A few Web-based tools are also available, including Trellix, that allows presentations to be made for the Web, teleconferences, and live electronic presentations all at the same time (links between pages become Web hyperlinks when placed on a Web site). Some designers use HTML editors, such as Microsoft's FrontPage or Macromedia's Dreamweaver, to make presentations that they deliver using a Web browser. The point is, whichever software tool you choose, there are certain basics that make the presentation work. The better tools include tutorials to help the novice locate features within the software application, and the various menu screens have a logic that novices can learn quickly. Advanced tools are designed presuming knowledge on the part of the preparer.

All electronic presentations share a common strategy, whether it be for the public at a press release or news conference, a boardroom presentation to the trustees, a departmental meeting with hundreds of employees, or a sales meeting with a client. Keep the presentation simple and clear, interesting but not overdone, and to the point. The presenter must always remember that the electronic media is part of the presentation—not the presentation itself.

The basics of electronic presentation that can be used in public and private meetings belong in one of two categories: design and content.

Design Basics for Presentations

Presentation tools have prepackaged **templates** and tools for modifying these templates. Each template has a variation for bulleted lists, charts, title pages, text pages, and so on. Company logos can be added to a template or the company's graphic artists can create a template with the company colors, logo, and even pages that are always to be included, which contain contact information and so on. Your organization may have a policy requiring that you use either the provided organization template or one approved by the information or graphic office. If you are fortunate enough to have a division devoted to preparing these kinds of support materials, they are probably capable of customizing a template for your department as well. (Having a specialized office for this kind of support does not mean that they can fix content errors that you create.)

Design basics include color choice, consistency of fonts and font sizes, spacing, letter case, number of lines and words per line, number of slides, and awareness of readability issues. The contrasts between font colors, background colors, and images placed on the template can cause vision problems. Color-blind individuals have a hard time with green print on a red background, and many people over forty discover that small print is difficult to read, especially if the color contrasts do not work well. Thus, yellow on green may not be the best color combination—even if your company logo features these colors prominently. The best thing is to develop a few options and show them to a variety of people. If you have an **Americans with Disabilities Act** (**ADA**) compliance officer, be sure to ask for a review of your template design and font formatting.

Some people like to develop a **signature template** that they always use when making a presentation. Some people like to use a specific border, others a favorite background color, still others have desired transitions. An icon or other special, "signature" emblem may be strategically located on the slide. Still, if you are not careful, you may get overly attached to the application. Subtly done, it can convey a level of professionalism that may be missing in the work of others. This is important if you are competing for a client or with other units for budgetary and project support. Too much activity on the screen can be distracting.

Content Basics for Presentations

To make sure that your content is sound, the best course of action is to prepare the content separately. Type the outline and notes with a word processor and then copy the outline into the outlining feature of the presentation application. Indeed, Microsoft and Corel products include spell checking in their presentation tools. However, it is essential that you realize that spelling- and grammar-checking abilities are minimally effective. If you include a split infinitive in the presentation, one or two people will be offended. If you include a spelling error, you can always blame the "typist" (though everyone knows that it was probably you who made the error). But, if you include a subject-verb agreement error, quite a few will think that you did not take the time and devote necessary attention to the presentation, or, worse, that you do not know better.

With a complete outline prepared and checked for errors, the next step is preparation of figures, graphs, photos, and illustrations. You can convert them for use in the application and place them appropriately, making sure that transitions and labeling guide your audience through the presentation.

Each page or *slide* (most applications refer to the pages as slides) should have a title, if it contains written material, or a caption, if it has visual materials. The most common layout employs bulleted lists and most pages should have no more than three bullets. Call this the **three-item rule**. Each item on the list should be six words or fewer. Single-word items require some kind of lead-in to establish a frame of reference. The title can be used to do this. For instance, to make your audience pause, a large, all-cap "THINK" would be a good start. You might have several well-placed "Review" or "Summarize" markers also.

If the outline has long items in it, the appearance on the slide in the *slide view* (the view that shows how the slide will look during the presentation) may need to be altered. Do not do this by squeezing long amounts of text into the space. You may need to switch to a text rather than a bulleted list slide layout and present the important phrase or sentence by itself on one slide. This single item on the slide actually strengthens the impact of your comment.

Do not hesitate to develop a brief outline on one slide and then devote slides or even a series of slides to expanding the points of that outline. Introduce the points much as you do when writing a report. The slide of an introductory outline for each main section of the presentation is like a paragraph of introduction for each main section of a report. Decide what you want to accomplish in the presentation and lead the audience through each step.

Quotations, charts, graphs, photos, and other visually dense material must be reviewed for clarity on the projection screen before inclusion. Generally, the strongest format for graphics is for each image to be placed on a single slide that fills the screen. There may be occasions when several images should be placed on the same slide, when you make side-by-side comparisons or even a fade from one image to another, but these occasions will be obvious after some practice.

In review, these basic rules should be easy to follow.

1. No more than three or four points per slide.
2. Keep each point statement as brief as possible.
3. Place long quotations or technical statements on individual slides.
4. Allow each critical graphic to have an entire slide and to fill the screen.

An electronic presentation serves to clarify, guide, and organize an otherwise verbal presentation. For the presenter, it is imperative to realize that the presentation is intended to make the speaker's comments easier to follow.

Common Mistakes

Sometimes, mistakes help pinpoint how an effective presentation can be prepared. The following are common errors:

- *Weird and distracting color schemes.* Even if you are sensitive to color blindness and other vision problems, the use of a strange color scheme can be distracting. An electric pink background with dark purple typeface may be perfectly clear, but the audience will devote some time to analyzing the color choice and not paying attention to the content.
- *Strange words and references.* Jargon can destroy an effort to make a clear presentation. Too many abbreviations, even with clear definitions of the abbreviations, make written items difficult to follow. More than one or two acronyms can be confusing as well. If acronyms or abbreviations are used and the presentation is long, you will need to reinsert the full term every half-dozen or so uses. Remember, your audience cannot scan back to the first use to remind themselves.
- *Too many bullets in the list.* Once you see a double-column of bullets, you will understand this problem immediately. New pages cost nothing, so why not put three bullets on each slide and add a slide with "Continued" marked on it? Some people fill a slide with bulleted items to the point that the list runs off the bottom of the slide. For clarity's sake, stick to three if you can (the three-item rule), four if you must. You might also consider numbering a long list so that your viewers will not get lost.
- *A point or item is so long that it requires three or more lines.* One method of defeating the three-item rule is to compound items. However, making items longer does not always help. If the concept being illustrated is already long and requires a full statement, devise an abbreviated statement for the bulleted list and then present the full statement in a detail slide following the list. Some people use several slides, moving from one to the next, expanding the point to its full statement, and then returning to an abbreviated statement. Figure 9.9 on page 282 illustrates this pattern.
- *Distracting and frequent transition effects.* They call it PowerPoint because the program gives you power over your presentation, but this does not mean that every moment of the presentation must be a show. Novices find the transition and animation effects (of which there are hundreds) and employ them for each bullet and every slide. This wears an audience down. Dazzle is not the goal for most professional presentations. The main point of a transition is to focus attention on the current point, not on the skill of the presentation author.

FIGURE 9.9
...

Sequences Details in a Presentation

Title of Slide

· · · · · · · · · · · · · · · · · ·

Subtitle

- This bulleted item has already been discussed, so it is faded about 50 percent

- This bulleted item has already been discussed, so it is faded about 50 percent

- **This bulleted item is currently being discussed, so it is full and larger than the others.**

Those already shown would be faded and may be just a short phrase. The item under discussion would be the larger, brighter, or bolder item with a fuller statement.

- *It looked really good on the computer screen.* Assume that you have just prepared a beautiful, appropriately understated presentation that your immediate supervisor is to deliver to the board of trustees and the CEO. The presentation starts and the beautifully understated hue of blue that you picked glares a fluorescent blue on the projector screen. It really looked good on your desktop, but now the laptop running the projector seems to have a mind of its own. Planning means that you run a few slides of the presentation pages through the equipment that will be used to make the presentation. We once watched a surprised university president make a presentation where all the bullets turned into silverware and food items. The laptop belonged to the nutrition department. This kind of error is not bad enough to stop the show, but it can be embarrassing.
- *Quantity is not quality.* Said the student about a carefully prepared course presentation, "But one-hundred-and-forty-eight slides only took thirty minutes when I practiced it." A slide per minute is a good guide, though that may be too many if you engage in any explanation or expansion of ideas. If the audience raises questions, one slide per minute will be far too many.
- *The presentation was more animated than the speaker.* Many people fail to understand that the presentation is a support, not the thing or an end in itself.
- *The presentation becomes a shield from the audience.* If your presentation is to make a formal announcement and then move on, this is not a problem. Too

often, though, the flow of the presentation prevents audience members from asking questions or contributing comments. Keeping the presentation simple and direct and allowing for pauses and opportunities for comments invites participation, if that is part of your plan.

- *Confusing pages of speaker notes for effective handouts.* Rarely do speaker's notes make good handouts. The best handouts would be like a press kit—an outline of the presentation printed on a few pages, with attached charts, graphs, and illustrations. You can always place the presentation on a Web site for those in your audience who need the exact material that you have presented. The useful materials will be the data analysis visible on a chart, map, drawing, or other visual aid.

Effective Presentations Skills

Learning to make effective presentations is an invaluable tool for professional success. Some people consciously work at improving their presentations each time they give one. Others seem oblivious to the value of a well-made presentation. An extension of effective managerial writing, presentations should be incorporated into your arsenal of managerial skills.

Even after years of making professional presentations, your skills should continue to improve. The tools, equipment, and access to information that presentation software employs continue to improve. To remain an effective presenter, you must take advantage of these improvements to continue to expand your mastery of this blended writing medium. When you reach the top of your profession and you delegate preparation of the presentation to others, you will still need to be confident with the technology, software, and content that you are presenting to others.

One way to attain a high level of proficiency is to be attentive to others, watching how they master or are mastered by presentation tools. Maintaining a critical eye provides opportunities to move ahead, increasing your mastery through observation and practice. Like all other aspects of managerial writing, the presentation—as well as the press release and its close relatives—are opportunities for increasing your success.

SECTION SUMMARY

Electronic presentation packages are commonplace. Successful use of the software requires the application of a few simple rules: avoid cluttering the screen, using jargon, and being wordy. Other frequent mistakes include strange color combinations, odd words without definition, too many points on a slide, dazzling yet confusing transitions from point to point and slide to slide, and confusing quantity with quality. Effective presentations are always clear and to the point.

CHALLENGE PROBLEM FOR REVIEW

Perception psychologists have conducted significant research into the effects of color on attention and mood. How might this information influence your decision to use certain color schemes to exert subtle influence on your audience? The Web is full of suggestions about color and mood, but where would you go for definitive suggestions about color schemes? Also, you may want to think about the extent to which you believe that design can have such an influence.

CHAPTER SUMMARY
...

An organization must have control over the news and information it possesses. This control is established and maintained through an information office, a public relations official, or a similar office. Each organization has its own style and approach to releasing information. To be successful, it should also have clearly stated policies and guidelines to help employees maintain professional relationships with the news media.

Press releases are among the most common ways that organizations have of getting important information to the public and ensuring that the media broadcasts or publishes the news. These news releases can also be in the form of product announcements and press kits. Information about new personnel appointments is released in this way as well.

Another means of making important information public or sharing it with other units of an organization is the electronic presentation. Software tools have made preparing a presentation look very professional, but the presenter must avoid a number of common mistakes in order to make an effective presentation.

EXERCISES
...

Prewriting Exercises
1. Collect several samples of press releases. (Companies often include news releases in annual reports, and the most popular place today is the company Web site.) Do these have all the necessary components?
2. Collect information about yourself that you think would be included in a press kit announcing your new appointment as the new vice president of _____ (you fill in the blank).
3. Find some examples from your courses of good and "less than good" presentations. Do these really serve the purpose, or are they merely short-hand outlines?

Writing Exercises
1. Think of an organization to which you belong or one of the companies for which you have worked. Write a one-paragraph statement expressing the information-sharing policy of that organization.
2. Use Prewriting Exercise 2 and write the press release announcing your appointment to the position you created.
3. Write a product announcement for a common item in your dorm room or household. Remember, you want to convince a customer base that they should buy this "new" product.
4. Using the common mistakes section of the text, develop an outline of the bulleted points and plan a presentation based on them. Be sure to determine how many slides and how many sub-points should be used for each major "mistake."

_____

_____

_____

_____

_____

_____

_____

_____

_____

_____

_____

_____

_____

_____

_____

_____

_____

_____

_____

_____

_____

_____

_____

_____

_____

_____

IN-BOX EXERCISE

...

IN-BOX

You have been appointed the information manager for Auto-Widgets International, Inc. Although it is not your long-term goal to be the manager of public relations, you understand that your role includes a public relations aspect and that this position is a stepping-stone to the corporate office. No one has stayed in this position very long, and it seems that the office is in some disarray. A-WII is located in Southern California.

ITEM 1: MEMORANDUM FROM KEN, SPECIAL PRODUCTS MANAGER.

We are glad to see you. That last guy was just marking time until he got a promotion. Too bad for him they sent him overseas again. He was so upset that he made no press releases during the last two months. I think we had record production and contracts reported last month. I know that Mr. Markoff wanted the news made public right away.

Your Response

Check one: ☐ Memorandum   ☐ E-mail   ☐ Letter   ☐ Note   ☐ Other

To: _____

_____

_____

_____

_____

_____

_____

_____

_____

_____

_____

_____

_____

_____

_____

_____

_____

_____

_____

_____

_____

_____

_____

_____

_____

_____

_____

ITEM 2: E-MAIL FROM KARL, ASSISTANT PLANT MANAGER. Our minority recruitment and training program has been a great success. You should publicize those numbers; they will make us look good. HR has all the details.

cc: HR Department.

Your Response

Check one: ☐ Memorandum ☐ E-mail ☐ Letter ☐ Note ☐ Other

To: _____

_____

_____

_____

_____

_____

_____

_____

_____

_____

_____

_____

_____

_____

_____

_____

_____

_____

_____

_____

_____

_____

_____

_____

_____

_____

_____

_____

_____

_____

_____

_____

_____

ITEM 3: E-MAIL FROM KARI, HUMAN RELATIONS STAFF. I have the complete report on our minority recruitment and training program. Almost a third of the trainees have quit or been hired by someone else. What's worse, the numbers are kind of odd. While we have higher than expected Asian immigrants, the African-American numbers were pretty dismal. Also, the Hispanic numbers were below the average local population. I know Ken wants to tout his program, but you better be cautious with the numbers.

Your Response

Check one: ☐ Memorandum   ☐ E-mail   ☐ Letter   ☐ Note   ☐ Other

To: _____

_____

_____

_____

_____

_____

_____

_____

_____

_____

_____

_____

_____

_____

_____

_____

_____

_____

_____

_____

_____

_____

_____

_____

_____

_____

ITEM 4: E-MAIL FROM CARLA, CHIEF DESIGN ENGINEER. We have completed the design of a revolutionary combination GPS/atomic clock. Not only does it locate the car on a map display screen, but the dashboard clock is updated and adjusted for time zone through the device every time the car is started. I can get you the specs and likely cost if you want. We need to announce this before someone else beats us.

Your Response

Check one: ☐ Memorandum ☐ E-mail ☐ Letter ☐ Note ☐ Other

To: _____

_____

_____

_____

_____

_____

_____

_____

_____

_____

_____

_____

_____

_____

_____

_____

_____

_____

_____

_____

_____

_____

_____

_____

_____

ITEM 5: NOTE FROM KAREN, EXECUTIVE ASSISTANT TO THE PLANT MANAGER. Markoff is going to Dayton for a big meeting and wants a press kit that includes recent contracts, sales figures, and new appointments. He wants to have a bio of you and the other executives promoted in the last two months. He needs them by next week.

Your Response

Check one: ☐ Memorandum ☐ E-mail ☐ Letter ☐ Note ☐ Other

To: _____

_____

_____

_____

_____

_____

_____

_____

_____

_____

_____

_____

_____

_____

_____

_____

_____

_____

_____

_____

_____

_____

_____

_____

_____

_____

_____

KEY TERMS

...

Americans with Disabilities Act (ADA) (p. 280)

Communications department (p. 260)

Corporate communications policy (p. 264)

Embargoed release (p. 267)

Filler (p. 277)

News release (see Press release)

Press kit (p. 274)

Press release (p. 261)

Product announcement (p. 269)

Signature template (p. 280)

Slug (p. 265)

Templates (p. 279)

Three-item rule (p. 280)

Vaporware (p. 270)

REFERENCES

...

Emert, Carol (January 30, 2003). "Bush Can't Pop Davis' Bottle; Wine Delivery Snafu Screws Up Governors' Super Bowl Bet," *San Francisco Chronicle*, A2.

Freiberg, Kevin and Jackie Freiberg (1998). *Nuts! Southwest Airlines' Crazy Recipe for Business and Personal Success*. New York: Broadway Books.

NASA. *STS-107 Columbia Mishap Update*, February 4, 2003. http://www.ksc.nasa.gov/columbia/hq0204brief.htm (accessed August 6, 2004).

CHAPTER 10
...
USING GRAPHIC IMAGES EFFECTIVELY

LEARNING OUTCOMES
...

Upon completion of this chapter, you will be able to accomplish the following tasks:

1. Describe the purpose for using graphics in a particular report, proposal, or other form of writing.

2. Select the most effective way to illustrate information, choosing among types of graphs, comparison charts, and flow charts.

3. Articulate a strategy for including or excluding illustrations of data and other graphic illustrations.

4. Identify the methods of preparing illustrations.

5. Select the most suitable electronic tools for preparing illustrations.

6. Know and distinguish the purposes of the different kinds of drawing and painting tools.

7. Describe the different means of converting an image to an electronic format and importing the image to a document.

8. Recognize the need to plan the preparation and placement of illustrations in the document.

9. Understand how to judge your final product and its impact.

10. Know the cautions offered concerning simplicity, clarity, and number of illustrations.

The power of today's graphic, illustration, and presentation software gives rise to two almost completely opposite effects. When used properly, the software can produce striking—often dazzling—effects. However, this same software appears to make everyone a professional graphic artist. Unfortunately, superficial appearances do not make professional artists. This should be clear to anyone who attempts to communicate using graphic illustrations and images.

The managerial writer can easily fall into several traps. The first is that of being smitten with the power of illustration software. In this circumstance, the writer becomes more excited about the tools than about the message. In a second trap, the writer under-develops critical elements of a graph, chart, or illustration while devoting significant development time to the showy parts of the illustration. The writer makes the assumption that images can convey the complete message. A third trap occurs when the writer fills the document with too many illustrations and graphic elements, and the audience quickly loses the flow of the narrative. As the cliché suggests, we cannot see "the forest for the trees." We stand in awe of the tree and what made it, and we get hung up in the making of the tree. Worse, we get lost in the trees themselves.

Examine your textbooks to see if you can find a page of beautiful graphics surrounding one line of text (probably lost somewhere on the page). Publishers use the term "over-developed" to refer to an excessive use of images, graphic illustrations (sometimes simply called *graphics*), boxes, and photos. In such a case, the preparer has failed to recognize the effect of this material on the reader.

Over-development may be a response to a popular view about learning styles. We fill pages with pictures and visual aids to help our visual learners. Because many people believe that they are visual learners, we consider that preparing information in a visual format is important. However, just as written information should follow a coherent narrative scheme, visual information should follow a coherent visual scheme. Not only should illustrations and images be prepared with an appropriate quality and clarity, they also should be placed in the text or appended as attachments in a way that provides information consistent with the report or presentation. Furthermore, images must not govern the message; instead, preparation and placement must be governed by the message being conveyed.

In this chapter, you will learn a simple strategy for organizing, preparing, and delivering information in a graphic manner. You will be exposed to several of the important tools used for preparing graphic illustrations and related art. Nevertheless, it is more important to focus on the message than on the format of the message. Unless you are truly a graphic artist, your role must be restricted to being the author of the message and a manager of information. Simple charts and tables can be powerful tools—if used effectively. For more than basic charts, tables, and similar kinds of data presentation, you should turn to a professional publication assistant whenever possible.

Strategies for Graphic Illustration

Effective graphic illustration is a result of careful planning focused on managing graphic resources rather than mastering them.

The term **graphic**, as used in writing and publishing, has its origin in the concept of making graphs. Originally, all graphs were numerical, and a graph was used to plot a set of numbers. This plotting of the numbers showed trends, illustrated formulae, or helped a problem solver visualize a solution. Today, a broader meaning of graphic includes visually explicit information; it often refers to outright exposure of usually unseen material. Thus, we refer to "graphic violence" and "explicit sexual content." This notion of graphic as "startling and direct expression" might be included in the idea of graphic illustration. The author wants to help the reader grasp the message quickly and easily. Graphic illustration provides a critical aid in achieving both dramatic effect and immediate communication. Illustrations can compress the complete message. By offering a complete or nearly complete expression of the message instantly, an illustration can provide a great impact.

Employing graphic illustrations effectively requires a strategy that balances the message with the impact of the illustration. This strategy first must come from a careful assessment of the role of the illustration. The writer must determine the purpose for using a graphic illustration. Establishing the purpose should take precedence over any other decision about the illustration process. Once the purpose has been established, the next step is placement of illustrations. For example, you can place all of the illustrations at the end of the manuscript or locate each illustration in proximity to its textual referent. Once purpose and placement have been determined, the final strategic step requires the creation of an illustration style. *Illustration style* is the basic layout and patterns used for graphs, charts, tables, figures, and photographs. This includes border style, font, and naming.

A well-planned strategy will result in efficiency and effectiveness. Even simple issues such as whether each table will be placed in a box within double or single border, if resolved prior to preparation of even the first table, can affect efficiency. Re-working even a few tables—each formatted differently—is a time-consuming process. However, the place to begin is determining your objective, both with the entire **illustration plan** and with individual illustrations. Essentially, you must be able to answer the question, "What is the purpose of this illustration?"

Establishing Your Purpose for Using an Illustration

Just as every word, sentence, paragraph, section, and chapter has a purpose and is carefully prepared to achieve that purpose, so must each illustration serve a coherent purpose. Typically, illustrations are effective tools for representing key ideas. With an illustration, you may present a large amount of information in a moment. A graph that is quickly and easily understood by the reader can show long-term trends or minor variations in data. Graphs and charts often provide an alternative means of stating information that would otherwise require clumsy numerical lists and details in the narrative. The illustration converts the numbers into a picture. Some readers may grasp the picture and use it to understand the numbers; others may understand the numbers and use the graph merely as a means of visualizing what the numbers are meant to show and the narrative is meant to say.

Illustrations can serve to summarize, too. They can minimize the need for reporting quantitative data in the middle of a narrative. In fact, charts and tables are often the sole means used to report data in reports and proposals. For writers and readers who deal with numbers frequently, viewing data reported in tabular form is commonplace. Even for this group, though, care must be taken not to allow the tables and charts to dominate the report at the expense of a clear and meaningful prose narrative.

Many companies with large publication needs, indeed most publishers, have graphic artists and illustrators on staff or readily available on a contractual or consulting basis. While you may find yourself in a situation without the luxury of outsourcing your graphics work, contracting a professional can be productive and cost effective. Still, even a professional will require a clearly designed illustration plan. The illustration plan must provide a set of specific guidelines for determining the nature of any particular illustration.

Illustrations can serve several purposes. Often an individual illustration is devoted to a single message. Of course, it is possible for one illustration to provide several key bits of information. The following includes the most common purposes for which an illustration might be utilized.

To Represent Data

Charts (such as pie and bar charts) are forms of graphic illustration and can be effective when used to show a collection of data, to organize the data, and even to serve as a primary record of data. Formally, **tables** are the specific form of chart that represents data in rows and columns. Sales volume, for instance, can be reported in a table using the most appropriate variable and covering all of the appropriate time frames. The table, organized in rows and columns, can be a record of sales figures for each person, district, or region for each day, week, month, quarter, or year. Usually, the sales report for an entire reporting period can to be placed on single page. When used to represent data, one chart or table serves as a summary for a series of charts and tables. In this format, and for the purposes of making an annual report, charts can be a record of everything that needs to be reported. Naturally, interpretive and analytic narratives guide the reader. For example, the reader should be told whether the chart represents good news or bad news. Table 10.1 shows a sample of a data table.

To Reveal Relationships

In presenting data, the preparer of a report should be aware of whether any key relationships need to be illustrated. One chart may summarize annual sales figures. Another

TABLE 10.1
...

Sample Data Table

Sales by Region, January 2004 through December 31, 2004 (in 10,000 Units)												
Region	1/31	2/29	3/31	4/30	5/31	6/30	7/31	8/31	9/30	10/31	11/30	12/31	Total
I	51	61	38	45	55	56	71	73	80	86	89	91	796
II	66	45	52	62	61	48	68	69	78	84	91	96	820
III	42	47	51	55	56	60	67	71	79	77	85	87	777
IV	63	64	68	69	71	72	71	75	88	89	91	98	919
V	55	58	59	63	64	64	68	72	77	81	80	91	832
VI	61	63	66	68	70	77	81	82	84	85	86	90	913
VII	72	48	81	80	35	55	67	48	81	91	37	92	787
VIII	22	37	48	52	61	66	73	75	82	93	99	102	810
Total	432	423	463	494	473	498	566	565	649	686	658	747	6,654

This is a very busy table, but the information is complete. The data has been simplified in Table 10.3.

chart can show the distribution of sales agents in various regions. Why not prepare a chart that illustrates related patterns between sales agents and sales figures? The question will eventually be whether three charts should be prepared, one showing the figures, another showing the agents, and yet another showing the relationship. At this point, skill at constructing charts is important. The relationship between agents and volume of sales would be presented most effectively and efficiently with a statistical correlation and a scatter plot. A **scatter plot** (or **scattergram**) is a graph of two variables that places a single point on the graph for each combination. The final graph appears as a set of clustered dots, each point representing two related data levels. It may be the case that in regions with more agents, each agent has a smaller sales volume due to the competition with other agents. This possibility is illustrated in Figure 10.1.

To Compare and Contrast

A simple comparison chart or table may have columns for each item being compared and another column for features. Table 10.2 on page 298 shows how this kind of chart can be used in promotional comparisons. In this case, the product with the most check marks is considered better because it has more features. This compare-and-contrast approach may not have much detailed information. It is unlikely that the check marks will suggest anything about the quality comparison that should be made. All three products may share a common feature, but do they all perform the feature equally well? A more detailed comparison can also be made based on performance. Often, features and performance are difficult to mix on the same chart.

To Show Trends

Trends are easy to illustrate. In western culture, our eyes normally scan from left to right. We usually view line drawings from left to right, with the scale indicated on the left and bottom of the chart. On a **line chart**, an upward-sloping line suggests an upward trend, a downward-sloping line suggests a declining trend, and a flat line suggests an unchanging pattern. Thus, upward lines are indicators for improving sales; a declining line is a good trend for waste, accidents, or customer complaints; the flat line suggests stability. When the graph is viewed, the interpretation should be quick and easy. Sometimes the most striking element of a graph provides an opportunity for discussion in the narrative.

FIGURE 10.1
...

Sample Scatter Plot

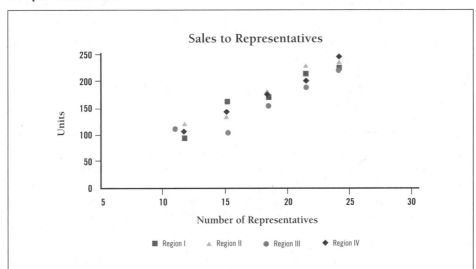

Note that the trend appears to show increased sales (*y*-axis) in relation to the number of representatives (*x*-axis).

TABLE 10.2
...

Comparison Table for Three Graphing Programs

Product Comparison Table Graphing Programs			
Feature	Basic	Deluxe	Premium
Draws vectors		✓	✓
Paints	✓	✓	✓
Preset charts	✓	✓	✓
Scatterplots	✓	✓	✓
Histograms	✓	✓	✓
Line graphs		✓	✓
Pie charts		✓	✓
Radar			✓
Bubble			✓
Surface			✓
Pareto			✓
High-low			✓
Exports to word processors	✓	✓	✓
Imports all databases		✓	✓
Preset figures		✓	✓
Organizational charts			✓
Action shapes			✓

The checks indicate that the program has the feature. When the feature is absent, a blank is usually all that is needed to indicate the missing feature.

If that element is missing in the narrative, the reader will be suspicious that you are trying to avoid addressing something important, even though you are technically making the required report of the data. This is true of almost every form of illustration. You should anticipate that someone will use the charts and data to perform his or her own analysis. Line charts are illustrated in Figure 10.2.

To Clarify Complex Patterns

Trends can be complicated and follow other trends or they may follow the timing of events. Sales figures may be seasonal or they may reflect broader economic trends (e.g., fewer cars are sold when interest rates go up and fewer are sold when the weather is cold). Also, complicated steps in a procedure, such as the process for filing a patent or complying with a federal regulation, can be shown with an illustration. In such an illustration, the sequence of events may be associated with the time necessary at each stop along the way. Even the physical place where the steps are completed can be illustrated simply with a picture, whereas the narrative description of the same event might be long and tedious. Table 10.3 on page 300 represents a simplification of the more cluttered Table 10.1.

FIGURE 10.2
...

Sample Line Chart

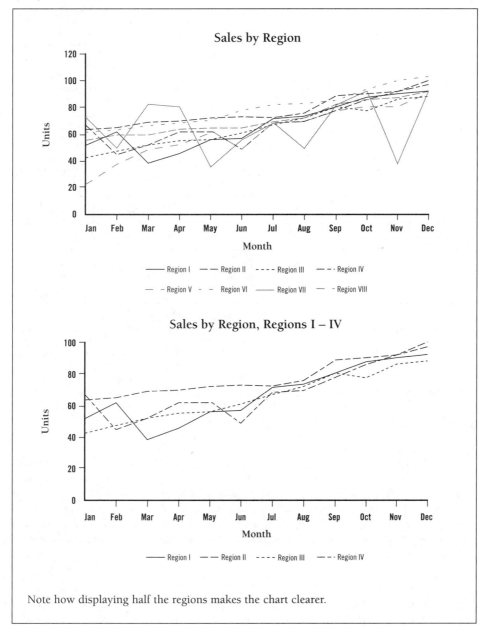

Note how displaying half the regions makes the chart clearer.

To Enhance Visualization of a Problem

We all hope that our writing will be so clear that no one needs aid in order to understand what we have said. Even so, the finest writing may benefit if the audience can
visualize critical concepts and issues. The single most important benefit of graphic
images must always be kept in mind: Graphic images provide readers with a means to
visualize instantly a problem, concept, sequence of events, or other critical information.
With graphic images, you can create a visual framework for everything that you want
the reader to construct and understand of your message. The challenge is to avoid using
the graphic image as a crutch to compensate for poor writing.

TABLE 10.3
...

Illustration that Simplifies

Sales by Region, January 1, 2004, through December 31, 2004 (in 10,000 units)					
Region	First Quarter	Second Quarter	Third Quarter	Fourth Quarter	Total
I	150	156	224	266	796
II	163	171	215	271	820
III	140	171	217	249	777
IV	195	212	234	278	919
V	172	191	217	252	832
VI	190	210	247	261	908
VII	201	170	196	220	787
VIII	107	179	230	294	810
Total	1,318	1,460	1,780	2,091	6,649

This table is a simplified version of Table 10.1. Rather than show each month, which would be extremely "busy," reducing the data to quarters makes it far more visually understandable. However, the data for Region VII that shows one month in three having extremely low production rates disappears when the months are added together. On the other hand, the dramatic growth in Region VIII becomes more obvious in this format.

A popular tool for illustrating relationships among a set of factors is the Pareto chart. The **Pareto chart** offers a graphic interpretation of the cumulative total of a measured event. For example, an illustration of all customer complaints can depict the total for each type of complaint, its percentage of the whole, and then show the accumulation of all types to 100 percent. This depiction also illustrates the relative frequency of each type of complaint. Figure 10.3 shows how a Pareto chart can illustrate complex relationships graphically.

To Reconstruct a Sequence of Events

If you expect an audience to develop a clear grasp of a sequence of events and the sequence is complicated, graphic illustrations provide an excellent format. A most common application is the **flow chart**. With a flow chart, symbols or schematized diagrams can be used to mark each stage of a sequence. Figure 10.4 provides an example of how symbols can be used to show the flow of events from the starting point to the end in a simple manufacturing process.

To Create a Context for Information

In 2000, the U.S. Census Bureau announced the new figures for the national census. On a very large chart, the bureau identified the population increase for each state (only a few had a decline). Because population determines the number of members from each state in the House of Representatives, some states that experienced an increase in population would, nevertheless, lose a representative or two because other states had even greater increases and would, therefore, gain representatives. The map that showed each state's

FIGURE 10.3
...

Pareto Chart

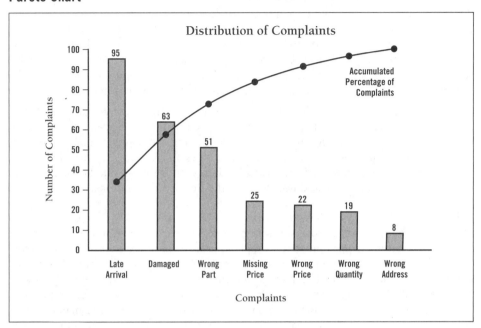

Distribution of Complaints

FIGURE 10.4
...

Chronological Flow Chart

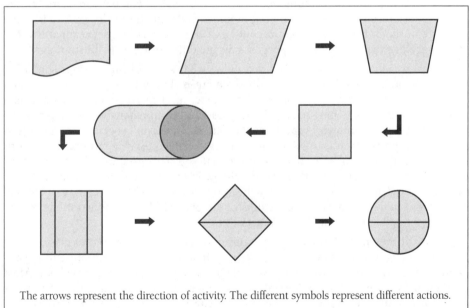

The arrows represent the direction of activity. The different symbols represent different actions.

increase also showed this information within the context of the even larger increases of other states. In the bureau's press conference, this large map provided a context in which the differences could be visualized and understood immediately. The census bureau's report described all of these changes in a narrative form. However, the context of this extremely important information was easier to follow after viewing the key charts and maps. (These maps can be viewed on the Web at the Census Bureau site, http://www.census.gov.)

Formulating a Strategy

Like other components in a document, the formatting and design of graphic elements requires preplanning. It may be easy with software to convert basic elements of a written document, including headings, page numbering, font style and size, and to alter these elements throughout the entire document. But, reconfiguring a large number of illustrations after they have been completed can be quite time consuming, even with the most powerful software tools. For this reason, preplanning graph elements is crucial for any effective strategy. Equally important in the use of graphics, the data and processes that are to be illustrated also require preplanning and collection—often before writing itself begins.

In the next section, we examine the tools involved in a process of developing graphic illustrations as well as ways that information can be organized for graphic illustration. In addition to these two important aspects of developing a strategy for graphic illustration, two criteria, inclusion and placement, must be established to guide the illustration process. These criteria provide rules for the kinds of graphs that should be included and general guidelines for where and how to place the finished illustrations.

Criteria for Inclusion

One rule of thumb for inclusion is: If information is unclear, use an illustration. As you might suspect, this rule may prove too simple to be as helpful as we desire. Other factors need to be considered. In deciding which information requires an illustration, you must consider the audience who will read your document and the purpose of that document. Documents filled with numbers or sequences of complicated operations require more illustrations and graphs than documents designed for sales purposes. The user manual for an automobile offers detailed information for a motivated, yet nontechnical audience. The manual is filled with illustrations, many of which are highly detailed and require study to decipher. If you want to change a fuse in your car, the manual directs you to the fuse box and to the correct fuse. A slick promotional brochure may include glossy photographs of many of the details of an automobile along with a detailed comparison chart, but the audience for this brochure does not need to know where the fuse is located. In fact, the audience of the brochure may soon become the audience for the user manual without any change in expertise. Differing purposes dictate different types of illustrations.

Several techniques may be used to determine what kinds of illustrations should be included in documents that are less easily distinguished than a car's sales brochure and its user manual. A sales report prepared for upper-level management can serve as a summary of each regional manager's detailed and comprehensive annual reports. Graphs used in the summary report may be derived from similar charts and graphs in the annual reports, but it is unlikely that a single detail would be appropriate. In short, you include illustrations that meet the goals that you have established for the manuscript. Information that strengthens your point or improves the way that your audience understands what you have written may be stronger if it is supplemented with a visual rendering. At a minimum, an effective illustration plan will have an illustration for each major point and at least one that summarizes the conclusion.

The use of presentation software programs discussed in Chapter 9 provides a model for illustrations in written documents. It may help to imagine yourself presenting your document orally. Which ideas would be difficult to convey without a visual aid? Most professional presentations include only a few, though quite powerful, graphic illustrations. Most of the presentation will be outline material that helps the presenter control and guide the audience. If a graphic illustration plan for your written document does not either lead to the reader's better understanding or guide the reader toward a conclusion, the illustration is not necessary.

Formulate meaningful criteria that are based on the specific objective of your written work. Although they may be fun, colorful, and even masterful, illustrations should not be done for their own sake. The rules that govern what you include in written form and guide what you say also must guide what you draw. Illustrations should be well integrated into the overall scheme of the written argument.

Criteria for Placement

Few illustrations break a paragraph. The most common placement format for tables, figures, and charts is at the end of the paragraph. Also, consider placing it at the first opportunity where it can be presented without being split by a page break. Photos and drawings—and, sometimes, small figures—can be inserted quite easily on a page so that the text wraps around the illustration, as in this textbook. If you are responsible for preparing **camera-ready copy**, you may want to experiment with the placement of illustrations. This experimentation will require you to be able to change the size and alter features like the "wrapping" of the text around the figures. A single page in a business magazine may have six or more charts with very detailed information on it. Such a concentration of charts is unusual, though. Often, the chart will be set aside in a box with additional explanation included in the box. This technique can be used effectively for a report or proposal that requires a large number of illustrations. With this method, illustrations can be placed in a group at the end of each section or even appended at the end of the report or proposal. If a several-page section has only one or two illustrations, they should be placed as close as possible to the narrative that addresses the concepts illustrated.

Readers have little tolerance for interpreting detailed illustrations, just as they have little tolerance for trying to follow a complicated narrative. You must judge the tolerance level of your audience. Their tolerance level will also help you determine a placement strategy.

SECTION SUMMARY

Graphic images are among the most powerful tools available to a writer. To use graphics effectively, your strategy must begin with establishing your purpose for using each illustration. This involves determining whether your purpose is to represent data, reveal relationships, compare and contrast, show trends, clarify complex patterns, enhance visualization of a problem, reconstruct a sequence of events, or create a context for information. Your next step is to formulate a strategy, which includes applying your criteria for inclusion and for placement.

CHALLENGE PROBLEM FOR REVIEW

A common effect used to show the difference between several items on a chart is to abbreviate the scales on the axes of the graph. For instance, the scale may start at a number other than zero. When comparing sales units and every representative has over 100 units, then starting at 100 makes sense—though this exaggerates the difference. The representative who sold 125 units will appear to have sold half as many as the representative who sold 150. Yet the difference is only 17 percent. This technique has the potential for great abuse. Examine charts in financial magazines to see if you can locate examples of these kinds of misleading details. What should be done to ensure that these kinds of space-saving techniques are not creating misinformation?

Processes for Preparing Meaningful Illustrations

Many software tools will help you prepare meaningful and effective illustrations. With each new generation of software, these tools become easier for the nonprofessional to master.

KEY CONCEPT 10.2
...

Select Appropriate Tools

You may think of the tools of illustration both as the forms that the illustration can take and as the software applications with which you create illustrations. In the following, we discuss both the types of illustrations and the processes that make them.

Graphs

Sometimes the terms graph and chart are used interchangeably, but graphs always have *x*- and *y*-axes (and sometimes a **z-coordinate** to represent a third axis). They may be **bar graphs** (also called **histograms**), line graphs (also called frequency polygons), scattergrams, **area charts**, and **pie charts**. A chart might be an **organizational chart**, a flow chart, a pie chart, or a data table. Table 10.3 summarizes the different types of charts and graphs.

TABLE 10.3
...

Types of Common Charts Summary Table

Area Chart or Pie Chart	A type of illustration that uses a geometric figure, usually a circle or a square, to represent the total distribution of a given variable, such as the total tax revenues or total sales, and then percentages of the total are represented as larger or smaller slices of the "pie" or sections of the total area.
Bar Graph or Histogram	Type of illustration that depicts each variable as a column or row that is filled from the base to the value being represented.
Chart	The broadest name for an illustration, it refers to graphs, tables, and free-hand illustrations.
Data Table	A type of chart that places data in rows and columns and allows sums and other analytic products (mean, standard deviation, etc.) to be placed in the summary rows or columns.
Flow Chart	A type of illustration that using various geometric shapes to symbolize a process or step and then drawing arrows or lines to show the order of the process.
Graph	A type of chart that uses a grid created by an *x*- and *y*-axis to illustrate regular or standard quantities and thus allowing comparisons.
Line Chart or Frequency Polygon	A type of illustration that locates related single values on the *x*-/*y*-grid and then connects the values with a line.
Organization Chart	A type of illustration that depicts the hierarchy of an company or agency by labeling boxes or other figures as either officers or offices and then showing the relationship between the offices with lines drawn between them.
Pareto Chart	A type of graph that represents the total distribution of a given variable, such as the total tax revenues or total sales, as a accumulation of all the depicted values.
Scattergram	A type of graph used for correlations that locates all the data points that have *x* and *y* values where the *x*- and *y*-axes indicate values of two variables that are being correlated.
Table	A type of chart that places data or classes of objects into columns and rows, where the position may reflect rank or importance but does not illustrate quantifiable difference based on position in the chart.

In a graph, the horizontal *x*-axis is called the *abscissa* and the vertical *y*-axis is called the *ordinate*. Traditionally, the *x*-axis is marked off in units of the variable, such as regional sales. The *y*-axis has coordinates for the amount or "frequency" of sales. A graph of customer complaints might show departments along the *x*-axis and the number of complaints on the *y*-axis. Another variation may be the month in which complaints are made, again shown on the *x*-axis, while the number of complaints (frequency) is shown on the *y*-axis. This is a guideline for creating graphs and variations are not wrong or inappropriate. A car dealership may want to show individual sales by placing miniature cars (using Velcro) on a chart that has each salesperson's name in a vertical column. The more cars to the right of the name, the more sales that individual has made. In this instance, the *x*- and *y*-axes are reversed, with the frequency dramatically announced along the horizontal axis. Table 10.4 illustrates this type of motivational chart. This is also a bar graph.

The auto sales graph shows how many discrete units individuals sell. What if the manager wanted to know what time of day sales occurred most often so that she could plan employee schedules more effectively? The mean might be 5:30 P.M. However, she cannot schedule everyone to be present at 5:30 P.M., or even from 5:00 to 6:00 P.M. Of course, there may be no sales at 5:30—the sales may be distributed at lunch and in the hour between 6:30 and 7:30 P.M. A clear picture of this situation requires a line graph. Also called a frequency polygon, the line graph shows the relative distribution, or frequency distribution, for a variable that is continuous. Time is a continuous variable, so a line graph would best represent sales distributed throughout the day. In the example described, the line graph will have two peaks, one at lunchtime, the other between 6:00 and 7:00 P.M. However, the line graph may show other patterns as well, perhaps with a small increase beginning around 4:00 P.M. (as people are getting off work). All of this data would be missed if a simple mean were used. A bar graph could be used, but it would need to be divided into the appropriate units. Divided into hour-long units, the evening sales might not be so apparent. Divided into half-hour increments, then it already looks like a line graph. Figure 10.5 on page 306 represents the graph used for scheduling.

The remarkable power of graphs to convey information succinctly and immediately is matched by the tools available for creating graphs. In an electronic form, data is typically stored in spreadsheets and databases. The most common of these found on a desktop computer are Microsoft's Excel, Corel's Quattro Pro, Lotus, and SPSS for PC. With each of these programs, you can create graphs that are exportable directly to a preferred software program. Presentation programs such as Microsoft's PowerPoint, Corel's Presentations, and Astound Presentations also create graphs. Once the data is entered

TABLE 10.4
...

Car Sales by Sales Representative

					Number of Cars							
Representative	1	2	3	4	5	6	7	8	9	10	11	12
Lian									🚗			
Thomas							🚗					
Miding								🚗				
Andrew				🚗								
Ann						🚗						
Jorge					🚗							

FIGURE 10.5
···

Scheduling Sales Representative

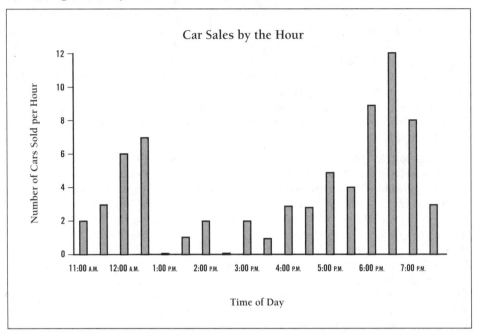

Car Sales by the Hour

into each of these spreadsheet and presentation programs, clicking the icon for the graph type chooses the format of the graph. A line graph can be switched to a bar graph; color or shading can be adjusted for each variable; and three-dimensional "shadowing" can be added. Each of these features requires only the act of selection; the program does the rest. You can try several variations to determine which one has the greatest impact. Illustration and layout programs such as Quark Express, Adobe Illustrator, Corel Draw, Adobe PageMaker, and Ventura not only can import graphs but to varying degrees can create graphs. The major word processors can import graphs prepared in their companion programs—and they can import graphs made in other programs, if they have been converted to a compatible file format.

With the variety of illustration programs and the expanding features of spreadsheets, presentation programs, and word processing programs, drawing a graph has become easy. Collecting and arranging the data will continue to be a chore. However, because drawing and illustrating functions have been integrated into the common way of storing data, a simple principle can be applied in the planning stages of any project: "Write once, read many times." That is, collect the data in a common format at the beginning, and you can manipulate, interpret, and report it many times without having to repeat the original collection process. Reporting requirements should be designed with the intention of future mining of the data. Skilled information technology personnel can design the appropriate combination of data storage and retrieval for almost any situation. In fact, managing data is a central task of the management information science (MIS) discipline. Remember, though: Good graphs require good data, which in turn require careful planning to facilitate data collection.

Illustration Tools

With the exception of highly specialized illustrations, such as medical illustrations and archeological records, the standard approach to preparing graphics is to use computer design tools. (Medical and biological illustrators use a wide assortment of electronic drafting, painting, and drawing tools, and they are highly qualified illustrators with specialized training.) Electronic illustration uses two basic formats: drawing and painting. Computer graphic artists use both formats, depending upon their needs.

Vector Drawing "Draw" programs use vectors, which are basically lines drawn between coordinates to create an image. The area within prescribed lines often is filled with color. Draw programs create images that can be expanded easily because they are created with various connected points that hold positions relative to each other. These are good tools to use for line illustrations and line art. Logos drawn with this kind of program can be expanded easily to billboard sizes without distorting the images. Adobe's Illustrator and Corel Draw are two commonly used desktop programs that create vector drawings, and there is a variety of engineering design software programs that work on the same principle. These design programs are called *computer-assisted design* or CAD programs. The evolution of processors and increased memory capacities of typical office desktop machines has made CAD programs more commonplace, though their use is still specialized.

Digital Painting "Paint" programs work on a different principle than vector drawing programs. Coloring each point in the image creates a complete picture. Coloring a straight or curved area makes lines as well. Because the images are created with color rather than filled geometric vectors, enlargement of some formats can result in distortion. The most common painting tool is probably Adobe's Photoshop, a program that has tremendous versatility. With an art pad and stylus, one can draw a picture as if working on a blank piece of paper. With an image captured through a camera, scanner, or even another program, Photoshop is an easy tool for manipulating an existing image. Unwanted background elements, such as telephone poles in a picture of the corporate headquarters, can be erased. While there are similar programs, Photoshop is the publishing standard. Also, although the software is designed with professional illustrators in mind, the amateur can create high-quality images with this tool.

Photography and Digital Imaging

New generations of digital still and video cameras have expanded illustration programs dramatically. Not only has the quality of the cameras steadily improved, but the ability to store and manipulate the images has improved as well. The memory stick of a camera that costs a few hundred dollars can store large numbers of photo images. These cameras are capable of producing photos that match and even exceed the quality and grain of thirty-five millimeter cameras. With photo manipulation programs, a novice can crop, rotate, touch-up, and insert photographic images into any desktop publication. Scanner technology continues to improve, and between these two technologies, virtually every barrier to image capture has been eliminated.

Digital Cameras Digital cameras are gauged by the maximum number of pixels (dots) in each picture. Common maximums for relatively inexpensive cameras are in the four and five million pixels range. These maximum-quality images produce files that are four to six megabytes in size, requiring the equivalent of four to six 3.5-inch diskettes. Cameras now have removable storage in several common formats: SmartMedia Card, Memory Stick, Compact Flash, and others. With typical storage, some of the cameras can store more than fifty of these high-resolution pictures. For more common uses, a slightly lower resolution generates photos that require one-eighth of the storage space. For example, 128 megabyte SmartMedia Card can hold 400 or more low-resolution images. Most cameras also store the photos in a variety of file types. The common Web-ready image is in one of two formats: gif ("graphics interchange format") or jpg (or jpeg which stands for "joint photographics experts group," an image format named after its developers). With photo-editing software, you can trim the file size of these formats from the four to five million bytes of the highest quality image down to a few thousand bytes. Depending on the desired application, the image can be prepared in a range of quality from the highest to the most compact.

Types of Files

The term *files type* refers to the way the graphic image is digitally constructed and stored. File types are important because certain files are more easily transmitted through the Web while other types are more useful in printed formats. For the Web, the primary concern is small storage and easy rendering on a computer terminal. The two most common static or still image file types for the Web are gif and jpg. These two file types are extremely compact. The jpg is best for photographs, while the gif is best for graphic art. However, when they are enlarged, they tend to lose quality and clarity. They have been termed "lossy" because of this characteristic. Contemporary digital cameras save the lowest grade images in one of these two types. The richest file types include tif (Tagged Image File Format) and bmp (Bitmap, the most frequently used format by Microsoft Windows). Each of the types—gif, jpg, tif, and bmp, are indicated on the file as file extensions. File names such as "myportrait.jpg" or "mylogo.gif" would indicate to the computer which program application to use to generate the screen image. The preferred digital format for professional publication is the tif file because many programs can use it and it can be manipulated without loss of image quality.

Digital video cameras have begun to match the quality of the digital still camera. While professional production cameras equivalent to professional film cameras are available, costs may be prohibitive for nonprofessional use with high-grade recording, as reasonably high-quality cameras are still just under $3,000. Many still cameras, however, can be used to capture brief video clips that play in the Quick Time or Windows Video Player formats. These are the same formats used by Webcams. For installation on a Web site, they are perfectly adequate. For presentation-quality video such as a brief clip to show in a business presentation, inexpensive analog to digital converters provide an alternative to an expensive digital video.

Software and hardware exist to capture VHS directly into the computer. The value of digital video is that it can be edited with software. DVD writers (sometimes called *burners*) are now affordable. Adobe Premier, for instance, can be used to create titles, edit video, and integrate other elements such as animation. For the managerial writer, the use of video is most likely the point at which one turns to an in-house specialist or a contracted professional.

Scanners The current trend in scanner technology is toward ease of use and minimum storage requirements for scanned images. Image quality continues to improve. Scanned images can be edited with the same image-editing programs used for digital photos. Another capability of the scanner is to capture text as an image, which, in turn, is processed through optical-character-reader software. This software converts the images of letters into a text-based format that can be imported into word processing programs. Materials that were written and published before electronic formats became commonplace can be converted to electronic storage. Not only does this kind of storage make life easier for future users of the material, but it also provides a means of reducing storage costs associated with large volumes of paper.

Scanner usage requires a warning, though. Recent legal decisions have established that the very creation of certain kinds of work automatically establishes copyright ownership, though the artist or author can officially register a copyright of images and text. Even casual use of a cartoon can infringe on the copyright owner's rights. When a presenter at a business meeting uses a *Dilbert* cartoon, for example, the owner of the *Dilbert* cartoon (Scott Adams) has specific rights. To use such an image properly, written permission must be acquired from the artist and the publisher. In most circumstances, a permission fee is required.

Drawing Tablets The most common tool for drawing an image in programs such as Microsoft Paint or Photoshop is the computer mouse, although computer graphic artists frequently use one of several types of drawing tablets. These tablets have several kinds of input devices, including a modified mouse and a stylus. Such tools are useful for both editing and free-hand drawing purposes. There are hundreds of enhancement software

Copyrights and Legal Concerns

Images, like written words, are protected from unauthorized use. The artist who creates an image, like the author who writes a sentence, is the original owner of the image. Use of the image requires permission and typically must be accompanied by an attribution to the artist or copyright owner. Images published in a newspaper, magazine, or book are copyrighted and require permission for use. They almost always require some form of payment or royalty, and the use is limited to a specified publication, such as a textbook or the textbook and its accompanying study guide. Use of an image that has permission for one type of publication may not include the reuse of the image in a sales promotion or as part of a Web site that promotes the book.

The author and the publisher follow strict guidelines both for giving and receiving permission to use an image. Unlike written material, of which an author can quote a small portion by giving proper citation to the original, no part of an image can be reproduced in this way. Even an art scholar must get permission to reproduce an image if the image is copyrighted, and images held in museums require reproduction permission to be used in a book or magazine article. Images do exist in the public domain, most typically from the government. Public domain means that they are free to use, but for most purposes, the source of the image should still be provided. Another level of availability is called "royalty free." Services that provide free images may do so for a subscription fee or are provided for sale as a collection (on CD-ROM or through an access code on the Internet). These may be in the form of "stock" photos or images, clip art, and even font types. More about these restrictions and the manner images can be used can be found on many Web sites discussing copyrights, public domain, and royalty-free issues. The best course of action will regularly include consultation with corporate counsel regarding intellectual property rights.

programs and add-ons as well. One remarkable three-dimensional-image-creation program is Bryce 3-D. The drawing "Twin Peaks" (shown here) was produced in several hours by a sixteen-year-old using an art pad and Bryce.

Vector drawing "Twin Peaks"

ERIK GARRISON

A method of digital-image capture worth mentioning is the use of screen capture software. **Screen capture software** takes a picture of the computer screen or an area of a computer screen and stores it in one of several image formats. For instance, instructions for using a new purchasing software application can be prepared by taking "pictures" of the various computer screens and then placing those "pictures" (called **screen shots**) in an instruction booklet. This booklet can be printed, published electronically, and e-mailed to all users of the software in the company. The company's information technology officer can optimize the transition to new software by merging these simple tools to create a brief but highly portable training tool.

Prepare the Information

Once you have command of the tools at your disposal and you have selected those appropriate for your project, there are several elements in the next step of preparing the information. These include collecting data, preparing sketches, looking for comparable samples from other works, and determining the placement in the document.

Collect Data

Collecting data can be the most time-consuming element in preparing information for inclusion in a report or publication. Some of the data may need to be researched; some of it may be held by other managers. The data must be in the right format for preparing graphs and tables. These steps take time, and they may need to be assigned to a single team member who becomes the custodian of the data.

Prepare Sketches

While the data is being collected, manual and electronic sketches can be drafted. Sketches help give a sense of the complexity and size of the finished tables, charts, and graphs. In a sketch, the data need not be complete, yet the number of variables should be accurate. The sketch helps us visualize the role of the illustration in the flow of the narrative. It can also be used to help us finalize the design of the illustration program.

Locate Samples

It is often good to collect samples from previous documents or from similar documents prepared by others. If you work with a team, these samples help others visualize the final product. If you work alone, they can give additional ideas for the look and feel of your document. With both the sketches and samples, a preliminary plan for the style and format of the illustration program should be made. In some companies, presentation formats are specified to ensure consistency. It is wise to check within your organization before beginning to prepare your presentation.

Determine Placement

Collect sketches and drafts of the charts and tables. With a complete, or nearly complete, list of the graphic illustrations planned, the next step is to prepare an outline of the document. The images can be matched to the outline headings. Once this is prepared, it should be used just as the outline of the narrative is used.

When Are Samples of Each Type of Illustration Needed?

If you are writing a five-page report that will be read by the management team and the CEO, the steps required to prepare a couple of graphs should be kept as simple as possible. Certainly, a comprehensive illustration program does not need to be devised, and the easiest forms of graphing will be adequate. You need to provide only a clear, accurate presentation of the information. Remember, a graph is useful because it provides a visual expression of the data. The management team should trust your information and its presentation.

In contrast, an annual report that will be shared with thousands of stockholders and future investors requires a different kind of preparation. Not only must certain information be presented in specific ways for legal purposes, but the information should be easy to grasp quickly by those who do not have expertise in this subject. This kind of project should be in the hands of a publication team. You may find yourself reviewing samples and approving them. The important criteria for this task are the ease of reading, ease of interpretation, and awareness of the audience.

Somewhere between these two kinds of reports is the project that requires the graphic preparation skills described in this chapter. These are the reports that do not require professional skills but do require professionalism. You or members of your team may need to make clean, clear, and attractive illustrations. Paper is cheap, and with these software programs a variety of samples can be generated with a few selections from the program's menus. After you have input the data into one of the planned graphs, print several variations. Share them with the team or show them to a colleague. Put them aside for as long as you can while you work on other aspects of the project. A fresh look, even a few hours later, may reveal problems with a layout or a preference for one over another.

Once a few samples have been approved, the complete program is ready to be made. Next, you will explore strategies for finalizing the project and assuring that the project has the desired impact.

SECTION SUMMARY

To prepare meaningful illustrations, you must start by selecting appropriate tools. The tools available include graphs (bar graphs, line graphs, scattergrams, area charts), illustration tools (vector drawing, digital painting), and photography and digital imaging (digital cameras, scanners, drawing tablets). Then you prepare the graphic: collect data, prepare sketches, locate samples, and determine placement.

CHALLENGE PROBLEM FOR REVIEW

Importing images, charts, and even what appears to be unadorned text from a variety of sources can produce nightmares for the person in charge of the final manuscript. You may have been required to compile the work of team members into a single report or presentation only to discover that the material seems to reformat itself with every new insertion or merge. What strategy can you suggest that would help you avoid the accumulation of hidden formatting information, automatic renumbering of outlines, and other odd behaviors?

The Final Product and Its Impact

KEY CONCEPT 10.3

The ultimate goal of the writing process is to create an effective product. The document must have graphic illustrations appropriate to the message and must elicit the appropriate, desired impact on the reader.

As with any form of writing, the final draft of a written document requires a close editorial review. The illustration program must be included in this review. All artwork, tables, charts, photos, headings, and numbering styles should be reviewed within the context of a completed package. Even the fonts used for the headings, captions, numbering system, and title page must be coordinated. Small details like this may have been overlooked or one partner in the process of preparing the document may have intentionally or accidentally altered the plan. The graphic images employed in the final product must be coordinated with the other style and formatting components of the product. The reason for this is simple: These components create regularity in the work and guide the reader. The patterns constructed and supplied by the consistency of the labels establish the foundation for the mental picture that the reader forms of the work. If you want to be considered a professional, every element of your writing product must be professionally produced and must look professional.

At times, line illustrations that looked smart when produced independently of the rest of the document take on a cartoonish appearance when they are placed in the final document. If the effect is appealing, that is fine, but if the work looks inappropriate when placed in its final context, changes must be made. If you are responsible for the presentation of the final document and you feel uncomfortable with an illustration, discard or rework that illustration. An illustration should not—*must not*—distract from your final product. If the project involves a team of people, the project leader has to be willing to discard something that may be close to the heart of another member. If you did the work by yourself, then you should not jeopardize the final product because you put time into an element that no longer fits. If you are especially fond or proud of something that must be left out, save it—you may be able to use it in another project later. The most critical criterion is that of the overall effect, the impact, of the final product.

Judging the Final Product

Who is to make such a crucial evaluation of the product? With a work of art, the artist must, on occasion, step back and take a look from a new perspective. The same is true of any written work. Unfortunately, the pace of work often dictates that things be completed at the last minute. The managerial writer rarely has time to put aside a project for a day or two and then return to it with fresh eyes. For this reason, many organizations have a designated editorial review process that places the responsibility for manuscript review in the hands of a capable person (or a team of qualified individuals).

There is a need for an independent, unbiased reviewer who is capable of recognizing the difference between good and bad writing and who can make constructive suggestions. Seek individuals on whom you can rely and take advantage of their expertise whenever possible and appropriate. Do not confuse a supervisor's reviewing your finished project with the critical need of close editorial review. However, if your supervisor does review the final document and complains that he or she does not understand the point of a particular illustration, then you have a clear signal that something is wrong. To avoid certain embarrassment, the final reviewer should not be the person for whom the document has been prepared. This makes the selection of the reviewer as important as the fact of having it reviewed. The key is in realizing how important the reviewer is to your project. The more information that you have presented in formats that are ancillary to the narrative, the more important this final review becomes. A few poorly conceived illustrations can undermine the best-composed manuscripts.

In professional publishing, the final judgment of the effectiveness of an illustration plan and its integration into a completed book rests in the hands of a project editor. For the most part, this judgment is subjective and depends on the editor's many years of experience. Little experience is required to detect poorly developed art and illustrations or inappropriately placed photos and figures, although simply judging that everything is correct and in the right place is not an evaluation of overall effectiveness. Such a simple judgment does not provide direction for improvement or enhancement of the overall impact. If your project is more than a routine report with prescribed charts and tables, it will benefit when you turn to someone who has experience in editing. Creating a consistent design strategy that incorporates all of the features of the finished product, including fonts and heading style as well as a common method for charts and graphs, gives even routine reports an accomplished feel. Documents that have a wider audience than the typical internal consumers of most managerial writing will benefit greatly from a coherent design and illustration strategy. The goal of this strategy is to optimize the visual impact of the final document *in balance* with the impact of the written narrative.

Cautions and Warnings

Given the time constraints that most managers face, the editorial review must be weighed against concerns for timeliness and efficiency. In the real world, even the best time managers are faced with enormous time constraints. Often, the time between being assigned a project and its expected completion date does not allow for all of the necessary steps to be undertaken with as much care and reflection as you would wish to take. The whole sequence from planning the illustration program to reviewing the finished product must be undertaken while the manuscript itself is being written. You may be tempted to write the content and prepare illustrations as each need arises. This pattern undermines the ideas of careful pre-planning and prewriting. In contexts that require significant amounts of writing, you can develop several illustration templates. For instance, if you issue numerous public reports, the value of this template approach is that recipients will recognize the consistency of the source. Using a template is probably the easiest means by which you can effectively write and illustrate a manuscript at the same time.

Unfortunately, managerial writers may engage in writing as if it were an area of expertise when, in reality, it is only a small part of their work. Overconfidence can ruin the final outcome. It can easily undermine the process if it leads to frequent revisions. Frequent revision results in a compressed schedule and the complications multiply. If the process involves several people, this time mismanagement can be highly disruptive and have lingering effects. To prevent this kind of damage, a project must begin with a coherent and easily understood strategy that includes a style sheet, a sample of each illustration form (table, chart, line art, and so on), and a list of anticipated tables and figures.

Once the project has reached near completion with the combination of text and graphics, a complete draft should be reviewed for consistency of both formatting style and presentation. During that review, a few elements related to impact should also be considered: simplicity, clarity, and scarcity versus overabundance. Although these elements are subjective, they are important. As important as these elements are, their effectiveness can be accurately evaluated only when you have the completed product in hand.

Simplicity

Simplicity refers to the number of elements depicted in a graphic illustration. Tables, charts, line graphs, bar graphs, photos, drawings, and flow charts can become difficult to grasp if they have even one too many elements. The simplest illustration depicts a characteristic of only one item. Still, many illustrations must be used to depict relationships between two or three elements. The more elements to be interrelated, the more difficult it becomes to produce a simple illustration. For complicated relationships, use a series of related illustrations with either the first or last showing the combined relationship set. At times it works well to show a complicated graph and then break it apart into component illustrations. The impact of this method can only be determined when a series has been completed. If the result is too complicated, the charts must be redone. An evaluation of simplicity can be made only with the completed product in hand.

Clarity

Clarity is a close relative of simplicity. However, the two terms are not identical. *Clarity* refers to the immediacy of understanding that the reader achieves when examining an illustration. If a humorous cartoon is placed in a manuscript and readers do not get it, then not only is the point lost, but the readers may feel that the author lacks the ability

to relate to them. So, a failure to be clear can result in more than a failure to communicate. In a more common case, the legend and captions of a chart may employ terms familiar only to the staff who regularly deal with them. Therefore, instead of referring to the "Northeast Region," the legend may refer to "Region 1." If the reader is required to search elsewhere to discover which region is Region 1, then the chart is unclear. The chart labeled "Last Quarter" will be clear and meaningful until this current quarter ends. If the chart is read next year, then the reader will be required to determine which quarter was "Last Quarter." A better label would be "Third Quarter 2005."

In addition to being a major concern in creating legends and captions, clarity must also apply to the content of graphic illustrations. Sometimes bar graphs do not emphasize key information as well as a line graph. Sometimes a line will imply continuity between one indicator and another. If the items being compared are independent, bar graphs are a better choice. If the graph is clear, there should be no ambiguity and no unintended implications created by the method of presentation. Fortunately, most graphing programs have a variety of graph templates that allow the preparer to change the graphing tool with a few key strokes or mouse clicks, so the switch between one presentation style and another when using charts and graphs is easy if the software has been mastered. Other forms of art, especially line drawings, may require more practice. Crucially important work may require professional assistance. In any case, clarity must be the rule.

Scarcity Versus Overabundance

No general rules exist that can be applied to the issue of scarcity or overabundance. Having no illustrations suggests that they are scarce, while having three or four illustrations per page suggests an overabundance of illustrations. You should develop a strategy based on the number of anticipated illustrations and the projected length of the document. Under most circumstances, the illustrations are distributed evenly throughout the document. However, if you anticipate five pages of narrative and thirty or forty illustrations, then it is likely that you have an overabundance problem. In this scenario, illustrations should be placed together as a separate appendix. The reader can then read the narrative uninterrupted and have the illustrations for immediate reference. The judgment of how many illustrations are appropriate for the length of the document or chapter is subjective. Again, a reviewer who has not worked closely on the project can be used to provide an unbiased reaction.

As with the issues of simplicity and clarity, judgments concerning the number of illustrations are best made when reviewing the completed draft. The scarcity judgment should be based not only on the visual appeal of the finished document but also on whether crucial information has been well illustrated and thoroughly explained. The problem of scarcity is simply a matter of too few visual aids; adding more will improve the reader's understanding. When there are too many illustrations for the length of the document, the problem may be due to the complexity of the information or the depth of analysis required of the report. Removing an illustration or collapsing several illustrations into one may not solve the problem. Still, if the problem of overabundance is one of too many aids, then removing some improves the clarity of the document. If overabundance results from having to cope with particularly complicated information, the author must judge this potential distraction and determine how to manage it, either by simplifying the illustrations or by adding an appendix. Knowing your audience for the finished product is extremely important in assessing scarcity and overabundance. Technical audiences expect more graphs and charts than do nontechnical audiences. Sales and marketing audiences tend to be more visual than engineers. There is a saying that to impress the audience, show the engineers lots of numbers in complicated charts and show the salespeople pictures.

A Concluding Note

Devising an illustration program that optimizes simplicity, clarity, and the number and distribution of the graphic aids in a manuscript does not guarantee that the illustrations will have the desired impact. Just as all good writing requires planning, practice, and revision, so does the illustration of ideas using graphics. Develop a strategy for each document and stick to it, know the tools that you have to help you make powerful images, and do not be afraid to remove clutter.

Properly constructed and well-designed graphic illustrations convey a sense of the author's mastery. Because the reader attains a more comprehensive understanding of the material, his or her confidence also increases. This subtle psychology of the look and feel of the document—along with being easy to grasp and understand—will strengthen the desired impact of the message that you are trying to convey. When combined with top-quality writing, the graphic image becomes a powerful communication tool.

SECTION SUMMARY

Because the impact of your final project is determined in part by who is judging it, you must, as always, be aware of your audience. The elements being judged include simplicity, clarity, and the balance between scarcity and overabundance.

CHALLENGE PROBLEM FOR REVIEW

Earlier, we suggested that there may be no simple rule of thumb for when to include an illustration. However, now that you have read this chapter, you probably have arrived at some ideas that will guide your future writing. Try to articulate the most important ideas. Can you defend them?

Checklist for Graphic Presentations

_____ Establish the purpose for the graphic illustration program.
_____ Formulate a strategy for including or excluding items from the illustration list.
_____ Select the appropriate tools for making the graphics.
_____ Prepare samples for other team members to examine and approve.
_____ Prepare the illustrations.
_____ Review the illustrations for clarity and appropriate number.
_____ Place the illustrations in the appropriate place in the manuscript.

CHAPTER SUMMARY

...

Because graphic images make a document easily understandable, they provide a powerful tool for managerial writing. To use this tool efficiently, you must establish the purpose for each illustration and determine where its placement is most effective, then you need to select the appropriate tools and prepare the data. Finally, you must be aware of the elements that will be judged by your audience in determining the impact of your graphics.

EXERCISES

...

Prewriting Exercises

1. Locate examples of illustration plans that may be less effective than intended. A good place to look is in introductory science and social science textbooks. Sometimes, there are so many illustrations that the actual text narrative gets lost. How might the examples be improved?

2. Find examples of misuse of graphics and charts. Were these errors accidental or were they meant to mislead?

3. Imagine that you were required to prepare a complex set of illustrations that involved scanner, cameras, drawings, and text art (for instance, you were just put in charge of the newsletter). Locate all these resources and determine what it would take for you to use them.

Writing Exercises

1. Using either real data borrowed from a report (data typically is not copyrighted—only the actual representation) or contrived data and produce a variety of graphic and tabular presentations. Do this by putting the data into a spreadsheet, database, or an illustration program, and then have the program produce the charts in different formats. Which of these formats best represents the data?

2. Using the data from Table 10.1 and Table 10.3, create a bar graph and a line graph for the quarters and an area chart for the totals. The bar and line graphs should show sales activity levels through the year while the area chart (a pie chart is best) should show the total sales activity as distributed across regions.

3. Use a drawing program to create your own company logo.

4. If you have access to a digital camera, take a series of pictures that illustrate how you prepare for and then undertake a writing project. Now, place this in a word processing document to tell the story in words and pictures.

5. Locate samples of different image file types and experiment with stretching, enlarging, cropping, and modifying the images. This activity will require access to software programs that will support the changes (such as Adobe Photoshop). Most cameras have a novice version of this kind of software.

6. In the next formal paper you write, try to incorporate illustration ideas. As you do so, formulate and articulate the strategy as it works for you.

IN-BOX EXERCISE

...

IN-BOX

You have yet another promotion. You are now the deputy chief information officer for the parent company, SHG International, and will manage all information gathering, corporate research, and public releases. Rather than a set of clearly delineated duties, your new position involves the "duties as assigned" by the chief information officer, Clarence House.

ITEM 1: E-MAIL FROM CHARLES, IT SPECIALIST ASSIGNED TO THE INFORMATION OFFICE. I heard you were going to do something about making everyone use the same software and file formats. This problem has gotten really serious. I think the problem is a training issue, because all the files used can be read by our standard computers.

By the way, I think the Richman girl told her dad about this. She was pretty upset because she thinks I lost some of her files.

Your Response

Check one:　☐ Memorandum　☐ E-mail　☐ Letter　☐ Note　☐ Other

To: _____

_____

_____

_____

_____

_____

_____

_____

_____

_____

_____

_____

_____

_____

_____

_____

_____

_____

_____

_____

_____

_____

_____

_____

ITEM 2: E-MAIL FROM CHERYL RICHMAN, SUMMER INTERN. I have cataloged all the official photos from the last two years. I had trouble opening a few of them using my computer, so I asked the IT people for help. I think they erased some of them. I cannot even find those files now.

Your Response

Check one: ☐ Memorandum   ☐ E-mail   ☐ Letter   ☐ Note   ☐ Other

To:

ITEM 3: E-MAIL FROM CRAIG, PRODUCTION ASSISTANT. I am having to redo every chart that is sent to me just to get it ready for the printer if the report is for release. The different divisions each have their own approaches. This will make it a mess later on when we try to maintain records of reports.

Your Response

Check one: ☐ Memorandum   ☐ E-mail   ☐ Letter   ☐ Note   ☐ Other

To:

ITEM 4: E-MAIL FROM CALLIE, PUBLIC RELATIONS. I have been on the job for two months now and I now have seen a different format for press releases from each SHG division. A-WII has even used two different formats in the same month. President Richman asked me why the releases always look different. I did not know what to say. He copied his e-mail to your boss to me. Then Mr. House told me to get with you about this problem.

Your Response

Check one: ☐ Memorandum ☐ E-mail ☐ Letter ☐ Note ☐ Other

To: _____

_____

_____

_____

_____

_____

_____

_____

_____

_____

_____

_____

_____

_____

_____

_____

_____

_____

_____

_____

_____

_____

_____

_____

_____

_____

_____

_____

ITEM 5: E-MAIL FROM FRANK RICHMAN, PRESIDENT, SHG INTERNATIONAL TO CLARENCE HOUSE. It has come to my attention that SHG International does not have a uniform document preparation guideline. I am confident that you can develop a satisfactory policy and present it to the executive leadership team. Our monthly meeting is in two weeks. We need to standardize all forms of media delivery and publications. Include standards for Web, press releases, press kits, graphics, and internal and external reports.

Across the bottom, a note to you: "Take care of this. CH"

Your Response

Check one: ☐ Memorandum   ☐ E-mail   ☐ Letter   ☐ Note   ☐ Other

To:

KEY TERMS

...

Area charts (p. 304)

Bar graph (**histogram**) (p. 304)

Camera-ready copy (p. 303)

Charts (p. 296)

Flow chart (p. 300)

Graphic (p. 295)

Illustration plan (p. 295)

Line chart (p. 297)

Organization Chart (p. 304)

Pareto chart (p. 300)

Pie charts (p. 304)

Scatter plot (**scattergram**) (p. 297)

Screen capture software (p. 310)

Screen shot (p. 310)

Tables (p. 296)

x-axis (p. 305)

y-axis (p. 305)

z-coordinate (p. 304)

...

THE NEXT STEP

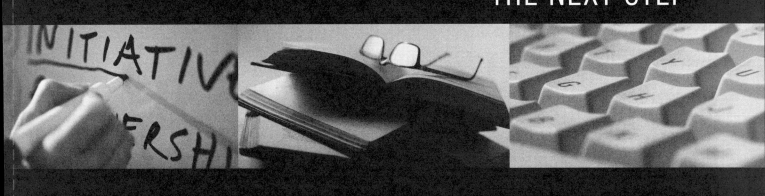

CHAPTER 11

Making a Career Move:
Seeking a New Job the "Write" Way

CHAPTER 11
...
MAKING *a* CAREER MOVE:
Seeking a New Job the "Write" Way

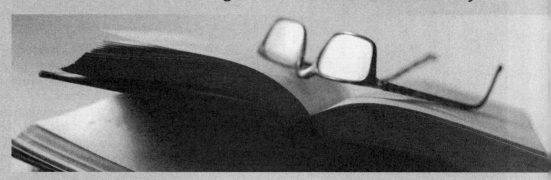

LEARNING OUTCOMES
...

Upon completion of this chapter, you will be able to accomplish the following tasks:

1. Assess your personal and professional goals in a manner that supports your job seeking.

2. Identify the resources available for researching a prospective employer and potential types and areas of employment.

3. Write an effective job application letter and a job inquiry letter.

4. Know the elements of an effective résumé.

5. Prepare a statement of goals and objectives for your résumé.

6. Prepare a one-page résumé highlighting your career plans and accomplishments.

7. Know the difference between a résumé, a curriculum vita, and a professional portfolio.

8. Understand how to prepare for a job interview.

9. Prepare responses to questions that you expect to answer and a set of questions that you plan to ask of an interviewer.

10. Develop a strategy for a follow-up letter.

"Résumés over there."

The average North American worker will make significant career changes five to seven times before retirement. For any given year in the United States approximately 35 percent of the workforce looks for a new job (FCIC, 2004). With so much change on the horizon, each time you enter a job search, you will benefit from knowing how to use research skills to locate a potential employer and how to use writing skills to obtain a job offer. Besides helping you obtain the job that you want, effective use of these skills can save time and money. The key to long-term success and personal fulfillment in a career often depends on the job seeker's ability to articulate, develop, and follow a clear career strategy. You must be proactive in your search. You cannot wait for something to happen or for someone else to find a job for you.

An essential first step on your path to a job is to be prepared. To begin, you must understand that creating a résumé and developing interview skills are but a small, though crucial, part of the process of landing a desirable job. You need to utilize these skills in landing a job that fits your personal expectations and life plans. Researching the nature of the job and the industry that it serves can help you be certain about your decision. Even the slightest amount of doubt, uncertainty, or self-questioning ("What am I doing here?") can diminish the energy that professionals expect to commit to their work. This pitfall can be avoided with carefully focused research into a prospective company and how it compares to market-leading industries. Even some job-preview activity such as talking to someone who does the kind of job you are seeking can help eliminate concerns that you have—or it may expose new concerns.

Planning a successful career move requires a fresh look at your career strategy and some thorough research into the prospects. This is true even if the move is a switch from one company to another in the same industry or even within the same company. In this chapter, you will learn how to appraise your goals and how to research a company that might hire you. You will learn how to write an application letter to capture a reader's interest. You will learn how to write a résumé that presents you in the best possible light, accentuating your positive features and minimizing any negatives that you may have. As an alternative to the traditional résumé, you will learn about the professional portfolio. Finally, you will learn how to prepare for an interview, how to perform during it, and what steps to take afterward.

Strategy: Opportunities and Introduction

Job searches must be guided by a career strategy. The job seeker must follow a two-pronged plan: "Know yourself; know the prospects."

Whether in the public or private sector, human resource (HR) and personnel managers must adhere to high standards for fairness in job selection processes, and there are professional organizations that oversee these standards. This does not mean that all managers are looking for the same type of employee. Each situation has its own parameters, and the guidelines for a position will vary from company to company. You cannot take it personally if you are "screened out," and above all, you should not place all of your hopes on a single opportunity. You can be sure that the job market does not reflect anyone's personal interest in you—it is indifferent and highly impersonal. When an employer is faced with hundreds of applicants, trivial details may govern the initial screening process. For instance, your résumé might be overlooked because the job description is so literally interpreted that some qualified applicants are excluded.

Suppose a company wants to hire a computer programmer. The personnel director reads the job description (which, in the computer industry, might require knowledge of odd or unusual computer languages), then culls everyone from the list of prospects who does not have the exact fit of languages. In many cases, having most of the programming language skills and a demonstrated ability to adapt and learn could be far more useful than specific language knowledge because programming languages change. If the personnel director does not understand this, capable applicants could be dropped from the list.

Recognizing how impersonal a job search can be helps you keep from taking things personally and becoming discouraged. It may become clear to you during an interview that you are not going to get the job. Immediately after the interview, make notes about what might have gone wrong. At a later date, when you can be impartial, review those notes—it may be that you did nothing wrong or you may see something that you can correct. If you are turned down for a job that you really wanted, as soon as you can do so gracefully, call the interviewer and ask if there is anything that you can do that might make you a stronger candidate the next time. You may find out that there were internal reasons for you not getting the job (e.g., a change in the job description). You may be told that your résumé needed clarification. You could even be told about a new job opening for which you are better qualified—and you already have an advantage since the interviewer knows you! In any case, you have a contact in the company. On the other hand, many interviewers and HR personnel will provide no feedback because of legal concerns. Applicants should not take such policies personally.

It also makes sense to keep several job possibilities available at the same time. If you have applied for a number of positions, you have to pay attention to the other possibilities and you do not have time to dwell on those that did not work out. Keep in mind that job seeking is an adventure, a learning experience, something that will lead to bigger and better things.

Because of the nature of the marketplace and the rigors of a job search, some seekers turn to career consultants who help evaluate their résumés and cover letters, conduct mock interviews, obtain leads, and help with negotiations. Because this is an expensive enterprise, because some job seekers have had excellent results but others have had disappointing experiences, and because you still have to do a considerable amount of work creating letters, résumés, and so forth, we mention this course of action only to make you aware that it is an option.

A job search must begin with a balanced, level-headed approach. A systematic approach starts with a review of your life goals and expectations. This includes an analysis of your professional strengths and weaknesses. Next should come careful research into the industry that you wish to enter, prospective companies, and their competition. Both you *and* the company must have a future together.

Develop Goals and Continually Reassess Them

Any time you begin a job search, you should recognize the opportunity to reevaluate your qualifications, personal goals, and objectives. Begin by being realistic. If your goal is to become a company CEO, do not expect to do so in your first job.

While it may be unnecessary to undertake a complete reassessment of values or engage in a soul-wrenching process of value clarification, the opportunity to reaffirm personal and professional goals should not be overlooked. Keeping these reassessed goals in mind should help you shape an effective résumé and guide you through an interview.

You can make goal setting a difficult chore or an enjoyable exercise. One method to make the exercise fun as well as insightful is to keep an activity record for a week or so.

In another approach, you prepare statements about what you would like to accomplish next month, next year, in five years, and in ten years. The first method reveals the distribution of activities in a given period of time. This forces you to ask questions about the relationship between the time spent on the activity and its value in regard to your personal and professional goals. Watching television twenty hours a week probably is useful only if you plan on becoming a screenwriter, news anchor, or something similar. Yet, if you discover that you spend a lot of time doing volunteer work or helping others, this activity may reveal an unarticulated goal or value. If you spend a lot of time reading or writing, then another set of goals may emerge.

The second approach to setting goals requires some imagination. Trying to imagine where you will be and what you will be accomplishing ten years from now means that you will be projecting your current ambitions and hopes into the future. Taken seriously, this task is not as easy as it seems. Simply declaring, "I want to be rich," is not adequately descriptive, even if it is a worthy goal. How will you become "rich"? What kind of riches? Those of us with happy, healthy, and successful children consider ourselves rich and blessed. Is this what you mean? Being forced to be specific and to offer details will make you more attentive to the complexities involved in developing achievable and realistic goals. The exercise is worthwhile. After establishing your benchmarks, review the daily activities you recorded for a period of time. Then, determine how you spent your time and ask whether this usage reflects your progress toward any of your goals. This exercise is provided in Prewriting Exercise 8.

Research a Company

This section applies most directly to the finishing student who is beginning a job search, but others can benefit from this advice, even those already employed in an industry and ready to move to positions of greater responsibility. For those just beginning, the decision on a specific industry that best fits your goals and abilities comes first. The next question that you may want to ask yourself is, "Whom do I want as my employer?" Consider how odd it is that while most students spend four or more years in college preparing for their first job, they approach graduation with only a remote idea of what they want to do. During college, they write research papers requiring hours of library research, yet these students often do absolutely no research when it comes to identifying a prospective employer. They usually accept a job with whichever company offers them a position first. A sensible job seeker spends a few hours inquiring about potential employers. Research helps every job seeker.

The college placement office is a good place to begin your research. The placement office is open to both current students and all alumni, whether they are recent graduates or not. Here you will find research materials about various companies, including their financial histories, their corporate reports, and even statistics on how many students from your school they have hired and what salaries they have offered in the past. Today, the Internet also provides a quick and easy means of learning about employers and jobs—both good and bad.

A counselor in the placement office can help you establish a placement file. This file includes letters of recommendation from some of your professors and general information on your college career. Many placement offices allow you to include letters from former and current employers or other pertinent sources as well. The counselor can help identify job-search areas in which students with your major have proven successful. If you have a business management major or computer information systems major, for example, you can probably locate several potential employers in the immediate area. For several years after you have graduated, the placement file can be updated with current letters from employers as well as additional information about employment. How long you maintain this file is up to you. If you plan to keep using it, however, you should make sure to keep it current.

The placement counselor may have copies of companies' annual reports or corporate handbooks that explain what they offer employees and what they expect. These are excellent resources. You might learn, for example, that some publishing houses require that those interested in becoming editors must first work as traveling sales representatives for up to two years (to get acquainted with the book list). A business major in a southern California college may be horrified to learn that a company that she always thought would be ideal for her requires all new account executives to go through three months of training in South Dakota and then to be willing to be transferred to New York City. On the other hand, a Hispanic computer science major might be delighted to learn that a major company that he or she has never considered has a special program to increase its number of minority employees, especially in the area of computer science.

The placement office should have a list of alumni who have worked for corporations that you are investigating. If no one has worked for a specific corporation, the placement advisor or alumni association should be able to locate a graduate from your institution who has worked in the same industry. These alumni are the best source of pertinent information for the early stages of a job search as well as the end stages when you are making a decision. At Duke University, for instance, there is a **networking** apparatus in place that puts students in touch with alumni in specific fields and informs alumni about graduating students who are qualified for positions in those fields. Even small, regional colleges such as Centre College in Kentucky and Hanover College in Indiana supply interested students with useful pamphlets about job searches, industries, and potential employers (especially local companies). Similar procedures are in place at most colleges and universities. You should plan to tap into the network of alumni no matter how long it has been since you graduated.

What other kinds of research can you undertake? Start by creating and maintaining a file folder on prospective employers. Newspapers often have special Sunday features on businesses and industries. Regular features in business magazines offer important information about changes in major industries. Many industries publish magazines devoted to their specific interests and are good sources for information about the industry and the companies that comprise it. Some of these magazines contain job information as well. You might want to watch business-oriented programs on cable or satellite television and check the Internet, too—and, don't forget that the reference librarian at your public library may be able to help you.

You will need to take notes, but conducting this research should ensure that your information will be current. Keep this information in the files that you create. Place in those files any local newspaper stories about companies in your field who have just hired new managers. These stories provide you with the manager's name and his or her department. This information can prove valuable later when you mount your campaign to meet and talk with actual managers instead of personnel department employees. The *Wall Street Journal* index provides an excellent resource, and computer search services are available in your library. Use them to research stories about companies you have considered as employers. (Not everything is on the Internet!) You will find articles that provide you with information that you can use later in your cover letters and in your interviews.

Your placement office has contacts with a number of employers who schedule interviews on campus, and the office probably hosts job fairs, too. You should take advantage of any opportunity to talk with these companies as well as to companies that you wish to contact yourself. Use your research skills to help prepare you to talk with these companies. When applicants are knowledgeable about a company, the impression they give is one of genuine interest combined with a self-starter's mentality.

Normally, in addition to being posted at the placement office, job fair notices and interview schedules are posted about campus, and most campus newspapers include these lists. Your placement counselor can probably put you on an e-mail list to receive these notices as well. Keeping up-to-date is important because it allows you to make an appointment in advance.

Appointments made in advance of a scheduled visit allow for preparation. A letter to the recruiter expressing interest in meeting and hearing more about an opportunity not only primes the recruiter, but it gives the letter writer the advantage of establishing familiarity and demonstrating interest and talent and provides a sample of your writing ability. Moreover, successful job seeking requires involvement in as many interviews as possible. The more experience you have in interview situations, the better equipped you are. You learn what questions might be asked, and you are forced to think about yourself and your abilities and goals more concretely than you might have up to now.

Frequently, the research-and-interview process reveals critical information about a company. This information can be both encouraging and discouraging. Your interest may be heightened, or you may drop the company from your list altogether. Use all of the resources at your disposal. Family, friends, and acquaintances (including clients or customers, if you already have a position) may know of job opportunities close to home. You can also check advertisements in newspapers (the library will have copies of current papers from other cities) and professional publications.

In today's Internet-connected world, many job searches are conducted online, whether through your college alumni office, a local Web site, or one of the national job placement companies on the Web (see Insight Box 11.1). This is a relatively easy and often successful approach and may not cost you anything but your time. The Privacy Rights Clearing House (http://www.privacyrights.org/) warns, however, that circulating your résumé on a Web site (even your personal site) makes you vulnerable to identity theft, a crime that affects millions of people each year.

Letters of Inquiry

Although your placement or employment office provides an excellent starting point, a **letter of inquiry** is usually the first crucial contact made with a potential employer. In the strictest sense, the letter of inquiry refers to a letter seeking information about the availability of positions. Often, job seekers send a résumé with the letter. Including the résumé at this point is questionable—even for desperate job seekers. Unless asked for by the employer, a résumé is needless material that must be dealt with (and thus is a time waster) and may suggest that the sender is either pushy or not knowledgeable.

A well-conceptualized letter reflects the writer's personality and qualifications in a brief format that serves the purpose of getting a response. To this end, you should use as many action words and keywords as possible and appropriate. A **keyword** is a term that carries special significance, and its use identifies you as a member of or knowledgeable about the target audience. Many large companies utilize software that identifies key-

INSIGHT BOX 11.1
...

Internet Job Search Resources

The Internet has become a force in job searches just as competitive solutions have for many other sectors of the economy. There are several major players in the job market search field, including Monster.com, CareerBuilder.com, Joblocator.com, and Careerjournal.com. The problem with the Internet is that it seems to result in few job offers for the applicants. According to Nick Corcodilos (2003), author of an online newsletter for headhunters, the job success rate is extremely low. In a well-researched special edition of his newsletter, he reports that only 1.5 percent of the online résumés result in a job. Of course, the Internet is still a great place to learn about potential employers and the industry you are trying to enter, even if it is a weak source for the jobs themselves.

Source: Corcodilos, Nick. "Job-Board Journalism: Selling Out the American Job Hunter," *Ask the Headhunter: The Insider's Edge on Job Search & Hiring,* June 17, 2003, http://www.asktheheadhunter.com/newsletter/OE20030617.htm (accessed July 5, 2004).

words on electronically submitted résumés, and it pays to give them what they are seeking. As an example, if you are seeking a position in the area of finance, you might talk about not only your accounting experience but also your analytical ability vis-à-vis trend analysis, results analysis, strategic planning, forecasting, and business policies. The same would be true of keywords used in the field of sales: contacts, lead generation, customer support, and account management. Many of these words are applicable to other areas as well. Among the terms or phrases that have universal applications would be "bilingual," "presentation skills," and "written communication skills." A response to your letter of inquiry creates the opportunity for you to write a more comprehensive yet tailored letter. This second letter can include the résumé or work portfolio. One of the truths about hiring is that there are frequently so many applicants that it is literally impossible for those in charge of choosing new employees to read all the applications. What takes place then, is that rather than trying to determine who is best, they begin looking for ways not to include applicants. Throwing out applications that are physically hard to read or which contain obvious errors or are in formats that they are not used to reduces the number that they have to read. Do not give anyone the chance to disregard your application for an easily avoidable mechanical error.

There are no set rules for the letter of inquiry. However, diplomatic candor and honesty are guidelines to follow. If you do not match up well with the company or vice versa, you do not want to work there and they do not want you. It is best to avoid the cost of time, money, energy, and emotions by determining this before a job offer is made. You are a qualified college graduate looking for a position with potential for a stable and productive future. You want to grow with a growing company. You are looking on the east coast or west coast, and so on. This can be said in one page of clear prose.

Such a letter can also be customized with an inquiry that reflects your knowledge of the company and even be personalized with an internal address to an actual person in the company. Letters with this attention to detail will get some kind of response—probably with equal timesaving candor and honesty. Sometimes the candor includes a bonus. Many executives and managers have broad networks of connections. You might get "We have no expansion plans, but an associate of mine at _____ told me that his company was planning to add employees in your area of expertise." It has happened.

How and when should a systematic job seeker include the letter of inquiry in the job search strategy? If schedules allow, send a letter of inquiry as a confirmation that you plan to be at a scheduled campus visit or job fair. If you have widened your search, use the letter of inquiry to introduce yourself to appropriate individuals at companies that you have researched. Use the letter as a means of following up on casual contacts and casual recommendations. If you go to a professional convention, for example, you will find that you can meet people in informal settings. Many of these people will know of openings in your field or will be willing to refer you to others who can be of help.

Material Should Look Good

The letters and résumés that are discussed in this chapter show you how to present yourself to someone who may have no prior knowledge about you. All of these communications should be typed or printed with an ink source that is dark, black, and clear, and they should be typed on good-quality paper (24 pound). Check your spelling and punctuation and not just with a spell and grammar checker—read what you have written! Limit the number and sizes of your fonts; you do not want your form to overwhelm your content. Avoid clutter; keep your documents clean looking by judicious use of space and margins.

Incidentally, if you go to a professional conference, take copies of your résumé with you. We have known students who did not do this, then received requests for their résumés from forty potential employers.

Use the interview at a job fair or the letter of inquiry to prepare the ground for a full-blown job application cover letter and résumé. At times, companies announce job availability and open positions in a manner that makes direct applications appropriate. In either case, the recipient of an application should have the sense that the letter and résumé were in one way or another invited. The letter of inquiry is typically uninvited. In either case, the tone of the letter should be complimentary and respectful.

To repeat what we have said numerous times, be careful with your word choice. This warning is truly germane in your letter of inquiry and your job application letter. Why? Because you only have one chance to make a first impression. A well-known mutual fund company boasts about its "proven performance." What does that mean? Every company has a proven performance record. The issue is, is the performance good or bad? We want to know whether the company has made good decisions or is its record characterized by poor management? Certainly, the advertisement is meant to suggest that the company's performance has been good, but the impression given by the advertisement reflects sloppy, imprecise thinking. This is not a characteristic that you want in a company with which you trust your money. With these thoughts in mind, let us examine the details of the application cover letter.

The Job Application Letter

The **job application letter** (also called a **cover letter**) is used for several purposes. First, the letter is an indication of your interest in a position. Second, it is a brief review of your qualifications for the position. Third, it serves as a cover letter for your résumé (the résumé—not the cover letter—provides a detailed description of your qualifications). Fourth, it expresses your willingness to be interviewed. The application letter also introduces you as a person; remember to consider your audience when you choose your wording and the specific information that you want to include. These letters require correct spelling, punctuation, and grammar. An error in any of these areas is unforgivable. Any error suggests to your prospective employer that you are careless, in a rush, uneducated, or some combination of these. Who wants an employee with these qualities working on projects in the company or representing them to clients and the public at large? You want to make the best impression that you can.

Application letters should be limited to one page. Many job seekers unwisely try to recreate the résumé in a narrative form or to repeat all of the information that is provided in the résumé. Avoid this error by including only pertinent highlights. You do not have to give your entire life story or work history in this letter, and there is no requirement that the items be listed in chronological order. If you have had one or two spectacular successes that are pertinent to the job for which you are applying, that is where your focus should be. You can exclude the rest. Employers may not have the time or interest to read much more anyway, especially in a large company where there can be hundreds of applications for each position and dozens of positions open. If the letter covers everything, why bore reviewers with redundant information in the résumé? At the same time, the job application letter provides a good opportunity for the employer to judge your ability to be concise and to determine the most important factors to emphasize. Thus, your thinking and writing skills, as well as your personality, may be appraised on the basis of this letter. Use it wisely to create a favorable impression.

Format

In Chapter 3, we discussed how to write business letters. Because a job application letter is merely another type of business letter, the basic approaches and principles that you learned apply in writing this kind of a letter. Figure 11.1 illustrates an approach that you might take when writing to a company about an advertised job.

FIGURE 11.1
...

A Response Letter

Street
City, State, Zip Code
Date

Name, Title
Department
Company
Street
City, State, Zip Code

Dear _____ :

In your first paragraph, state the job (by title) for which you are applying. Try to begin the first sentence with something other than "I." For instance, "Please accept my application for . . ." or "In response to your announcement . . ." or "Information that I have received from . . . ."

In the second paragraph, indicate how you fit the requirements for the job as detailed in the ad or by the employer or another information source. When there is little specific information, you may fill in what you think they are looking for, but be careful not to be overimaginative.

In the third paragraph, you might address more details indicated in the job announcement or expand on why you are well-suited for the position or how you will find career satisfaction in this or expected further positions with them that would be part of a normal advancement pattern. You may indicate something about the company that especially impresses you. Do not write something merely to be writing something. It is better to be brief than wrong, and it may be useful to add more details during your interview.

In the fourth paragraph, indicate that you are enclosing a copy of your résumé and that you are interested in providing any further information that they may need. The references should be as local to your prospective employer as possible. The name, title, employer, business address, working hours, and telephone number should be included. Three to four references are usually sufficient. However, before you include their names in your letter, you should first ask their permission, and you should give them a copy of your résumé for their own reference.

The fifth (and last) paragraph should contain a thank you for the attention given to your application and a comment about your willingness to see or talk with them about the specifics of the job. You might also indicate that you will be in their area at such-and-such a time and would like to contact them, if that is all right. Alternately, you might say that you would like to call them at a specific time later about the possibility of talking with them personally or setting up an interview.

Sincerely,
[Your handwritten signature]
Typed Name

Enclosure

In the application letter, you explain how you meet the advertised criteria for a position. Since clerical staff often screen cover letters and résumés before managers see them, if your résumé does not show actual required experience (in sales, for example), you will need to explain this disparity in order to keep your résumé from being placed in the rejected pile. The screeners may be looking for certain key words that reflect the criteria of the advertised position.

The type of application letter written as an application for a specific job announcement is also known as a **response letter**. Write response letters when you know that there is a position open and you are responding to an advertisement or request of some sort. One of the main purposes of this type of letter is to obtain an interview; therefore, you want to provide the details about yourself that will help the company decide that they may want to hire you rather than one of the other job applicants.

A second kind of cover letter, the **blind cover letter**, is used when you do not know whether there is an opening but you want to let a company know that you are interested in any appropriate positions that might come open. In effect, the letter is a request that your information be placed on file for future possible openings.

Although larger companies maintain files of prospects, smaller companies may not be able to devote much time to maintaining such files in an organized manner. With these companies, you may be better off with a letter of inquiry. However, there is no harm in blanket mailing blind cover letters to dozens of companies involved in the kind of work that appeals to you or which frequently use people who work in your area of expertise and training. Usually, these letters are sent to a number of companies and are either not tailored to a specific company or are only minimally tailored using the mail merge feature of a software application (see Chapter 8). Therefore, with focused brevity, you express your interest in doing the kind of work that the company does, explain why you are interested, and suggest some of your personal goals. Even if a company has no present openings for someone with your qualifications, letters of this kind may impress an employer with your initiative and lead to further contact, if it is personalized to that company. If you do interview for a position later, your name will be familiar to those who do the hiring, which is your advantage over other applicants. Still, blanket mailings may be ineffective for several reasons. They are expensive and time-consuming (with little promise of paying any dividends), they are discouraging for the sender, and they are usually an annoyance to employers. Some experts believe that this type of letter should be used only if an individual has a contact or a lead with a company. Moreover, each letter, whether three or three hundred, should be personalized to the company.

The blind cover letter has the smallest success rate of any type of job search technique (calling the company employment office is not included in this assessment and generally is not recommended). A job seeker may have only a 1 to 3 percent response to such an approach. Still, in a tight market, any chance is worth a try, and a well-planned total approach in seeking a job can include some broadly cast blind letters. Employers actually expect to receive a certain volume of these unsolicited letters and have standard practices for coping with them.

If there is anything that distinguishes your background from other recent graduates, you should include this information in the blind cover letter. You may have an unusual combination of skills or be the only female minority student graduating from your school in your field. In Figure 11.2, notice that Hal Pinter calls attention to his work experience. While managing a pizza parlor may not seem an ideal experience for a high-tech marketing position, Pinter wisely calls attention to those skills that are transferable—his personnel, financial, and language skills. He also emphasizes his ability to manage his time successfully; he is able to maintain a 3.5 GPA while working thirty hours a week. Personnel managers find this kind of concrete detail attractive.

The **request for assistance letter** provides the platform for seeking help or information from someone already employed in your field. This letter must be addressed to a specific individual. With rudimentary research, you can discover the name of the per-

FIGURE 11.2
...

A Blind Cover Letter

4000 West Fifth Street
Phoenix, AZ 85044
October 12, 2004

Mr. T. Stoppard
Director of Personnel
Arcadia Corporation
11222 High Tech Parkway
Phoenix, AZ 85002

Dear Mr. Stoppard:

It is clear to me that Arcadia Corporation encourages its employees to display their initiative and problem-solving skills and that the corporation rewards hard work. During the past two years, I have carried a full course load at Arizona State University while working 30 hours a week as a manager at Pizzasogood. On two separate occasions, our regional office has selected me as employee of the month. I have full responsibility for hiring, training, scheduling, and our store's bottom line. During this time, I maintained a 3.5 GPA (4.0 = A) while pursuing a BS degree in marketing. I will graduate next month.

As the enclosed résumé indicates, I have three years of experience as a data consultant. Please note that I minored in computer science and am comfortable with spreadsheet, database, and electronic spreadsheet software. You will also see that I took a number of courses in Spanish. My fluency in this language might prove an asset to Arcadia Corporation should it want to reach the large Hispanic community here in Arizona as well as nationally.

Please consider me for any appropriate marketing position. In the meantime, I would appreciate any information you could send to me regarding possible future openings. I look forward to hearing from you.

Thank you for your consideration.

Sincerely,

Hal Pinter

Hal Pinter

Enclosure

son to whom the letter should be addressed. This information is available in a number of places, and one of the most effective methods of learning what you need to know is simply to call the company and ask the receptionist. The letter may include a request for assistance regarding how to learn about openings, whether the company has a formal application process or form, and to whom applications should be sent. Many people welcome the chance to provide this information, and these kinds of questions become a part of your networking system. You can easily include comments describing your experience and the kind of work that you would like to do. Consequently, the letter serves as a letter of inquiry as well.

To decide what kind of letter you need to prepare, ask yourself what you intend to accomplish with the letter. Consider these questions:

- Do I know of a position at this company?
- Do I know the name and position of the person who will read this letter?
- What kind of response do I expect from this letter?
- Do I need to create a reason for additonal contact?

Table 11.1 provides a set of questions that will help you determine what type of letter you should use.

Cover Letter Writing 101

Before you can begin writing any letters, however, you must understand the basics of these types of letters. All job application cover letters contain four fundamental parts: the identification, the statement, the request, and the close.

The Identification In the first paragraph, explain why you are writing. This means that you identify the position for which you are applying and how you learned of the position opening. In order to let your prospective employer know that you are applying to work in a specific company and not just writing to everyone in the industry, include some information that conveys this. You can find out about companies from many of the same sources that led you to apply for the job in the first place. If the company is located in your community, you can ask friends or people who already work there about the company. You can also check with the local chamber of commerce, state or local Better Business Bureaus, or similar organizations. Remember, information about most major companies can be found at your library in various reference books and at the company's Web site on the Internet, as well.

The company's annual report provides an excellent source of information. Because you want to investigate any company for which you might work, this research serves two purposes. First, you learn whether you want to work there. Second, you can refer to pertinent facts in your cover letter to let the potential employer know that you are serious about the position, that you have the initiative to determine your suitability for it, and that you will fit into the organization itself. In addition, you will have begun your preparation for the interview.

TABLE 11.1
...

Which Type of Letter Should You Use?

Do I know of a position at this company?	If yes, use a response letter. If no, use a blind cover letter.
Do I know the name and position of the person who will read this letter?	If yes, use a response letter. If no, use a blind cover letter.
What kind of response do I expect from this letter?	If a follow-up opportunity is sought, use a response letter. If further information is needed, use a request for assistance letter.
Do I need to create a reason for additional contact?	If yes, use a request for assistance letter. If no, use a response letter.

The Statement In your second and third paragraphs, discuss what you understand the position to include and how your skills and training fit the position. In the third paragraph, expand on a few details about your skills and experience and explain how these apply to the position that you are seeking. These two core paragraphs constitute a "statement" about how you match the announced position and how you would be excited to undertake the opportunity it represents. This statement can be made in one paragraph, but as one paragraph, it has the potential for becoming too long. Again, this is not a summary of your résumé; you are highlighting pertinent facts and establishing the relationships among them. This carefully devised outline of your background must emphasize those elements that meet the employer's advertised requirements or preferences. These elements can be school related and/or past job related. They also may require some thinking "outside the box." A shift manager at a local coffee shop is still a management role, even if it only involved overseeing several people each work shift. Every job you have is important and provides important lessons for the future. However, do not overwork this inspired view of your work history. Find one simple and direct example or skill to build your case.

The Request In the fourth paragraph, indicate a willingness to be interviewed and to provide additional supportive material. You might suggest that you feel confident about the announced position and your ability, and that an interview would strengthen your claims. Add that you are willing to offer more detailed information about projects you have completed in which they may have an interest. Identify the other types of supportive evidence you could send. These may include testimonies from clients, coworkers, other team members of a project, supervisors, and professors. Unfortunately, letters of reference and other reference contacts have become highly restricted in the workplace. Professors continue to write detailed and extensive letters of reference or support for their students, but employment-based references have dwindled to verification of employment and highly structured (and brief) telephone interviews. Approach this supporting material with caution.

Close Close by expressing your appreciation for being considered for the position. Different types of letters may require different styles of closure. For instance, in the case of a request for assistance letter, the reader should understand the request clearly.

INSIGHT BOX 11.3
...

What It Was Like

Some of your professors may have written their dissertations before desktop computers were available, even before photocopying was commonplace. Their 150- to 200-page-long dissertations were typed on a manual typewriter (electric, if they were lucky), and each page (along with five or six carbon copies) had to be perfect. A single misspelling or punctuation or spacing error meant that the entire page (and carbon copies) had to be retyped. You do not have to be so careful and exacting in many of your managerial writing projects, but you must be vigilant to make sure that no document leaves your desk with a single error in it. Errors reflect badly on your thinking, on your credibility, on your carefulness, and on your attitude toward your project and your audience. In addition, some projects require the same level of exactitude that was imposed upon your professor's dissertation. It makes sense, then, to practice that kind of care with all of your writing projects; to make that kind of care a habit. You will avoid the easy pitfalls if you do this, and you will reap rewards that are worth the time spent cultivating this habit.

With regard to the number of paragraphs to be included in these types of letters, the number may vary. Earlier, we described how five paragraphs can be used (they could easily be collapsed into three paragraphs). Some people consider the standard paradigm to be the three-paragraph model, which covers the following questions: Why am I writing?; How do I meet the requirements of the prospective employer?; What do I want to happen next? Of course, it is permissible to use a four- or five-paragraph structure, if it is necessary to do so because of what you are trying to communicate.

Notes on Content

Employers are not impressed with obvious form letters, especially those that come in the form of photocopies on which you have typed their names and addresses. They want someone who has taken care and effort in preparing an application, for this is seen as a reflection of the personality of the person applying for the position and his or her attitude about the position and the company. It is vital, then, that you make sure that you use the job application cover letter to emphasize those areas in your background that specifically relate to the position you are seeking and demonstrate a knowledge of the role of that position in the company.

SECTION SUMMARY

A systematic job search must start from a base knowledge of your strengths and weaknesses and the nature of the current job market. Begin by articulating or reassessing your goals. This can be followed by research to find a company that fits your needs and vice versa. Having identified such a company or companies, you then write letters of inquiry and job applications.

CHALLENGE PROBLEM FOR REVIEW

Assess the research tools you have at your disposal for investigating a company that has a job opening you would fit. Most job seekers want to go to the Internet immediately, but the information on the Internet is often unfiltered and often highly biased. What about the public library? Would you contact the Better Business Bureau? What is your tolerance for negative information; that is, at what point would you decide not to continue an application with a company that has a few negative reviews?

Process: Identify Yourself Through Your Résumé

KEY CONCEPT 11.2
...

Employers form opinions of job applicants based on initial impressions created by the letters and résumés they receive. A successful job candidate presents the best possible and most appropriate impression.

When an employer reviews potential employees, the candidate provides the major evidence considered. This evidence takes the form of a letter, résumé, portfolio, or even a video. A **curriculum vita** is primarily used when applying for graduate or professional school and contains, in outline form, a list of academic achievements. Although a résumé is the document preferred by most human resources people, a **professional portfolio** has the advantage of providing samples of a candidate's actual work. A collection of work samples can be especially relevant for those with significant work experience or who are in graphic arts. A portfolio may also help illustrate examples of work you have done, such as a sample business plan or press release. A portfolio contains: (1) a heading with your name, postal address, telephone number, e-mail address, and

Web page; (2) a table of contents; (3) a work chronology; (4) a statement of your career goal; (5) a summary, no longer than one page, of your education and other training and a list of your business-related skills presented in categories (communications, graphics, interpersonal); (6) a list, no longer than one page, of your interests and work objectives; (7) a list of your major accomplishments, including a brief narrative for each using action words (coordinating, leading, negotiating, risk taking) providing evidence of the quality and value of your achievements (stress those that best display your creative talents or in which you were an initiator); and (8) a bullet-point list of your strengths, particularly as related to your accomplishments. Where appropriate, samples of work or other evidence may be included (along with accomplishments, for instance, press releases about a completed project).

For the most part, the impressions given by the letter and résumé provide the most information about your professionalism. Thus, these materials must be developed and prepared with care. From the beginning, you should be aware of the way that the recipient (your prospective employer) will review and interpret the materials. Each piece of information must be tailored with the perspective of this reviewer in mind.

The Résumé

A résumé is not a curriculum vita or a professional portfolio. **Résumés** are created according to long-standing conventions for format and presentation. While you may feel particularly clever and creative in how you convey your information, you must remember that those who review résumés have certain expectations about them.

Content

Your résumé should include clear, concise, and complete information about you as a person—your training, interests, and so forth—that is pertinent to the position for which you are applying. This content provides the employer with an overview of your abilities and character. The information should be convincing and should lead the employer to arrange an interview with you.

Format

There are two basic formats for a résumé: the chronological outline form and the functional narrative form. There is also a "hybrid" that combines these two formats. The nature of the position for which you are applying and the amount and nature of your experience will determine which form is appropriate.

In either case, the résumé essentially has an outline structure. The difference between the chronological and the functional formats is that a straight outline (chronological) résumé is merely a list of your accomplishments in chronological order within categories, while the narrative (functional) résumé is an expanded form of the outline résumé in which you explain in some detail what your experiences have entailed.

For younger, recently graduated applicants (or anyone with little or no professional experience), the preferred form of résumé is organized following the chronological outline form. As with your letter of application, keep your résumé to one page or less in length. This allows you to highlight your experience, shows the employer that you can be succinct and selective, and is more likely to be read thoroughly than would be a longer document. In fact, employers are sometimes suspicious, especially in the case of newly graduated applicants, if a résumé is more than one page long. They fear that it may have been padded.

Expanding into the narrative (functional) format is primarily to explain previous job duties. The narrative must flow; the active voice best conveys a lively and energetic image. Writing in the active voice is a challenge, but it increases your chance for success. For instance, rather than saying, "Edited the college newspaper; served as student body vice president; lead developing and then directed a community service program for the English department," you would say, "My activities included editing the college newspaper, serving as student body vice president, and developing and directing an English department community service program."

We all want to make the best impression possible and we are tempted to list everything that we have done that might—even in the remotest way—make us a more attractive candidate. As your career progresses, you will experience increasing difficulty as you try to limit yourself to a one-page résumé. One way around this dilemma is to use both a short outline résumé and a narrative résumé. Another alternative is the functional format, a listing and description of the various functions you have performed. You can indicate in your letter of application that you are enclosing an abbreviated form for your résumé and that you will be happy to provide a copy of the comprehensive, detailed version if the prospective employer so desires. This saves the employer time and you money (you do not incur high duplicating and mailing expenses, because you supply the full résumé only to those who are seriously interested in your application). A request for the detailed narrative version of your résumé informs you that you are under serious consideration, allows you to present your full qualifications, and gives an opportunity to write another letter in which you can point out additional facts that you think are important. Remember, each time the employer sees your name, you become more real in that person's mind. Following a letter or résumé with more detail at the request of the employer helps separate you from other job applicants.

Typically, employers do not expect to see references on a résumé (or even included with one) unless the job description calls for it. Moreover, some résumé experts now suggest that the phrase "References Upon Request" should not be included, because it is assumed that if an employer asks an applicant for them, you will happily supply them. Also, a former employer has tight legal restrictions when writing references. In short, they may open themselves up for trouble if they write something negative. As a potential employer or supervisor, you need to be aware of this.

Before you include anyone on your list of references, be sure that they have agreed to provide a reference for you. When you approach them for permission to use their name as a reference, you might also phrase your request in such a way that you can determine how good the reference will be. You might say, for instance, "I would appreciate it if you would write a letter of recommendation for me, if you feel that you can do so, though I will understand if you would prefer not to." It may be helpful to offer a draft letter or summary of key points to the person you are asking to write a reference. This practice has the dual benefit of reducing the work the potential reference agrees to take on while simultaneously providing an opportunity for you to supply facts that he or she might not recall. Occasionally, someone writing a letter of reference will write a damaging letter that makes it difficult for you to secure a position. It is helpful, therefore, if you can obtain a copy of the reference letter from the writer. Furthermore, you should take advantage of your campus placement office. This allows you to gather your letters together in one easily accessible file, gives your prospective employer the opportunity of requesting your file personally, and removes the need for your references to write numerous letters. Moreover, some placement services are willing to read your letters as they are submitted and to alert you if there is one that you might want removed because it is not useful. Incidentally, some references feel more at ease if they are writing for a confidential file, which means that you are not allowed to see the letter. Some employers prefer such files because, presumably, the letters contain the references' honest assessments and opinions. Remember, though, unless you waived the right, you can review letters written about you.

Some experts in the field feel that it is best to list your references on a separate sheet of paper rather than including them in your résumé; others consider a list of references an integral section of a résumé. The overall length of your résumé may help determine which approach you choose. Either way, if there is room on your résumé, you should include the address of your institution's placement office so that your prospective employer knows who to contact for a copy of your file (if your résumé is too short, this gives you an opportunity to fill out the page with important information; you can still name your referees in a list of **letters on file**). You might want to include your references' telephone numbers as well. Again, some employers feel that they can solicit a more honest opinion directly from a reference over the telephone than they can get from an all-purpose letter in a placement file. This can work to your advantage, especially if your reference thinks highly of you. A telephone contact allows your reference to expand upon the comments contained in the letter of recommendation and specifically address your qualities that are well suited to a particular job, including personal traits that otherwise might not be considered.

Your letter of application and résumé are two of the most important documents you will ever create. It is imperative that you review each carefully to make sure you have made the most effective, accurate, and mechanically correct presentation possible. Recently, several coaches at high-profile colleges lost their jobs when it was found that they had exaggerated or lied in their résumés. Refer to the following list as a guide as you are writing your letter of application and résumé. It also serves as a checklist after you have finished them.

- Responses to published advertisements should be mailed within three days of the appearance of the advertisement.
- Your letter and résumé should be on 8½-inch × 11-inch white bond paper.
- Both the letter and the résumé should be brief, clear, accurate, positive, and to the point.
- Your letter and résumé should be completed on a word processor.
- Proofread your letter and résumé carefully.
- Check to make sure that your address, telephone number, e-mail address, and other contact information is present and correct.
- Date your application letter.
- Sign your application letter.

When examining your résumé, an employer will look for the following specifics: your telephone number (include your e-mail address; it shows that you are technologically in tune); action verbs; numerical details; relevant work history; and honors, awards, or extracurricular activities that provide a fuller picture of you as an applicant. After all, the employer is trying to determine who will be most productive and best fit into the organization. As for numerical details, this includes all types of numbers and quantities, such as how many television or radio stations ran the advertisement that you designed, over what period of time and the percentage of sales increase that followed the advertisement—and note, "May to June 2004" is more impressive and clearer than "5-6/04."

As might be expected, you should avoid the reverse of this list. In other words, do not photocopy or use a form cover letter (the employer appreciates being considered a person as much as you do), do not mail your résumé without an application letter, and do not try to impress someone with cute or unusual salutations ("Dear People" or "Gentlepersons," for example) or use an employer's first name by itself. Use the title and last name of the addressee, if it is known. If you are writing to someone whose name is gender neutral (such as Shannon, Terry, Pat, or Ashley) or whose name is from a culture that is unfamiliar to you (Japanese, Arabic, Mayan), it is best to use the addressee's first and last names alone rather than taking a chance on which title to use and writing to Mr. So-and-So when the employer is a woman. If you do not know the specific name of the addressee, then address the letter to the "Director of Human Resources" or a similar department. Avoid the use of "To Whom It May Concern." The now outdated phrase reminds one of form letters prior to the age of word processing. The digital age means that every letter can be customized.

Do not make demands related to salary or vacation time or other fringe benefits. These can be discussed later and you do not want to offend your prospective employer or give the impression that these items are more important to you than the job. In fact, you should allow the interviewer to bring up the matter of salary. If this does not occur, bring it up only as a matter of inquiry at the end of the interview, an experience discussed in the next section.

Do not type your letter in capital letters. Some experts believe that using letterheads from current or past employers is unwise—again, in this digital age, you can make your own letterhead. This can create a professional look. You may choose to create your own letterhead instead of right justifying your address and the date for a more professional look. With the word-processing capabilities available today, you can develop creative (but business-conservative) letterheads that state, "I am a professional career person, not just a student looking for a job." The old custom of attaching a photograph of yourself is no longer being followed; you do not want an employer to react to the limited information available in a photograph. Similarly, do not send a transcript of your schoolwork with your résumé unless the employer specifically requests one, although you should be able to make a transcript immediately available to any employer who wishes to obtain a copy. This means that you need to check with the registrar's office at your school to find out how to make sure that this is done, what the cost will be, and whether you will be required to pay in advance.

Notes on Order of Materials

If you use common sense in constructing your cover letter and your résumé, you will make a good impression. You want to demonstrate that you have the ability to produce. Therefore, you should stress those experiences that best indicate this, whether educational, job related, or off the job. Sometimes this means deleting information from or adding information to your résumé. Here are some ideas:

- Your résumé layout should be clear.
- If you lack experience relevant to the job for which you are applying, stress your skills instead of your experience.
- Use the language of business; rather than saying "term paper," say "research report."
- Remember to use action verbs and avoid errors.

If you are preparing a large number of résumés to be used in pursuing several different kinds of positions, you probably cannot compose an all-purpose summary statement of your job or career objectives to place at the beginning of your résumé. Any statement that you make may sound so vague, unoriginal, or trite that it will be ignored (or worse, counted against you). In this case, it would be prudent to omit the summary statement from your résumé and incorporate a tailored statement in your cover letter or to type a statement of your job objectives on a separate piece of paper; this permits you to speak directly to those aspects that apply to the position in question. Figure 11.3 provides a very simple, unadorned résumé.

Some counselors think that statements of goals or objectives are counterproductive. They sound trite and like everyone else's, and they may include something that could cause the reader to lose interest in you. If you want to include supplemental information, like a section on unusual personal experiences (such as spending two years in Americore or living in a foreign country for several years) or additional training (which might be included if that training increases your ability to perform the tasks included in the job description), place this information at the end of the résumé. Surveys have shown that the following order of inclusion is the most effective: personal contact information, education, work experience, general supplemental information (hobbies, interests, achievements, honors, and awards, if relevant to the position), and references. Part-time work and extracurricular activities are oftentimes of interest to employers because they reveal the breadth of your interests and your ability to structure your time efficiently. Personal data (age, gender, race, geographic origin), much of which cannot be requested by the employer, is becoming less commonly offered by the applicant. Also, be aware that some items (hobbies) might not appeal to your employer. If you have decided that you want to work only where your interests match those of your employer, you may include items that

FIGURE 11.3
...

A Sample Functional Résumé of a New Graduate

Linda Mansfield

School: Apt. #12   **Permanent:** Box 510
3345 Farralone Ave.   Rt. 5
San Francisco, CA 94103   Durham, NC 27711

Telephone: (919) 555-2134 (rings on cell and home)

E-mail: lmansfield@yourmail.net

JOB OBJECTIVE: To apply business administration and production experience in the technical division of a communications corporation

EDUCATION: University of California, Berkeley, 2001–2005, B.A. in business communications and marketing

WORK EXPERIENCE:

2001–2005	**KSEG-TV** (UC Berkeley television station), all production areas. Scheduled guests for interview shows; wrote news script; assisted camera operators; and prepared announcements for campus activities.
Summer 2002	**Ashley's Department Store**, accounts receivable department. Processed invoices and payments.
2001–2004	**UC Berkeley School of Business**, undergraduate student research assistant. Collected data from intranet and library.
Summer 2000	**Heather's Pizza**, delivery. Took phone orders and delivered pizza.

COMMUNITY SERVICE:

Neighborhood Association for Adult Literacy. Assisted in creating television commercials to attract new students and tutors. 1999–2003

Berkeley Humane Society volunteer. Worked with animals in the shelter and with adopting families. 2000–2005

HONORS:

UC Berkeley School of Business, Outstanding Senior Business Administration Student Award, 2005

California State Regents Scholarship. 2001–2005

Charles Roland Automotive Scholarship, 2001

will exclude you from some positions. This is a personal matter, but as long as you understand the potential consequences, it is your choice.

Although some counselors believe that the standard chronological résumé stressing work history is no longer required and that it is better to use your résumé to communicate exactly who you are, most employers prefer the standard approach. This is especially true for recent graduates or people with little or no professional experience.

Within each section of your résumé, you should list your activities or experiences in reverse chronological order (starting with the most recent and working backward in time). The advantages to this format are that it shows what you have been doing most recently, it illustrates your increasing expertise, and it establishes a pattern of continuing work history related to your career objectives and the employer's needs.

Two final notes: First, when you have finished your résumé, have it reviewed by your advisor or someone who has experience in working with résumés (perhaps someone with whom you have had contact in the personnel department or upper management of a company for which you have worked). Second, continually review your résumé to be sure that it is up-to-date and to improve it, to make it more effective.

SECTION SUMMARY

Presenting the best picture of yourself to your prospective employer is crucial. This may be done in a standard format résumé. Careful organization, together with simplicity, clarity, accuracy, and a correct format and clean presentation are essential.

INSIGHT BOX 11.4
...

Good Writing Pays

Besides making you a better writer, a careful and knowledgeable use of words provides benefits that are not so obvious. Fairly or not, your reader may judge your intelligence and level of education by the way you use words. Learn when to use "me" or "I," don't say "upping" if you mean "increasing," avoid slang and jargon, know the rules of punctuation, and be aware of subject-verb agreement and other grammatical mine fields.

In Chapter 8, you learned about spell-check and grammar-check programs on your computer, but these checks sometimes miss things or misinterpret what you are trying to say. If you are in an area of accounting, the use of the word "physical" rather than "fiscal" will bring a derisive reaction from your reader. The substitution of "facial" for "fascia" by someone in the construction trades would elicit a similar response. In order to avoid humiliation, keep a dictionary, a thesaurus, and a grammar handbook on your desk as part of the regular tools of your trade.

George Orwell, one of the great stylists in English literature, wrote a famous essay on usage called "Politics and the English Language." In this essay, Orwell explained how to use language effectively no matter what kind of writing you do. He listed six rules: "(1) Never use a metaphor, simile or other figure of speech which you are used to seeing in print. (2) Never use a long word where a short word will do. (3) If it is possible to cut a word out, always cut it out. (4) Never use the passive [voice] where you can use the active. (5) Never use a foreign phrase, a scientific word or a jargon word if you can think of an everyday English equivalent. (6) Break any of these rules sooner than say anything outright barbarous." The last of Orwell's axioms is rephrased in a humorous quote attributed to Winston Churchill in rebutting the rule that a sentence should not end with a preposition: "This is the sort of English up with which I will not put."

Sources: Orwell, George. (1945); *Shooting an Elephant and Other Essays.* New York: Harcourt Brace Jovanovich; and *Bartlett's Familiar Quotations* (1980). Boston, MA: Little Brown.

CHALLENGE PROBLEM FOR REVIEW

Quite a few people work for McDonald's during their high school years. The experience is so common that *McJob* has found its way into the *Merriam-Webster's Collegiate Dictionary*, 11th ed. List all those McJobs you have held in the past. Can you convert them into relevant experiences for the positions you will soon hold as a managerial professional? After framing these work experiences, imagine yourself in the position of someone who must interpret these experiences to determine whether or not to make an offer. Would you give yourself a job based on these accomplishments?

Product: Interview and Presentation

KEY CONCEPT 11.3
...

A job search culminates with a successful interview followed by a job offer and salary negotiation. The successful interview requires effective self-presentation.

Employers typically require an inescapable component of the job search, the interview. Everyone from the lowest-paid, least-skilled employee to the president and chief executive officer undergoes an interview. In small companies, the CEO or president may actually interview finalists for most positions. A face-to-face meeting remains central to the hiring process. As with the letter and the résumé, careful preparation precedes successful execution.

Preparing for the Interview

The quality of your résumé influences whether you are invited to an interview. However, the interview frequently determines whether you are hired. As with the résumé, common sense is your best guide to how to conduct yourself during an interview.

Many factors that influence the interview are not within your control. If the employer needs something that you cannot provide or if your personalities do not mesh, the interview is not likely to result in a job offer. This is perfectly acceptable. You do not want to be where you are not wanted or where you will not fit. There are many things you can do prior to an interview to improve your chances, however. Be sure to investigate the company thoroughly. You should have completed a quick review of company information when the first letters were composed, but once an interview is scheduled, you should conduct more thorough research. Research can reveal important information that may be invaluable in a discussion with the employer. Your knowledge demonstrates your interest and your ambition.

The most important single element, though, may be another kind of preparation, the kind of preparation that begins with self-assessment. The well-developed and clearly articulated goals discussed previously are critical. These goals help you know what you want, know the abilities that you have and do not have, and know how well you match the company's needs. Once you have determined your skills and goals, it is useful to predict what questions you will be asked and to practice answering them. Have specific details and figures ready to use as evidence. The more practice you have in answering potential questions (for example, "What relevant experiences have you had?" "What are your career goals?" "What would you do if . . . ?"), the more secure you will feel as the interview progresses. Some of the questions may be the same as those you have asked yourself, such as "Where do you want to be in five years?" and so on. Practice makes your answers smoother and gives you both confidence and the appearance of confidence.

The most frequently asked questions are easy to anticipate. A question like "What was your major in college?" may be first. This could suggest that the interviewer has not read your résumé. Do not overinterpret this event. It may be that the interviewer is trying to put you at ease or he or she may want to see how well you handle a subject that you know well. Often, subordinates preselect résumés and candidates, and the interviewer reads key material during the interview. The best interviewers do this, but they do it without the interviewee being aware that they are doing it.

In any case, questions with short answers can be opportunities for you to elaborate with more details. You might be asked about the classes you took and which classes you liked most, or you might be asked about special internships and similar experiences. You will definitely be asked about previous and current employment—especially anything that is perceived to have prepared you for working with the company. Interviewers ask about least favorite tasks and whether you encountered any problems on your last job. This can be followed by a question about how you dealt with those tasks or handled those problems. For those who are not recent graduates, the big question to be prepared for is why you are interested in changing jobs. No matter why you are applying for this job, be prepared to answer the question of why you choose to apply to work for this company. It is important to realize that these questions tell you something about the interviewer and his or her interests.

Nearly all interviews involve four basic questions, even if they are not phrased as questions:

1. Why are you interested in this type of work?
2. Why do you want this particular job? or Why do you want to be an assistant manager in our new widget-adjusting plant?
3. What interests you about our company?
4. What can you tell me about yourself that is relevant to this job?

In responding to these and any other questions, be sure that you answer the question asked. Your answers should be short, although they must include information beyond a simple "yes" or "no." For instance, you might suggest that you have been interested in widget manufacturing since your uncle gave you a widget for your birthday when you were twelve. (By the way, historically, a widget was any tool difficult to describe, such as the special tool in the seventeenth century for making round rungs for a ladder or chair. Today a widget is a specialized software tool.) Also, this position involves work similar to what you did at your most rewarding summer job. The combination of summer work experience and widget production is exactly what you have been seeking. Whether you expand on these answers will depend on the interviewer's reaction.

Before you speak, ask yourself what the interviewer wants to know. Interviewers do not want to know everything that you have ever done; they want to know what kind of a person you are and if you are trained to do what they want you to do. Your answer should take this into account. Your college experiences can work for you. There are times when you can make the question fit your answer, and you can supply the interviewer with the type of information that is required. You need to know what you are talking about in case the interviewer asks you for details. However, it is also important for you to convince the interviewer that you understand what the job entails and that you have the motivation and abilities needed to be successful in the position. In fact, it is recommended that interviewees hold mock interviews and that they do so several times before an actual interview takes place. Check to see if your placement office or employment center arranges this sort of activity.

It is no accident that the members of one of the most successful professions—law— conduct mock trials as part of their regular training in graduate school. They continue this practice throughout their careers. Knowing the answers and knowing how to react are important factors in successful interviews. Physical and mental rehearsal proves successful in many contexts. Sports teams practice for this reason.

When rehearsing for an interview, start at the beginning, with your entrance into the room, and go through the entire process, including your exit. These are important but frequently overlooked steps. You need to know in advance what you are going to do with your overcoat, your briefcase, purse, and anything else you might be carrying. During actual interviews, interviewees have dropped their files on the floor while trying to take off a scarf or jacket. They have dropped bags containing their lunches, knocked over table lamps trying to balance résumés on their laps, and spilled coffee on themselves. Do you think that cup of coffee or glass of water is worth the possibility of spilling?

Sit where the interviewer indicates you should sit. Have a pad of paper (with the time and date of the interview and the company and interviewer's names already written on it) so you can write down thoughts and questions to ask during the interview as the interview progresses. Record what is said for your follow-up letter.

The most common mistake job applicants make is that they fail to be prepared to ask questions about their prospective employers. The interview works both ways; just as an employer would not want to hire someone about whom little or nothing is known, you should not want to work for a company about which you know very little. The interview is the best time to learn what you need to know. Actually, good interviewers usually ask if you have any questions. Your questions may impress the interviewer favorably.

Here are some examples of questions that you should plan to ask:

- What kinds of advancement opportunities are available in your company for someone with my education and work experience?
- How would I be evaluated?
- What qualities are typical in your employees?
- Are there any opportunities or problems that the company is confronting that might affect my position?
- What is the work environment like?
- How is promotion determined?
- What is the employee turnover rate?
- What is the next step in the employment process?
- Is there anything that I might not like about this job?
- What do you enjoy about working for [name of company]?
- When might I expect to hear from you? Should I contact you if I have not heard anything in two weeks?

It helps if you can phrase some of these questions so that it is evident that you know something about the company and/or position (the number of employees in the department in which you would work, the company's leading product, sales figures, potential competitors and their products, and so on). It is useful, too, to involve the interviewer personally in your questions. You might ask, "What is the work environment like?" and similar questions. One of your last queries could be the most revealing and the best one to end the interview because it lets the interview conclude on a positive note: "What do you enjoy most about working for [name of company]?"

Another aspect of preparation involves how you present yourself. Your physical appearance is part of that crucial first impression. Dress as though you are applying for a position one step higher than the one for which you are applying. In both your dress and your answers, you need to consider your audience. It would not be fitting to arrive at an interview for a managerial position with a *Fortune* 500 company dressed in college casual clothing any more than it would be smart to show up at an interview for the position of a U.S. Department of Agriculture field inspector at a meat-packing plant dressed in a three-piece suit (a three-piece suit is uncommon at any level of government today).

If you are not sure about what to wear, be conservative. Tailored separates, jacketed suits, and business dresses are almost always acceptable for women, and men should wear dark blue or gray suits; white, long-sleeved shirts; conservative ties; tall, dark socks for men, neutral hose for women; and a good pair of well-shined leather shoes.

Proper grooming and cleanliness are musts. Smoking and chewing gum are unacceptable in an interview situation, and if the interview takes place in a restaurant, a light meal that will not be messy to eat is favored. Liquor normally should be avoided; you do not want to risk the tension of the circumstances causing the alcohol to have a greater effect than you are used to. Order a glass of water, juice, or iced tea instead.

Finally, keep in mind that often the interviewer is *trying to impress you*. The company is probably trying to recruit you as much as you are trying to secure a position with the company. In fact, they may have allocated quite a few resources to a current staffing need, so they are making a special effort. Pay attention to these efforts. Let the interviewer make suggestions, especially on small things such as a dish that the restaurant makes particularly well, and so on. Be cautious, but be ready to try the local favorite or specialty.

The Interview Experience

Undoubtedly you have already learned many of the social graces that are important in the interview itself. You may not have realized how important these were, though. Research indicates that there is a *halo effect* that occurs during an interview (the halo effect is the tendency to rate someone at the same level on all items of a scale). This effect is created by your first impression on the interviewer. In fact, the most important thirty seconds in an interview are most often the first thirty seconds, for by the end of that time the employer will already have a first impression. Whether it is positive or negative, that impression will set the tone of the interview and affect the interviewer's evaluation of your answers and general demeanor. It is almost impossible to change someone's initial impression during the short course of an interview.

Remember the warning about controlling whatever you may be carrying. Still, it may be useful to have an extra copy of your résumé, samples of your work, or copies of letters of recommendation on hand during the interview, so consider whether you might be able to use them. However, bring no possible distractions into the interview room. Because dropping objects is not conducive to making a good impression, rather than worry about that possibility, you may want to leave elsewhere anything that you would have to carry. Under no circumstances should you take something into an interview that might be disruptive. *Leave your cell phone and laptop in the car or hotel.* (As an aside, especially if you travel in your job search, keep accurate, dated records; you may be able to qualify for tax deductions. Check with your tax consultant.) If you have luggage because you expect to leave for a flight following the interview process, ask a receptionist for a safe place to store the luggage; then leave the cell phone and pager turned off and in the luggage. It is important to treat all of the people you meet at the interview site professionally and properly. Interviewers will hear from staff who are disdained or subjected to abuse of any kind. The interviewer may also hear if you are friendly and courteous.

When you enter the room to meet your interviewer, project an image suitable for the position. Walk in with your head up, smiling, and confident. You know about yourself and the company and that you are well dressed. Because these details can be addressed in advance, you do not have to worry about them as you enter the interviewer's office. Select what you will wear at least a day before the interview and be sure that it is clean and that you feel comfortable wearing it. You may even want to check yourself in a full-length mirror to make sure that your appearance is what you want it to be. This kind of preparation is not vanity; it is common sense.

Eating before an interview can be problematic, depending on what time the interview takes place. If you do not eat, you may hear your stomach answering questions before you do or your blood sugar may drop and you will be tired. Eating too much can be a problem, too, because digestive noises may erupt or you may lose your concentration due to a change in your blood sugar. Eat lightly at least an hour ahead of your scheduled meeting. The American Dietetic Association recommends a slice or two of whole-grain bread with peanut butter, fruit such as oranges or bananas, or something of this nature.

The interview will probably open with a handshake. Do not worry about having cold, clammy hands. This is a natural reaction for people under stress and cannot always be avoided. However, to counteract this reaction, stop at a restroom first and hold your hands under the hot-air dryer or run warm water over your hands and then rub them thoroughly dry. This helps keep your hands reasonably warm until you get through that first moment of meeting. Your quick visit to the restroom also allows you to check your hair, get a drink of water, and do anything else that you might want to get out of the way for the next fifteen minutes or so. To ensure that your hand remains warm, you might keep it in your pocket or hold a tissue in it. When you enter the interview room, though, make sure that your hands are empty and not in your pockets. Your handshake should be firm yet not tight. Avoid the crushing "death grip" and the "limp-fish" shake. Applicants should know that female interviewers expect to shake hands with them just as male interviewers do.

Once you are in the office, you will be invited to sit down. If possible, choose a seat beside the desk rather than in front of it so that there are no barriers between you and the interviewer. A seat on the interviewer's left is preferred; because people are used to gathering information in a left-to-right direction, they pay more attention to things on their left than on their right. If there is no desk, try to sit in a chair (or on a couch) facing, and slightly to the left, rather than next to the interviewer. If you are carrying a briefcase or papers that you might want to refer to during the interview, place them where they will be out of the way but where you can get to them easily if necessary. An attentive interviewer will notice this kind of professional preparation and the impression that you are making may be enhanced.

Do not appear awkward when you talk. Body language can be significant in helping you present yourself well. Sit straight on your chair, with your hands and feet relaxed. Be attentive. Do not change seats or wander around the office. Do not cross your legs. Columnist Sylvia Porter once even advised against inquiring about materials on the interviewer's desk. Presumably, though, she had in mind business files, because a comment on a photograph, an art object, a trophy, or something of that nature may serve to break the ice or to form a bond with the interviewer.

Numerous psychological and sociological studies have found that eye contact plays a vital role in establishing relationships. Accurate or not, folklore holds that people who look you straight in the eye when they are conversing are honest, reliable, and confident. William Shakespeare's *Othello* was intended to disprove this concept over four hundred years ago, but it is certainly still current in our society. The importance of looking at the interviewer when a question is being asked and when you answer cannot be overemphasized.

Let the interviewer take the lead in the interview. You might want to be prepared to make a comment about a topical, business-related news item in case there is an awkward moment of silence to bridge, but most of the time you should take the role of the respondent. Once the questions begin, be open and honest. Answer as completely as you can any questions about your education, previous work experience, career plans, and what your strengths and weaknesses might be. Weaknesses can be noted, then shown to be assets, such as when you admit that you are quiet in nature but that you are effective in negotiations because you can be depended upon to listen well, to gather pertinent facts, and to present them logically and in a reasonable manner. With litigation mounting and workers' rights being widely advertised, it is becoming less and less likely that you might be asked a question that by law you are not required to answer, such as your age, race, political or religious affiliation, marital status, financial position, or the nature of your military discharge. On occasion these questions are asked in a disguised form ("What is your maiden name?"). If you are asked such a question, do not accuse the interviewer of doing something illegal or immoral; you may even want to answer the question. If you do not want to answer the question, you can politely inform the interviewer that, although you do not object to answering the question, you understand that you are not required to answer. The following topics cannot be questioned in an interview:

- National origin or descent
- Citizenship
- Age
- Marital and/or family status
- Personal characteristics (height, weight, etc.)
- Disabilities
- Medical conditions
- Affiliations
- Arrest record
- Military status

Finally, a technique that helps prepare you for your interview is to look at the situation from the other side. Pretend that you are the interviewer. What would you ask the interviewee? Four characteristics that you would want to see in a prospective employee include:

1. a concern for timeliness
2. the ability to be a self-starter
3. the acceptance of the team-player concept
4. the vision, know-how, and ability to follow through that characterizes an initiator or change agent

To these, you must add the ability to do the job tasks associated with the position. These might include analyzing data, programming computers, applying international standards, and so forth. What you would not want to hear is: "I really need this job," "This represents a good career move for me," or "I have no questions." The interviewer may question why the company would need the prospective employee, wonder if the hire would benefit the company, and assume that the lack of questions represents a lack of preparation, a lack of imagination, or both.

As an interviewer, you probably want to know the answers to some of the questions just mentioned. Additional questions might depend on the circumstances that develop during the interview:

- If the prospective employee is leaving a job, what reason is given for leaving? Is the rationale reasonable; does the employee express a sour-grapes attitude or bad-mouth the former employer? The answer could well suggest the attitude that might be brought to the new company.
- What did the employee like about the last job? Was there anything that could have been improved? This may reveal what positive things may be brought along, although the questions must be asked carefully or they invite improper responses.
- What is the most interesting project that the employee has been involved in? People who enjoy challenges can be detected by their answers to this question.
- What kind of people does the employee like to work with and what are the traits of those who annoy the employee? The character traits that the employee is most likely to emulate and those that the employee does not possess, as well as the employee's sensitivity to coworkers, may be divulged in the answers to these questions.
- What kinds of things in the employee's last position caused a missed deadline or forced a schedule change? It is possible to assess the candidate's degree of flexibility and willingness to work hard by the answer to this question.

Politeness and good manners are critical in an interview. When the interviewer indicates that the interview is concluded, express your thanks for the opportunity to learn about the position and the company, your appreciation for any materials that you might have been given, and your gratitude to the interviewer for having taken the time to see you. This leaves a good final impression, and if you go to work for the company, it is nice to be on a friendly basis with someone whom you have met previously.

A follow-up letter sent within a day or two, reiterating your interest and repeating your appreciation, solidifies this final good impression. According to surveys, only 10 to 15 percent of interviewees send thank-you notes, so taking the courteous, correct action could set you apart. The note can be short, yet one precaution to take, regardless of the length, is to write out a draft of what you want to say before putting words on paper.

Another way of making a good impression with a thank-you letter is to include a comment that you have some ideas about the job that you would like to discuss (be sure that you do). If you do this, be careful that what you say is not construed as being too presumptuous. This also gives you an opening for a follow-up call, which, if meaningful, can be to your benefit.

It cannot be stressed too much that common sense should be your guide in the interview process. Think about how you would appear to yourself if you were the interviewer. Be prompt. This means finding out ahead of time exactly where and when the interview will be and where you will park if driving. Making sure that you can get there before you are due may require a trial run the day before. Follow any procedures outlined by the company. Act naturally. Listen to the interviewer and allow the interviewer to do the talking, except when you are clearly expected to respond. You want to get your points across, but people tend to believe that good listeners are intelligent.

Occasionally, more than one person will conduct an interview. If you encounter this situation, do not be concerned. Make sure that you address the answer to a question to the person who asked it, but also make sure that you periodically establish eye contact with everyone in the room. On rare occasions, more than one person might be interviewed at the same time (this might also be one of those instances when there are multiple interviewers). This is a poor interview practice, and all you can do is the best that you can. In the final analysis, you may be better off not working for a company that does business this way. Other items to keep in mind for an interview include:

- Do not become tense; remember that if your qualifications are appropriate, it will be to the employer's benefit to hire you and, while you do not want to be arrogant, if you do not get this job, there will be other opportunities for jobs that may be even better.
- Do not become emotional during the interview.
- Do not try to oversell your case. This makes the interviewer think that you are trying hard because you have little to represent.
- Do not make promises about performances that you cannot keep.
- Do not try to be funny, overbearing, overly aggressive, or a know-it-all; that kind of person does not appeal to you and is not likely to appeal to the interviewer.
- Do not stress salary and fringe benefits demands unless prompted to by the interviewer.

When the interview is about to end, you might summarize any points you think are worth repeating or that you want to make sure are understood. If the interviewer does not indicate when you might hear about his or her decision, it is appropriate to ask when you might learn about the decision or if it is all right to contact the company if you have not heard within a given time period, say one or two weeks.

To recapitulate: Be sure that you know your own strengths, that you have articulated your goals, that you are informed about the company, and that you can enthusiastically present a picture of how all of these elements fit together.

Thank Yous and Multiple Interviewers

We noted that it is wise to send a follow-up thank you note to the person who interviewed you. Often you will meet briefly with many of your potential collegagues, and you would not be expected to write to each of them, although it is prudent to collect their business cards for future reference—to help you remember who they are and to give you contact information.

But, to whom should you address the note on the rare occassion when you are interviewed extensively by more than one person? One of our daughters was interviewed by the person who invited her for the interview and will make the hiring recommendation, the corporation's CEO who approves the hiring, and five other people in the division, all for at least half an hour each. Her field, medical physics , is a small one and, even if she does not work for this company, it is likely that she will meet these people at professional conferences, so she wants to establish a good relationship with them.

There are several options. A thank you could be sent to: the person who invited her for the interview, the inviter and the CEO, or to each of those with whom she met. Alternatives might be to write a note to the inviter and ask that he pass on her gratitude for the time and information that everyone provided individually; she might write a note to the inviter and send copies to each of the others with personalized hand-written messages on the copies; she might write a letter to the inviter and short thank yous to the others whom she met. Combinations of these approaches are additional possibilities. For instance, she might write the letter to the interviewer and then if she takes the position she could send short notes to the others telling them how much she enjoyed meeting them and letting them know that she is looking forward to working with them.

The final decision is a personal one, in part determined by your own personality and what you feel comfortable doing and in part determined by circumstances. You may be limited by time or the number of interviews you have. In a small organization, the blanket approach might be more appropriate than in an extremely large company, or vice versa, depending on the culture/climate of the organization. In some corporate settings, any of the above options might be delivered via email; in other corporations, handwritten or typed missives are preferable. If you can determine during the interview which of these factors is applicable, you will have a double step up.

SECTION SUMMARY

The interview is a critical element in a job search. Preparation is the key to a successful interview. This includes knowledge of the company, reviewing your personal assessment, practicing answering and asking questions, and wearing proper attire. Your bearing and conduct during the actual interview are extremely important.

CHALLENGE PROBLEM FOR REVIEW

There are many excellent sites on the Internet that address illegal interview questions. These sites offer suggestions for how to handle the questions as well as examples of proper questions that get at the intent of the question. For instance, the issue of family status arises from the need the employer may have for you to go on weekend trips, work late, and be available in an instant. Rather than ask if you are prepared to do all this, he or she asks if you have children. The recommendation is to answer the intended question: "I am available to do the job and give it my complete attention." Explore these sites and determine how you might answer the two or three most difficult questions for you. One of the more helpful sites is the following "About" site: http://job searchtech.about.com/od/interview/. Another site is http://www.job-interview.net/.

CHAPTER SUMMARY

...

Getting a suitable job requires attention to a few simple details. To start, you need to know enough about yourself and the position for which you are applying to be sure that there is a good match; then you need to write letters of inquiry and make job applications that reflect this. The next step is to present a good, accurate picture of yourself by means of a properly prepared résumé. Finally, for a successful interview, you must be carefully prepared, your demeanor and attire must be appropriate for the occasion, and you must make good first and last impressions.

EXERCISES

...

Prewriting Exercises

1. Brainstorm I: List five specific skills you have that will either qualify you for a particular position or will help you determine what kind of position for which to search.
2. Brainstorming II: List five specific personal qualities you possess, as evidenced by your activities over the past three or four years, that would fit with either of the lists developed for Brainstorm I.
3. Brainstorming III: List your major accomplishments in school and work over the past five years.
4. List all of the activities that you enjoy or are good at and would like to continue to do for the rest of your life—research, sales, travel, sports, the arts, anything that you can imagine.
5. Combine as many of the items as you can from the lists compiled for Prewriting Exercises 1 through 3. This should help you concentrate on the job area that is most appropriate for your interests, talents, and major preferences. Do not forget to take advantage of your institution's career counseling office, your state or local employment office, job search companies such as Drake Beam Morin, Inc., or human resources outplacement services for help in this area. Even after you have chosen a field, there may be an infinite number of job possibilities from which to choose.
6. List your priorities (in order of priority) for your ideal position. This list should include both the type of work and the type of company for which you would like to work.

7. In separate lists, detail your strengths and weaknesses as they relate to the position and company type that you decided upon in Exercise 6.

8. Complete the goal-setting exercise, Figure 11.5.

FIGURE 11.5
...

Goal Setting

Here are four simple steps that can be undertaken to begin a goal-setting process.

Step 1: Clarify Values

Rank (1 is the highest) the values in the left column in terms of their importance to you, then in the right column describe something you do that reflects how you value each of the top four items in the left column.

____ Character	1. _____
____ Friends	
____ Work	
____ Family	2. _____
____ Place of Worship	
____ Home	3. _____
____ "circle" of close friends	
____ Play	
____ Spouse/Significant Other	4. _____
____ Other (specify): _____	_____

Is there something you could do differently to reflect your values more consistently?

Step 2: Set Concrete Goals

First, what do you hope to accomplish in the next ten years?
- Where will you be?
- What will you be doing that is different from today?
- Name something that you will do in ten years that you do not do today.

Second, what do you hope to accomplish in the next five years?
- Where will you be?
- What will you be doing that is different from today?
- Name something that you will do in five years that you do not do today.

Third, what do you hope to accomplish in the next few weeks or months?

Step 3: Assess Your Skills

Skills you possess:	Skills you need for your goals:
Which skills are you underutilizing?	How can you build these missing skills?

FIGURE 11.5

...

continued

Step 4: Evaluate Your Self-Management

For the following activities, is your performance rated as novice, apprentice, proficient, or distinguished?

	Novice	*Apprentice*	*Proficient*	*Distinguished*
1. Rate yourself as a time manager:				
2. Rate yourself as a money manager:				
3. Rate your ability to enjoy your free time:				
4. Rate yourself as a person manager:				
5. Rate your past success in reaching your goals:				

Name specific things that you could do to improve your ratings on the items on the left:

Writing Exercises

1. Read the following memo carefully. Compose a memo to President Richman in answer to his memo and provide him with a summary of your qualifications for the position. This is your opportunity to ask questions or to make observations if you want to do so.

MEMO

To: You
From: Frank Richman, President
Re: Possible promotion
Date: Last Tuesday

I am currently considering some restructuring of the marketing division. Molly Dulcinea and Fred Tony [your immediate supervisor] may exchange places, or I might move Fred into a new associate vice president's position. I have been pleased with your handling of the Maurice account, and if I decide upon the latter approach, I would like to know if you would be interested in taking over Fred's current responsibilities. Please let me know your thoughts by the end of next week.

2. Examine the job advertisements in a trade journal, in a local newspaper, or on the Internet. Evaluate these postings to find one or more that suit your qualifications and career aspirations.

3. Analyze your strengths and weaknesses relevant to the job description(s) in the previous question.

4. Write a cover letter applying for the position of your choice.

5. Design a résumé that can be adjusted to be used for any position for which you might apply (for instance, you could include the most likely variations).

6. Design a résumé that is specifically applicable for the position for which you wrote a cover letter.

7. Write a letter thanking a potential employer for an interview.

8. In a local newspaper, a newspaper from an area where you would like to relocate, or on the Internet, read an article or story about a company that interests you. Find out the president's name and address (hint: most company Web sites include this information) and write a letter outlining your abilities as you think they might be appropriate to that company and indicate your interest in pursuing the possibility of employment there.

9. In 2003, a national television commercial run by the Ford Motor Company included the claim that Ford was "recognized for having the most repeat buyers of any other make." What does this mean? That more than any other brand's repeat buyers, Ford's repeat buyers buy Fords? That is not what the advertisement says. If the words convey any rational meaning, it is that Ford's repeat customers buy any other brand more than they buy Fords. Pretty funny—and, pretty embarrassing for Ford. As in Jay Leno's "Headlines" segment on *The Tonight Show*, examine print and television advertising for similar goofs. Correct them. Avoid this kind of error in your own writing by reviewing it carefully before making it public.

_____

_____

_____

_____

_____

_____

_____

_____

_____

_____

_____

_____

_____

_____

_____

_____

_____

_____

_____

_____

_____

_____

_____

_____

_____

IN-BOX EXERCISE

...

IN-BOX

You have been in your new job as deputy chief information officer at the headquarters of SHG International barely a few hours, and you have been authorized to create a new position. The position is that of editor for the print media which your office generates. The company president is eager for the position to be created and filled, so you need to get the process started as soon as possible.

ITEM 1: FORMAL MEMORANDUM FROM CLARENCE HOUSE, CHIEF INFORMATION OFFICER [YOUR SUPERVISOR]. You are authorized to create a position of information specialist with duties for editing all the printed media we create in our office. Please develop the job description and job analysis as soon as possible. We want the job filled within the month if at all possible. Contact the human resources department for procedures to create the position, set the salary, locate an office and office equipment, and so on. The CFO will be adding funds to our budget to cover the cost of this position. I will need to know the total cost for the position and the office in about two weeks. We can be flexible with the salary, because we want an experienced person in this position. President Richman believes that we can save money by reducing preparation time and fewer outsource expenses for the printers. This person will be expected to oversee our new guidelines for printed media and make our publicly released materials more consistent.

If you need any help in the process, contact the human resources manager or my assistant, Pat.

Your Response

Check one: ☐ Memorandum   ☐ E-mail   ☐ Letter   ☐ Note   ☐ Other

To: _____

_____

_____

_____

_____

_____

_____

_____

_____

_____

_____

_____

_____

_____

_____

_____

_____

_____

_____

_____

_____

_____

ITEM 2: E-MAIL FROM PAUL, HR SPECIALIST. I got a copy of House's memo, so I thought I should let you know that the process is a bit complicated and we need a few items right away if you are going to make his deadline. In a few weeks we will need an account number for the position in payroll even before the person is hired. We have to charge the position development costs, including advertising the position and the interview costs, to the position account. Mr. House will probably conduct the interview with you even though you will be the immediate supervisor. You will need to review the regulations. To get started, I need a job description and a preliminary list of job duties. Keep in mind that some of these duties may be reassigned from other people in the information office.

Your Response

Check one:　☐ Memorandum　☐ E-mail　☐ Letter　☐ Note　☐ Other

To: _____

_____

_____

_____

_____

_____

_____

_____

_____

_____

_____

_____

_____

_____

_____

_____

_____

_____

_____

_____

_____

_____

_____

_____

_____

ITEM 3: E-MAIL FROM PAMELA, INFORMATION SPECIALIST I. I heard about the new position. I have been doing most of the editing of everything we send out for the last year. I was really getting tired of it because it was taking too much of my time. Let me know if you need any help. I want to be sure to hand over all the duties.

Your Response

Check one: ☐ Memorandum   ☐ E-mail   ☐ Letter   ☐ Note   ☐ Other

To: _____

_____

_____

_____

_____

_____

_____

_____

_____

_____

_____

_____

_____

_____

_____

_____

_____

_____

_____

_____

_____

_____

_____

_____

_____

ITEM 4: E-MAIL FROM PETER. Here is the name and address of my contact at the employment agency we use for most of our job searches. I used him last year when I added a position. If you can get a list of desired skills and experiences you need, he can tell us what is out there and maybe you can tailor the description a little more specifically. I wasn't careful and my job description was too broad so I got all kinds of applications. HR made me screen them all because I did not set the right minimum qualifications. (Something about creating qualifications after the fact.) So, if you can get a list to Phil he can suggest how hard it will be to find someone or whether you will get hundred of applicants. If you do it right, HR will screen the unqualified out of the pool (they even did a few for me, but I still had to read about 200 resumes).

Your Response

Check one: ☐ Memorandum   ☐ E-mail   ☐ Letter   ☐ Note   ☐ Other

To: _____

_____

_____

_____

_____

_____

_____

_____

_____

_____

_____

_____

_____

_____

_____

_____

_____

_____

_____

_____

_____

_____

_____

_____

_____

_____

ITEM 5: MEMO TO YOU FROM VICTOR MARKOFF. I heard at a meeting that SHG would be getting an in-house editor. That is great news; we sure have needed one. One of my friends from college has been doing this kind of stuff in the publishing industry and she may be looking for another job. I will get her to send you a resume.

Your Response

Check one: ☐ Memorandum ☐ E-mail ☐ Letter ☐ Note ☐ Other

To: _____

_____

_____

_____

_____

_____

_____

_____

_____

_____

_____

_____

_____

_____

_____

_____

_____

_____

_____

_____

_____

_____

_____

_____

_____

_____

_____

_____

_____

KEY TERMS

...

REFERENCES

...

Federal Citizen Information Center (FCIC) of the U.S. General Services Administration. "Life Advice About Changing Your Job" http://www.pueblo.gsa.gov/cic_text/employ/change-jobs/changjob.htm (accessed August 17, 2004).

GLOSSARY

. . .

A

Administrative control (p. 73): A manager must offer clear direction for subordinates who have been assigned to provide feedback and include the form of the feedback and the time it should be given. The three main components for directing others are delegation, feedback, and time frame.

Americans with Disabilities Act (ADA) (p. 280): A federal law requiring that services, workplace opportunities, and educational opportunities have equal access for individuals with differing disabilities.

Analogy (p. 42): A type of comparison that examines likenesses between members of different classifications and is useful in clarifying and explaining difficult or abstract concepts.

Analysis (p. 42): The process of identifying the relationships between and among different components of an argument or a process of reasoning.

Analytic report (p. 108): A document detailing an analysis of the components of a whole in order to provide an understanding of that whole.

Area charts (p. 304): A type of graphic illustration that uses a geometric figure, usually a circle or a square, to represent the total distribution of a given variable by dividing the figure into percentages of the whole thus illustrating the relative distribution of each part.

Argument (p. 9): A rhetorical device for reaching a conclusion by arranging evidence, logic, and reasoning in order to support the claims being made and the conclusion reached.

Arrangement task (p. 38): The approach to problem solving that involves taking existing elements and placing them in a meaningful pattern.

Assertions (p. 10): Claims made without evidence or substantiation, often made by declaring them to be true.

Assessment (p. 208): The collection of data about a particular project, event, process, team, or individual.

Assessment center (p. 213): A specialized environment in which trained professional evaluators (called assessors) observe an employee or job applicant undertaking carefully controlled activities, utilizing job-oriented simulations to document and rate an individual's skills and potential for leadership.

Asynchronous (p. 248): Not at the same time, for instance, referring to schedules of employees who work at different times of the day and night and in different places.

Asynchronous communication (p. 234): The exchange of information and messages that occurs over time, with participants sending messages on their own time rather than in a face-to-face format like a personal discussion or a teleconference.

B

Bar graph (histogram) (p. 304): Type of graphic illustration that depicts each variable as a column or row that is filled from the base to the value being represented.

Basic order (p. 39): The type of general-to-specific order in which a general topic is introduced and then specific evidence or aspects of the issue are considered.

Behavioral approach (p. 6): An approach to writing that depends upon the principles of observational learning through observation and imitation of a successful model.

Behaviorally anchored rating scale, (BARS) (p. 211): A system that identifies a set of critical incidents and records the levels of performance of an employee on each critical incident.

Blank page approach (p. 5): An approach to a writing project completely "clean"; without any planning or rewriting, in a kind of stream-of-consciousness mode.

Blind cover letter (p. 336): A communication used as an introduction to an application when an applicant does not know whether there is an opening but wants to let a company know of interests in any appropriate positions that might come open.

Buddy lists (p. 236): The directory of names of contacts in an instant messaging system.

Bureaucratic style (p. 85): An approach to management that appears officious and impersonal.

Business case (p. 108): A study covering a problem or opportunity and a recommended response; involves details of a real situation.

C

Camera-ready copy (p. 303): The term for the end product of desktop publishing in which case the final copy is printed on a laser printer or other high-quality printer and then sent to the print shop for reproduction and binding.

Case study (p. 108): The educational or training equivalent of an analytic report.

Causal chain (p. 47): A sequence of causes and effects that occurs when one cause leads to an effect that in turn leads to a new cause and again to a new effect.

Central route persuasion (p. 135): The strategy used to address specific issues by utilizing authoritative information, reasoning, and analysis.

Chart (p. 296): A form of graphic illustration used to show a collection of data, to organize the data, and even to serve as a primary record of data.

Chat rooms (p. 234): A real-time discussion page on the Internet. "Chat rooms" can include hundreds of people in a "live," typed discussion.

Chronological analytic report (p. 110): A document that focuses on the time line of a problem to reveal elements of the organization and the context of work that contribute to the problem.

Coaching (p. 203): The act of directing another person to do a task, usually in a one-on-one setting.

Common ground (p. 7): The shared aspects of a communication, including language, shared goals, cultural background, and shared experiences.

Communication channel (p. 7): The mode— oral, written, nonverbal, electronic, and so forth—through which a message is sent.

Communication process (p. 6): The process of moving meaning from one place to another, first constructing a message, sending the message, and then receiving a message.

Communications department (p. 260): The office of a company or organization charged with disseminating information to the public and monitoring the exchange of information within a company or organization.

Comparison (p. 42): Analysis that is focused on points of similarity.

Comparison and contrast (p. 42): An analytic approach exposing each item to common descriptions and similar treatments to illustrate differences or similarities between things.

Complex question fallacy (p. 53): The most well-known form of begging the question, e.g., "When are you going to stop beating your spouse," "When did you stop cheating on your taxes?" and so on, which suggests that you are guilty of the charge.

Conformance (p. 125): The concept of contents corresponding in form or appearance.

Contrast (p. 42): Analysis that is focused on points of dissimilarity.

Controlling idea (p. 5): An overarching thought or intention that guides an action in the most general sense; in writing, the way of thinking about a writing task that incorporates both the purpose of the writing and the strategy required to achieve that purpose.

Cooperative principle (p. 7): An axiom that states that communication is a process of sharing information in which the creator of the message is making an honest attempt to be understood.

Corporate communications policy (p. 264): Statements that govern how an employee can use corporate identity to send messages to others as well as rules governing to whom and what kind of information the organization will share with the public.

Critical events (critical incidents) (p. 211): Actions or work procedures that are considered representative of a larger group of work activities.

Critical incident analysis (p. 111): Focus of the examination of a problem that is on a single, illustrative or significant event.

Critical thinking (p. 56): The formal application of logic in the problem-solving process through a process of evaluating ideas, arguments, and claims of others by first analyzing the material and assessing its validity.

Culture (p. 12): A group of people who share common goals, physical spaces, and shared experiences.

Curriculum vita (p. 340): An academic résumé that lists, among other professional experiences, one's educational history, publication activities, and other accomplishments.

D

Decision sciences (p. 116): The systematic exploration of psychological, sociological, technological, and organizational factors that influence how conclusions are reached.

Decision systems approach (p. 116): A methodology used to analyze the manner in which judgments are reached within an organization.

Deductive reasoning (p. 51): The process in which the conclusion necessarily follows from the stated premises.

Delegation (p. 201): The process of assigning responsibility to a subordinate who then acts, within the restrictions of the assigned role, as an agent for the person making the assignment.

Direct message (p. 141): A clear statement of the key elements of the recommendation at the beginning of the body of the report; written in active language.

Discussion forums (threaded discussions or discussion boards) (p. 236): Media on which participants post messages that become available for review by any visitor to the Web site; allows each visitor to post a follow-up response or create a new message sequence. (See also Online Forum.)

E

E-mail (p. 234): The method by which communication similar to a letter or a memo can be sent via a computer network or the Internet.

Embargoed release (p. 267): The hold placed on a news release that tells the recipient that the information in the release cannot be made public until the specified.

Employee development (p. 209): The process for worker improvement of performance based on acquiring and training skills, both improving existing skills and adding new ones.

Empowerment (p. 15): The extension of responsibility and authority from higher management to workers at all levels of the corporate hierarchy.

Encoding process (p. 7): The act of giving a message a form that can be sent in the chosen mode of sending messages.

Equivocation (p. 54): This reasoning error takes place when a meaning is applied to a word that is either different from the meaning of the word when it is used elsewhere in the message or when the word is used in an ambiguous manner.

Ethics (p. 20): A set of guidelines for a profession or for life in general intended to govern conduct by declaring appropriate behavior and affirming which actions are right or wrong..

Evaluation (p. 208): Using data collected through assessment to make a judgment about how well the project, event, process, team, or individual is progressing toward a desired end.

Executive summary (p. 173): A statement that provides a brief overview of all of the major points included in a proposal.

Expert system (p. 116): A computer program that analyzes a data set and makes an assessment.

F

Feasibility report (p. 150): A document that provides managers with all of the information necessary to make an informed decision. Should provide a conclusion based on the research within it.

Filler (p. 277): Potentially distracting and unnecessary information or details that expand the size of the communication.

Findings (p. 125): The results of information gathering and analysis.

Flow chart (p. 300): A form of graphic representation that uses symbols or schematized diagrams to mark each stage of a sequence of events or steps in a process.

Formal-structural analytic report (p. 110): A document that examines the organizational arrangement and its official procedures and work processes in order to identify and account for a specific problem.

Formative evaluation (p. 208): The use of assessment to develop employee skills and knowledge while improving employee performance.

Formula approach (p. 6): The use of templates for each major form of communication, also for developing tone and content of types of messages.

G

Goal (p. 206): A general statement of direction in contrast to a specific measurable objective, such as, "maintain high productivity" (a goal) versus "sustain or exceed last year's productivity levels" (a measurable objective).

Goal-directed strategy (p. 198): An approach to control of an organization and its members through the objectives and outcomes sought.

Graphic (p. 295): A visual representation of a concept; as used in writing and publishing, the concept has its origin in the idea of displaying numbers as coordinates on a lined illustration (called a graph).

Graphic rating scale (p. 209): An evaluation system that has been formatted to illustrate numeric evaluations (called ratings) or rankings in a graphic manner.

H

Headhunter (p. 332) : A professional hired to search for qualified candidates for specific positions.

Human resource approach (p. 115): A methodology using information about existing personnel to develop a comprehensive analysis of an organization.

I

Illustration plan (p. 295): The arrangement that establishes guidelines for determining the nature of any visual representation placed in a document and directs the preparation and publication of supporting graphics for a document, manuscript, or book.

Immediate causes (p. 46): Those events that bring about effects that are most obvious, usually because they are close to the effect in time or space.

Indirect messages (p. 141): Communication used to divert attention from the author by using passive language. A presentation of the reasoning, evidence, and analysis in a manner that is to be the same, step-wise manner undertaken in the actual preparation of the assessment or recommendation.

Inducing-structure task (p. 38): The approach to problem solving that involves the creation of a structure or organization where none exists.

Inductive reasoning (p. 52): A conclusion is reached about all members of a category from studying only a few members of that category as the analysis proceeds from the particular to the general.

Inoculation (p. 140): Presenting information that anticipates challenges and inquiries, to provide an anticipatory "preemptive strike."

Instant message (IM) (p. 236): Small dialogue screens allow typed communication between two people at a time.

Interface (p. 239): The format and protocol of a computer screen or other electronic device that support the interaction between the machine and the user.

Internal entrepreneurship (p. 15): Units within an organization that operate like independent business units and market their services to other units within a company.

Intranet (p. 237): An internal Internet with access restricted to specified personnel, often in a secure environment.

J

Jargon (p. 85): Specialized terminology used by people who share a common field of interest (such as accountants, computer scientists, physicists, and scholars).

Job analysis (p. 115): A detailed description of each employee's workplace activities. Also, a description for activities required to perform a specific task.

Job application letter (or **cover letter**) (p. 334): A letter that indicates your interest in a position and provides a brief review of your qualifications for the position.

Journal (see Work diary).

K

Keyword (p. 332): A term that carries special significance for a specific audience and alerts that audience that the author is a member of their group.

L

Lateral thinking (p. 56): The solution to a problem is sometimes best determined when the problem is looked at from a different or alternative perspective.

Law of parsimony (p. 49): The axiom that states that when faced with two equally valid and acceptable answers to a given problem, you should use the simpler one.

Least-to-most-important order (p. 39): The means of organizing items that creates a series that moves from subordinate and less critical points, issues, or reasons to the most critical points.

Letter of inquiry (p. 332): A communication requesting information about the availability of a position.

Letter of transmittal (p. 171): A document that "hands over" or transmits a sales proposal to a potential customer.

Letters on file (p. 343): A list of references that are held by an agency or with a college placement center.

Line chart (p. 297): Also known as a line graph or frequency polygon. A graphic illustration in which data is represented by a line that connects discrete data points as if they represent a continuum between the points; an upward-sloping line represents an upward trend, a downward-sloping line represents a declining trend, and a flat line suggests an unchanging pattern.

Local area network (LAN) (p. 232): A computer linkage and communication system that employs secure wiring or a wireless system through an office, a building, or a set of neighboring buildings, linking a wide variety of personal computing and mainframe platforms.

Logos (p. 87): A graphic emblem that represents a company or person.

M

Macroculture (p. 4): The broadest level of social order in a given context.

Major-to-subclass order (p. 39): The type of general-to-specific order in which something is divided into units that are examined separately, though usually in relationship to each other and to the whole.

Management by objectives (MBO) (p. 198): A system for directing others based on clearly articulated, quantifiable goals and monitoring collective progress toward those goals rather than individual work performance.

Memorandum or memo (p. 71): The most common form of intraorganizational, written communication.

Memorandum of understanding (p. 82): This communication records a formal agreement. Typically signed by all parties involved, it carries the weight of a contract.

Mentoring (p. 203): The relationship of a senior employee to a lower-level employee that results in a coaching and guidance of the lower-level employee.

Microculture (p. 4): The local social order and its associated values, beliefs, and behavioral habits.

Mind map (p. 41): Graphical representation of how to think about a topic, created by connecting circles of information or points with logical connections.

Mnemonic device (p. 35): A technique used to improve memory by either elaborating items to be recalled or organizing them in such a way that they are easier to recall.

Most-to-least-important order (p. 39): The organizing approach that places the most critical or most convincing element of the argument at the beginning and follows with points of decreasing impact.

N

Needs assessment (p. 112): A determination of the current and future financial, technical, and human resources required to accomplish a specified goal.

Networking (p. 331): A process for obtaining help or advice through personal connections.

News release (see **Press release**): See Press release.

O

Objective (p. 206): A measurable form of a goal. The goal may be "decrease workplace accidents"; the objective would be "reduce workplace accidents by 15 percent in the next quarter."

Online forum (p. 234): A page on the Internet that allows visitors to post responses and initiate discussions, which occur over time; also called a discussion forum or discussion thread.

Organization Chart (p. 304): A type of illustration that depicts the hierarchy of a company or agency by labeling boxes or other figures as either officers or offices and then showing the relationship between the offices with lines draw between them.

Organizational analytic report (p. 112): A document used to provide a comprehensive review and analysis of as many aspects of an organization as practical.

Organizational culture (p. 13): The values, beliefs, and behavioral habits of a company or institution.

Outline (p. 34): The overall organization of a piece of writing that provides the order in which points are made and their relationship to one another; it serves as the major unifying element of the writing.

P

Paradigm (p. 71): A standard model or template to be followed in shaping or controlling an action or event.

Pareto chart (p. 300): A graphic illustration constructed by ranked the data in frequency of occurrence and bars plotted in descending order and used to determine what characteristic is the major contributor in a process.

Peripheral (p. 249): The add-on devices that accompany a computer and help access a variety of other forms of information.

Peripheral route persuasion (p. 135): The strategy that involves using indirect approaches for changing the behavior (mostly purchasing and voting behavior) of an intended audience.

Personal data assistant (**PDA**) (p. 233): A small electronic device that replaces a paper personal planner and incorporates features that may include Internet access and a range of information necessary for the busy executive.

Pie charts (p. 304): An area chart drawn as a circle, where each region looks like a pie wedge.

Preproposal (p. 182): A brief description of intended activities sent to a foundation or a grant agency in order to get feedback concerning whether or not the foundation or agency would be interested in the proposal or whether the foundation or agency supports this type of activity.

Press kit (p. 274): The material made available at a press conference or when a press release is made.

Press release (p. 261): A public announcement made available to the media for purposes of broader dissemination.

Prewriting (p. 5): The process of preparing for writing: collecting supporting materials, developing an outline of ideas, and selecting the appropriate form of presentation.

Principle of parallelism (p. 44): The expectation that features will be analyzed and compared in the same order from item to item.

Problem-focused analytic report (p. 109): A specific problem, event, or challenge is explored in order to uncover causes and ramifications of the event as well as the means to avoid or prevent it from recurring.

Process-oriented management (p. 197): An approach to control of an organization and its members through the procedures, functions, and actions used.

Product announcement (p. 269): A form of news or press release that indicates the arrival or pending arrival of new merchandise or manufactured good.

Professional portfolio (p. 340): A free-form approach that combines both the résumé and the vita and is intended to display specific accomplishments such as successful projects and skills.

Proposal (p. 164): A description of a project meant to address the requirements of a company, nongovernmental nonprofit organization, or a government organization. The preparer is often competing for the contract to undertake the project.

Q

Quality circles (p. 200): Special groups that are composed of team members, team leaders, and group leaders that explore ways to improve quality and productivity in a plant.

R

Reasoning (p. 9): The process of using logic to organize evidence and analysis in reaching a conclusion.

Report protocol (p. 121): A term used to refer to the content and form of a document together with the method for making adjustments and the means of its delivery.

Request for assistance letter (p. 336): A communication seeking help or information from someone already employed in your field.

Request for information (RFI) (p. 167): A published announcement that asks potential suppliers how they would approach solving a problem, including whether the problem can be solved in its current form, as well as gathering preliminary information about the suppliers.

Request for proposal (RFP) (p. 165): A formal statement of needs, requirements, technical specifications, and time frames prepared by an organization so that vendors and other service providers can compete for the contract.

Response letter (p. 336): A communication that is a reply about an open and advertised position.

Résumés (p. 341): A listing of credentials and job experiences, especially professional positions held.

S

Sandbagging (p. 92): Offering additional and unnecessary justification beyond the actual reason for firing.

Scatter plot (scattergram) (p. 297): A graph of two variables that places a single point on the graph for each combination. The final graph appears as a set of clustered dots, each point representing two related data levels.

Screen capture software (p. 310): A program that takes a picture of the computer screen or an area of a computer screen and stores it in one of several image formats.

Screen shot (p. 310): A "picture" gathered by screen capture software and saved for later use.

Self-directed team (p. 199): An organization of people wherein a group of workers is given a project and develops its own organization and distribution of work.

Self-managed team (p. 200): An organization of people wherein the group of workers accepts responsibility for management tasks such as performance assessment and project selection.

Sequential (chronological) order (p. 38): The presentation of a series of events in time order that moves from first to last in order of time.

Signature template (p. 280): A format of a presentation, including background colors, logos, button styles, and font styles, that is used for all of the presentations made by a individual or group.

Simple-to-complex order (p. 39): Basic concepts are presented first, often in the form of an overview, followed by a more detailed, in-depth discussion of the points.

Slug (p. 265): A one- or two- word title used on press releases that is used with the page number on any more than one-page releases.

Solicited proposal (p. 177): A type of request in which the contracting organization is seeking applications for the contract.

Solicited recommendation report (p. 142): A response to a management request for a report on an aspect of the company's affairs. These documents can be solicited from internal or external sources.

Spam (p. 238): Named for the Hormel processed meat, these are unwanted e-mail messages that are sent to large numbers of recipients and are often scams, marketing of unusual products, attachments with viruses, and other malicious electronic clutter.

Spatial order (p. 38): The movement from one object or physical location to another in a reasonable manner that may include a description of the physical relationship of the items being described.

Strategic planning approach (p. 117): An analytic approach used when focusing on goals rather than on procedures.

Strategy (p. 5): The organizing conceptualization of a project used to achieve a specific goal; this involves resources, information, analysis, and delivery that fit the message to the audience for optimum effect.

Subject line (p. 238): The e-mail text area that corresponds to the "RE:" of a paper letter.

Summative evaluation (p. 209): A review of performance for a previous period, often six or twelve months, almost always linked to salary increases.

Systems approach (p. 115): An methodology for analysis in which individual units within an organization are treated as a whole entity constructed of interacting and interdependent parts.

T

Table of contents (p. 172): The listing of the items that appear in a manuscript, showing the order of each and the page where each item begins.

Tables (p. 296): The specific form of chart that represents data in rows and columns.

Teleconference (p. 237): Simultaneous two-way audio and visual interaction from a distance.

Templates (p. 279): Pre-made formats that include a thematic variation for bulleted lists, charts, title pages, text pages, and so on.

Three-item rule (p. 280): The rule of thumb suggesting that slides in a presentation should have no more that three elements.

Title page (p. 170): The cover of a document that lists, according to the nature of the document or manuscript, key details that identify the document.

Training (p. 204): A form of teaching that focuses on a specific skill or job task that typically requires learning tasks and procedures rather than concepts.

Transformation task (p. 38): This approach to problem solving takes an existing order and analyzes it in order to convert it into another order.

U

Underlying (or **ultimate** or **root**) **cause** (p. 46): Often a more remote event that initiated or contributed to a chain of events leading to the event currently being examined. Also, the fundamental event that leads to all other related events.

Unsolicited proposal (p. 178): A type of application for financial support to undertake a project or a presentation to a company for consideration of a product or service that has not been sought by the organization.

Unsolicited recommendation report (p. 142): A analysis that is not requested, but is generated by an employee who recognizes a new opportunity, a new risk, or a newly discovered procedure or managerial oversight that needs to be brought to the attention of higher management.

V

Values clarification (p. 17): A process of articulating personal interests and ambi-tions in such a way as to recognize them as important guiding forces in one's life.

Virtual office (p. 249): An employee workspace that is a collection of hardware and software, including a laptop, cell phone, PDA, and other options that makes having a physical office unnecessary; allows the employee to be entirely mobile.

Virtual private network (p. 237): A communication system that typically links remote users and one or more LANs using the Internet as the primary carrier of the electronic signal; it differs from a WAN in that it uses the Internet rather than leased or publicly switched lines.

Vugraph (p. 135): The slide of a presentation that includes a visual representation, usually of data or performance trends.

W

Whiteboard (p. 237): A software tool allowing each participant to alter on text or graphics that are being viewed by all the participants in a teleconference or Web-based conference.

Whole-to-part order (p. 39): The type of general-to-specific order in which an overview of the entire situation is provided, with subsequent attention being paid to the components.

Wide area network (WAN) (p. 237): A form of computer communication system utilizing dedicated, often leased, lines or direct telephone dial-up for communication between and among remote sites and linking one or more LANs; allows completely isolated users to dial into the system through the telecommunication system.

Wizard (p. 244): A common term for software tools that automate a series of steps in preparing a document or converting material from one format to another.

Work diary (p. 206): A written record in daily format of activities and accomplishments related to work typically maintained by an individual, but also for a team or other group.

Writing portfolio (p. 207): A collection of personal samples of written work assembled in an organized manner to illustrate something about the collection or the writer, often for the purpose of review and to improve writing skills.

X

x-axis (p. 305): In a graph, this horizontal axis called the abscissa; traditionally, the *x*-axis is marked off in units of the variable, such as regional sales.

Y

y-axis (p. 305): In a graph, the vertical axis is called the ordinate; traditionally, the *y*-axis has coordinates for the amount or "frequency" of sales.

Z

z-coordinate (p. 304): In a graph, a third axis that represents a third variable and is represented as perpendicular to the *x* and *y* axes of the graph.

INDEX

...

A

ABCD rule of managerial writing, 172
Ability, proposal topic, 166, 168
Abscissa, 305
Abstract, for unsolicited internal proposal, 180
Accountability, proposal topic, 166, 168
Acknowledgment of message, 8
Acrobat Reader, 243
Acronyms, 78, 85, 281
Action memos, 71, 81–82
Action request letters, 88, 89
Active voice, 141
Adams, Scott, 145, 309
Address books (electronic), 240
Ad hominem, 53
Administrative control, 73
  See also Control
Adobe Acrobat, 243
Adobe Illustrator, 306, 307
Adobe PageMaker, 306
Adobe Photoshop, 307
Adobe Premier, 308
Ad populum, 53
Advertising
  central route persuasion, 135
  peripheral route persuasion, 135
Air Transport Association, 111
Alphanumeric structure, 38
Alta Vista, 240
Americans with Disabilities Act (ADA), 280
America Online (AOL), 236
Analogy
  analytic report tool, 126
  as comparison, 42–43
  false, 55
  reasoning by, 126
Analysis, logic and, 52–56
Analytic report, 4, 107
  analogies and, 126
  analysis tools, 125–126
  bad news with a solution, 136
  checklist, 127
  consultant format, 123–124
  criteria analysis, 120–121
  data collection and organization, 124–125
  decision systems approach to preparing, 116, 117
  defined, 108, 109
  executive summary format, 124

external, 118–120
findings, 125
formal format, 121–122
human resource approach to preparing, 115, 117
informal format, 123
internal, 118
organizational, 112–114
organizing, 120–126
problem-focused, 109–112
protocols for, 121–124
resources, 126
solutions, 126
strategic planning approach to preparing, 117
strategies for, 114–117
systems (organizational) approach to preparing, 115, 117
Analytic tools
  cause and effect, 46–48
  comparison and contrast, 42–46
Analyze, defined, 108
Anderson, Sparky, 55
Announcements, 238
Annual reports, 310
ANSII, word processing format, 243
Apology, 73
Appeal to authority
  as fallacy in logic, 53–54
  in persuasive writing, 141
Appeal to pity, 54
Appearance
  for interview, 349–350
  of letters, 333
Appendixes
  in a formal report, 122
  in sales proposals, 173
Application letter
  See Job application letter
Approaches, to writing
  behavioral, 6
  blank page, 5–6
  formula, 6, 8
  structuring of material, types of, 38–40
  systematic quality, 40–41
Appropriateness, of directions, 196
Arabic numerals, in outlines, 36–37
Area charts, 304
Argument

assertion distinguished from, 32, 9–10
data collection and organization and, 125
defined, 9
persuasion distinguished from, 52
  See also Reasoning
Aristotle, 36
Arrangement task, in organization, 38
Arthur Andersen, 123–124, 260
Assertion
  argument distinguished from, 32, 9–10
  defined, 10
  objectivity and, 49
Assessment, in employee evaluation, 208
Assessment and recommendation reports
  See Persuasive reports
Assessment center, for employee evaluation, 213–214
Assigning specific tasks, 202
Associational elements, 50
Astound Presentations, 305
Asynchronous communication, 234
Asynchronous work schedules, 248
Attachment, to business letters, 87
Attribution, importance of, 51
  See also Plagiarism
Audience
  aspects of, 11
  awareness (readiness to understand), 46, 47
  of business letters, 85–86
  characteristics of, 137
  of memos, 72, 73
  for persuasive writing, 139–140
  prejudice of, 140
  receipt of message, 4
  secondary, 80
  of solicited recommendation reports, 143
  for transmittal letter, 92
  view of presenter, 139
Authority
  ABCD rule, 172
  delegating of, 15, 73, 201–202
  empowerment and, 200
Auto correct, 242–243

Joblocator.com, 332
Job search, 328
  college placement offices, 331
  goals for, 329–330
  Internet resources, 332
  job application letter (cover
      letter), 334–340
  letters of inquiry, 332–334
  research a company, 330–332
  See also Interview and presen-
      tation; Résumé
Joint external-internal analytic
    report, 113–114
Jonson, Ben, 35
Journals, as means to incorpo-
    rate writing into mentoring
    relationship, 206–207
jpg (jpeg; joint photographics
    experts group), 307, 308

K

Kallick, Rob, 248
Kamen, Dean, 270–271
Keeler, Wee Willie, 55
Kelleher, Herb, 261
Kennedy, John F., 122
Keyword, 332–333
Kirschenbaum, Howard, 18

L

Language, formal, 85
Lateral thinking, 56–57
Law of parsimony, 49
Layout patterns (word process-
    ing), 246
Least-to-most-important order,
    39, 40
Legal issues
  bad news letters, 92
  electronic signatures, 87
  externally produced analytical
      reports, 119
  fax correspondences, 87
  in graphic illustration, 309
  illegal interview questions,
      351–352
  memorandum of understand-
      ing, 82–83
  written communication, 21
Length
  business letters, 87
  executive summaries, 124
  job application letters, 334
  letter of transmittal, 171
  report memos, 80
Letters, 15
  appearance of, 333
  bureaucratic style, 85
  from individuals, format of, 87
  rejection, 70
  See also Business letter; Job
      application letter;
      Memorandum (memo);
      specific types of letters
Letterhead
  business letters on, 86

electronic form, 246
  in information release, 264
  memos on, 74
  personal, 87
Letter of inquiry, 332–334
Letter of transmittal
  for proposal seeking founda-
      tion support, 183
  for sales proposal, 171–172
Letters, alphabetic, in outlines, 36
Letters on file, 343
Lexmark, 115
Line charts, 297, 299
Line graph, 306
Local area network (LAN), 232,
    248
Local culture, 13
Logic, 51
  electronic form, 246
  of evidence, 49–50
  evidence as support for, 51–52
  fallacies in, 52–56
  in persuasive writing, 141
Logically unconnected ele-
    ments, 135
Logo
  as addition to templates, 279
  on consultant-provided
      reports, 123
  in information release, 264
  vector drawing and, 307
"Lossy," 308
Lotus, 305
Lowe's Home Improvement, 13

M

Macroculture, of the workplace,
    12–14
Macromedia's Dreamweaver,
    279
Macro program (word process-
    ing), 244
Major-to-subclass order, 39
Management by objectives
    (MBO), 198–199
Management process, 8
  control of work, 9
  information flow, 9
Management tools, for written
    directions
  assigning specific tasks, 202
  delegating authority, 201–202
  feedback, 202
  monitoring progress, 202
  recognizing success, 203
  time frame, establishing, 202
Managerial writing, strategies in
  approaches, 5–6
  audience, 11
  behavioral approach, 6
  blank page approach, 5–6
  communication ethics, 20–21
  communication process, 6–8, 9
  communicator, 10–11
  context, 6–8
  corporate goals, 14–15

culture, 21–22
  ethics, 21–22
  formal process, 15–16
  formula approach, 6
  informal process, 15–16
  management process, 8, 9
  message, 11
  microculture, organizational
      culture, macroculture,
      12–14
  personal goals, 17–19
  preliminary decisions, 4–5
  professional conduct and per-
      sonal success, 17–22
  reasoning, argument, and
      assertion, 8–10
  role of, 5–11
  self-image and corporate
      image, 19–20
  strategy, defined, 5
  workplace, understanding of,
      12–16
Managerial writing, technical
    writing versus (table), 198
Managing by memo, 77–78
Marcus, Bernie, 12–13
Maslin, Michael, 145
Matrix (outline), 35, 36
McGuire, W., 140
Meeting notes, as means to
    incorporate writing into
    mentoring relationship,
    205–206
Memorandum (memo), 15
  action, 71, 81–82, 234
  audience for, 72
  checklist, 95–96
  defined, 71
  formatting, 74–76
  group (electronic), 238, 240
  impact of, 73
  importance of, 71
  informational, 71, 76–78, 234
  memorandum of understand-
      ing, 71, 82–83, 234
  message of, characterizing,
      72–73
  purpose of, 71–72, 76–83, 234
  record, 71, 78, 79, 80, 234
  reminder, 76–78, 79
  report, 71, 80–81
  results, specifying, 73
  tone of, 71–73
  transmittal, 234
  unsolicited, 80
  for unsolicited internal pro-
      posal, 180
Memorandum of understand-
    ing, 71, 82–83, 234
Memory Stick, 307
Mentor, 204
Mentoring
  See Coaching (mentoring),
      with written communi-
      cation
Merchant of Venice, The,
    (Shakespeare), 145